Camp TV of the 1960s

Camp TV of the 1960s

Reassessing the Vast Wasteland

Edited by
ISABEL C. PINEDO and W. D. PHILLIPS

Oxford University Press is a department of the University of Oxford. It furthers
the University's objective of excellence in research, scholarship, and education
by publishing worldwide. Oxford is a registered trade mark of Oxford University
Press in the UK and certain other countries.

Published in the United States of America by Oxford University Press
198 Madison Avenue, New York, NY 10016, United States of America.

© Oxford University Press 2023

All rights reserved. No part of this publication may be reproduced, stored in
a retrieval system, or transmitted, in any form or by any means, without the
prior permission in writing of Oxford University Press, or as expressly permitted
by law, by license, or under terms agreed with the appropriate reproduction
rights organization. Inquiries concerning reproduction outside the scope of the
above should be sent to the Rights Department, Oxford University Press, at the
address above.

You must not circulate this work in any other form
and you must impose this same condition on any acquirer.

Library of Congress Cataloging-in-Publication Data
Names: Pinedo, Isabel Cristina, 1957– editor. | Phillips, W. D. (Wyatt D.), editor.
Title: Camp TV of the 1960s : reassessing the vast wasteland /
edited by Isabel C. Pinedo and W. D. Phillips.
Description: New York, NY : Oxford University Press, [2023] |
Includes bibliographical references and index.
Identifiers: LCCN 2023004928 (print) LCCN 2023004929 (ebook) |
ISBN 9780197650752 (paperback) | ISBN 9780197650745 (hardback) |
ISBN 9780197650776 (epub)
Subjects: LCSH: Camp (Style) on television. | Camp (Style)—United
States—History—20th century. | Television programs—Social
aspects—United States—History—20th century. |
Television broadcasting—Social aspects—United States. |
LCGFT: Television criticism and reviews.
Classification: LCC PN1992.8.C35 C36 2023 (print) |
LCC PN1992.8.C35 (ebook) | DDC 791.450973/09046—dc23/eng/20230207
LC record available at https://lccn.loc.gov/2023004928
LC ebook record available at https://lccn.loc.gov/2023004929

DOI: 10.1093/oso/9780197650745.001.0001

Isabel and Wyatt dedicate this work to their parents, respectively, on whose televisions they first saw most of these shows in all their original (Isabel) and syndicated (Wyatt) glory.

Contents

Acknowledgments	ix
Contributors	xi
About the Companion Website	xv

Introduction: Camp(ing) in the 1960s   1
W. D. Phillips and Isabel C. Pinedo

1. Gilligan and Captain Kirk Have More in Common Than You Think: 1960s Camp TV as an Alternative Genealogy for Cult Television   23
Isabel C. Pinedo and W. D. Phillips

SECTION I: LAYING THE (CAMP)GROUNDWORK

2. *Fractured Flickers* (1963–64), Camp, and Cinema's Ab/usable Past   51
Andrea Comiskey and Jonah Horwitz

3. Wearing French Cuffs to a Gunfight: Camp and Violence in Hanna-Barbera's *Snagglepuss* (1961)   75
Emily Hoffman

SECTION II: CAMP TV'S TENTPOLES

4. They're Creepy and They're Campy: Camping the American Family on 1960s Horror Television   97
Jamie Hook

5. Spellcasting Camp: *Bewitched* (1964–72)   120
Andrew J. Owens

6. How the West Was Fun: *F Troop* (1965–67) and the American Frontier   137
Cynthia J. Miller

7. "Holy Fruit Salad, Batman!": Unmasking Queer Conceits of ABC's Late-1960s Branding 154
Benjamin Kruger-Robbins

8. "We're Being Passed off as Something We Aren't": Authenticity versus Camp on *The Monkees* (1966–68) 176
Dan Amernick

9. Straight Male Spies, Queer Camp Vistas: The Evolution of Non-Normative Masculinities in *The Avengers* (1961–69) and 1960s British Spy-fi TV 195
Craig Haslop and Douglas McNaughton

SECTION III: OTHER CAMP(TV)SITES

10. Can TV Music Be Camp? Notes from the 1960s 215
Reba A. Wissner

11. *Flipper*'s (1964–67) Dark Camp 236
Nicholas C. Morgan

12. Camp TV, *The Beverly Hillbillies* (1962–71), and Flip Wilson's (1970–74) Geraldine Jones: Negativity, Trans Gender Queer, and the Comedy of Manners 256
Ken Feil

13. "Far Right, Far Left, and Far Out": Mainstreaming Camp on American Television 277
Moya Luckett

Afterword: Questions of Taste and Pre-cult/Post-cult 297
Matt Hills

Index 309

Acknowledgments

This book project started when Isabel peer-observed Wyatt's course, "Cult TV and Its Audiences," at Hunter College in 2013. That session, centered on camp and the TV programs *Pee-wee's Playhouse* and *Batman*, led to an email exchange and then a conversation, which led to a Society for Cinema and Media Studies (2015) conference paper and the 2018 article reprinted as Chapter 1. It has now led, ultimately, to this collection.

Throughout this process, we have benefited from feedback from conference audiences and colleagues, as well as from university and college funding support. Early drafts of some material were presented at the Society for Cinema and Media Studies Conference in Seattle, 2019. We're grateful for the attention, encouragement, and helpful comments we received, particularly from our panel respondent Aniko Bodroghkozy. We also want to acknowledge the anonymous reviewers at Oxford University Press for their helpful criticism of the book, and reviewers at *Cinema Journal* and *Journal of Popular Television*, as well as editor James Leggott, who offered valuable criticism in crafting the journal article. In addition, we want to thank two research assistants—Noah Waldman who provided assistance on the journal article, and Sumaita Hasan who helped design the Gantt chart (Plate 1)—as well as our indexer, Kaelene Hansen.

Last, but not least, we are grateful to the wonderful scholars who contributed chapters to this collection.

Isabel has benefited from a 2020–21 PSC–CUNY Award, jointly funded by The Professional Staff Congress and The City University of New York. She is indebted to her writing support group Deb Schutte, Shorna Allred, and Davida Pines, for their advice and comradery. She is grateful to her friend Wyatt, the best collaborator ever, and sends her heartfelt thanks, as always, to Frank and Heather for their abiding generosity, love, and kindness.

This collection also benefited from a subvention award granted by the Humanities Center at Texas Tech; Wyatt thanks the faculty and staff there for their assistance. He also wants to recognize the contribution of the intrepid ILL/Document Delivery staff at TTU Libraries who were able to assist in providing many of the books and DVDs utilized in researching and compiling this collection. Further, he thanks his colleagues and students in the Film and Media Studies program and the English Department for their support over the last eight years. Finally, Wyatt thanks Isabel for her easy collegiality and long friendship and Robin, Zola, and Josie for their love.

Our thanks to Norman Hirschy, our editor at Oxford University Press, who has been an enthusiastic supporter of our work since the CFP went out, and to the editorial staff at the press.

Chapter 1 is a modified version of an article previously published under the same title in the *Journal of Popular Television*. Our thanks to the journal for permission to republish this essay.

Contributors

Dan Amernick is an assistant professor of Film & Television at Marist College, having completed his MA in Media Studies and his PhD in Mass Communications from the S.I. Newhouse School of Public Communications at Syracuse University. Prior to going back to college, Amernick spent many years working in Los Angeles, notably as a writer on the CBS sitcom *The Nanny* from 1995 to 1999. Previous Publications include "The Not-Ready for Archive Players: The Lost Seasons of 'Saturday Night Live.'" *Journal of Popular Film and Television*, vol. 46, no. 2 (2018).

Andrea Comiskey is a visiting scholar at the University of Pittsburgh. Her research and teaching interests include animation aesthetics and film and television narrative. Her publications include articles in the journals *Post Script* and *Iluminace* and the collections *The Classical Hollywood Reader* and *Special Effects: New Histories, Theories, Contexts*.

Ken Feil is an assistant professor in Emerson College's Visual and Media Arts Department. Recipient of an NEH "Enduring Questions" grant (2016/2017), Ken is the author of *Rowan and Martin's Laugh-In* (2014) and *Dying for a Laugh: Disaster Movies and the Camp Imagination* (2005), in addition to essays in *Our Blessed Rebel Queen: Essays on Carrie Fisher and Princess Leia* (2021), *Reading the Bromance* (2014), and the journal *Celebrity Studies* (2017). Ken's newest book, *Fearless Vulgarity: Jacqueline Susann's Queer Comedy and Camp Authorship*, was recently published by Wayne State University Press.

Craig Haslop is a senior lecturer in Media at the University of Liverpool. Prior to his academic career, he spent eighteen years working in the cultural industries as a PR consultant in both the charity and the commercial sectors. His current research interests focus on representations of LGBTQI+ people in the media, in particular the relationships between the industrialization of cult TV and shifts in LGBTQI+ representations, and of young people's experiences of gender and sexual identity on social media.

Matt Hills is a professor of Fandom Studies at the University of Huddersfield. He is the author of six sole-authored research monographs, starting with *Fan Cultures* in 2002 and coming up to date with *Doctor Who: The Unfolding Event* in 2015, as well as publishing more than a hundred book chapters and journal articles in the areas of media fandom, fan studies, cult film/TV, and audiences in the digital era. Most recently, he has co-edited *Doctor Who: New Dawn* (2021) for Bloomsbury Academic.

xii CONTRIBUTORS

Emily Hoffman is a professor of English at Arkansas Tech University, where she teaches film and television studies, creative writing, and literature. She has published on a variety of pop culture topics, including *Mad Men* and Michelangelo Antonioni in *The Legacy of Mad Men: Cultural History, Intermediality, and American Television*; *Mary Tyler Moore*; *A Place in the Sun*; and Paul Newman's screen persona in *Iconoclasm: The Making and Breaking of Images*.

Jamie Hook received his PhD from the Department of Communication and Culture at Indiana University, Bloomington. His research explores the intersections of adaptation, taste politics, film history, and representations of gender and sexuality. He has published work in Routledge's *Porn Studies* journal, the Palgrave Studies in Adaptation and Visual Cultural series, and Edinburgh University Press's ReFocus: The International Directors Series.

Jonah Horwitz is a visiting lecturer at the University of Pittsburgh. He has published essays on European silent cinema, *Directory of World Cinema: France*, and midcentury US television, in the journal *Cinéma(s)*.

Benjamin Kruger-Robbins is a visiting assistant professor of film and media at Emory University. He holds a PhD in visual studies from UC Irvine, and his research concerns queer involvement within the American television industry and TV audience cultures. His writing has appeared in *The Velvet Light Trap, Refractory, Sexualities*, and *Flow* as well as in the edited anthology *The Politics of Twin Peaks*.

Moya Luckett is the author of *Cinema and Community: Progressivism, Exhibition and Film Culture in Chicago, 1907–1917* (Wayne State University Press, 2014) and coeditor of *Swinging Single: Representing Sexuality in the 1960s* (University of Minnesota Press, 1999). She is currently writing two books, one on the relationship among celebrity, economic recession, and foreclosed social mobility, the other on femininity and popular media. Her work on femininity in popular media, 1960s film, TV and popular culture, celebrity culture, British cinema, and early film has appeared in such journals as *Screen, Feminist Media Studies, New Review of Film and Television*, and *Celebrity Studies* as well as in several anthologies. She teaches at NYU's Gallatin School of Individualized Study.

Douglas McNaughton is a senior lecturer at the University of Brighton's School of Media, where he is also a member of the Screen Studies Research and Enterprise Group. Recent publications in *Historical Journal of Film, Radio and Television, Journal of British Cinema and Television*, and *Critical Studies in Television* explore the interplay of the poetics of space and place, with a particular interest in representations of place, the politics of labor, social spaces, and performance.

Cynthia J. Miller is a cultural anthropologist specializing in visual media. She teaches in the Marlboro Institute for Liberal Arts at Emerson College, and is the editor or co-editor of seventeen scholarly volumes, including the forthcoming *Journeys into Terror* (2023). She serves on the editorial board of the *Journal of Popular Television*, and also edits the Film and History book series for the Rowman & Littlefield Publishing Group.

Nicholas C. Morgan is a postdoctoral Core Lecturer in the Department of Art History and Archaeology at Columbia University. He is currently at work on two book projects, one considering art of the 1980s and 1990s in relation to the AIDS crisis and another on theories of labor and sociality in the filmic and artistic undergrounds of the 1960s. Recent journal articles include an essay on the Brazilian artist José Leonilson's queer use of the newspaper in *ARTMargins*, another on the video art of Vaginal Davis in *TSQ: Transgender Studies Quarterly*, and a review essay (co-authored with Ksenia Soboleva) on museum commemorations of the Stonewall riots in *QED: A Journal in GLBTQ Worldmaking*. His writing on art for broader audiences has appeared in *Harper's Bazaar*, *Artforum*, *Hyperallergic*, the *Financial Times* Sunday magazine, *Garage*, and several exhibition catalogs.

Andrew J. Owens is a lecturer in the Department of Cinematic Arts at the University of Iowa. His teaching and research interests include global film and television history, media historiography, LGBTQ+/critical race theory, genre studies, and media industry studies. His first book, *Desire After Dark: Contemporary Queer Cultures and Occultly Marvelous Media* (Indiana University Press, 2021), constructs a cultural and industrial history of queer occult media from the 1960s to the present.

Wyatt D. Phillips is an associate professor of Film and Media Studies in the English Department at Texas Tech University. His work primarily engages questions related to the political economy and industrial practices of visual media. He has published in *Film History*, *Genre: Forms of Discourse and Culture*, *Journal of Popular Television*, and *Historical Journal of Film, Radio and Television* as well as contributing chapters to half a dozen collections. He recently finished co-editing, alongside Justin Wyatt, *Screening American Independent Film* (Routledge, 2023) and is currently completing a monograph that considers the historical relationship between the business culture of the early twentieth century and the role that genre has long played in Hollywood and American mass media.

Isabel C. Pinedo is a professor of Film and Media Studies at Hunter College, CUNY. She is the author of *Difficult Women on Television Drama: The Gender Politics of Complex Women in Serial Narratives* (Routledge, 2022) and *Recreational Terror: Women and the Pleasures of Horror Film Viewing* (SUNY University Press, 1997). Her work focuses on feminist television studies, the horror film, and social theory. Her writing has appeared in *Television and New Media*, *Journal of Popular Television*, *Jump Cut*, *Journal of Film and Video*, and various collections. She is currently working on a hybrid project, a book that combines the history of her immigrant family with a history of the horror film written from an immigrant perspective.

Reba A. Wissner is an assistant professor of Musicology at the Schwob School of Music at Columbus State University. She received her MFA and PhD in musicology from Brandeis University and her BA in music and Italian from Hunter College of the City University of New York. She is the author of three books, *A Dimension of Sound: Music in The Twilight Zone* (Pendragon Press, 2013), *We Will Control All That You Hear: The Outer Limits and the Aural Imagination* (Pendragon Press, 2016), and *Music and the Atomic Bomb on American Television, 1950–1969* (Peter Lang, 2020). With Katherine Reed, she has co-edited *Music in Twin Peaks: Listen to the Sounds* (Routledge, 2021).

About the Companion Website

https://www.oup.com/us/camptv

Oxford University Press has created a website to accompany *Camp TV of the 1960s: Reassessing the Vast Wasteland*. Materials that cannot be made available in a book, namely television clips from scenes discussed in the chapters, are provided here. The reader is encouraged to consult this resource in conjunction with the chapters. Examples available online are referred to in individual chapters as videos (e.g., Video 1.1) and indicated in the text with Oxford University Press's symbol ⏵. In addition, you can find a comprehensive bibliography of the sources cited in the individual book chapters.

Introduction

Camp(ing) in the 1960s

W. D. Phillips and Isabel C. Pinedo

In late March 1966, the character *The New York Times* referred to as "the caped crusader of camp" landed squarely on the cover of *TV Guide* (Stone). The accompanying article—"Batty over Batman?"—quoted the managing editor of *Status* magazine as saying "Yes, *Batman* is in. A most amusing show. It is mass camp . . . the best kind of camp" (Whitney 16). Yet when *Batman*'s producer, William Dozier, was interviewed for that same *Times* piece at the beginning of the year, he emphasized instead the longer history of camp, leaning into middlebrow culture's timorous, pejorative association with genderqueer performativity. "In Hollywood," he complained, "they're calling me the 'King of Camp.' I hate the word 'Camp.' It sounds so faggy [*sic*] and funsies."

Clearly at mid-decade the understanding and valuation of camp were still heavily disputed. What is not disputed, however, is that camp was, during the 1960s, very much in the midst of a significant transformation and a move from the margins to the mainstream. *Batman*'s premiere in January 1966, and the rampant success that immediately followed, is generally recognized as one of two watershed moments in the popularization of camp; Susan Sontag's publication of "Notes on 'Camp'" in the fall of 1964, approximately a year and a half earlier, is the other. Sontag, however, had used the word before. In a film review published earlier that year, she used "camp" twice as an adjective to describe an aesthetic style, though both times locking it safely behind a pair of scare quotes. Notably, within those few intervening months, she had expanded her definition, removing the quotes (aside from the title) and elevating it through capitalization—from "camp" to Camp. Describing it now as a "sensibility (as distinct from an idea)," she here added a reading position to her explication: "Camp taste," "the Camp eye," "the lens of Camp"—all of these indicate her recognition of camp as also a mode of reception (275–281). Marrying the two, number three of the fifty-eight "Notes," which she offered in lieu of a direct definition, stated: "Not only is there a Camp vision, a Camp way of looking at things, Camp is as well a quality discoverable in objects and the behavior of persons. There are 'campy' movies, clothes, furniture, popular songs, novels, people, buildings" (277), and—as this collection of essays will make clear—Camp TV shows.

Sometimes reduced to the overly simplistic "so bad that it is good" (e.g., Whitney 16), camp more significantly "converts the serious into the frivolous" (Sontag 276). But it also functions—and this is true of camp as both a mode of expression, or aesthetic style, and as a mode of reception—to activate forms of cultural resistance "anchored in the reversed use of cultural tools (images, functions, contexts) to spread suspicion toward normalcy, by promoting the queer . . . understanding of things" (Malinowska 4). Importantly here, "queer" is understood to engage both of its familiar meanings: genderqueer (or anti-straight) and non-normative. Camp, as we argued in the 2018 article, "Gilligan and Captain Kirk Have More in Common Than You Think: 1960s Camp TV as an Alternative Genealogy for Cult TV," that prompted this collection of new scholarship (included here as Chapter 1), is therefore both a style or aggregation of textual features that focuses on, *and* a reading strategy that looks for, "the artifices of the social world . . . simultaneously displaying and critiquing the constructedness of all images . . . variously associated with incongruity, irony, parody, humor, aestheticism, performativity, and theatricality" (Phillips and Pinedo 25). The genre characteristics we focused on in that article—satire, intertextuality, reflexivity, and gender fluidity—nominated for us a body of televisual texts from the mid- to late 1960s that shared these features, which enabled forms of dual address. This duplexity allowed these programs to appeal to multiple audiences—juvenile and adult, mainstream and countercultural—at the same time. Produced in a period of both cultural transformation (some would say upheaval) and industrial change (in the move to full-color primetime lineups), the TV programs we studied there—including *Batman* (1966–69), *The Monkees* (1966–68), *Green Acres* (1965–71), *Get Smart* (1965–70), *The Man from U.N.C.L.E.* (1964–68), *Gilligan's Island* (1964–67), and *F Troop* (1965–67)—have all strangely endured the ravages of time (more or less) and continue to draw the attention of viewers and critics (and scholars). As such, they have remained uniquely relevant pieces of American pop culture well into the twenty-first century.

A number of other television programs clearly warranted similar consideration in that article, but the space available to us there and the nature of the argument precluded further consideration. Happily, this collection allows for exactly this kind of expansion, and here we are pleased to present work that not only continues our consideration of those programs but adds other key shows such as *The Addams Family* (1964–66), *The Munsters* (1964–66), *The Beverly Hillbillies* (1962–71), *Bewitched* (1964–72), *Lost in Space* (1965–68), and *Rowan & Martin's Laugh-In* (1968–73). Examples of camp in British TV in *The Avengers* (1961–69), *The Prisoner* (1968–69), *Department S* (1969–70), and *Jason King* (1971–72), and Camp TV precursors, such as *Fractured Flickers* (1963–64) and *Snagglepuss* (1961), are importantly added here as well, as are relevant televisual outliers that only dabbled in or were later appropriated as camp, such as *Star Trek* (1966–69) and *Flipper* (1964–67). There is still certainly more work to be done (the genre-bending of *The Wild Wild West* [1965–69] and the campy humor of *Hollywood Squares* [1966–81] both come to mind), but here we have collected a significant amount of new research that productively expands the scholarship on this body of television programs, many of which were and are still notably understudied. This new collection then carries forward our intention, laid out in that earlier article (22), to recuperate, for scholars, both the programs and viewing practices associated with 1960s Camp TV.

This introduction will offer additional contextualization of 1960s camp beyond what we were able (or inclined) to include in our article. This is due in large part to the different objectives of the two pieces. While both clearly engage in what Rick Altman and other genre theorists call "regenrification"—establishing a new context of other works within which a given work can be read (81–82), there we aspired to present an unrecognized precursor to cult television; here we aim to frame and introduce the essays assembled in this volume by emphasizing their concordance and synthesizing the collection's overall contribution. With the range of programs closely considered here, it might be productive to return to our title—Camp TV—and consider its terminological application to such a disparate range of shows. In our initial article, we emphasized a subset of key textual characteristics that opened onto dual address (satire, intertextuality, etc.) for what we there referred to as "active viewers." Second-level meaning systems, while necessary for understanding Camp TV (and camp more generally), are not alone sufficient for differentiating camp texts from all other texts, and in fact it was this similarity to Cult TV texts that led us to focus on strategies of dual address initially.

Other genres, too—such as children's programming and cartoons—often open out to an intended multiplicity of meaning, something the chapter on *Snagglepuss* in this collection takes up directly. Yet we maintain that, in relation to its dual address, the aggregation of textual features in conjunction with the cultural context, its ubiquitous deliberateness, and the pertinence of color combine to mark Camp TV as a distinct form.

Additionally, the brief duration of 1960s Camp TV raises the question as to whether "genre" is the best theoretical paradigm and categorical term for this body of televisual texts. Film genre scholars have offered key studies of film cycles, which they define as "a series of similar [works] produced during a limited period of time, often sparked by a benchmark hit" (Grindon 32). Looking at the Gantt chart in Plate 1, which presents the temporality (along a shared timeline) of each of the television series addressed in this collection, a period of high-volume production matching that of a genre cycle is clearly on display beginning with the 1964–65 season (the shows that premiered in September 1964) and then tapering off by the end of the decade. If strictly applied, however, this definition of a genre cycle falters for our object of study since no one show could arguably be assigned the "benchmark" status. *Batman*, probably the best remembered Camp TV program and one with a clear influence on the use of color in American prime-time television (Phillips and Pinedo 26), appears too late in the cycle and produced too few camp imitators. Nonetheless, *cycle* seems to fit nicely with the quick rise but brief temporality of Camp TV.

To a certain degree, our study of 1960s Camp TV has been modeled on studies of film noir. James Naremore states directly that "nobody is sure whether the films in question constitute a period, a genre, a cycle, a style, or simply a 'phenomenon'" (9). Yet his and other studies of noir regularly identify and analyze those works not solely on their textual affinities but also on the industrial circumstances and cultural contexts that surrounded and informed their production, circulation, and reception—a triangulation of analytical perspectives we similarly took up previously and that our contributors, in various ways, continue herein. One final genre-related concept warrants attention as possibly relevant to our notion of the categorization of 1960s Camp TV or, rearranging the terms and broadening the scope, camp in 1960s TV. In Christine Gledhill's study of melodrama, she argues that this term marks not a cinematic genre, but rather a modality or "culturally conditioned mode of perception and aesthetic articulation" that, like comedy and romance, regularly underlies many films and even other film genres (227–229). We can recognize here significant overlaps with Sontag's understanding of camp as a "sensibility" that is legible in a wide array of cultural objects. Following this, we note that, in a number of the television programs considered closely here, camp is working perhaps less like a fully formed set of genre conventions and more like a sensibility that becomes manifest in some of these programs in specific and limited ways, such as in the subverted representations of gender roles (e.g., *F Troop*, *The Avengers*) or in playfully reflexive treatments of the sitcom as a genre (e.g., *The Munsters*). Returning to the Gantt chart and looking at the programs closely considered here, this kind of camp modality appears significantly in the shows that ultimately lead up to the success of mainstreamed camp in programs like *Get Smart*, *Batman*, and *The Monkees*. Based on prevalent theories of genre formation (Altman 54–68), this is exactly as we would expect.

Looking back at the history of camp, Sontag's was not, of course, the first articulation of that term; several scholars—including the authors here—have elsewhere traced various instances of the term and concept from its entry into the popular vernacular of the 1960s backward through its earlier articulations and manifestations, most often associated with homosexual male subculture, from Christopher Isherwood to Oscar Wilde to Louis XIV's brother (Phillips and Pinedo 24–25). Several writers (Meyer; Babuscio) have taken umbrage at scholars or critics such as Sontag that disassociate camp from its genderqueer origins, yet as Greg Taylor has effectively argued, "Camp . . . is ultimately bigger than sexuality or sexual identity, and identifying it as an essentially queer activity may limit our ability to recognize its importance and influence as [a much] broader strategy of vanguard cultural resistance" (167n4; see also Cleto 16–22).

Taylor's focus on the vanguard draws our attention also to one of the other key formative lineages for 1960s camp: avant-garde or underground cinema. In fact, it was Jack Smith's *Flaming Creatures* (1964) that Sontag was reviewing (after it was seized by New York City police on the grounds of indecency!) in the pre-"Notes" publication already mentioned. There she employed the term to describe the film's "rich collage of 'camp' lore" and "the modern 'camp' way of relishing mass culture" (376—note the scare quotes). Smith was a key player in this period, but other filmmakers such as Kenneth Anger and George Kuchar were important contributors as well (Tinkcom 73–74; Mathijs and Sexton 88–89). Andy Warhol, famous already for his role in Pop Art, established his Factory and began experimenting with making films in 1963. Before the end of the 1960s, Warhol had made well over one hundred films, some of which circulated through art house theaters but many of which played only at his own events and art openings. Often remembered for his experiments with cinematic time (*Sleep* [1963], *Empire* [1964]) and engagement with New York City's gay subculture (*Blowjob* [1964], *My Hustler* [1965]), Warhol also continued his fascination with the detritus and ephemera of American culture—including those individuals it casts off—as well as its celebrity, consumer, and popular cultures, all critical elements of the camp aesthetic (Tinkcom; Ross). Lesser-known Warhol films such as *Soap Opera* and *Batman/Dracula*, both from 1964, mark significant overlaps with the key aspects of camp's burgeoning popularization. Notably here, between Sontag's "Notes on 'Camp'" and ABC's premiere of *Batman*, Warhol produced and premiered *Camp* (1965), a series of vaudeville-esque performances by several Factory regulars that traded on the sudden wider legibility of the term-as-title for its "commercial" appeal (though the film only played at Warhol's events). Near the end, the film includes a scene in which Jack Smith invites the viewer to "open the closet, can we?" as the camera pans to find a *Batman* comic hiding there on the shelf (Tinkcom 97–99).

Mainstream cinema also caught on to camp, and that same late-1960s period saw a number of examples of deliberate camp, such as the camping of James Bond by both *Our Man Flint* (1966) and Dean Martin's Matt Helm series (starting with *The Silencers* [1966]). *Barbarella* (1968), Roger Vadim's adaptation of an erotic science-fiction comic strip starring Jane Fonda, and *Beyond the Valley of the Dolls* and *Myra Breckenridge* (both in 1970) regularly warrant mention in discussions of intentionally produced camp. Certainly a range of 1960s cultural production beyond the audiovisual also directly engaged camp, including pop music (e.g., Teddy and Darrel's 1966 release *These Are the Hits, You Silly Savage*); stand-up comedians and their comedy albums (e.g., Paul Lynde's *Recently Released* [1960]); and a wide gamut of print materials, including sources for several of the films mentioned above, the queer camp parodies of Bond mentioned in our article (27), and—of course—*MAD Magazine*. For some cultural critics, deliberate camp "willingly forfeits its own dignity in order to invite a distanced, liberated play with its textual meanings." However, "the game is now rigged, with the artist still controlling spectator response" (Taylor 168n7). Thus, though all camp invites the spectator to respond in some way, recognizing if not necessarily understanding the subaltern meanings (drag is a good example here), in deliberate camp the subtext is designed to (co-)exist on the surface. Consequentially, to do so, the artist or producer intentionally places themselves above the spectator again in terms of controlling the interpretation of meaning, reducing or even removing for some camp's essential joie de vivre.

Camp's move from subcultural sensibility to mass culture object through the blast furnace of commercial exploitation is also a key feature of this book. Many histories of camp note its transformation within popular culture and popular discourse across that decade, but there has yet to be a more careful consideration of that move as it was both reflected in and promoted by the *television programs* of the 1960s. A medium with the reach of television would seemingly have been absolutely consequential to the popularization and then mainstreaming of camp, the result of which is variously known (here and elsewhere) as "mass camp," "pop camp," "het[erosexual] camp," "de-politicized camp," and "democratized camp" (Hook 249). Yet aside from the regular name-dropping of programs such as *The Monkees* and especially *Batman*, the role of television in this has not been seriously considered.

"Gilligan and Captain Kirk," which argued for a genre (or cycle) of mid-to-late-1960s television programs (as an unrecognized predecessor to the more thoroughly studied "Cult TV") has already laid the groundwork for such an intervention. There we defined our object of study as:

> a larger body of work that we identify as 1960s Camp TV, produced under historically specific industrial conditions and characterized by a clearly identifiable camp style that connects these shows. As with any genre cycle, a single show displays some, though not necessarily all, of the traits in the cluster. In line with other applications of camp, these shows employed narrative strategies such as parody and satire, intertextuality, self-reflexivity, and an overt emphasis on performativity that included (but was not limited to) the treatment of gender. Individually, but especially collectively, these characteristics of Camp TV both allowed for the mobilization of an active viewer and enabled that viewer to recognize the contestability of the texts' surface-level representations. (27)

Camp TV of the 1960s: Reassessing the Vast Wasteland, as a new collection of original essays, expands the scope of that study by including readings of other critically overlooked or underestimated 1960s American prime-time programs that drew significantly on aspects of camp, offering novel readings of key 1960s programs in relation to a developing cycle of Camp TV, investigating television precursors that exhibited key aspects of camp early in the decade, and bringing new methods and approaches to bear on this newly recognized TV genre. Collectively, this opens out the discussion of just how consequential *television* was to mainstreamed camp and the degree to which individual shows engaged or advanced that process.

At the same time, this collection offers new perspectives on the history of American television's translation from "vast wasteland" at the beginning of the decade to its "turn toward relevance" ten years later. Speaking to the National Association of Broadcasters on May 9, 1961, for the first time as the new Chairman of the Federal Communications Commission (FCC), Newton Minow clearly understood himself to be one of President John F. Kennedy's "New Frontiersmen." He articulated his charge to those in the audience that day: "I am in Washington to help broadcasting, not to harm it; to strengthen it, not weaken it; . . . to stimulate it, not censor it." However, he immediately added: "Above all, I am here to uphold and protect the public trust." In that latter role, he took this opportunity to exhort the *television* broadcasters to better serve the American public. After praising a small handful of programs including "Astaire Time" (1960), *The Twilight Zone* (1959–64), and *The Valiant Years* (1960–61), he complimented some of the work done in the most recent season: "When television is good, nothing—not the theater, not the magazines or newspapers—nothing is better." However, to motivate them to improve, he had to make a rhetorical shift and denigrate, to an even greater degree, the current televisual landscape. The fuller context of his infamous jibe continued:

> But when television is bad, nothing is worse. I invite each of you to sit down in front of your television set when your station goes on the air and stay there, for a day . . . until the station signs off. I can assure you that what you will observe is a vast wasteland. You will see a procession of game shows, formula comedies about totally unbelievable families, blood and thunder, mayhem, violence, sadism, murder, western bad men, western good men, private eyes, gangsters, more violence, and cartoons. And endlessly, commercials—many screaming, cajoling, and offending. And most of all, boredom.

Though Minow was ostensibly speaking of the entire day of programming, the genres and tropes he explicitly denotes skew clearly toward prime time. As FCC chairman, he generally understood his charges—"almost 180 million Americans gathered around 56 million sets"—as requiring safeguarding from vapid or, worse, deleterious programming. In doing so, he reinforced the patriarchal role of both government and industry and offered broadcasters an infantilized characterization of their viewers and, by extension, the American public.

Describing the activities of CBS and its president, Bob Wood, some ten years later, Todd Gitlin, in *Inside Prime Time*, relates what he terms "the turn toward 'relevance'" (203). At the start of the 1971–72 season, previous rural-themed network successes like *Mayberry R.F.D* (1968–71), *The Beverly Hillbillies*, *Green Acres*, and *Hee Haw* (1969–71) were purged from the network's lineup and "young, urban, and more 'realistic'" (209) fare like *The Mary Tyler Moore Show* (1970–77) and *All in the Family* (1971–79) added. This sudden shift at the dawn of a new decade is generally attributed to a new emphasis on demographics in courting advertisers—with *who* was watching (in terms of buying power) rather than *how many* were watching taking over as the operative selling point.

Industrial shifts and marketing trends notwithstanding, the young, urban, educated consumers that CBS, NBC, and ABC all imagined they could court through innovative programming were there already at the end of the previous decade and hence available to lure to the newly relevant TV shows of the 1970s. This is in sharp contrast to the audience imagined by Minow and projected to that room full of broadcasting decision-makers at the beginning of the 1960s. So how did the audience change so notably in the course of ten years? What programs, still often characterized as part of an enduring "wasteland" on American television, were those viewers watching during this decade? How did TV shows of the intervening era entertain but also entice this newer population of viewers? How consequential for Camp TV was the emergent viewership of young, educated baby boomers and the youth rebellion that Aniko Bodroghkozy and others have already studied in relation to 1960s TV? At one point in his speech, Minow stated that it was time for American television to "grow up." America itself saw a radical transformation during this era, one that was reflected, refracted, and projected onto its television screens. How can we trace both this metaphorical maturation process of television and the radical shift in America and Americans through the TV shows of the 1960s? What role did the programs we read under the sign of camp play in these various processes? It is these questions, and others related to this key transitional period in America and American television, that this collection also works to consider.

Despite our emphasis here, and in our title, on "the 1960s," the neat borders of decades are, of course, a historian's construct. The 1960s perhaps as much as any decade in recent American history demonstrates the forced nature of such broad characterizations; the zeitgeist as well as the cultural products of 1963, for example, are arguably more similar to 1958 than to 1968. Tracing the history of both camp and Camp TV bears this out as well. Our previous study of the genre cycle of Camp TV focused primarily on shows that premiered (and often were also cancelled) between 1964 and 1969. The middle section of this collection ("Camp TV's Tentpoles") more or less aligns with this periodization. This lets us mark the shift from shows that, according to Cynthia J. Miller in her chapter on *F Troop*, "not only reassured and grounded viewers caught up in the confusion of change, but also gently nudged them forward" (142), to those like *Rowan & Martin's Laugh-In* or even *The Monkees* which, as Dan Amernick argues in this volume, began to aggressively (if still playfully) challenge mainstream views. The beginning of this periodization again situates nicely alongside the publication of Sontag's treatise on camp and marks the beginning of this cycle as well as the end of the previous one. In the introduction to their collection of essays *Sontag and the Camp Aesthetic: Advancing New Perspectives*, Brian Peters and Bruce Drushel note that this periodization (1954–64) has been referred to by design critic Thomas Hine as "the campiest decade in American history" (viii). Echoing this, we have elsewhere commented on camp's "move from the margins to the mainstream in the decade between Christopher Isherwood's 1954 novel of queer identity awakening, *The World in the Evening*, and Susan Sontag's 1964 'Notes on "Camp"'" (Phillips and Pinedo 25). Furthermore, this also appears to fit well with Quinlan Miller's separate historicization of Camp TV.

After our 2018 article, two additional scholarly works devoted to a consideration of Camp TV appeared within two years, though none were aware of the presence of any of the others. Miller's monograph, *Camp TV: Trans Gender Queer Sitcom History*, was published in spring 2019; approximately a year later, Ania Malinowska's 2200-word entry on "Camp TV" was published in *The International Encyclopedia of Gender, Media, and Communication*. Significant to our work here, Miller's book focuses on "the 1950s and 1960s and on the commercial art form of the sitcom" and therein identifies regular and arguably regularized instances of queer gender, predominantly in the casting and characterization of guest stars. These performances marked the shows, according to Miller, as "a form of camp that . . . was a part of popular culture in advance of the late-1960s, before the time that scholars have, so far, expected it" (3). Even more neatly, his study of guest star casting and characterizations hews closely to this

1954–64 periodization: his chapter "Camp TV and Queer Gender: Sitcom History" starts with an "exemplary instance" from a 1954 episode of *The Martha Raye Show* (1954–56) that guest starred Paul Lynde, Wally Cox, and Charlotte Rae, "all luminaries of queer gender" (27); the first episode Miller cites specifically in his introduction is a 1964 episode of *The Patty Duke Show* (1963–66). To study this earlier form of camp on American television, Miller develops a new critical construct he christens "trans gender queer." As "a placeholder for the genderqueer within pop culture products that are supposed to be exclusively cis," this approach to critical viewership offers scholars and others "the possibility of reading gender cues that are more specific than male and female, masculine and feminine" (3). This can be a powerful analytical tool for recognizing moments of camp coding and hence engaging in camp as a historically valid reading strategy in comedies that were not otherwise heavily invested in camp as a style, genre, or mode of production. Several of our contributors here, including Ken Feil and Emily Hoffman, draw on this aspect of Miller's work in addressing camp's capacity for skewing and skewering traditional strategies of gender representation within the context of the sitcom and more broadly within American television.

However, in comparison to our work (2018 and here), Miller is predominantly tracing just one aspect of camp into American TV and tends to use the term "camp" to cover any of a number of related aspects—parody, reflexivity, satire, irony—that also appear in the presence of queer or trans performers/performance. As such, he argues that camp was always a part of the sitcom since these elements appear there from the very beginning in television's process of appropriating the forms as well as the personnel from other media and entertainments. Much of this had come via the performance history of variety programming, specifically those related to what Miller calls "'vaudeo' . . . vaudeville by way of television broadcast" (35). His study does much then to help place the energies of Milton Berle, the Three Stooges, and other similar camp-like elements of pre-1960s TV that are important to our history (Phillips and Pinedo 33) but which were already in place in television in the early 1960s and/or imported from other media such as vaudeville or Hollywood. These traditions continue to appear in the some of the more obvious aspects of cross-dressing we pointed out in *The Monkees* and *Gilligan's Island* where audiences easily recognized the costume play but the characters within the diegesis seemed blind to it. To his credit, for Miller, this is only the most obvious form, "the most conventional understanding of drag in narrative fiction" (13).

This analytical approach relates as well to our own period of focus, but our definition of Camp TV is notably more encompassing and does not reduce to gender or sexuality, though it fully recognizes and includes both. It might then be beneficial to consider this as one strain of camp that, when it shows up in 1960s Camp TV, was already part of its televisual lineage, imbedded within the conventions of the sitcom prior to the mid-1960s. Interestingly, if we combine our timeline with his, we are able to observe a more complete trajectory of camp, and particularly trans gender queer camp, from the margins to the center of American culture. Paul Lynde—well known for his presence in both Miller's era of sitcom guest stars and our own Camp TV of the 1960s (perhaps best known as Uncle Arthur on *Bewitched*, Lynde appears briefly in three of our contributors' chapters)—could figuratively model this translation, as his own position within American television moved from the margins to the center, from guest star roles in short-lived programs to the center square in the gameshow *Hollywood Squares* (a position he assumed in 1968 and then held for more than a decade).

Noteworthy here as well is Miller's observed "dip in camp TV in the very late 1950s and early 1960s" that was a result of industry reactions to mid-1950s political energies (mostly the House Un-American Activities Committee [HUAC]) that "brought pressure from sponsors, the FCC, journalists, lobbyists, set manufacturers, and other investors in the network system to purify the airwaves of potentially offensive content" (37–38). This then helps to differentiate our periodization of Camp TV from his, which carries over this "dip" but remains consistent in terms of the conventions he associates with camp television and thus as a specifically genderqueer—or trans gender queer—activity. For our period, the end of his "dip" in the early 1960s coordinates with the broader introduction of other aspects we recognize as markers of camp. In particular, this includes Pop Art's multiplicity of meaning built on recycled consumer images, with which early 1960s television shows such as *Fractured Flickers* (studied here) were also beginning to play. Critics and audiences were, as a result, becoming increasingly familiar with new meanings drawn from familiar images. At the same time, the cultural and political tensions of the 1960s made such dual-address structures steadily more relevant (and popular) for mass entertainment. These became even more readily available to and desired by TV producers in the widespread infusion of color recording and broadcasting, which further activated audience awareness and built toward mass camp as a style both legible and palatable for mass dissemination (Phillips and Pinedo 23–24).

Malinowska, without being familiar with either Miller's or our studies, also recognized the 1960s as a key starting point, yet her references there are just a small part of her argument of televisual camp's origins in the "open homosexuality" of several music icons, such as Dusty Springfield, which led into the 1970s disco era's "flexibility of gender" (2). She ultimately argues that *Dynasty* (1981–89) "is the first TV show recognized for its camp traces," something both Mark Finch (1999) and Jane Feuer (2005) have similarly claimed. The campiness of British sitcoms such as *Absolutely Fabulous* (1992–95) were, for Malinowska, inspired by *Dynasty*, particularly Joan Collins's Alexis. Working in the register of "feminist camp" (Robertson), she also points to shows such as *Xena: Warrior Princess* (1995–2001), *Buffy the Vampire Slayer* (1997–2003), and *Desperate Housewives* (2004–12) as key texts of camp television from the last twenty-five years. Finally, she highlights the popularity of *RuPaul's Drag Race* (2009–present) as a contemporary example.

Malinowska's periodization highlights for us one of the predicaments of studying any short-lived genre or production cycle: what happens after the run of success and high-volume production ends? Further, we should also ask: what are the reasons for its fall from grace? Beyond the dispersed energies of a fully "democratized" camp (Booth), Moya Luckett also argues in our final chapter that the conservative movement in America at the end of the 1960s—Richard Nixon's so-called silent majority—appropriated camp for its own purposes, diluting its political valence and cultural use-value for the audience/s that had initially found it attractive. This coincided, as we noted in our 2018 article, with a resurgence of interest in camp by the subculture out of which it initially emerged: "the 1969 Stonewall riots and the resulting revision of gay identity politics in the early 1970s resulted in camp being reclaimed, to a degree, by and for that subculture" (Phillips and Pinedo 25n8; Cleto 88–92). The two most famously campy texts of the 1970s—John Waters's *Pink Flamingos* (1972) and *The Rocky Horror Picture Show* (1975)—of course skewed back toward this genderqueer subculture, but now the cult energies of midnight movies competed with and, for some viewers, dominated the camp nature of these two films. Like camp, cult affinities seek pleasure in secondary, subaltern, often transgressive meaning systems. Unlike camp, however, cult tastes tend to gravitate toward an "oppositional connoisseurship" of the detritus or at least excesses of mass culture, a connoisseurship that relies on and relishes the viewer's "ability to discern (and define) authentic aesthetic material lurking in low culture products" (Taylor 51).

For cinema scholars, camp reifies a viewing position that seeks pleasure in creative control, reading out obscured (though not necessarily unintentional) meanings. Moreover, cult film enthusiasts value, appreciate, and take pleasure in the detritus (not all of it, but those designated via the specialized "cult" tastes), perhaps purposefully and even gleefully reading it against its original intended meanings (as with the diegetic viewers of *Mystery Science Theater 3000* [1988–99]). Concepts such as Jeffrey Sconce's theory of "paracinema" attempt to create an umbrella under which all of these cinematic viewing positions (cult, camp, midnight, etc.) and their corresponding film texts can fit; though useful to a degree, such an umbrella is not always or fully successful (Mathjis and Sexton 89–94). Television scholars, though, understand Cult TV texts somewhat differently, as those that engage and at times encourage a distinct participatory culture in a small but notable subset of the viewers. Not surprisingly, given the close kinship between viewer agency in Cult TV and Camp TV that was the impetus behind our 2018 article, the TV programs of the 1990s and early 2000s noted by Malinowska as examples of Camp TV are also regularly found in the scholarship on Cult TV, with *Buffy* occupying a particularly important space (Abbott; Lavery; Gwenllian-Jones and Pearson). Cult TV also falls, more generally, into the era of postmodernity, and scholars such as Harry Benshoff have noted that "true to the polemics of the postmodern economy, the camp sensibility . . . has perhaps become just another hip stance or lifestyle practice available for purchase," diffusing its energies further beyond what we observe in the initial wave of "mass camp" in the 1960s (205; see also Phillips and Pinedo 27n13).

To conclude this brief historical purview, we would be remiss if we failed to mention also the almost uncanny persistence of Camp TV within American pop culture across the intervening half-century. Beyond the *Batman* juggernaut and the TV syndication (and then VHS/DVD compilations) which kept these programs in circulation for later generations, nearly every show mentioned, from *The Man from U.N.C.L.E.* to *The Addams Family* to *Lost in Space*, has received a Hollywood adaptation. *Bewitched* even made it into the mythology of the Marvel universe with its inclusion in *WandaVision* (2021). Looking back over the long history of television, these programs—more than most—continue to stand out and draw attention. As we said at the beginning of this introduction, there is something about these shows that keeps viewers coming back. This collection aims to help us understand why.

Chapter Summaries

The first chapter is a reprint of our 2018 article. We have chosen to include it here, despite the initial framing of that argument in relation to the established paradigm of Cult TV, as it contains numerous analytical aspects which connect implicitly or explicitly to the work in this collection. (Readers should note that all citations of that essay in this collection refer to the page numbers in the original *Journal of Popular Television* publication rather than the reprinted version in Chapter 1.) Following that, the new essays included here are divided up into three sections. The first, "Laying the (Camp)Groundwork," includes two chapters that look at television programs that preceded and hence laid additional groundwork for mid-1960s television's rush toward mass camp. We start with Andrea Comiskey and Jonah Horwitz's chapter on *Fractured Flickers*. Produced by Jay Ward, who was also behind the campy humor of Rocky and Bullwinkle (*The Adventures of Rocky and Bullwinkle and Friends* [1959–64]), *Flickers* re-edited older footage, mostly from silent films, to create new, absurdist replacement narratives and comic montages. Rather than simply mocking older films, *Flickers*, they argue, repurposed them in a complex, reflexive mode that combined sincere affection and gleeful travesty. Its sophisticated camp approach both echoed contemporaneous avant-garde found footage cinema, such as Bruce Conner's *A Movie* (1958), and presaged later Camp TV such as *The Monkees* that utilized silent-film techniques and iconography. In the process, *Flickers* tutored its baby boomer audiences in camp appropriation of popular culture and the logistics of dual address.

Emily Hoffman's chapter on Hanna-Barbera's *Snagglepuss* follows. Although Snagglepuss's homosexuality has long been assumed, Hoffman expands her analysis beyond a character study to specifically consider the series of shorts from *The Yogi Bear Show* (1961), which has received little attention. She finds that *Snagglepuss* repeats a storyline centered on the protagonist's efforts to navigate iconic masculine communities (the Wild West, the mafia, the Knights of the Round Table), but that to do so, he must rely on disguises that obscure his flamboyant pinkness and performance of non-normative masculinity. Hoffman further argues that Snagglepuss represents classical Hollywood's history of closeted gay labor and, as such, allows us to read its violent slapstick comedy as a cautionary tale about the consequences of passing as straight in mid-century Los Angeles.

The middle section of this collection focuses on "Camp TV's Tentpoles," and here our contributors look both at key programs that have been understudied by television scholars, such as *The Addams Family* and *F Troop*, and bring new insights to well-studied works of camp television, such as *Batman*. Jamie Hook's chapter on *The Addams Family* and *The Munsters* compares these two iconic television texts of the 1960s that united family-centered narratives with horror through the representation of family units comprised of literal monsters. While both are situation comedies, Hook notes that they are further unified by strong camp sensibilities as they intentionally camped American middle-class mores as well as the generic tropes of the sitcom itself. Sitting at the crossroads between the mainstream and the subcultural, comedy and horror, and competing modes and meanings of camp, these shows constructed an image of the American family as simultaneously monstrous and endearing during a cultural maelstrom in which the institutional politics of the family were being reconsidered and renegotiated. The resulting programs, according to Hook, thus offered both mainstream values and countercultural pleasures through the language of camp. We see here then a form of Camp TV more closely resembling the broader mainstreamed camp or conservative camp that Moya Luckett will argue for in our last chapter as opposed to the more aggressively countercultural camp of shows like *The Monkees*.

Andrew J. Owens's chapter on *Bewitched* continues this focus on the sitcoms that drew on fantastical elements to create humor in its reading of the ways in which *Bewitched* refracted 1960s occultism through the lens of camp. Here he examines the show as part of a transitional moment across both the industrial and programming landscape of 1960s American television and other forms of "occult media" in the United States. While Sontag denied any true political potentialities of approaching the world in a campy way, Owens argues that *Bewitched* nevertheless used its love of "artifice and exaggeration" (Sontag) to assemble, in the 1960s, a generative ideological ground for American television's capacity for social critique, especially in relation to changing mid-century mores of gender and sexuality.

In the sixth chapter, Cynthia J. Miller continues this inquiry into comedic critique of masculinity and patriarchy as she looks closely at *F Troop* and its use of camp's repertoire of self-conscious humor—parody, satire, irony—along with the physical comedy of vaudeville. This sitcom, Miller argues, both mocked and reinforced white patriarchal notions of Manifest Destiny and the Myth of the Frontier in its comedic take on life in a frontier cavalry fort. Her chapter situates the series in the sociopolitical context of the 1960s and examines the ways in which *F Troop* and its cast of misfits and shady characters poked fun at canonical US history, authority, social class, and normative gender roles, as well as racial and ethnic stereotypes.

In Chapter 7, Benjamin Kruger-Robbins locates *Batman* in the broader context of network programming strategies. He re-evaluates ABC's reputation as a venue for what network executive Harve Bennett famously called "Wild-Ass Programming" by analyzing reception, production, and distribution artifacts surrounding *Batman* in conjunction with those relating to explicitly gay-themed episodes of the short-lived detective procedural *N.Y.P.D.* (1967–69). In this way, the deliberate camp of *Batman* is seen to form part of a complex and occasionally affirmative, if also socially problematic, overture to "new" audience demographics. Kruger-Robbins's comparison here reveals a dual branding strategy that positioned ABC as an emerging venue for "quality" adult gay content while tightening the network's grip on "adolescent" entertainment for young families.

Chapter 8, by Dan Amernick, considers the Monkees' attempts, starting in the latter part of the first season but taking on notable significance during the second, to distance themselves from the Camp TV image that had been crafted in the initial batch of episodes. He argues that, following the off-camera skirmishes between the band's creative personnel and music supervisor, Don Kirshner, many of the episodes began to reflect the growing backstage tension. Though neither the band nor the television program were ultimately able to shed the powerful associations of camp performativity, Amernick reads specific episodes within the context of the band's efforts to achieve authenticity and explores *The Monkees*' endeavors to develop a kind of televisual authenticity that existed in contradistinction to, though always alongside of, the aspects of the program that remained anchored in Camp TV.

In Chapter 9, the last chapter of this section on the "tentpoles" of 1960s Camp TV, Craig Haslop and Douglas McNaughton expand our study to British television and survey developing representations of masculinity in British "spy-fi" series such as *The Prisoner*, *Jason King*, and especially *The Avengers*—arguably the best known of these British programs. In particular, they investigate these shows' use of pop camp to subvert hegemonic masculinity and articulate shifting discourses of gender performativity in the 1960s. Here they find, for example, that John Steed's persona in *The Avengers* shifted from hard-boiled, trench coat–wearing *noir* detective to effete dandy, sipping champagne and wearing Pierre Cardin suits. Moreover, his female associates became ever more capable at physical combat as the Steed character became more camp. This is particularly relevant to this collection as, at this stage in its run (the Emma Peel/Diana Rigg episodes) and at the height of Camp TV on American television, the series played in syndication in the United States (see Plate 1). The subversion of masculinity by camp in these British spy-fi programs reached an apotheosis, Haslop and McNaughton claim, at the end of the 1960s, with Jason King of *Department S* (1969–70) and *Jason King* (1970–71), whose protagonist is a sybaritic, womanizing novelist who glides through unlikely crime-fighting adventures in a range of flamboyant outfits. Drawing on the concept of "macho drag," they argue that the King character intentionally draws attention to the constructedness of hegemonic masculinity.

In the final section of this collection, titled "Other Camp(TV)sites," our remaining contributors expand on the work presented to this point, apply new methods to the study of Camp TV, and engage programs not immediately legible as camp. In this way, the final section opens out beyond just a study of already-canonical Camp programs and connects certain lines of inquiry that initiate or run through 1960s Camp TV to later trends in television and post-1960s culture. Reba A. Wissner's chapter, "Can TV Music Be Camp?," examines the musical scores of 1960s space operas *Star Trek* and *Lost in Space*, and spy shows *The Man from U.N.C.L.E.* and *Get Smart*, to reveal certain affinities with Camp aesthetics: exaggerated style, unique instrumentation and instrumental combinations, and outlandish musical vocabularies. By examining the musical constructions common to these series, this chapter extends the emerging definition of the Camp style in 1960s television *music* to other contemporary series such as *Batman*, to better allow us to understand the role of music in Camp television. All televisions at the time were equipped with relatively consistent sound technology even as there were major disparities in image quality due to color versus black/white sets; Wissner's study contributes to a better understanding of the ways in which producers communicated and audiences received and interpreted meaning via sound within Camp TV's system of dual address, even when watching these shows in monochrome.

Nicholas C. Morgan's chapter unpacks the ways *Flipper* would have been legible as camp to certain viewers at the time, showing how its multiple campy villains and frequent use of nature documentary camerawork interwove queer subtexts and camp aestheticism. From this angle, Morgan demonstrates the persistence of naïve camp in the mid-1960s and the way the broader cultural dissemination of camp in that decade facilitated a form of dual address even in a program that articulated itself in opposition to camp's irony and insincerity. He then turns to *Flipper*'s reception among fans, writers, and artists since the early 1990s. These receptions explore a current of "dark camp" wherein stigma and perversion exist alongside the cheerful glamor more often emphasized in accounts of camp. Resultantly, Morgan identifies *Flipper* as a cultural site in which this dialectical relationship between negative and positive affects was accessible to queer viewers within the broader mediasphere of 1960s television.

In Chapter 12, Ken Feil approaches Camp TV by addressing the correspondence between camp and the comedy of manners. The violation of conventional "good taste" and its reflection in gender performance and sexual orientation comprises a camp comedy of manners that Feil argues helped set the stage for both the programs and fans of Camp TV. However, camp theory historically has remained colorblind and, as a result, replicates the white, gay, male, and middle-class historical norms of camp. Feil works to find ways to address this oversight and applies recent critical paradigms forwarded by Quinlan Miller and Racquel J. Gates in his analyses of camp manners comedy in both the sitcom *The Beverly Hillbillies* and Flip Wilson's drag performances as Geraldine Jones on *Rowan & Martin's Laugh-In* and *The Flip Wilson Show* (1970–74). As a result, Feil's chapter works to address the deficiencies in camp theories for addressing gender nonconformity and especially race.

In the final chapter in *Camp TV of the 1960s*, Moya Luckett explores how 1960s television programs such as *Green Acres*, *Get Smart*, and *Batman* used camp's playful, performative qualities and its love of artifice for more conservative ends. Further, she works to understand how American television's adaptation of camp allowed the medium to capitalize on the period's new (and sometimes radical) youth culture without fundamentally disturbing its genres, aesthetics, economics, and address. She further investigates how camp's ambivalence allowed mainstream viewers to negotiate and even resist cultural change while still courting more progressive and newly valuable youth audiences. As the Metropolitan Museum of Art's popular "Camp: Notes on Fashion" exhibition demonstrated as recently as 2019, the mainstream still often finds camp irresistible. Placing her study at the end of the 1960s and focusing on a more conservative, cynical camp sensibility found in shows like *Rowan & Martin's Laugh-In*, Luckett argues that even as camp's political and subcultural allegiances mock, question, and sometimes threaten accepted norms, its aesthetics incorporate aspects of mainstream American taste (in particular, its *bad* taste) displaying its capacity to reinvent the mundane—a quality particularly attractive to TV networks during the 1960s.

Matt Hills's Afterword completes and concludes the anthology. Here Hills positions this study of Camp TV in relation to other scholarly considerations of subcultural forms and audiences. He calls forth Susan Sontag as well as, notably, Pierre Bourdieu in discussing the cultural and subcultural capital of Camp TV. In doing so, he expands broadly into issues of cult, kitsch, paracinema, trash, and other "admixtures of textual content and contextual/audience activations" (303) which have helped to determine the theoretical approaches found throughout this collection. Rather than analyzing and contextualizing Camp TV itself—which is the work of this collection's chapters, Hills uses his Afterword to contextualize the *scholarship* on Camp TV by placing the work done here within the broader scope of subcultural analyses both inside and outside of television studies.

Stepping back, this anthology suggests the need for analyses of Camp TV programs not spotlighted in this volume, including the aforementioned *The Wild Wild West* and *Hollywood Squares*. It also indicates a range of further research questions yet to be explored. Both *Hogan's Heroes* (1965–71) and *F Troop*, read closely here in terms of its skewering of traditional representations of masculinity by Cynthia J. Miller, also significantly turned perpetrators of state genocide into objects of camp humor. *Hogan's Heroes* in particular used camp to neuter our collective memory of the Nazi menace, and did so in part by featuring three actors directly affected by Nazi aggression: Robert Clary (Cpl. LeBeau) survived concentration camp internment and Werner Klemperer (Col. Klink) and John Banner (Sgt. Shultz) fled Germany and Austria, respectively (Williams). Additionally, various chapters discuss the on-screen and off-screen exchange of talent across Camp TV shows. Cynthia J. Miller points out that on *F Troop*, medicine man Roaring Chicken was played by Edward Everett Horton, who plays a similar role, Chief Screaming Chicken, on *Batman*. Horton is introduced in this volume by Comiskey and Horwitz as the narrator of "Fractured Fairy Tales" on the Jay Ward production, *The Adventures of Rocky and Bullwinkle and Friends* (1959–64). A social network analysis of on-camera and behind the scenes labor that analyzes the circulation of acting, producing, and writing talent between Camp TV shows of the period and its precursors would shed light on the production culture of the period, the exchange of knowledge, and collaborations that coalesced into 1960s Camp TV. Such an analysis could be further extended to the British programs, including but not limited to those addressed in Chapter 9.

In conclusion, these chapters collectively rethink the blanket characterization of 1960s prime-time programs as constituent of a vast wasteland and complicate our understanding of mid-century television's invocation of dual address through their consideration of such conventions of Camp TV as same-sex drag, innuendo and double entendre, exaggerated musical coding, and the use of vibrant color. These practices generated multivalent meaning systems that allowed audiences to derive pleasure from programs that to varying extents challenged normative views. As new pleasures are continually derived from revisiting these older Camp TV programs, we hope the chapters will yield not only new pleasures but also new scholarly directions for understanding television history, its (sub)cultural (under)currents, and—to quote William Dozier once again—the "funsies" associated with camp's many possible meanings.

Bibliography

Abbott, Stacey, editor. *The Cult TV Book: From* Star Trek *to* Dexter, *New Approaches to TV Outside the Box*. Soft Skull Press, 2010.

Altman, Rick. *Film/Genre*. BFI, 1999.

Babuscio, Jack. "Camp and the Gay Sensibility." 1977. *Camp Grounds: Style and Homosexuality*, edited by David Bergman, University of Massachusetts Press, 1993, pp. 19–38.

Benshoff, Harry M. "Camp." *Schirmer Encyclopedia of Film*, vol. 1, edited by Barry Keith Grant, Thomson Gale, 2007, pp. 201–205.

Bodroghkozy, Aniko. *Groove Tube: Sixties Television and the Youth Rebellion*. Duke University Press, 1991.

Booth, Mark. *Camp*. London: Quartet, 1983.

Cleto, Fabio, editor. *Camp: Queer Aesthetics and the Performing Subject—A Reader*. University of Michigan Press, 1999.

Feuer, Jane. "The Lack of Influence of *thirtysomething*." *The Contemporary Television Series*, edited by Michael Hammond and Lucy Mazdon, Edinburgh University Press, 2005, pp. 27–36.

Finch, Mark. "Sex and Address in *Dynasty*." Cleto, pp. 143–159.

Gates, Racquel J. *Double Negative: The Black Image & Popular Culture*. Rutgers University Press, 2018.

Gitlin, Todd. *Inside Prime Time*. 2nd ed. University of California Press, 2000.

Gledhill, Christine. "Rethinking Genre." *Reinventing Film Studies*, edited by Christine Gledhill and Linda Williams, Arnold, 2000, pp. 221–243.

Grindon, Leger. *Knockout: The Boxer and Boxing in American Cinema*. University Press of Mississippi, 2011.

Gwenllian-Jones, Sara, and Roberta E. Pearson, editors. *Cult Television*. University of Minnesota Press, 2004.

Hook, Jamie. "Willful Infidelities: Camping Camille." *Queer/Adaptation: A Collection of Critical Essays*, edited by Pamela Demory, Palgrave Macmillan, 2019, pp. 241–260.

Lavery, David, editor. *The Essential Cult TV Reader*. University Press of Kentucky, 2010.

Malinowska, Ania. "Camp TV." *The International Encyclopedia of Gender, Media, and Communication*, edited by Karen Ross, John Wiley & Sons, 2020, pp. 1–6.

Mathijs, Ernest, and Jamie Sexton. *Cult Cinema*. Wiley Blackwell, 2011.

Meyer, Moe, editor. *The Politics and Poetics of Camp*. Routledge, 1994.

Miller, Quinlan. *Camp TV: Trans Gender Queer Sitcom History*. Duke University Press, 2019.

Minow, Newton N. "Television and the Public Interest." 1961. *American Rhetoric Online Speech Bank*, www.americanrhetoric.com/speeches/newtonminow.htm. Accessed July 14, 2021.

Naremore, James. *More Than Night: Film Noir in Its Contexts*. University of California Press, 1998.

Peters, Brian. M., and Bruce. E. Drushel. "Introduction: Some Notes on 'Notes.'" *Sontag and the Camp Aesthetic: Advancing New Perspectives*, edited by Bruce E. Drushel and Brian M. Peters, Lexington Books, 2017, pp. vii–xv.

Phillips, W. D., and Isabel Pinedo. "Gilligan and Captain Kirk Have More in Common Than You Think: 1960s Camp TV as an Alternative Genealogy for Cult TV." *Journal of Popular Television*, vol. 6, no. 1, 2018, pp. 19–40.

Robertson, Pamela. *Guilty Pleasures: Feminist Camp from Mae West to Madonna*. I.B. Tauris, 1996.

Ross, Andrew. *No Respect: Intellectuals & Popular Culture*. Routledge, 1989.

Sconce, Jeffrey. "'Trashing' the Academy: Taste, Excess, and an Emerging Politics of Cinematic Style." *Screen*, vol. 36, no. 4, 1995, pp. 371–393.

Sontag, Susan. "A Feast for Open Eyes." Review of *Flaming Creatures*, directed by Jack Smith. *The Nation*, April 13, 1964, pp. 374–76. Reprinted as "Jack Smith's *Flaming Creatures*." *Against Interpretation and Other Essays*, Octagon Books, 1982, pp. 226–231.

Sontag, Susan. "Notes on 'Camp.'" 1964. *Against Interpretation and Other Essays*, Octagon Books, 1982, pp. 275–292.

Stone, Judy. "Caped Crusader of Camp." *New York Times*, January 9, 1966, p. 75.

Taylor, Greg. *Artists in the Audience: Cults, Camp, and American Film Criticism*. Princeton University Press, 1999.

Tinkcom, Matthew. *Working Like a Homosexual: Camp, Capital, Cinema*. Duke University Press, 2002.

Whitney, Dwight. "Batty over Batman? Holy Horticulture, Batfans, Here's How Batmania Bloomed!" *TV Guide*, March 26, 1966, pp. 15–20.

Williams, Alex. "Robert Clary, Who Took a Tragic Journey to 'Hogan's Heroes,' Dies at 96." *New York Times*, November 17, 2022, www.nytimes.com/2022/11/17/arts/television/robert-clary-dead.html. Accessed December 14, 2022.

1

Gilligan and Captain Kirk Have More in Common Than You Think

1960s Camp TV as an Alternative Genealogy for Cult Television

Isabel C. Pinedo and W. D. Phillips

Everyone agrees that camp is a style (whether of objects or the way objects are perceived is debated). (Bergman 4–5)

Introduction

On January 6, 1966, six days before ABC's premiere of *Batman* (1966–69, ABC), its televisual adaptation of the comic-book hero, the *New York Times* ran a background story on the show titled "Caped Crusader of Camp," an early nod to the style forever associated with the program.[1] Paying particular attention to the economics of prime-time programming in American television's network era, the article claimed that "ABC could not afford to put the show into the [7:30–8 p.m.] time slot if it only appealed to children" (Stone 75). The tactic developed by the show's executive producer, William Dozier, to reach a wider audience (or in the sportive language of Judy Stone, the article's author, "everyone from the milk to the martini set") was "to apply the pop art technique of the exaggerated cliché, laying it on to the point where it becomes amusing for adults" (75). In her study of "Pop, Camp, and the *Batman* Television Series," Sasha Torres notes that "formulations like 'To

---

Originally published in *Journal of Popular Television*, vol. 6, no. 1, 2018, pp. 19–40. © 2018 Intellect Ltd Article. English language. doi:10.1386/jptv.6.1.19_1. We have reversed the order of the authorship in this reprinted edition to reflect the fully collaborative nature under which it was researched and written.

Isabel C. Pinedo and W. D. Phillips, *Gilligan and Captain Kirk Have More in Common Than You Think* In: *Camp TV of the 1960s*. Edited by Isabel C. Pinedo and W. D. Phillips, Oxford University Press. © Oxford University Press 2023. DOI: 10.1093/oso/9780197650745.003.0002

the kids it's real, to the adults it's camp' were repeated so often in the popular press, that they became a kind of public interpretive mantra" (254n21). A mantra, we might add, which clearly foregrounded the dual address that constructed, and was constructed for, that show's imagined, split audience. In a fan letter to Norman Felton, executive producer of television's *The Man from U.N.C.L.E.* (1964–68, NBC), we find evidence of a comparable bifurcation as a result of that show's explicit irony, a narrative technique similarly associated with the broader camp style. Christopher Brown from Toronto, Canada, penned: "all the time that I have been a fan I have wondered why—at the end of a show—you put 'We wish to thank the United Network Command for Law & Enforcement [U.N.C.L.E.] for without whose assistant [*sic*] this program could not be possible.'"[2] Clearly this fan recognized U.N.C.L.E. as a narrative construct, of a kind with other superspy fiction influenced by Ian Fleming's James Bond stories, yet he nonetheless failed to grasp the ironic nature of the humor inherent in the inclusion of such a false credit.

Like *Batman* and *The Man from U.N.C.L.E.*, a number of mid-1960s prime-time television programs seemed to not just allow, but *encourage* viewing practices that transcended the infantilized conceptualization of television audiences commonly associated with the "vast wasteland" of network television in the 1950s and 1960s.[3] This chapter argues that such shows constitute a significant and unhistoricized set of predecessors to contemporary Cult television. Analyzing both audience interpretive practices and a set of textual characteristics that facilitated and encouraged such participatory and interpretive activities—a two-pronged methodological approach drawn directly from recent scholarship on Cult TV—we also identify a televisual genre cycle comprised of a relatively cohesive group of programs, all of which premiered on American television in the mid-1960s, that we here retrospectively nominate as "Camp TV."[4]

The existing literature on Cult TV—or shows like *Twin Peaks* (1990–91, ABC), *The X-Files* (1993–2002, Fox), *Buffy the Vampire Slayer* (1997–2003, WB/UPN), and *Lost* (2004–10, ABC)—focuses, in its genealogical account, almost exclusively on the science-fiction programs of the 1960s, such as *Star Trek* (1966–69, NBC) in America and *Doctor Who* (1963–89, 2005–present, BBC) and *The Prisoner* (1967–68, ITV) in Britain. Roberta Pearson recently referred to television's *Star Trek* as the "fount and origin of all things cult" ("Observations" 9). Through its avid viewership in first broadcast and then syndication, its letter-writing campaign to stave off cancellation, its establishment of a constellated community of fans via fanzine publication and circulation, the actual congregation of that community at fan conventions, and the continued activation of that community through a multi-media, multi-text, shared universe, *Star Trek* did, in many ways, "establish the pattern for the cult television program" (Gwenllian-Jones and Pearson xvi) and serve as a "prototype" (Reeves et al. 25) for later Cult TV.

Yet in emphasizing such histories, the scholarship on the genealogy of Cult TV has ignored another set of televisual texts that offer a complementary lineage. This alternative history includes a consequential and arguably influential group of pre-Cult televisual texts which, like those later Cult TV programs, possess a distinguishable correlation of mutually informing textual features, reception practices, and differentiation from the mainstream. These programs we collectively identify as Camp TV: prime-time television shows such as *Gilligan's Island* (1964–67, CBS), *F Troop* (1965–67, ABC), *Get Smart* (1965–70, NBC/CBS), *The Man from U.N.C.L.E.*, *Green Acres* (1965–71, CBS), *Batman*, and *The Monkees* (1966–68, NBC) that aired in America in the mid-1960s and contained in most, if not all, of their episodes, camp elements such as irony, farce, performativity, and theatricality. Additionally, all of these programs were either part of their respective network's transition to a full-color prime-time line-up or were moved to color as a part of that shift (Plate 2).[5]

The lack of attention to these programs, as well as the "rocketman" and other television programs of the 1950s with atypically participatory fan behavior, by Cult television scholars can be partly justified by the historical conceptualization of the television audiences for these shows as either specifically juvenile or infantilized by the networks' audience discourse of that era. The absence of Camp TV programs (individually and collectively) in the accepted pre-history of Cult television and the identification of 1960s science fiction/fantasy programs as the dominant predecessor of Cult TV allowed scholars to differentiate between the higher-order *interpretive* viewing strategies and the merely *participatory* audience practices associated most often with juvenile cult fandom.[6] And, in fact, television programs like *The Monkees*, *Batman*, *Green Acres*, and *Get Smart* were produced and scheduled to appeal to younger audiences. Yet, as this chapter demonstrates, other elements of these shows clearly indicate the presence of textual features such as irony, satire, and parody intended to foster interpretive practices specific to adult viewers capable of recognizing secondary meaning systems. Such features, we argue, can be grouped in this period of television history under the sign of camp. Arguing for this distinction, this chapter considers some of the circumstances and mechanisms that led to the ascendance of Camp TV in the 1960s and then performs a close reading of certain manifestations of that camp-ness that encouraged alternative reading practices. Its use of satire and parody to address contentious subjects, its playful treatment of gender as performative and fluid, its self-reflexive consciousness, and its intertextual cross talk between concurrent programs all positioned 1960s Camp TV to produce a more active viewership, one that perceived the dual address of those shows. These viewing strategies, which directly affect how we historically interpret these programs, are remarkably similar to those that have been used to identify and define Cult television. If the scholarship on Cult TV has recuperated, for scholars, both those programs and the viewer practices associated with them, this chapter helps initiate a similar action for mid-1960s Camp TV.

Defining Cult TV

Definitions of Cult TV initially grew out of but also developed in counterpoint to the scholarship on cult cinema. Many such early studies worked to identify the textual properties of programs that distinguished them individually and ultimately marked them as a cohesive group. For Cult TV scholars, the demonstration of a unique compendium of textual qualities including seriality, intertextual and intratextual density, a hyper-diegetic mythology, and an expansive metatextual universe has been crucial for the differentiation of Cult TV programs from both cult films and non-Cult television (Pearson, "Kings"; Wilcox; Gwenllian-Jones and Pearson xvii). According to Mark Jancovich and Nathan Hunt, for the producers of Cult TV, it has also been crucial to differentiate their programs "in opposition to the mainstream" (27). Ultimately, the critical distinction for Cult TV has been that such an act of differentiation is located in the construction of its audience as well as the production of its texts.

The growth of Cult television during the 1990s in such shows as *The X-Files* and *Buffy* corresponded with media studies' developing focus on reception practices and paradigms (Gwenllian-Jones and Pearson xvi; Jancovich and Hunt 39–41). This correlation resulted in the recognition that Cult TV programs were made (by the audience), not born (by producers). Though it occasionally overemphasized the efficacy of the audience, the application of this analytical approach contributed to the understanding of Cult TV as a unique field, one not fully definable through textual analysis, and is now universally recognized as a (and often *the*) key attribute of Cult television.

More specifically it is the active presence of avid viewers that, through their behaviors and practices in response to individual shows, create a community—be it constelled (via fanzines), virtual (via online groups), or actual (via conventions). If not larger in size than the fan base for other programs, this audience is at least more significant in relation to the overall fan community of a specific program and the broader media and cultural perception of its fans. Moreover, this community is not only participatory (writing fan mail, blogging affections, purchasing merchandise) but also *interpretive*—approaching the textual plenitude of Cult TV programs with not just passive acceptance of the explicit meaning, but actively seeking out supplemental meaning(s) through extensive critical analysis and discussion. Furthermore, numerous members of this community also actively produce additional, sometimes oppositional, meanings through the creation of "tertiary texts such as fan fiction, scratch videos, cultural criticism essays, filk music, Web sites, and fan art" (Gwenllian-Jones and Pearson xvi).

The "Pop" in Color Television

To provide the necessary context for the emergence of Camp TV as a significant presence on mid-1960s American televisions, to clarify the definition of this body of televisual texts, and to elucidate its relation to later Cult TV, we revisit the introduction of color to American programming and then address the history of camp, relating its mid-1960s emergence into popular culture to the voguishness of Pop Art. These two artistic styles were applied in an intertwined and—to a degree—subversive form to American television in this period in a manner that altered the historical trajectory of camp by effectively, if never fully, commercializing it for the masses.

Color, for many, seemed to emerge fully formed onto American airwaves, if not actually most television sets, in the middle of the 1960s. By the fall season of 1966, all of America's regular prime-time broadcasting was in color, up from approximately 15 percent two years earlier. This complete and sudden shift, unsurprisingly, spurred the sales of color TVs; still, by the end of fall 1966 less than 20 percent of homes had the capacity to see these shows in color. Those numbers increased steadily, and in 1972 the number of homes with color finally outnumbered those with only black and white. Nevertheless, this clearly indicates that the vast majority of Americans originally experienced these 1960s programs not in the colors intended by the in-house producers, directors, set and costume designers, etc., but rather in the same black-and-white spectrum as every other earlier program. We can see this situation inscribed, for example, in fan responses: a fan letter for *The Man from U.N.C.L.E.*, which switched from black and white to color at the beginning of its second (1965–66) season, effuses: "Broadcasting the show in color was a great idea [. . .] even though our family doesn't yet have a color TV" (Harper).

This use of color was an important factor in the development of Camp TV. As executives sought out programs for their new all-color schedules, story ideas that particularly benefited from a colorized treatment arguably became increasingly valuable. Still, the vibrant colors in shows such as *Get Smart*, *Batman*, and *The Monkees* did not develop without a precedent, but rather could also be found in television commercials as advertisers looked for any advantage to make their products stand out and the networks looked to increase advertising revenues. The clear inspiration for many of these vibrant color schemes throughout the advertising world—not just television but especially print ads—was the bright, aggressive colors of Pop Art, which began to appear in periodicals such as *New York Times Magazine* and *Cosmopolitan* in abundance in 1964 (Whiting 138, 261n75; Spigel).

Pop Art emerged in the late 1950s and early 1960s partly as a response, within the art world and by artists, to the elitist tone of abstract expressionism. Artists such as Andy Warhol and Roy Lichtenstein made appropriation their key strategy, yet they rendered the quotidian, mass-culture objects they drew on—advertising, comics, celebrity images—in ways that marked them as extracted, separated from that mass culture. Emphasizing and manipulating the color palette was one such method. While these artistic choices were done seemingly in an effort to reduce or eliminate the distance between high culture and popular culture, the ironic and satirical commentary—directed largely at the increasingly prevalent postwar consumer culture—continued to separate professional appreciators of art from the majority of viewers who more simply appreciated familiar images defamiliarized through bold color schemes, expressive typefaces, and collage techniques. As such, the role of the spectator assumed an increased relevance for these artists. As Paloma Alarcó, curator of a 2014 Pop Art exhibition at the Thyssen—Bornemisza Museum argues: "If for Pop Art the fundamental question was to transform modes of perception [. . .] the viewer's participation in the work of art became the crucial element" (17). However, print advertisers' commodification of this Pop Art aesthetic in the mid-1960s in magazines aimed at middle- and upper-middle-class women can be seen to have helped mark it as largely "safe" for dissemination to television's mass audience. As television made the shift to prime-time colorization, producers and network executives both would have likely felt safe applying such color schemes to their prime-time programs, as the political implications of Pop Art had, for television's mass audience, already been flattened, stripped of their socially critical meanings.

Camp Style and the 1960s

It is our contention that while the satire and irony originally critical to Pop Art's impact on the art world had, by the mid-1960s, been largely reduced by advertisers to its flamboyant color palette, the narrativization of Pop Art aesthetics in television programs re-opened a space for second-level meanings to emerge. And it is here that we can recognize the importance of camp as a concomitant movement that engaged Pop Art's bold color schemes and similarly foregrounded its ironic and satiric treatment of mainstream culture. Unlike Pop Art, which was a response, in many ways, to the postwar commodification of culture, scholars, particularly those from queer studies, have produced histories and epistemologies of camp that extend back through the twentieth century and beyond.[7] According to Moe Meyer's convincing argument, it was with the trials of Oscar Wilde in 1895 that dandyism and campish posturing, rhetoric, and the implications thereof became associated with queer theatricality and differentiation.

The idea behind camp in the first half of the twentieth century largely involved subcultural communication, as the male homosexual community employed camp as a means of differentiating themselves from the hegemonic, heteronormative culture while simultaneously mocking the assumptions and perceptions of that dominant, exclusionary society; yet such a position required both the sender and the receiver of the message, via the camp expression, to "speak" the same language. Furthermore, such camp expressions—drag, for example—gained subcultural power as a result of their unfamiliarity to the mainstream. Those spectators unaware of the codes of camp could certainly recognize difference, but could make little sense of the intended meaning of that difference. The term appears to begin its move from the margins to the mainstream in the decade between Christopher Isherwood's 1954 novel of queer identity awakening, *The World in the Evening*, and Susan Sontag's 1964 "Notes on 'Camp.'" More generally, the term—as well as the cultural form it labeled—seems primed to be opened out to greater usage in the early 1960s, appearing in the pages of *Time*, *Life*, the *New York Herald Tribune*, and other popular magazines and newspapers around the same time as Sontag's contribution (Cleto, [Section I] 45; Thomas 990). By 1966, the use of the term had moved so much toward the center that ABC and the *New York Times* had embraced the term in the advance marketing of *Batman* (Stone 75). Scholars in both queer studies and media studies have addressed how "pop camp" (Cleto, "Camp") or "mass camp" (Klinger) of this period depleted, to a degree, the political thrust of gay camp, keeping the presentational techniques but evacuating the subcultural meaning(s). This "mainstreaming of camp" (Cleto, [Section II] 89), in which American television played a major role, continued throughout the 1960s and into the 1970s.[8] However, as the second part of this chapter will show, Camp TV programs maintained a politicized edge, though one distributed across a broader cultural context.

Sontag's avoidance of any singular definition of camp via her series of fifty-eight "Notes" expressed what the queer subculture already knew about the robustness yet slipperiness of the term. The difficulty seems to be due to the unique split in the identity of the concept between a mode of expression exhibited by the object or performer and a mode of reception possessed by the spectator. As a mode of expression, camp often indicated the artifices of the social world by employing the bold colors associated throughout the 1960s with Pop Art.[9] It is this focus on artifice, simultaneously displaying and critiquing the constructedness of all images—in both art specifically and life generally—that underpins camp style, a style variously associated with incongruity, irony, parody, humor, aestheticism, performativity, and theatricality (Sontag; Newton; Babuscio; Kleinhans).

As David Bergman's quote that serves as the epigraph for this chapter indicates, the question as to whether camp is a style associated solely with the object or a style reliant on viewer perception is one that has long been debated, with the more convincing arguments locating it in a combination of the two. Camp, by its nature, therefore relies on spectatorial foreknowledge to a greater degree than most modes of expression, yet at the same time tends to make the recognition of difference as easy as possible for the audience. For Camp TV, color was a key part of that explicitness. ABC's *Batman*, still for many the primary cultural reference for camp, is illustrative here. The immediate and enormous success of this show indicated an effective application of color to mid-1960s television. As a result, both producers and television executives would have looked to repeat such a success through an appropriation of its noteworthy traits. Following the simple model of Rick Altman's "Producers' Game" (38), its Pop Art aesthetics and camp sensibilities were identified as key elements of that success, extracted and then re-applied in the conceptualization of new programs.[10] Moreover, it was the example of *Batman* as a show that *emphasized* its color scheme and made it a part of the show's meaning system that network producers could recognize as one route to success. Hence, the employment of the campy colors associated with Pop Art carried into certain aspects of prime time in the mid-1960s a more pervasive camp style that emphasized the newly available color schemes as well as other elements long associated with camp performance. Yet, as our research has already made clear, many viewers watched these programs without the saturated colors and the meaning systems they were intended to evoke (Plate 3). The unintended effect of this loss was to complicate the official purpose of the garish colors and to turn a significant section of the audience's attention to these shows' other distinguishing camp characteristics, namely their absurdity, farce, and irony—textual features that were capable of stimulating a unique form of audience participation.

Both Cult TV and camp (TV and otherwise) hinge significantly on the presence of interpretive audience communities. However, as their broader scholarly considerations have indicated, this is—in both cases—but one aspect of their overall defining characteristics. What emerges in the comparison of the definitions of cult and camp is the significance of their theoretical intersections, with both hinging on a symbiosis of textual properties and audience awareness and agency in the construction of a purposeful differentiation from mainstream texts and behaviors.[11] The nature of this symbiosis of the object and the audience in scholarly analyses of both camp and cult texts is strikingly similar and further supports our argument that Camp TV of the mid-1960s should be added as a complementary lineage in the development of Cult TV.

Moving beyond this analytical similitude, we further inquire if the audiences for Camp television of the 1960s provide any specific evidence of cult-like behavioral patterns. Can we recognize aspects of such an active viewer in the historical audiences of these shows that compares, perhaps, to *Star Trek*'s oft-cited community-based fandom? To a degree, the answer is, in fact, yes. *Batmania*, a Batman fanzine published originally between 1964 and 1967, is one such example. Though its publication pre-dates the debut of ABC's *Batman* by roughly two years, that significant media-crossing moment for Bat-fans was heavily reported in its pages and energized its circulation, at least temporarily. Coincidentally, the first example of "Bat fiction" to appear in its pages also corresponded closely with that January 1966 debut, published just one month later, in issue nine (Fagan 12–13).[12] Similarly, *The Man from U.N.C.L.E.*, which demonstrated numerous camp-like elements in its second and third seasons, also spurred several examples of what we now identify as derivative works closely related to contemporary forms of fan fiction: an article printed in *Photoplay* magazine is obviously built around partially real, partially concocted interviews wherein the fictionalized female interviewer is wooed by Sean Connery/James Bond in the bedroom and *U.N.C.L.E.*'s Robert Vaughn/Napoleon Solo in the living room (Hoffman); the comic strip "Harry Chess: That Man from A.U.N.T.I.E." (recognized as "the first gay comic strip"), which ran in a Philadelphia homophile newspaper in 1965 and 1966 (Murphy 22); and—notably for our study here—a series of nine gay-themed paperbacks by Victor J. Banis (as Don Holliday) published between 1966 and 1968, the first of which was titled *The Man from C.A.M.P.*

Camp TV and the Active Viewer: Four Traits

In identifying such programs and their associated viewing behaviors as an unhistoricized lineage of Cult TV, we are also arguing for a larger body of work that we identify as 1960s Camp TV, produced under historically specific industrial conditions and characterized by a clearly identifiable camp style that connects these shows. As with any genre cycle, a single show displays some, though not necessarily all, of the traits in the cluster. In line with other applications of camp, these shows employed narrative strategies such as parody and satire,[13] intertextuality, self-reflexivity, and an overt emphasis on performativity that included (but was not limited to) the treatment of gender. Individually, but especially collectively, these characteristics of Camp TV both allowed for the mobilization of an active viewer and enabled that viewer to recognize the contestability of the texts' surface-level representations.

Explicit Satire and the Campification of Aggressive Political Ideologies

On the surface, the Camp TV programs we discuss here can be seen to have offered 1960s national audiences a domesticated version of contemporary cultural animosities—the counterculture in *The Monkees*, Cold War geopolitics in *The Man from U.N.C.L.E.* and *Get Smart*, the urban-rural divide in *Green Acres*, and military colonization of Native Americans in *F Troop*. These programs addressed aggressive political ideologies at a time of social unrest by making them palatable, first, by de-politicizing those animosities, and second, through their broader "campification." In the process, the latter opened up other readings, allowing for audience interpretations that were not completely recuperated by that act of domestication.

As writer Buck Henry attests, *Get Smart* was designed (like other camp texts) with a dual address to the audience, here with "the slapstick for the kids and the political satire for the adults."[14] Occasionally these moments of explicit satire appeared within these shows in ways that barely masked their meanings for adult audiences. *Get Smart* took jabs specifically at the CIA. In "Island of the Darned" (S2 E11, 1966), Max tells the villain: "We're Control agents [. . .]. We're trained to be very loyal and very stupid." And after Agent 86 (Max) has killed the KAOS agent by lobbing a grenade at him, Agent 99 laments:

99: Oh, Max, how terrible.
86: He deserved it, 99. He was a KAOS killer.
99: Sometimes I wonder if we're any better, Max.
86: What are you talking about, 99? We have to shoot and kill and destroy.
   We represent everything that's wholesome and good in the world.

In a similar fashion, *Batman* deployed its excessive adherence to conformity to critique the electoral process. In "Hizzoner the Penguin" (S2 E17, 1966)—broadcast just before Election Day in 1966—when Batman runs for mayor, he opts for an issue-driven campaign, as opposed to the Penguin's flashy but effective campaign. "I'm convinced," Batman announces, "the American electorate is too mature to be taken in by cheap, vaudeville trickery." Then, breaking the fourth wall, "After all, if our national leaders were elected on the basis of tricky slogans, brass bands, and pretty girls, our country would be in a terrible mess, wouldn't it?" Like Buck Henry, *Batman*'s co-creators Lorenzo Semple Jr. and William Dozier wanted adults to see the satire. Matt Yockey, in his monograph on *Batman*, states: "viewers were encouraged to be engaged participants in the show's skillful deconstruction of the tropes of television, the superhero genre, and America itself" (1–2). Thus, even as a part of the supposedly de-politicized 1960s mass camp, Camp TV still participated actively in the larger challenge to normative values and institutions.

Satire was aimed at the federal level in the *Green Acres* episode "A Star Named Arnold is Born: Part 2" (S3 E30, 1968). After piglet Arnold Ziffel lands a starring role in a Hollywood movie, the horse he replaced, who was holding out for more money, appeals to Arnold's conscience by saying he was going to use the money to send his son, a foal, to Stanford. Arnold immediately understands the stakes, "But if he doesn't go to college they'll draft him." Faced with this new insight, Arnold feels guilty and relinquishes the part (see Video 1.1) ▶. This play on the word "draft" bears ideologically contradictory meanings, the thin pun on the farm labor of work horses was clearly at home in the world of Hooterville, but the threat of the military draft, whose deferment helped to drive up college enrollment throughout the show's late 1960s and early 1970s broadcast run, was clearly at home in the world of the American viewer.

Intertextuality and Cross Talk

As these shows implicitly acknowledged that television viewers came to the set already situated in a contentious political context, they also nodded to viewers' familiarity with other TV programs of the period. As such, the intertextuality employed in 1960s Camp TV shows of this period is clearly of a kind with the intertextuality of later Cult television. *Get Smart* directly spoofed *The Man from U.N.C.L.E.* in "The Man from YENTA" (S2 E21, 1967), in which CONTROL agents 86 and 99 are assisted by their Israeli counterpart from YENTA. And in a wink to *Gilligan's Island*, produced by Sherwood Schwartz, on "Schwartz's Island" (S4 E13, 1968), 86 and 99 end up stranded on a desert island whose location is unknown because it was built by KAOS. Similarly, the *F Troop* episode "Spy, Counterspy, Counter Counterspy" (S1 E22, 1966) references *Get Smart* with a secret agent named B. Wise who uses Maxwell Smart's (i.e., M. Smart) idiosyncratic speech inflections, mannerisms, and espionage tools—not a shoe phone, but a shoe gun. Though *The Man from U.N.C.L.E.* episode, "The Bat Cave Affair" (S2 E28, 1966), revolves around a Bela Lugosi–like count in Transylvania, the title plainly evokes *Batman*, which premiered three months prior to the episode's airing. The coincidence suggests the episode was (re)christened to capitalize on the popularity of the new show.

"Monkees Get Out More Dirt" (S1 E29, 1967) not only headlines Julie Newmar, who played Catwoman on *Batman*, but also visually references

Thing from *The Addams Family*, boasts repeated verbal references to *Get Smart*, and includes a character named Dr. Sisters, based on Dr. Joyce Brothers, who doles out advice to the lovelorn on television, as Video 1.2 shows ⓟ. In "Captain Crocodile" (S1 E23, 1967), *The Monkees* spoof a series of TV shows, including again *Batman*, in the form of Frogman (Peter) and Reuben the Tadpole (Davy), clad in orange sharkskin suits, capes, and "frog" emblems (Plate 4). When they battle criminals, it is framed—like many of Batman's fight sequences—in a Dutch angle and punctuated by graphics such as "rumble" and "bang." At the end, they argue over who gets to say Batman's famed tag line: "Crime does not pay."

Performativity and Self-Reflexivity

In addition to nodding to other Camp TV programs, the shows followed in the long tradition of camp by addressing certain "knowing" viewers through particular types of performativity, including the self-reflexive acknowledgment of their status as television shows—or their own performance as fictions—as well as, significantly, the performance of gender.

Throughout its run, performance was central to the episodic plots of *Gilligan's Island*. As Walter Metz observes, in almost a third of all episodes the castaways put on a show, whether it be a diegetic film, stage play, beauty contest, rock concert, or dream sequence that placed the cast in other story worlds (71). In "The Second Ginger Grant" (S3 E24, 1967), which manifests multiple versions of Sontag's "Being-as-Playing-a-Role" (280), the performative character of identity extends beyond gender switching. Because the professor advises everyone to play along with Mary Ann after she gets hit on the head and thinks she is Ginger, Ginger (already a simulacrum of Marilyn Monroe) has to play Mary Ann so that Mary Ann can play Ginger. The show's self-reflexive turn was also evident in the Skipper's Brechtian look at the camera (a recurring feature across the series) when exasperated by Gilligan, which not only breaks the fourth wall, but hints at the particular performative dynamic of Laurel and Hardy. Even the name of the ship, the *SS Minnow*, is a sly reference to FCC Chairman Newton Minow, whose 1961 condemnation of television as a "vast wasteland" still stung in 1964 when the show was created (Metz 21).

Similarly, in the *Green Acres* episode, "Das Lumpen" (S3 E10, 1967), when Lisa interrupts Oliver's account of how they met (an account with multiple permutations throughout the run of the series), the flashback scene of his account flickers like a celluloid film that has been stopped mid-projection. And on "A Star Named Arnold Is Born: Part 2," when the piglet Arnold Ziffel and a horse talk, the dialogue is shown in subtitles as they snort and neigh. The subtitles continue into the next scene only stopping after Lisa looks down at the subtitles and declares: "We don't need those words anymore" (see Video 1.1) ▶. Production credits were also sometimes incorporated into the diegetic space of *Green Acres*, appearing, for example, on Lisa's hotcakes. Characters also remarked on them. In one episode, Lisa wakes up and, responding to the executive producer's on-screen credit, says, "Oliver! Who is Paul Henning?"[15] These acts of complicity with the audience drew attention to television devices, the zany comedy, and the communal sense that the audience was in on the joke.

The self-awareness of *Batman* is similarly evident in "The Penguin's a Jinx" (S1 E4, 1966) where a character intones, "Batman never lends himself to commercial enterprises." Though this episode aired at the start of the series in January 1966, the statement alluded to the merchandising power of the brand in a year when *Batman* products, combined with that of James Bond, accounted for approximately 25 percent of the US licensing business (Santo 70). Moreover, consider Andy Medhurst's contention that Fredric Wertham's (1955) reading of Batman and Robin's relation as homoerotic influenced public perception of the series. It suggests the self-reflexive turn of Robin's feminine mannerisms and walk in "Smack in the Middle" (S1 E2, 1966), discussed at greater length below; this was the series' second episode, making the characterization explicit from the beginning (see Video 1.3) ▶. Likewise, in "The Devil's Fingers" (S2 E15, 1966), when camp icon Liberace, clothed in his own signature costumes, plays a pianist and "famous ladies' man" who courts Dick Grayson/Robin's Aunt Harriet, the already conspicuous dual audience address of *Batman* is compounded by the parallel between Liberace's thinly closeted persona and the transparency of Bruce and Dick's secret identities. For Matt Yockey, "Liberace confirms Wertham's assertion that the secret life of the superhero is akin to that of the homosexual" (94). This reading may not have been accessible to kids, but in the overdrawn manner of the camp sensibility, it was served on a silver platter for adults.

Self-reflexivity also marked *The Monkees* with its regular use of direct reference to the production process as well as to the audience. The show's tag sequences regularly broke from the story frame to present interviews, audition tapes, musical numbers, outtakes, and at times involved calling production personnel on camera or referring to the manufactured nature of the band. On "Monkees Blow Their Minds" (S2 E25, 1968), Mike, impersonating Frank Zappa, rails against how commercial the Monkees are to Zappa, who in turn wears Mike's trademark wool cap. The program's blatant awareness of or complicity with the audience is also conveyed through the boys speaking directly to the camera, as when in "The Monkees in Paris" (S2 E22, 1968), Mike stops in mid-scene to complain to "Jim" (series director James Frawley) about the script's oft-repeated plot device, which leads Frawley to walk on camera to defend the script (see Video 1.4) ▶. As Laura Goostree observes, this drew attention to "aspects of the television industry with which the audience was not necessarily familiar in 1966" (52).

The Monkees took a further deconstructive turn by consistently transgressing television conventions. The show regularly employed discontinuous cuts, disregarded continuity errors, incorporated experimental techniques such as fast motion, and inserted surreal elements, particularly during fantasy sequences or musical romps.[16] In addition to its anarchic character, the program made carefully crafted references to the youth counterculture. The boys' psychedelic print shirts, love beads, and long hair, in addition to their rock music and lack of jobs, were all cultural signifiers of hippiedom. The series celebrated youthful energy and showed youth as capable in a world of utterly inept adults (Bodroghkozy 68; Goostree 57).

"The Chaperone" (S1 E5, 1966) is exemplifying in this regard, combining cross-dressing with a critique of military authority. Micky dresses as Mrs. Arcadian to convince the general to allow his daughter to attend a house party. The general, who lounges in jungle camouflage and plays with toy soldiers and tanks, is instantly smitten with Mrs. Arcadian. Both the warrior and his war are depicted as absurd, and incompatible with the freedom of youth culture embodied by the show. At a time when prime-time television largely presented the military as heroic, and on a broadcast channel whose parent company, RCA, was involved in defense contracting with the Pentagon, the general is scolded by his daughter for his "medieval attitudes" (Bodroghkozy 73–4; Bindas and Heineman 23). Though *The Monkees* campified social conflicts by reducing free love to chaste kisses and anti-militarism to making a fool of the general, its deconstructive tendencies, anarchic energy, and fun sense of mayhem suggested a breakdown of the normal value system, all of which appealed to a youth audience culturally primed to look for and hence recognize the implicit meanings otherwise lost on older or unsympathetic audiences.

Performativity and Gender Fluidity

The shifts in cultural notions of gender and gender representation in the 1960s were also being performed on Camp TV shows of that period—namely gender passing on *The Monkees* (as illustrated above), gender impersonation on *Batman*, cross-dressing on *Gilligan's Island*, and the figure of the adult tomboy on *F Troop* and *Green Acres*. We will consider how this playful gender bending on mainstream television, in a period of turbulent social change and challenges to dominant culture, contributed to the development of the types of active viewership that later came to be considered a defining trait of Cult television.

At a time when normative ideals of a consumption-oriented suburban nuclear family life were being questioned by movement activists and the counterculture, the rampant use of cross-dressing in Camp TV opened opportunities for the further destabilization of gender norms. In *The Monkees*, as soon as a male character put on a wig, dress, heels, and assumed more demure mannerisms, seemingly heterosexual men were so convinced of the cross-dresser's female gender status—despite the unshaven sideburns, ill-fitting wig, unshaven legs, and hairy arms wearing bulky wristwatches—that they sought to woo her. The sexual advance functioned as a testament to how convincing the disguise was, despite obvious visual evidence to the contrary. The cross-dresser was designed to fool other characters, but not the audience, who was in on the joke. For the diegetic suitor, the cross-dresser conformed to Judith Butler's performative notion that gender is constituted by doing, not being. Gender is actualized through the repetition of socially regulated and embodied acts. And though these parodic performances have their limits, they still manage to denaturalize gender through parody.

In *The Monkees*, female impersonations are frequent and self-consciously poorly performed. "Fairy Tale" (S2 E16, 1968), an episode-long fantasy sketch played on minimalist cutout cardboard sets with deliberately amateurish production values, presents the most sustained instance of cross-dressing (Plate 5). In addition to all the Monkees playing male characters, Davy plays Gretel and Little Red Riding Hood, Micky plays Goldilocks, and Mike plays princess-in-distress Gwen, whose beauty captivates the boys, especially Mike himself, who via shot/reverse-shot editing is particularly taken with Gwen's long sideburns (see Video 1.5) ▶.

In her book on cross-dressing, Marjorie Garber traces the trope of the intentionally poorly disguised man in drag back to the Christmas pantomime figure of the Dame. For Peter Ackroyd, this figure is parodying "himself as a male actor" (102). The influence of the Dame has been passed down to television through vaudeville. Early television brought the performance styles of vaudeville to television in the form of the variety show, which combined song, dance, skits, and monologues (Murray 97). Vaudeville-headliners-turned-TV-stars such as Milton Berle (*Texaco Star Theater*, 1948–55, NBC) were adept at playing with ethnic and gender cues in the construction of the multiple characters they played, some in drag.[17] Garber argues that Milton Berle's performance in drag served to defy the stigmatization of the Jewish male as effeminate, "deploying gender parody [as] an empowering strategy" to recuperate this maligned image (233). Similarly, Patricia Mellencamp argues that Lucille Ball's efforts to escape domestic containment in *I Love Lucy* (1951–57, CBS) may have failed narratively by the end of each episode, but succeeded as comic spectacle; Lucy's virtuoso performance of physical comedy often entailed disguising herself as various male figures (for instance, celebrities such as Harpo Marx) but also a Martian, even a chair, all to advance a scheme, settle an argument, or break into show biz. Following in this tradition, Camp TV shows of the 1960s employed cross-dressing to challenge notions of hegemonic masculinity, the fixity of identity, and restrictive gender norms. It is crucial to note, however, that the vaudevillian tradition of male cross-dressing appropriated by mid-1960s prime-time TV producers was done so in a different cultural moment, thus producing different meanings; youth here is key to such a reading as The Stooges and Berle were not only from an older entertainment era but also significantly older men in comparison to, for example, Burt Ward or Micky Dolenz. Moreover, pushing beyond the model provided by these earlier programs, Camp TV shows—which aired during a period of collective press for social change on multiple fronts—also introduced the more direct homoerotic element of a man falling in love with the wigged cross-dresser.[18]

Garber discusses specifically the transformative role of wigs in establishing social status (213); in *The Monkees*, we see a different variant of "the magic of the wig" in which merely putting on a wig is enough to confer female status in the eyes of fellow characters. The performance is by design unconvincing to the audience, a self-parody, and therein lies the humor. Similarly, in the *Batman* episode, "Caught in the Spider's Den" (S2 E55, 1967), Black Widow, played by aging camp icon Tallulah Bankhead, announces she is going to use makeup to "look exactly like Robin." When we next see the Boy Wonder, Burt Ward mimes Tallulah Bankhead's voice and mannerisms to deliver a deliberately unconvincing impersonation of Robin by Black Widow. This ploy is a replay of one used in the earlier episode, "Smack in the Middle," in which Molly, the Riddler's assistant, dons a mask to pass as Robin (see Video 1.3) ⊙. In one shot, Molly, played by Jill St. John, is dressed in a copy of Robin's disguise, holding the mask and wig. After a reverse shot of the Riddler, the camera cuts back to Burt Ward, hand on hip, head tilted, performing Molly playing Robin (Plate 6).

Gilligan's Island features a mix of cross-dressing similar to that used in *The Monkees* and the cross-gender miming of *Batman*. In "Gilligan the Goddess" (S3 E30, 1967) a tribal king arrives on the island looking for a "white goddess" to sacrifice to the volcano god (see Video 1.6) ⊙. The four men cross-dress to shield the women (Plate 7). In "The Friendly Physician" (S2 E29, 1966), a mad scientist uses a device to transplant the mind of one character into the body of another; notably, three of the four pairings involve opposing genders. Though all identities are restored at the end, the episode plays with the malleability of identity, its performative character. Gender-crossing here, as in *The Monkees* and *Batman*, could be understood differently by different audiences—both as playfully safe campified transgressions ensconced within these contained diegetic communities but also as indicative of a loosening of rigid gender norms in 1960s youth culture.

The figure of the adult tomboy on Camp TV also challenges the normative terms of the gender binary. On *F Troop* the tomboy is quick-tempered, buckskin-clad Angelica Thrift, aka Wrangler Jane, who runs the trading post, delivers the mail, outshoots the soldiers at the fort, and woos the bungling Captain Wilton Parmenter. As a frontier woman, she is rendered safe due to her rural strangeness, regularly stepping outside the narrow gender strictures of domesticity and crinoline dresses.[19] On *Green Acres*, Ralph Monroe, regularly clad in overalls, cap, and pale lipstick, is the female half of carpenters-for-hire, the "Monroe Brothers" (Ralph and Alf), so named to attract clients who might be reluctant to hire a woman even though, ironically, the people in small-town Hooterville all know each other. Ralph is Alf's "brother" in the same story world in which Arnold the piglet is Fred Ziffel's "son."

Agent 99, though not a tomboy, subverts gender norms on *Get Smart* as an independent working woman who knows karate and routinely outsmarts her partner Maxwell Smart. Similarly, Catwoman's challenge to normative femininity, her authority over her henchmen, and resistance to Batman suggested female power for some of the women Lynn Spigel and Henry

Jenkins interviewed about their memories of watching the show as children (138). As with the transgressive cross-dressers or gender impersonators of *The Monkees, Batman,* and *Gilligan's Island,* the adult tomboys and independent women of *F Troop, Green Acres, Get Smart,* and *Batman* pointed to ruptures emerging in normative culture but did so within the confines of a playful diegesis. The purposeful malleability of gender representation that was associated with camp generally, and recognizable specifically within a number of Camp TV shows of the 1960s, corresponded with a unique fluidity in audience identification practices. These practices are the same as those recognized in audience behavior commonly associated with Cult TV.

Conclusion

The surreal humor of *Green Acres,* satire of *Get Smart,* "exaggerated clichés" of *Batman,* and anarchic character of *The Monkees* appealed to a youth audience at a time when 41 percent of the US population was underage and watched a lot of television (Bindas and Heineman 24). Color acted as the engine that delivered into American prime-time television all of the other aspects of mid-1960s camp—both aesthetic and thematic predilections—some of which were particularly well positioned to produce a more active viewership. But even, and perhaps especially, in black and white, Camp TV's playful theatricality, deconstructive tendencies, and satire lent themselves to multiple readings and viewing practices clearly similar to those that would come to greater fruition with the later development of Cult TV.

In conclusion, our study has demonstrated that television audience interpretive and participatory practices more commonly associated with programs and viewers in the TVII (post-network cable) and TVIII (digital content delivery) eras, within which Cult TV first developed and now thrives, can also be found productively in TVI (network era) environments. Moreover, our analysis of reception practices coupled to specific features of the texts has been utilized to identify a televisual genre cycle we recognize as Camp TV, the textual similarities of which were necessary but ultimately not sufficient at the time to support a generic label. Nonetheless, the cultural specificity of Camp TV that we have described here both indicates that the complexities of society at the time were inflecting on a certain subset of television programming and serves as validation for the close study of this period of TV history. Although studies of some individual programs have been carried out, these television shows have not previously been brought together, as we have done here, to recognize their reinforcing cluster of traits and to address why, beyond the 1960s ascendance of mass camp within American popular culture, they emerged at this particular historical moment. Finally, this chapter productively illustrates that the received and established media lineages standardized by cultural historians are often incomplete and need to be complemented by further consideration, as we have done here with our analysis of Camp TV in relation to Cult TV.

Notes

1. Support for the article was provided by a 2015 President's Fund for Faculty Advancement Award at Hunter College of the City University of New York. Noah Waldman supplied valuable research assistance.
2. Brown was writing as the show began to enter more widespread syndication; the role of syndication on the reception and development of both Camp TV and Cult TV is worth additional consideration, but is beyond the scope of this chapter.
3. Federal Communications Commission (FCC) Chairman Newton Minow coined this phrase in a 1961 speech and was thus referring primarily to 1950s television programming. Once available, however, critics regularly applied the term when deriding later programs, including many of those we consider here.
4. Thomas Andrae, in his study of the American import version of *The Avengers* (1966–69, UK:ABC), similarly applies this term to "shows like *Batman* and *U.N.C.L.E.*" (122) as part of his description of the cultural background for the American reception of Diana Rigg's feminist spy, but does not broaden his purview any further; his description of mid-1960s camp (122–126) complements that which we provide here. Jane Feuer also uses the term "'camp' TV," but uses it to describe a strand of prime-time serial television originating in the 1980s that she generally refers to as "prime-time melodrama" (27).
5. *Gilligan's Island*, *F Troop*, and *The Man from U.N.C.L.E.* each ran for one year in black and white before switching to color. Other programs that could be considered either a part of, or influential for mid-1960s Camp TV, but that we did not analyze for this article, include the animated *Rocky and His Friends/The Bullwinkle Show* (1959–64, ABC/NBC); *The Addams Family* (1964–66, ABC) and *The Munsters* (1964–66, CBS), neither of which converted to color; and the British *The Avengers* (1961–69, but specifically with Diana Rigg from 1965 to 1968). Later comedy-variety shows that have been interpreted in terms of a camp style—such as *The Smothers Brothers Comedy Hour* (1967–70, CBS) and *Rowan & Martin's Laugh-In* (1968–73, NBC)—also fall outside our purview here. *U.N.C.L.E.* is a special case for our study; though it ran for four seasons, only the second and third can reasonably be considered a part of Camp TV (Kackman 84–96; Jenkins 16).

6. Adult viewers of Camp TV notably participated with the texts in ways previously uncommon, though not unheard of, for American prime-time television. Perhaps the behavioral patterns "taught" by the 1950s programs to young audiences can be seen to have carried over to adult baby-boomer viewers in the mid-to-late 1960s; at the very least such behavior was culturally acceptable and, in certain cases, encouraged.
7. The term "camp" has been attributed multiple lines of development, most convincingly, the French *camper*—related to military exercises in general, but particularly influenced by those under Louis XIV and his brother, Monsieur, who extended to military camp life the exaggerated, performative aesthetic of Versailles (Booth 78).
8. Both Cleto and Klinger pick up on Mark Booth's discussion of "democratized" camp. The 1969 Stonewall riots and the resulting revision of gay identity politics in the early 1970s resulted in camp being reclaimed, to a degree, by and for that subculture, though mainstream camp would continue, more or less separately, thereafter (Cleto, [Section II] 88–92, and "Camp").
9. Several scholars have argued effectively that such a formulation is inverted and that Pop Art should be recognized as a particular manifestation of a gay camp aesthetic (Thomas).
10. In the case of *The Man from U.N.C.L.E.*, this logic arguably played a role in the show's mid-series revision.
11. Nonetheless, cult and camp are clearly not synonymous, with the textual features, the meanings intended by those features, and the purpose of the differentiation from the mainstream all distinctively marking one from the other (even as they sometimes overlap). Certainly camp is the more politically charged, involving—as it does—the issues of queer identity politics (despite the attempt by Sontag and others to de-emphasize that relationship). Jeffrey Sconce develops another, similar concept in his definition of "paracinema," though Mark Jancovich has, in his own consideration of cult movies' subcultural capital, effectively critiqued some of Sconce's paracinema/camp binarisms. These attempts to differentiate such terms and the concepts they signify can be recognized as manifestations of the critical hierarchies inherent within much scholarship, including our own interpretive/participatory distinction.
12. Comics had already established their own cultish fan behaviors; see, for example, the comics fanzine *Alter Ego*, first published in 1961.
13. Fredric Jameson argues that under postmodernism, parody loses its political bite and morphs into pastiche—mimicry without the satiric impulse. Postmodernism can more accurately be described as a structuring presence in later Cult TV shows such as *Twin Peaks* than in the programs discussed here.
14. Notes and memos produced early in the development of the pilot episode explicitly refer to the potential program as both "James Bond Satire Series" ("James Bond") and "Parody Spy Series" (Honeystein).
15. Henning also produced *The Beverly Hillbillies* (1962–71, CBS) and the rags-to-riches (or riches-to-rags) schema he employed necessitated an emphasis on social performance which, as we read it here, extended beyond the original class-based binary.

16. Producers Bob Rafelson and Bert Schneider were new to television production and deliberately hired mostly inexperienced production personnel who would not insist on conventional norms (Bodroghkozy 70; Goostree 50).
17. In addition to Berle's move to TV, *The Three Stooges* film shorts began playing on television at the end of the 1950s.
18. A number of the Warner Bros./Bugs Bunny cartoons, which appeared on American TV in the early 1960s, enacted similar courtships. However, not only were these appropriated from a previous media context (the cinematic short film), but this homoerotic element was also clearly sanitized for mass/juvenile audiences through the use of animation and anthropomorphized animals.
19. *The Beverly Hillbillies*'s Ellie Mae provides a similar example.

Bibliography

Abbott, Stacey, editor. *The Cult TV Book: From* Star Trek *to* Dexter, *New Approaches to TV Outside the Box*. Soft Skull Press, 2010.
Ackroyd, Peter. *Dressing Up*. Simon and Schuster, 1976.
Adams, Val. "N.B.C. Will Boost Use of TV Color." *New York Times*, March 9, 1965, p. 71.
Alarcó, Paloma, editor. "Pop Art Myths." *Pop Art Myths*. Madrid: Museo Thyssen-Bornemisza, 2014, pp. 14–49.
Altman, Rick. *Film/Genre*. BFI Publishing, 1999.
Andrae, Thomas. "Television's First Feminist: *The Avengers* and Female Spectatorship." *Discourse*, vol. 18, no. 3, 1996, pp. 112–136.
Babuscio, Jack. "Camp and the Gay Sensibility" [1977]. *Camp Grounds: Style and Homosexuality*, edited by David Bergman, University of Massachusetts Press, 1993, pp. 19–38.
Beard, Jim, editor. *Gotham City 14 Miles: 14 Essays on Why the 1960s* Batman *TV Series Matters*. Sequart Research and Literary Organization, 2010.
Bergman, David. Introduction. *Camp Grounds: Style and Homosexuality*, edited by David Bergman, University of Massachusetts Press, 1993, pp. 3–16.
Bindas, Kenneth J., and Heineman, Kenneth J. "Image Is Everything: Television and the Counterculture Message in the 1960s." *Journal of Popular Film and Television*, vol. 22, no. 1, 1994, pp. 22–37.
Bodroghkozy, Aniko. *Groove Tube: Sixties Television and the Youth Rebellion*. Duke University Press, 2001.
Booth, Mark. *Camp*. Quartet, 1983.
Brown, Christopher. Letter to MGM, July 23, 1971, Fan Mail 1967–1971, Norman Felton Papers, The University of Iowa Libraries, box 22.
Butler, Judith. "Gender Trouble, Feminist Theory, and Psychoanalytic Discourse." *Feminism/Postmodernism*, edited by Linda Nicholson, Routledge, 1989, pp. 324–340.
Cleto, Fabio. "Camp." *Routledge International Encyclopedia of Queer Culture*, edited by David A. Gerstner, Routledge, 2006, pp. 121–124.
Cleto, Fabio, editor. *Camp: Queer Aesthetics and the Performing Subject: A Reader*. University of Michigan Press, 1999.
Cleto, Fabio. "Introduction" [to Section I: Tasting It]. Cleto, 44–49.

Cleto, Fabio. "Introduction" [to Section II: Flaunting the Closet]. Cleto, 89–95.
Coleman, Donald F. "Advertising in Color." *Color Television: The Business of Colorcasting*, edited by Howard W. Coleman, Hastings House, 1968, pp. 159–171.
"Color TV Set Makers Turn Sales Volume Up." *Business Week*, no. 1847, 1965, pp. 144–146.
Fagan, Tom. "Study in Schizophrenia (Bat-Fiction #1)." *Batmania*, no. 9, 1966, pp. 12–13, http://comicbookplus.com/?dlid=11955. Accessed March 13, 2015.
Feil, Ken. *Rowan & Martin's Laugh-In: TV Milestones Series*. Wayne State University Press, 2014.
Felton, Norman. "The Man from U.N.C.L.E. . . . and How It All Began," 1982, Norman Felton Papers, The University of Iowa Libraries, box 90.
Feuer, Jane. "The Lack of Influence of *thirtysomething*." *The Contemporary Television Series*, edited by Michael Hammond and Lucy Mazdon, Edinburgh University Press, 2005, pp. 27–36.
Garber, Marjorie. *Vested Interests: Cross-dressing and Cultural Anxiety*. Routledge, 1992.
Garvey, Daniel E. "Introducing Color Television: The Audience and Programming Problem." *Journal of Broadcasting*, vol. 24, no. 4, 1980, pp. 515–525.
Goostree, Laura. "The Monkees and the Deconstruction of Television Realism." *Journal of Popular Film & Television*, vol. 16, no. 2, 1988, pp. 50–58.
Gwenllian-Jones, Sara, and Roberta E. Pearson, editors. *Cult Television*. University of Minnesota Press, 2004.
Gwenllian-Jones, Sara, and Roberta E. Pearson. Introduction. Gwenllian-Jones and Pearson, pp. ix–xx.
Harper, Jim. Letter to Norman Felton, September 18, 1965, Fan Mail 1964–1966, Norman Felton Papers, The University of Iowa Libraries, box 22.
Henry, Buck. "Interview" [2006]. *Get Smart*, Season 1, Disc 5, DVD, New York: HBO Studios, 2008.
Hoffman, Jim. "Connery & Vaughn: Bedroom Spy vs. Living Room Spy." *Photoplay*, vol. 68, no. 3, September 1965, pp. 33–39, 70–71.
Honeystein, Karl. "Mel Brooks—Parody Spy Series," April 13, 1964, David Susskind Papers, Wisconsin Historical Society Archives/Wisconsin Center for Film and Theater Research, folder 6, box 73.
Isherwood, Christopher. *The World in the Evening*. Methuen, 1954.
Jancovich, Mark. "Cult Fictions: Cult Movies, Subcultural Capital and the Production of Cultural Distinctions." *Cultural Studies*, vol. 16, no. 2, 2002, pp. 306–322.
Jancovich, Mark, and Nathan Hunt. "The Mainstream, Distinction, and Cult TV." Gwenllian-Jones and Pearson, pp. 27–44.
"James Bond Satire Series—Notes—April 24, 1964" David Susskind Papers, Wisconsin Historical Society Archives/Wisconsin Center for Film and Theater Research, folder 5, box 73.
Jameson, Fredric. *Postmodernism, or the Cultural Logic of Late Capitalism*. Duke University Press, 1992.
Jenkins, Tricia. "Feminism, Nationalism, and the 1960s' Slender Spies: A Look at *Get Smart* and *The Girl from U.N.C.L.E.*" *Journal of Popular Film and Television*, vol. 43, no. 1, 2015, pp. 14–27.
Kackman, Michael. *Citizen Spy: Television, Espionage, and Cold War Culture*. University of Minnesota Press, 2005.
Kleinhans, Chuck. "Taking out the Trash: Camp and the Politics of Parody." Meyer, pp. 182–201.

Klinger, Barbara. *Melodrama and Meaning: History, Culture, and the Films of Douglas Sirk*. Indiana University Press, 1994.

Madoff, Henry, editor. *Pop Art: A Critical History*. University of California Press, 1997.

Medhurst, Andy. "Batman, Deviance and Camp." Pearson and Uricchio, pp. 149–163.

Mellencamp, Patricia. "Situation Comedy, Feminism, and Freud: Discourses of Gracie and Lucy." *Studies in Entertainment: Critical Approaches to Mass Culture*, edited by Tania Modleski, Indiana University Press, 1986, pp. 80–95.

Metz, Walter. *Gilligan's Island: TV Milestones Series*. Wayne State University Press, 2012.

Meyer, Moe, editor. *The Politics and Poetics of Camp*. Routledge, 1994.

Meyer, Moe. "Under the Sign of Wilde: An Archaeology of Posing." Meyer, pp. 75–109.

Miller, Cynthia J., and A. Bowdoin Van Riper, editors. *1950s "Rocketman" TV Series and Their Fans: Cadets, Rangers, and Junior Space Men*. Palgrave Macmillan, 2012.

Murphy, Michael J. "The Lives and Times of Harry Chess." *The Gay & Lesbian Review Worldwide*, vol. 21, no. 2, 2014, pp. 22–24.

Murray, Susan. "Ethnic Masculinity and Early Television's Vaudeo Star." *Cinema Journal*, vol. 42, no. 1, 2002, pp. 97–119.

"Pay-off for NBC Color Next Fall?" *Broadcasting*, March 1, 1965, pp. 32, 34.

Pearson, Roberta E. "Kings of Infinite Space: Cult Television Characters and Narrative Possibilities." *Scope: An Online Journal of Film and Television Studies*, November 2002, pp. 1–12, http://www.nottingham.ac.uk/scope/documents/2003/november-2003/pearson.pdf. Accessed February 20, 2016.

Pearson, Roberta E. "Observations on Cult Television." Abbott, pp. 7–17.

Pearson, Roberta E., and William Uricchio, editors. *The Many Lives of Batman: Critical Approaches to a Superhero and His Media*. Routledge, 1991.

Reeves, Jimmie L., et al. "Rewriting Popularity: The Cult Files." *"Deny All Knowledge": Reading* The X-Files, edited by David Lavery et al., Syracuse University Press, 1996, pp. 22–35.

Santo, Avi. "*Batman* Versus *The Green Hornet*: The Merchandisable TV Text and the Paradox of Licensing in the Classical Network Era." *Cinema Journal*, vol. 49, no. 2, 2010, pp. 63–85.

Sconce, Jeffrey. "'Trashing' the Academy: Taste, Excess, and an Emerging Politics of Cinematic Style." *Screen*, vol. 36, no. 4, 1995, pp. 371–393.

Sontag, Susan. "Notes on 'Camp.'" 1964. *Against Interpretation and Other Essays*. 1966. Picador, 2001, pp. 275–292.

Spigel, Lynn. *TV by Design: Modern Art and the Rise of Network Television*. University of Chicago Press, 2008.

Spigel, Lynn, and Henry Jenkins. "Same Bat Channel, Different Bat Times: Mass Culture and Popular Memory." Pearson and Uricchio, pp. 117–148.

Stone, Judy. "Caped Crusader of Camp." *New York Times*, January 9, 1996, p. 75.

Thomas, Joe A. "Pop Art and the Forgotten Codes of Camp." *Memory & Oblivion: Proceedings of the XXIXth International Congress of the History of Art*, Amsterdam, September 1–7, 1996, edited by Adriaan Wessel Reinink and Jeroen Stumpel, Kluwer Academic, 1999, pp. 989–995.

Torres, Sasha. "Caped Crusader of Camp: Pop, Camp, and the *Batman* Television Series." *Pop Out: Queer Warhol*, edited by Jennifer Doyle et al., Duke University Press, 1996, pp. 238–255.

Walker, Cynthia W. "Mr. Bond's Neighborhood: Domesticating the Superspy for American Television." *James Bond and Popular Culture: Essays on the Influence of the Fictional Superspy*, edited by Michele Brittany, McFarland & Co., 2014, pp. 80–102.

Ware, James Redding. *Passing English of the Victorian Era: A Dictionary of Heterodox English, Slang, and Phrase.* George Routledge & Sons, 1909.
Wertham, Fredric. *Seduction of the Innocent.* Museum Press, 1955.
Whiting, Cécile. *A Taste for Pop: Pop Art, Gender, and Consumer Culture.* Cambridge University Press, 1997.
Wilcox, Rhonda V. "The Aesthetics of Cult Television." Abbott, pp. 31–39.
Yeazel, Lynn A. "Color it Confusing: A History of Color Television." *American Broadcasting: A Source Book on the History of Radio and Television*, edited by Lawrence Wilson Lichty and Malachi C. Topping, Hastings House, 1975, pp. 72–79.
Yockey, Matt. *Batman: TV Milestones Series.* Wayne State University Press, 2014.

Television Programs

The Addams Family. 1964–1966. Television Series. Seasons 1–2. USA: ABC.
The Avengers. 1961–1969. Television Series. Seasons 1–6. UK: ABC (Associated British Corporation).
Batman. 1966–1969. Television Series. Season 1–3. USA: ABC.
    "Smack in the Middle" (January 13, 1966).
    "Fine Feathered Finks" (January 19, 1966).
    "The Penguin's a Jinx" (January 20, 1966).
    "Hizzoner the Penguin" (November 2, 1966).
    "The Devil's Fingers" (October 26, 1966).
    "Caught in the Spider's Den" (March 16, 1967).
The Beverly Hillbillies. 1962–1971. Television Series. Seasons 1–9, USA: CBS.
Buffy the Vampire Slayer. 1997–2003. Television Series. Seasons 1–7, USA: WB/UPN.
Doctor Who. 1963–1989, 2005–present. Television Series. Seasons 1–39. UK: BBC.
F Troop. 1965–1967. Television Series. Seasons 1–2. USA: ABC.
    "Spy, Counterspy, Counter Counterspy" (February 15, 1966).
Get Smart. 1965–1970. Television Series. Seasons 1–5. USA: NBC/CBS.
    "Island of the Darned" (November 26, 1966).
    "The Man from YENTA" (January 28, 1967).
    "Schwartz's Island" (December 21, 1968).
Gilligan's Island. 1964–1967. Television Series. Seasons 1–3. USA: CBS.
    "The Friendly Physician" (April 7, 1966).
    "Gilligan the Goddess" (April 17, 1967).
    "The Second Ginger Grant" (March 6, 1967).
Green Acres. 1965–1971. Television Series. Seasons 1–6. USA: CBS.
    "A Star Named Arnold Is Born: Part 2" (April 10, 1968).
    "Das Lumpen" (November 8, 1967).
I Love Lucy. 1951–1957. Television Series. Seasons 1–6. USA: CBS.
Lost. 2004–2010. Television Series. Seasons 1–6. USA: ABC.
The Man from U.N.C.L.E. 1964–1968. Television Series. Seasons 1–4. USA: NBC.
    "The Bat Cave Affair" (April 1, 1966).
The Monkees. 1966–1968. Television Series. Seasons 1–2. USA: NBC.
    "The Chaperone" (November 7, 1966).
    "Captain Crocodile" (February 20, 1967).
    "Fairy Tale" (January 8, 1968).
    "The Monkees in Paris" (February 19, 1968).

"Monkees Blow their Minds" (March 11, 1968).
"Monkees Get Out More Dirt" (April 3, 1967).
The Munsters. 1964–1966. Television Series. Seasons 1–2. USA: CBS.
The Prisoner. 1967–1968. Television Series. Season 1. UK: ITV.
Rocky and His Friends/The Bullwinkle Show. 1959–1964. Television Series. Seasons 1–5. USA: ABC/NBC.
Rowan & Martin's Laugh-In. 1968–1973. Television Series. Seasons 1–6. USA: NBC.
The Smothers Brothers Comedy Hour. 1967–1970. Television Series. Seasons 1–3. USA: CBS.
Star Trek. 1966–1969. Television Series. Seasons 1–3. USA: NBC.
Texaco Star Theater. 1948–1955. Television Series. Seasons 1–6. USA: NBC.
Twin Peaks. 1990–1991. Television Series. Seasons 1–2. USA: ABC.
The X-Files. 1993–2002. Television Series. Seasons 1–11. USA: Fox.

SECTION I
LAYING THE (CAMP) GROUNDWORK

2
Fractured Flickers (1963–64), Camp, and Cinema's Ab/usable Past

Andrea Comiskey and Jonah Horwitz

Unjust, Unfair, and Completely Uncalled For

On the screen, Quasimodo, perched perilously atop the Notre Dame cathedral, taunts a crowd gathered below. But from the speakers, an adenoidal voice chants, in sync with his lurching movements, "One, two, red, white, and blue! We are the boys from Southern Cal U!" Onlookers point upward and exclaim, "It's Dinky!"

So it is that the classic 1923 film adaptation of *The Hunchback of Notre Dame* is transformed into "Dinky Dunstan, Boy Cheerleader" (Video 2.1) ▶. The angry mob, pitchforks and torches in hand, becomes opposing football squads and their fans. Lon Chaney's hunchback becomes mascot Dinky, whose fight song fails to cheer USC to victory (they lose, 99–0, and he sulks back into the belfry). This bit of *détournement* is probably the most in/famous segment from the 1963/64 TV series *Fractured Flickers*, which re-edited footage from silent films and added a bevy of comic voicework to create new, absurdist replacement narratives (S1 E5, 1963). A creation of Jay Ward Productions, responsible for the characters Rocky and Bullwinkle, *Flickers* featured not only the studio's stable of actors and writers—Bill Scott, the voice of Bullwinkle, is Dinky—but also the impertinent, allusive, lightly topical, and reflexive humor characteristic of Ward's animated series.

Although *Flickers* may be more weird than funny, we hold that it is significant in several ways. With its dense weave of references to popular culture old and new, arch self-mockery, eccentric parade of icons, subversions of anything serious, and, above all, fusion of travesty and affection—travesty *born of* affection—*Flickers* merits inclusion as an early entry in what W. D. Phillips and Isabel Pinedo have identified as "Camp TV," a group of 1960s series that offers an "alternative genealogy" for the cult TV of later decades (21). If *Flickers* is not wholly camp by the most stringent definitions, it certainly belongs to the moment of camp's emergence into the mainstream, its "democratization" (Cleto 122) to which Susan Sontag's 1964 "Notes on 'Camp'" bore witness.

Flickers is also a place where a camp sensibility intersects with several other genealogies of popular media. One is that of "riffing," which can include the practice of comics talking over, mocking, cheering, re-narrating, and/or reediting older audiovisual media—typically texts construed as "bad" in some fashion. To the extent that *Flickers* is referenced in media histories, it is as a precedent for and perhaps influence on such phenomena as Rifftrax and *Mystery Science Theater 3000* (1988–99) (see, e.g., Carrier 103). Rather than an origin point, however, *Flickers* is a pivot between a body of now-obscure 1930s and 1940s burlesques of silent movies, and later, better-known examples of audiovisual remixing and riffing. It is also adjacent to traditions of found-footage media-making, which *Flickers* hails in the form of an unexpected borrowing from Bruce Conner's *A MOVIE* (1958). Finally, *Flickers* belongs to a 1950s and 1960s silent-cinema revival. Silents abounded on postwar TV, from slapstick scenes allowing Howdy Doody a bathroom break in the morning, to *Movie Museum* (1954–c. 1957) filling holes in late-night schedules. *Flickers*, both the most ballyhooed and badly behaved of these revivals, earned reproof from Lon Chaney Jr., who contemplated a lawsuit over Ward's "unjust, unfair and completely uncalled for" destruction of his father's screen legacy ("They Fractured My Pa"). *Fractured Flickers* endured as a watchword for the "abusive" treatment of film history (Schickel 32).

But as we will demonstrate, *Flickers*'s relationship to its silent films and mode of address to its audiences were slier and more riven with contradictions than such condemnations allowed. Transcending mere mockery, it was admiring *and* irreverent, disrespectful *and* curatorial. In the first sections of this essay, we reconstruct a history of reuses of silent cinema dating back a century, culminating in the medium of television providing a venue for the re-presentation and rediscovery of silents. We then describe how *Flickers* transformed the varied attitudes seen in these earlier appropriations in a new mode, one of mainstreamed camp, and in the process brought in techniques adjacent to those of the cinematic avant-garde.

We argue that *Flickers* helped to fashion, for a post–World War II generation, an ab/usable cinematic past. Beyond that, it modeled a generative connoisseurship by which all manner of cultural texts and norms could be gleefully mis/appropriated, re/mixed, and de/re/contextualized to upturn existing meanings and create new ones.

Hollywood's Reuse of Silent Cinema

Flickers was hardly the first instance of American film and television repurposing silent cinema. Recent work by media historians and amateur and professional archivists has excavated examples dating back to the end of the silent era itself, revealing not so much a sustained tradition across the decades but rather a series of brief and quickly forgotten efforts. To the contemporary viewer, these instances strikingly prefigure later instances of riffing, replacement narratives, montage, and the like. But they pointedly lack the richly contradictory attitude that characterizes camp. Instead, they seem alternately sappy and ungenerous.

To begin with, historian William Drew has described the "Old Time Movie Show," a name given in the early 1920s to the alternative exhibition practice of screening older, nickelodeon-era shorts, often with an invitation for the audience to poke fun. This was, Drew writes, a "conscious attempt to send up the cinema's 'primitive' past by intentionally exposing it to ridicule" (xiv). This sense of cinema's past as "primitive" informs most of the dozens of short subjects assembled in the 1930s from otherwise unrenumerative reels of silents slumbering in studios' vaults. These derivatives came chiefly in two distinct modes. One was of sincere, sometimes syrupy, nostalgia. Warners' "Thrills of Yesterday" (1931), subtitled "Serious Moments from Serial Days," overlays snatches of short films from cinema's first decades with apologetic narration ("Those were the struggling days of the movies") and the old-fashioned sounds of a barbershop quartet. The other mode was of brazen defilement. "The Unshod Maiden" (1932), one of Universal's "Brevities," treats the sufferings of the heroine of Lois Weber's *Shoes* (1916), which it radically condenses, as the occasion for suggestive jibes and verbal eyerolls at its moments of pathos. The most elaborate examples of this tendency—and those that most clearly prefigure *Fractured Flickers*—were MGM's "Goofy Movies," produced by Pete Smith. Smith used voice-over, antipathetic sound effects, and, as Eric Hoyt observes, "cutting between films from different genres" to manically mock, and provide flaky replacement narratives for, 1910s silents (83). "Goofy Movies No. 4" (1934) turns a William S. Hart Western (which we haven't been able to identify) into "The Passions of

Horse-Pistol Pete." When he tires of mocking outmoded performance styles ("Now Peter remembers his school of acting and strikes pose B"), Smith interpolates shots of a smiling monkey or a ridiculous flying machine. The once-famous Hart goes unmentioned, an act of either mercy or sacrilege.[1]

Later "remixes" of silent films, such as RKO's 1940s "Flicker Flashbacks" and the 1945 compilation feature *Gaslight Follies*, alternated between—but did not truly synthesize—these modes. The former follows nostalgic montages and accoutrements (sing-a-longs, lantern slides) with abridgments of films of the 1910s. The latter's cinematic techniques and earnestly melodramatic plotlines are mocked in voice-over ("Gads! What drama, what emotion!"). After a long "those were the days" chronicle constructed of old newsreel clips, *Follies* showcases Biograph's early feature *East Lynne* (1915), adding not only the familiar voice-over quips but also sound effects (a cash register rings, unseen audience members yawn) and such indignities as the film appearing to get stuck in the gate and briefly playing upside-down.

Not all of Hollywood's references to the silent era were relegated to such ephemera. The silent era was the subject of several major studio features, though, as David Bordwell observes, it was usually portrayed in a mode of "patronizing nostalgia" (434). Along with the marginal product discussed above, these features treat *datedness* as the silents' fundamental attribute. Even when these films do not attack the silents directly and instead use them as an occasion for wordplay and audiovisual puns, they often convey the impression that whatever entertainment value they once had has been irretrievably lost. In part, this attitude was self-congratulatory: a triumphant American film industry reminding its audiences just how far it had come. However, Bordwell records a partial exception to this general attitude: even as they often derided silent drama as crude and embarrassing, critics and audiences still enjoyed, even revered, silent comedy. Films by Chaplin, Lloyd, and Sennett were all revived in the 1940s, circulating widely in both cinemas and home collections (432–433). Silent comedy would eventually become a mainstay of postwar American television, and its treatment in *Fractured Flickers* was notably ambivalent.

Mischief Makers and Movie Museums

By the late 1940s and 1950s, film studios' interest in revisiting the silent era was on the wane. The work of bringing silent cinema to the attention of a new generation—by means both admirable and disreputable—would fall largely to the new medium of television. The saturation of silent cinema on American TV would crest in—and allow for—the allusions to silent-film syntax and iconography in mid-1960s camp series like *The Monkees, Batman,* and *Gilligan's Island*.[2]

With growing numbers of stations, each with numerous broadcast hours to fill, postwar US television had an insatiable appetite for content. Much of that content would be old movies, which were both in ample supply and, as Hoyt has documented, reliably popular with TV audiences (150–151). Before the mid-1950s, however, the major studios were reluctant to license their sound films for broadcast, seeking to hold out until the new industry matured and could offer them a greater return. As a result, the airwaves, particularly outside of prime time, were filled with alternative fare—including silents. Hoyt notes that some TV viewers "found pleasure" in the datedness, or putative badness, of much of this product, watching them "with a sense of irony" that he links to camp (188–189).

TV audiences' relationships to slapstick, by far the genre of silent film most abundant on postwar TV screens, were more complex. As Rob King writes, the trickle of prewar theatrical revivals of silent comedy became "a geyser" on 1950s TV (16). Silent comedy would be repackaged and resold to TV *ad infinitum*. It was almost always served up as marginal kids' entertainment, inserted into episodes of morning variety shows or used to fill brief programming gaps. Silent slapstick shorts—shorn of titles and credits, ruthlessly edited, sped up, outfitted with sound effects and zany voice overs—were repackaged under names like "Chuckleheads," "Comedy Capers," "The Funny Manns," and "Mischief Makers." King notes that these "cutdowns" of silent comedy amounted to an "infantilization" of the style (198), reducing the originals to their most antic, violent, and outré elements for a perceived audience of attention-challenged tykes. Yet in these reedited versions, presented in adrenalized, almost nonnarrative bursts, slapstick shorts seem less like dated subjects for ridicule and more like hyperstylized emanations from another universe, with their own laws of physics and behavior. For many baby boomers, the allure of this alternate universe was strong, producing a "second-order" nostalgia for this revised version of silent comedy that would resonate not just in the youth cultures of the 1950s and 60s, but for decades after (King 196–197).

Silent dramas sometimes appeared on postwar TV. New York City's ABC affiliate broadcast a series of silent features, including *Husbands and Lovers*

(1924) and *The Son of the Sheik* (1926), on Sunday evenings in 1948 and 1949 ("Old Silent Films"). Similar programs followed on other stations, often in the wee hours. But aside from comedy cutdowns, silents' most visible presence on 1950s and 1960s US TV, in or just outside of prime time, was courtesy of Paul Killiam. Killiam was a New York–based radio announcer and comic who, in the mid-1940s, ran the Old Knickerbocker, a kind of *Gaslight Follies* in the flesh that featured bygone forms of live entertainment in a cabaret format. Musty stage melodramas (performed with tongue securely in cheek) mixed with novelty acts, including one in which Killiam accompanied silent shorts with his comic monologues. In the 1950s, he brought this routine to his own, short-lived WCBS series and to network talk shows. In an undated clip from *The Steve Allen Show* (1956–64), Killiam re-narrates an excerpt from D. W. Griffith's *Man's Genesis* (1912). The reflexive conceit is that, with TV stations in danger of running out of product, Killiam's "company" has "worked out a technique for making 'new old' movies," using a lens that would give that "stale, washed-out look" audiences had come to expect. The humor relies on self-consciously groan-inducing and stale puns, ethnic jokes, and double entendres, and derives mostly from the incongruity between the prehistoric setting of the film, depicting life among cavemen, and the re-narration, which tells of a "modern romance" between "Jim and Joan" using urbane, contemporary references. It is scarcely a reverent treatment, but the bit depends less on direct mockery of his source than a winking acknowledgment of the desultory quality of the entire performance.

Killiam, a film collector, eventually sought to expose audiences to silents in what critic Richard Schickel called more "respectful" ways (33). He did so through a string of syndicated series that sought to bring the TV audience an awareness of the historical and aesthetic values of America's silent film heritage. The first of these was *Movie Museum*. Its fifteen-minute episodes—over 100 within a year of its debut in fall 1954—began with stately piano music over a shot from Griffith's *Intolerance* (1916). They presented digests of single films and surveys of a particular figure or genre. Killiam offers wall-to-wall narration, mixing jokes, synopses, gossip, and the occasional semi-scholarly insight.[3] After *Museum* was the short-lived *Hour of Silents* (late 1950s) and the higher-profile, half-hour *Silents Please* (1960–61), featured on ABC in late prime time. The opening credits boasted a montage of silent stars, promising "the excitement, the thrills, the laughter, and the heartbreak of Hollywood's golden era." Episodes offered, with musical accompaniment and limited narration, condensations of Griffith's *Orphans of the Storm* (across two episodes) from 1921, *The Perils of Pauline* (1914), *Nosferatu* (1922; billed as *Dracula*), and *The Hunchback of Notre Dame*, among others. In these and later specials and series, Killiam brought the discoveries and insights of film archivists and curators at the Museum of Modern Art and the George Eastman House to the TV public. In its second season, *Silents Please* was hosted by Ernie Kovacs, who, cigar in hand, began each episode with a brief lecture delivered from his den laden with books, hi-fi equipment, and movie memorabilia. Kovacs, a paragon of cult TV, offered midcentury audiences a celebrity model of the cultured, conscientious, canny silent-film lover.

In their efforts to reacquaint postwar audiences with silent cinema, Killiam and Kovacs were not pontificating in a vacuum. Lynn Spigel has observed that Kovacs's network specials offered televisual play with sound and silence in a way conspicuously inspired by silent cinema (178–180, 188–196). His experiments took place amid a TV trend of allusions to and parodies of silent films, extending to entire episodes of sitcoms and a "silent" interview with Sessue Hayakawa on *The Steve Allen Show* before which the host "wisecracked over" a clip from *The Typhoon* (1914) (Spigel 205–206). Buster Keaton, Gloria Swanson, and other veterans of silents were newly visible as mainstays of variety, talk, and game shows. Beyond the tube, a popular series of theatrically released compilation features of the 1950s and 60s, several edited and narrated by Robert Youngson, represented silent comedy—and sometimes other genres—to grander effect than the TV cutdowns. These compilations tied excerpts of silent comedies (sourced from high-quality prints in the studio vaults) together with celebratory, even purplish narration. Publishers brought out mass-market "pictorials" like *Classics of the Silent Screen* (1959). Across the pond, the radio series *The Goon Show* (1951–60) and its TV and film offshoots featured silent-film references and parodies. For instance, Peter Sellers collaborated with Richard Lester on the silent-comedy pastiche *The Running Jumping & Standing Still Film* (1959), which eventually led to Lester directing The Beatles in *A Hard Day's Night* (1964) and *Help!* (1965), both peppered with appropriations of silent-film grammar and iconography. *The Monkees* (1966–68) would follow suit, helping to consolidate silent-film allusions and iconography at the center of 1960s youth culture. Indeed, the visual citations of silent cinema found in numerous mid-60s series were legible to youth audiences *as* citations largely thanks to the profusion of slapstick cutdowns and other silent-cinema ephemera on TV in the preceding fifteen years.

The World of Jay Ward

Fractured Flickers certainly is one link in the chains previously described. But for its original audiences, the primary association would likely have been to the animated TV series created by Jay Ward Productions. These displayed a pervasive comic knowingness and detachment, as well as a willingness to poke at totems of postwar culture (from cold warriors to he-men), that gave them a "peculiar appeal bordering on the subversive" (Christon K6). Their aesthetic has often been likened to—and sometimes identified with—camp. Riffing on silent cinema was an integral component of this aesthetic, setting a crucial precedent and context for *Fractured Flickers*.

Beginning with *Crusader Rabbit* (1950–51, 1959), Ward animations were distinguished by their memorable character designs and voice acting, rudimentary animation, farcical storylines, and nonstop punning. Its flagship series, known initially as *Rocky and His Friends* (1959–61, ABC) and then as *The Bullwinkle Show* (1961–64, NBC), featured several recurring segments, including the adventures of the titular squirrel and moose, "Fractured Fairy Tales" (in which Edward Everett Horton narrates parodies of classic children's stories), "Peabody's Improbable History" (a "genius" talking dog and his loyal human boy travel in time), and "Dudley Do-Right" (a hopelessly earnest Canadian Mountie battles the dastardly villain Snidely Whiplash).

Ward's series—whose sensibility was equally the responsibility of head writer and voice actor Bill Scott—were often described as having a knack for reaching both children and adults. This split "kidult" appeal was key to midcentury prime-time animation (Mittell 70). For children: cute animals, funny voices, (proudly) dumb jokes, and lots of cartoon violence. For adults: all those things, plus a torrent of cultural and topical allusions, puns, and parodies, spanning the obvious and the arcane. A similar duality was central to the programs Phillips and Pinedo place in their canon of Camp TV, from *Batman* to *Get Smart* to *The Monkees* (20–35). Not coincidentally, the syndicated Ward series mostly appeared in the same early-evening time slots, 7:00 and 7:30 p.m., as several of those later programs—an after-dinner hour when both parents and children were dependably plunked down in front of the TV set.

Among the more obviously campy elements of Ward's cartoons were parodic amplifications and ironic inversions of gender. *George of the Jungle* (1967–70, ABC) is a riff on the Johnny Weissmuller Tarzan movies—already staples of camp appropriation. The nearly preverbal George boasts a barrel chest and a peanut brain, and often requires rescuing by quick-witted Ursula and erudite jungle critters. George was himself a variation on the earlier character Dudley Do-Right, a dim-witted, cowardly incompetent who occupies, to hilarious effect, the traditionally heroic lead role. Dudley's hyperbolic "squareness" (he trills chivalrous maxims in a high-pitched voice and calls Lawrence Welk "real toe-tapping music") and his less-than-enthusiastic courtship of ostensible love interest Nell (who is romantically interested only in Dudley's horse) loudly echo the coded, "trans gender queer" depictions that Quinlan Miller argues saturated 1950s sitcoms (1).

The "Dudley Do-Right" skits are only the most obvious examples of a string of silent-film references in Ward's shows. In one "Fractured Fairy Tales" installment, characters continually mistake the name of one silent-era cowboy star, "Harry Carey," for another, "Hoot Gibson." Other sequences name-drop mostly forgotten silent players Evelyn Brent and Elmo Lincoln (whose 1918 version of *Tarzan of the Apes* would be fodder for *Flickers*). Apart from such in-jokes, the governing allusions are to stage and silent-film melodrama, evident in typography, character designs, a rinky-dink piano score, irises, and frequent intertitles. The go-to cliché of silent melodrama—the hero races to rescue his lady, who has been tied to the railroad tracks—recurs over and over. Probably more people alive today have been exposed to this trope via Jay Ward cartoons than by any silents that include it. Hans Conried, voice of the moustache-twirling Whiplash, mimicked silent and sound superstar— and noted ham and axiom of camp—John Barrymore (Scott 170). As the precision and frequent obscurity of such references suggest, Ward, Scott, and writer-collaborator Chris Hayward were all silent-film aficionados.[4] The trio took part in the midcentury effort to give silents more dignified exposure. In the mid-1960s, Ward purchased theatrical rights to films by Mack Sennett, Laurel and Hardy, and D. W. Griffith, with plans to mount retrospectives and assemble compilation features. Ward regarded such items "with a collector's reverence" (Bart).

We Offend Everyone

Fractured Flickers was thus an extension of the Ward crew's infatuation with silent film. It was Hayward's brainchild, originally conceived for *The Watts Gnu Show*, a puppet-centric revue that never got past a 1959 pilot. *Flickers*'s pilot was prepared from late 1960 to early 1961. Hayward, Scott, and Allan Burns wrote most of the segments. Raymond Rohauer, famous for helping to revive the fortunes of Buster Keaton, programming revivals and avant-garde screenings at the Coronet in Los Angeles, and playing fast and loose with copyright, furnished the vintage source material for a per-episode flat fee (Scott 226–227). Rohauer's collection gave the *Flickers* team access to a wide and deep archive of cinema history. Films chosen for fracturing were duped, edited, and then dubbed by members of the Ward stock company, primarily Scott, June Foray, and Paul Frees. Conried appeared in the flesh—between the flickers—as host. This cast, along with the animated credits sequence that mixed likenesses of Harold Lloyd, Sennett bathing beauties, Keystone Kops, and Douglas Fairbanks with types similar to those from "Dudley Do-Right," connected the show to the familiar Ward TV universe.

Flickers had a lengthy gestation. Initially proposed as a CBS network series, it was briefly courted by the British Independent Television Corporation, which facilitated the production of six or seven additional episodes. In late 1962, it was picked up by Desilu Productions, then the most powerful independent TV producer in America. The deal demanded twenty-six episodes, and the Ward team had to race to reach that number (with consequences discussed below). Desilu mounted an aggressive sales campaign, taking out full-page ads in trade papers timed to the 1963 National Association of Broadcasters convention. Ads mimicked the series's conceit, with a caption reading "Desilu will have these beautiful Gaslight Club girls as hostesses in Room 311" under a photo of Chaney in his Quasimodo makeup (Advertisement, April 1, 1963). Ward himself promoted the show with his patented ironic ballyhoo. A promo kit, made up like a lascivious fan magazine, featured stickers with the comic visage of Snub Pollard and noted that *Flickers*'s main ratings competition included "The National Oboe Hour" and "How Zinc Is Made" (Harris). Ward organized an elaborate travesty of film culture, the "Coney Island Film Festival," in which *Flickers* was the only thing in competition and, naturally, received all the awards. Guests arrived on a vintage subway train placed back into service for the event and drank Prohibition-style bootleg hooch ("'Rhinestone' Jay").

Whether because of such antics or simply the reputation of Ward's animations, *Flickers* was a near-instant success. ABC bought it for its owned-and-operated stations, giving it prime exposure in major cities, and this was followed by purchases for over one hundred domestic and overseas markets. Like previous Ward series, *Flickers* was typically scheduled for the early evening hours, with Desilu making an explicit appeal to "laughers of all ages" (Advertisement, May 13, 1963). In its original run, *Flickers* was often among the top ten syndicated shows in markets like Boston, Chicago, Detroit, and San Francisco.[5]

The show's reception was mixed. Aside from Chaney Jr., who worried that the show "leaves a disrespectful image in the minds of children" and argued that it was a violation of "'moral' principle" ("They Fractured My Pa" 31), objections were brooked from Joan Crawford (Scott 226). Similarly, a column in the magazine *8mm Collector* sneered that "the very idea of the series is repulsive to me" (Haven 138). But complaints, real or imagined, made good publicity. In an interview with Ward, the *Los Angeles Times* conjured a vivid image of loyal readers of *Cahiers du Cinéma* leading "a peace march to Hollywood" in protest. In response, Ward cheerfully boasted, "We offend everyone" (Gardner). Reviews largely praised the series's inventiveness and extension of the familiar Ward brand of humor (Scott 228). Few, however, acknowledged its place in the lineage of recycling. As for responses from original "regular" viewers, there's little but traces. Notably, one correspondent to the *Chicago Tribune* hinted that the show *enhanced*—rather than desecrated—the "fun and old-fashioned comedy" of the source material (R. H.). A disappointed *Variety* review suggested that the show's "pedestrian gaggery" would appeal mostly to kids ("Review" 34). But an Anaheim housewife complained to the *Los Angeles Times* that its early-evening slot—a time when she was "doing dishes, washing children, etc."—would mean that "I never get to see what's going on" (qtd. in Smith). Such comments are evocative of the show's dualities: its affection for and merciless "fracturing" of cinema heritage and its address to both children and adults.

Camp Personae and Camp Address

Fractured Flickers, like *The Bullwinkle Show*, is constructed from short, modular units—most notably the "flickers" themselves. But these are wrapped by segments featuring Conried, including one celebrity interview per episode. As in other Ward shows, in *Flickers* everything is fodder for comic ironizing and nothing is played straight. But what binds the show's disparate elements is not simply a comic mode. Rather, it is in the show's engagement with camp that we can locate a coherent aesthetic linking the interviews, Conried's introductions, and the flickers.

The obviously scripted chats are playful, self-conscious travesties of celebrity interviews, with guests engaging in self-parody, serving as "straight men" for Conried's performance of an incompetent, out-of-touch host, or professing disdain for the very series on which they are appearing. Paul Lynde feigns discomfort as Conried repeatedly mistakes him for a different guest (S1 E18, 1963). Conried and Anna Maria Alberghetti politely argue over whether or not she is expected to sing during her segment (S1 E19, 1963). Fabian claims ignorance of *Flickers* but professes his love for "old films" like *Gidget Goes Hawaiian* (1961) (S1 E2, 1963). Bob Newhart pickets his own interview, citing offenses to himself (*Flickers*'s voice artists mimicked Newhart's stand-up persona) and other talent living and dead (S1 E24, 1964).

Among the participants we find a who's-who of stars known for their glamor, exaggerated performance of gender, and/or other camp affinities: alums of beach-party films (Annette Funicello, Deborah Walley), sopranos (Alberghetti, Vivien Della Chiesa), sex goddesses and burlesque performers (Diana Dors, Gypsy Rose Lee), erstwhile "Latin lover" Cesar Romero, and icons Lynde, Zsa Zsa Gabor, and Rose Marie. Edward Everett Horton, who began his career in the 1920s and was later known for playing prissy bachelors, offers not just camp appeal but a direct link to silent cinema. In sum, *Flickers*'s interview subjects trace a clear arc from early- to mid-twentieth-century camp personae.

This sending-up of "excessive"—and especially *sexually* excessive—stars and character archetypes also shapes the show's engagement with silent cinema. A core tenet of camp is that historical distance defamiliarizes personae and styles and that this detachment renders them ripe for camp appreciation. Theda Bara is an axiom of this phenomenon. The fabulous excess and artifice of her 1910s vamp persona was underlined by the passage of time, making it ripe for camp enshrinement within a few decades (Babuscio 124–125). Bara takes pride of place in *Flickers*. Her cartoon likeness graces the credits, and her portrait, defaced with a moustache, hangs on the wall behind Conried (see Figure 2.1). In one episode, Conried and Ursula Andress commune with Bara's spirit via Ouija board, learning of her fury at a mysterious "FF" (S1 E25, 1964). Like *George of the Jungle*, *Flickers* burlesques the hypermasculine Tarzan. Though an interview with camp icon and sound-era Tarzan Johnny Weissmuller ultimately went unused, the show's first episode fractures an earlier incarnation, Elmo Lincoln in *Tarzan of the Apes*. In a typical gesture, Paul Frees's voicework makes the husky "Tarfoot" a burlesque on a more up-to-date hypermasculine

Figure 2.1 Hans Conried, standing in front of a defaced portrait of silent "vamp" Theda Bara, introduces an episode of *Fractured Flickers*. "Rose Marie" (S1 E1, 1963, *Fractured Flickers*, Jay Ward Productions).

type: a Brooklyn-accented meathead who promises Jane "liverwurst, lox and cream cheese" (Video 2.2) ▶. Tarfoot's husky body is rendered absurd by juvenilization. A feat of strength is said to earn "a merit badge for sure" and a lustful pass at Jane becomes a request to "rub noses."

Flickers mobilizes the dual address central to both camp TV and Ward's brand. Kids might be amused by the bad puns and silly sound effects, while adults might be flattered to get more cerebral jokes and intertextual references. One persistent subject is *Flickers*'s hardly exalted place within commercial TV's "vast wasteland" (a phrase Conried invokes at least once) (S1 E4, 1963). In the segment "What Is Jay Ward Really Like?" a captain of industry and some browbeaten employees from a 1910s film are refigured as Ward and TV writers "Rob Sterling" and "Reginald Nose"—more-than-obvious references to Rod Serling and Reginald Rose (S1 E7, 1963). The replacement narrative makes these avatars of serious, "quality" TV servile to Ward, a purveyor of junk. The segment also sends up the writers' leftish reputations, with Ward accusing them of "Bolshevism—worse, liberalism" for asking for a day off.

Ward is handed a copy of next fall's prime-time lineup, which features "Sing-along with Yma Sumac," "77 Gaza Strip," and "Peter Watergunn."

The posture of self-mockery seen in "What Is Jay Ward Really Like?" is pervasive. The bulk of Conried's jokes are at the expense of the putative awfulness of his own show. He describes it as "a mess" and the production staff as "four monkeys with scissors and crayons" (S1 E5, 1963), regularly references a churn of lawsuits supposedly filed by rightly aggrieved viewers and filmmakers (e.g., S1 E7, 1963), and reports that an episode was broadcast backward without viewers noticing (S1 E3, 1963). This insistence on the show's cheapness and incompetence, recalling Killiam's act, is joined to occasional laments over and apologies for *Flickers*'s unjust butchery of cinematic history. This comic reflexivity serves as a hedge by signaling (sincerely or not) a lack of commitment to or confidence in its own material. But it also creates a distance that renders more complex and ambivalent the show's attitude toward its source material. To mockery, it adds shades of appreciation, affection, and sympathy. This is a camp sensibility.

Silent Cinema and Camp Ambivalence

Flickers marshals all the strategies for remixing the cinematic past developed by its antecedents. Some segments, including "Dinky Dunstan," radically abridge and re-narrate a single film. This approach was the show's founding conceit, although only occasionally is it extended to a full ten-minute segment. In episode one, Conried tutors the viewer in this method using a sequence from *Blood and Sand* (1922). But within the first few episodes, some segments go beyond simple elision to include other forms of comic re-editing. For instance, "Cornell Goes Wilde" repeats *ad absurdum* a brief shot of Richard Barthelmess practicing a field goal from *The Drop Kick* (1927), rendering the action ridiculous (S1 E2, 1963) (Video 2.3) ▶. Some segments stitch together fragments from multiple films. After the first few episodes, this multi-source approach becomes more common and more ambitious, resulting in the manic, quasi-avant-garde style discussed below. Near-continuous "looping," the term the crew used for the added soundwork—whether by a narrator, voice actors playing characters, or both—is crucial to all the "flickers" segments.

Flickers mines various genres and tones. This often means that it adds comic soundwork to an already comedic film. For instance, the segment

"The Cut-Away" purports to present unearthed behind-the-scenes audio of an exasperated director alongside footage from his set (S1 E5, 1963). The escalating comic calamities of the actual source (starring forgotten comic Billy Dooley, "The Misfit Sailor") are rewritten as disasters from the set of the (fake) *Creep in the Deep*. In a series of gags evoking the camera-switching of live TV, the director continually tries to salvage things by cutting to a view of a ship that, by the end, is sunk—weighed down by "too many extras." At one point, the director asks, with Newhart-esque stammering, to see "some he-man lovemaking." After the female co-star gestures grandly, he despairs: "Not you, Vera! Uh, cut away, Morrie!" Here we see how the gender performance/play already in silent slapstick is further twisted and inverted, adding layers of masquerade. Even when *Flickers* is aiming for a similar affective register as the source material, the replacement narrative reorients the locus of humor and, like the re-editing of *The Drop Kick*, manufactures an impression of "failed seriousness" (Sontag 287).

But the targets of *Flickers*'s most elaborate replacement narratives are mainly dramas like *Hunchback*. The show took particular interest in fracturing dramas featuring extremely stylized performances ripe for camp appreciation, from Chaney to German expressionism to John Barrymore. "Do Me A Flavor" turns *Dr. Jekyll and Mr. Hyde* (1920) into a "stirring saga of the soft drink industry" (S1 E2, 1963). Barrymore's Jekyll becomes Dr. Seltzer, inventor of a double-chocolate seltzer formula. The grotesque throes of the Jekyll-Hyde transformation become evidence of the formula's revitalizing powers. Standing, Barrymore juts his arms out, fingers splayed, and waves them up and down convulsively (see Figure 2.2). The narration turns these movements into Dr. Seltzer miming his "play-the-piano-mood." In an example of *Flickers*' brand of "sick" humor, Hyde bludgeoning his fiancé's father to death is mickey-moused to the tune of "The Seltzer Song." Over a concluding shot of Hyde's crazed, agape visage as he crouches over his victim, Bill Scott sustains a cheery note for six seconds (Video 2.4) ▶.

The use of "excessive" performances like Chaney's and Barrymore's to set up bold (perhaps cheap) comic incongruities exemplified, for some viewers, the program's disrespect for its sources. And it is easy to see why those committed to respectful, open-hearted, and context-sensitive presentation of silent cinema would react with some mix of horror, sadness, and anger at the travesties served up by *Flickers*. Conried's intros are sometimes dismissive: "Of course, from our vantage point of forty years later, we can easily see how trite and threadbare some of the situations were and how

Figure 2.2 In the segment "Do Me a Flavor," voice-over transforms Dr. Jekyll's anguished convulsions into limp-wristed "piano playing." "Fabian" (S1 E2, 1963, *Fractured Flickers*, Jay Ward Productions).

unbelievably bad some of the acting was" (S1 E4, 1963). Such comments, and the fracturings described above, appear consonant with the strain of riffing culture that positions its sources as obviously "bad" and deserving of mockery.

But the explicit and implicit attitudes toward silent cinema expressed by *Flickers* are not as straightforward as "isn't this terrible?" or even "it's so bad it's good." As noted above, the films are often represented as undeserving and unfortunate victims of the show's ham-fisted "mutilation." Immediately after his assertion about "unbelievably bad acting," Conried tempers his condescension with a playful acknowledgment (not unlike Sontag's) of how time affects standards of realism and taste: "Isn't it comforting to know that in the year 2000, someone will do the same thing for *The Loretta Young Show*? [1953–61]?" And Conried's introduction to a segment that makes hay of the performances in *The Hands of Orlac* (1924) pitches the original not as dated or inept, but as a "marvelous film" starring "the great European actor Conrad Veidt" (S1 E5, 1963). He calls *Hunchback* a "masterpiece." Horton's discussion with Conried is the most sincere of the interviews; he introduces a segment fracturing the romance *Young April* (1926) by means of waxing nostalgic about Ruritanian farces (S1 E6, 1963).

Fractured Flickers mutilates *and* celebrates. We can consider its re-editing and re-narrating not as simple mockery, but rather as a means to exploit the abundant opportunities for comic incongruity between sound and image. Only in rare instances does a replacement narrative serve as a vehicle for direct, sneering commentary on the alleged badness of the original film's acting, themes, or emotional appeals (as in "Horse-Pistol Pete" and *Gaslight Follies*). *Flickers* largely eschews direct commentary and instead offers more elaborate editing and soundwork that, at its best, embraces the allusive, punny, and absurdist wit we associate with Ward productions. To rewrite *Hyde* as a story about a singing soda scientist, or to turn Veidt's trancelike gestures in *Orlac* into a form of massage, is certainly to trivialize—but not necessarily to denigrate. Nor does it suggest that silent films are exhausted of all value except an ability to serve as an object of our derision. While viewers might cultivate misinformed and condescending attitudes, the show's approach leaves open possibilities for other kinds of appreciation. Fracturing is as much, if not more, about using the source films to create something zany, frivolous, and new as it is about offering strong judgments of silent films—other than that they have been somewhat defamiliarized by the passage of time and happen to be cheaply available for playful appropriation.

Cinema's Rummage, Camp Collage, and the Avant-Garde

Over the course of its run, *Fractured Flickers* gradually abandoned the practice of making replacement narratives from single films in favor of briefer, even more manic collage sequences. These take not just from silent fiction films but from seemingly anything rummaged from Rohauer's vast collection, from masterpieces to ephemera: silent- and sound-era newsreels, ethnographic documentaries, "thrills and spills" compilations, and even talkies. The mock campaign ad "Return Marvin D. Snark to Washington" lasts three minutes and contains material from over a dozen sources (S1 E18, 1963). When the narrator cites Snark's "flood control bill" (which "provides a controlled flood" to homeowners), we glimpse the inundated bedroom from *Fatty and Mabel Adrift* (1916). A reference to Snark's denunciation of Calvin

Coolidge "as a red" accompanies 1927 footage of Coolidge donning a Lakota eagle-feather headdress. Over a brief clip of Marlene Dietrich from *The Blue Angel* (1930), her song "Falling in Love Again" is replaced with a warbly rendition of "Voting for Snark Again"—complete with added noise to approximate, on the soundtrack, the beaten-up quality of the old print. We also see an escape artist dangling feet-first from a crane, bombs issuing from a plane, chorus girls, Buster Keaton, a Lady Godiva imitator, a patient wildly resisting a team of surgeons, mustachioed men in kimono performing magic, blindfolded men conferring around a table, a frail woman being throttled, a prisoner restrained by the neck, early flying machines, and more.

Why this shift to this collage aesthetic? While early episodes were made in the span of weeks or months, later ones were made in haste after the show began airing. The luxury of time on the early episodes allowed the voice actors, effects artists, and editors to develop extended replacement narratives and carefully match new dialogue to on-screen lip movements. This process was especially time-intensive (Scott 228–230). The method for later episodes involved ransacking Rohauer's archive for any bits of film that could be spliced together and then binding them, loosely, with narration. With less ambitious sound–image relationships and less pretense of a narrative through line, the collage segments were likely easier to assemble at breakneck speed.

The humor of these segments seems to reflect the frenzy of their making. Puns, "sick" jokes, and allusions come blindingly fast. Some approach the surreal in their feverish non sequiturs, bizarre juxtapositions, and nonsense. There is still a camp ethos here—say, in contemplating the sublime ridiculousness of experimental flying machines, or the "failed seriousness" of Coolidge's headdress ceremony. But the bewildering heterogeneity of their source materials, including many shots from actualities, shifts the locus of humor, and of appreciation/derision, from the outmoded representational codes of silent cinema toward cinema writ large as a vast repository of the bizarre, the inane, the terrible, the trivial, and everything between. In so doing, *Flickers* announces its affinity with some unexpected contemporaneous works of cinematic collage: on the one hand, the everything-goes Italian "Mondo" features (*Mondo Cane* [1962] would have been in release around the time later episodes of *Flickers* were being put together), and on the other, an avant-garde tradition of found-footage film—an example of which the series brazenly appropriates.

In one remarkable sequence, "Mother's Day," Scott adopts the vocal shtick of entertainer Eddie Lawrence, specifically his "Old Philosopher" character (S1 E7, 1963). A typical Lawrence routine involves the weary, warbly Philosopher reciting a series of woes, punctuated by cacophonous bursts of ballyhoo and brass music. In one high-energy section, Scott's ersatz Philosopher exclaims, "Keep smiling, be happy, don't sulk, and whatever you do, remember: Rome wasn't built like your mother!" On the image track is an eight-second flurry containing fourteen shots. Among them are an explosion, a wagon train, a speeding locomotive, Teddy Roosevelt's quaking jowls, a water-skier's wipeout, and a military tank cresting a hill (Video 2.5) ▶. Later there is a second flurry that constructs a POV sequence—and a dirty joke—through consecutive shots of a sailor peering through a periscope, a woman posing seductively in black underwear on a mattress, and a speeding torpedo. If these sound familiar, it is because they appear in Bruce Conner's 1958 found-footage film *A MOVIE*. This is definitely not a coincidence, as a full twenty-four of the thirty shots composing the segment's rapid-fire montages are in (or from) *A MOVIE*.

How did substantial chunks of this landmark of avant-garde cinema end up on 1960s prime-time TV? The most likely answer involves Rohauer's role as a distributor and exhibitor of experimental film. *A MOVIE* screened in Los Angeles on programs Rohauer organized through his Society of Cinema Arts (Lanza 136–138). Ward, too, was part of this cinephilic milieu. Surely one of them recognized the affinities between *A MOVIE* and *Flickers*. (It is probable that Rohauer, known for unauthorized dupings and screenings, failed to inform Conner of this use of his film.) The excerpts from Conner's film—that is, excerpts of excerpts—are at once an example of the show's policy of wanton appropriation *and* an homage—a hailing of one practitioner of audiovisual trawling and camp resignification by the makers of another.

The Afterlives of *Fractured Flickers*

After its first and only season concluded in 1964, *Flickers* stuck around in syndication for decades. Befitting its multi-generational appeal, it was sometimes programmed alongside cartoons on weekend mornings and other times late at night for insomniacs and third-shifters. Not long after its initial run, Ward and Rohauer packaged a selection of *Flickers* segments with W. C. Fields and Laurel and Hardy compilations for theatrical release. This program became a staple of revival theaters and college film series well into the 1970s. In the 1980s and 1990s, *Flickers* could be seen on cable networks

Showtime and Ha! (a progenitor of Comedy Central). By that point, other TV series partly inspired by *Flickers* had appeared. *Mad Movies with the L.A. Connection* (1985–86) featured a comedy troupe re-narrating classic Hollywood sound films. The cast of *Mystery Science Theater 3000*, which debuted in 1988 and continues today, poked direct fun at various low-budget midcentury features (echoing the likes of "Goofy Movies" and "Flicker Flashbacks"). The enduringly popular *MST3K* has inspired other series and innumerable live riffing events, and helped to further mainstream a taste culture based around the ironic appreciation/mockery of "trash" cinema.

We can also posit *Flickers* as a forerunner of a variety of more outré found-footage practices. It may be fanciful to connect the maniacally repeated kicks of "Cornell Goes Wilde" to the manipulations of Martin Arnold's *Passage à l'acte* (1993), which turns an innocuous breakfast-table scene from *To Kill a Mockingbird* (1962) into a spastic purgatory. But the madcap methodology of *Flickers*'s collages resembles, and likely inspired, later "mash-ups," from Joe Dante's *The Movie Orgy* (1968) to internet-era compilations by Everything Is Terrible!, which project a simultaneous awe and revulsion at the excretions of late-twentieth-century VHS and TV cultures.

Despite its initial notoriety, decades-long presence on TV, and prefiguring of an ever-expanding world of riffing and found-footage manipulations, *Flickers* is seldom recalled by journalists or scholars, except, as noted, as an "unhappy memory" for having "desecrated" silent films (Thomas). Mention of the show can arouse the ire of cinephiles today. But reviews of its 2004 DVD release situate *Flickers* not as a disgrace to cinema history but as an appendage to it, something with particular appeal to film buffs. Indeed, the web is rife with testimonies of baby boomers and younger fans for whom the series was an introduction to the splendors of silent cinema. For example, a member of the Nitrateville online community wrote that "far from making me have a bad opinion of silent film, [*Flickers*] enchanted me with [its] visual riches, and so successfully whetted my taste for more, and as originally presented" (odinthor). Might the naughty *Flickers* have done as much to keep silent cinema in popular consciousness as the well-behaved *Silents Please*?

Echoing Phillips and Pinedo, we have conceptualized *Fractured Flickers*'s address to its adult and youth audiences, and its attitude toward silent cinema, as "split" or "dual"—as if distinct. But in practice, cult texts like *Flickers* often serve as a bridge between one mode, or one attitude, and another—or, to use a more charged mixed metaphor, a "gateway drug." For a small group, its contradictory stance toward silent films led them to a rich appreciation of that art form. But the series's affinities with other, mostly later camp series on 1960s TV hint at a greater legacy. *Flickers* drew in young viewers thanks to the Ward connection, its time slot, and its broad comedy. Much like *MAD Magazine*, it tutored them in sophisticated, "adult" viewing strategies: the celebratory, satirical, even subversive possibilities of audiovisual remixing, and in the masquerades, double meanings, and sense of play associated with camp.

Notes

1. These shorts made of recycled materials were themselves recycled for later series; the version of "Horse-Pistol Pete" we first viewed came from a 1941 short, "Flicker Memories."
2. In 1965's "Castaways Pictures Presents," Gilligan and the Skipper find a stash of vintage filmmaking equipment; the jodhpur-clad millionaire ("Cecil B. Howell") directs a silent picture replete with stock characters, pancake makeup, undercranking, and wild pantomime. For more on *The Monkees*, see Amernick, Chapter 8, in this volume.
3. The Killiam series benefited from the research and writing of June Bundy Csida, an entertainment journalist and publicist, and the collector and film historian William K. Everson (Stein Haven, 119–120). Kevin Brownlow credits Everson with pushing Killiam toward a more serious, scholarly presentation of silents (Brownlow).
4. Hayward later created the cult (and camp) TV series *My Mother the Car* (1965–66).
5. It is not clear why a second season was never produced, but the creators' exhaustion and sense that the conceit could not be extended further probably had something to do with it.

Bibliography

Advertisement for *Fractured Flickers*. Broadcasting, April 1, 1963, p. 111.
Advertisement for *Fractured Flickers*. Broadcasting, May 13, 1963, p. 43.
Babuscio, Jack. "The Cinema of Camp (aka Camp and the Gay Sensibility)." *Camp: Queer Aesthetics and the Performing Subject: A Reader*, edited by Fabio Cleto, University of Michigan Press, 1999, pp. 117–135.
Bart, Peter. "Films by Sennett and Griffith Sold." *Los Angeles Times*, August 28, 1964, p. 18.
Bordwell, David. *Reinventing Hollywood: How 1940s Filmmakers Changed Movie Storytelling*. University of Chicago Press, 2017.
Brownlow, Kevin. "Obituary: William K. Everson." *The Independent*, April 16, 1996, www.independent.co.uk/incoming/obituary-william-k-everson-5619936.html.
Carrier, David Ray. "Cinemasochism: Bad Movies and the People Who Love Them." *In the Peanut Gallery with Mystery Science Theater 3000: Essays on Film, Fandom, Technology and the Culture of Riffing*, edited by Robert G. Weiner and Shelley E. Barba, McFarland, 2011, pp. 101–108.

Christon, Lawrence. "Tales of Jay Ward and the Bullwinkle Gang." *Los Angeles Times*, November 13, 1988, pp. K6–7, K50–52.
Cleto, Fabio. "Camp." *Routledge Encyclopedia of Queer Culture*, edited by David A. Gerstner, Routledge, 2006, pp. 121–124.
Drew, William M. *The Last Silent Picture Show: Silent Films on American Screens in the 1930s*. Scarecrow, 2010.
Gardner, Paul. "'Fractured Flicks' Flourish." *New York Times*, October 27, 1963, p. 125.
Harris, Harry. "Wacky Promotional Kit Introduces Series Titled 'Fractured Flickers.'" *Philadelphia Inquirer*, August 9, 1963, p. 11.
Haven, Lisa Stein. *Charlie Chaplin's Little Tramp in America, 1947–77*. Palgrave Macmillan, 2016.
Hoyt, Eric. *Hollywood Vault: Film Libraries before Home Video*. University of California Press, 2014.
King, Rob. *Hokum!: The Early Sound Slapstick Short and Depression-Era Mass Culture*. University of California Press, 2017.
Lanza, Tim. "Raymond Rohauer and the Society of Cinema Arts (1948–1962): Giving the Devil His Due." *Alternative Projections: Experimental Film in Los Angeles, 1945–1980*, edited by David E. James and Adam Hyman, Indiana University Press, 2015, pp. 129–140.
Miller, Quinlan. *Camp TV: Trans Gender Queer Sitcom History*. Duke University Press, 2019.
Mittell, Jason. *Genre and Television: From Cop Shows to Cartoons in American Culture*. Routledge, 2004.
odinthor [Brent C. Dickerson]. "Re: What got you into old silents and talkies?" *Nitrateville*, June 24, 2020, www.nitrateville.com/viewtopic.php?t=29956&start=30#p237471. Accessed October 3, 2020.
"Old Silent Films Are Booked for WJZ Video on Sunday Nights Starting Next Week." *New York Times*, October 1, 1948, p. 50.
"Paul Killiam on the Steve Allen Show." *YouTube*, uploaded by MVerdoux, November 22, 2011, www.youtube.com/watch?v=cuYKgDsgavw.
Phillips, W. D., and Isabel Pinedo. "Gilligan and Captain Kirk Have More in Common Than You Think: 1960s Camp TV as an Alternative Genealogy for Cult TV." *Journal of Popular Television*, vol. 6, no. 1, 2018, pp. 19–40.
Review of *Fractured Flickers*. *Variety*, October 2, 1963, pp. 34, 52.
R. H. "TV Mailbag." Letter. *Chicago Tribune*, March 7, 1964, p. B2.
"'Rhinestone' Jay Ward's Coney Island Cotillion for 'Fractured Flickers.'" *Variety*, July 24, 1963, p. 48.
Schickel, Richard. "The Silents Weren't Just Voiceless Talkies." *New York Times*, November 28, 1971, pp. SM32–33, 54, 57, 59–60, 62, 64.
Scott, Keith. *The Moose That Roared: The Story of Jay Ward, Bill Scott, a Flying Squirrel, and a Talking Moose*. Thomas Dunne, 2000.
Smith, Cecil. "And Now a Word from Our Sponsor." *Los Angeles Times*, December 26, 1963, p. C14.
Sontag, Susan. "Notes on 'Camp.'" *Against Interpretation and Other Essays*, Farrar, Straus & Giroux, 1966, pp. 275–292.
Spigel, Lynn. *TV by Design: Modern Art and the Rise of Network Television*. University of Chicago Press, 2009.
Thomas, Kevin. "Bewitching, Live Score Joins Silent 'Dr. Caligari' at Nuart." *Los Angeles Times*, August 24, 1988, p. H1.

Media

Batman. 1966–1968. Television Series. Seasons 1–3. USA: ABC.
Blood and Sand. Directed by Fred Niblo, Famous Players-Lasky/Paramount, 1922.
The Blue Angel. Directed by Josef von Sternberg, UFA, 1930.
The Bullwinkle Show. 1961–1964. Television Series. Seasons 3–5. USA: NBC.
Crusader Rabbit. 1950–1951, 1959. Television Series. Seasons 1–3. USA: first-run syndication.
Dr. Jekyll and Mr. Hyde. Directed by John S. Robertson, Famous Players-Lasky, 1920.
The Drop Kick. Directed by Millard Webb, First National, 1927.
East Lynne. Directed by Travers Vale, Biograph, 1915.
Fatty and Mabel Adrift. Directed by Roscoe Arbuckle, Keystone, 1916.
Flicker Memories. MGM, 1941.
Fractured Flickers. ca. 1963–1964. Television Series. Season 1. USA: first-run syndication.
Gaslight Follies. Directed by Gaslight Follies Co., 1945.
George of the Jungle. 1967. Television Series. Season 1. USA: ABC.
Get Smart. 1965–1970. Television Series. Seasons 1–5. USA: NBC, CBS.
Gidget Goes Hawaiian. Directed by Paul Wendkos, Jerry Bresler Productions, 1961.
Gilligan's Island. 1964–1967. Television Series. Seasons 1–3. USA: CBS.
"Goofy Movies No. 4." MGM, 1934.
The Goon Show. 1951–1960. Radio series. UK: BBC.
The Hands of Orlac. Directed by Robert Wiene, Pan-Film, 1924.
A Hard Day's Night. Directed by Richard Lester, Water Shenson Films/Proscenium Films, 1964.
Help! Directed by Richard Lester, Walter Shenson Films/Subafilms, 1965.
The Hunchback of Notre Dame. Directed by Wallace Worsley, Universal, 1923.
Husbands and Lovers. Directed by John M. Stahl, First National, 1924.
Intolerance. Directed by D. W. Griffith, Triangle, 1916.
The Loretta Young Show. 1953–1961. Television Series. Seasons 1–8. USA: NBC.
Mad Movies with the L.A. Connection. 1985–1986. Television Series. Season 1. USA: first-run syndication.
Man's Genesis. Directed by D. W. Griffith, Biograph, 1912.
Mondo Cane. Directed by Gualtiero Jacopetti, Paolo Cavara, and Franco Prosperi, Cineriz, 1962.
The Monkees. 1966–1968. Television Series. Seasons 1–2. USA: NBC.
A MOVIE. Directed by Bruce Conner, 1958.
The Movie Orgy. Directed by Joe Dante, 1968.
Movie Museum. 1954–c. 1957. Television Series. Season 1. USA: first-run syndication.
My Mother the Car. 1965–1966. Television Series. Season 1. USA: NBC.
Mystery Science Theater 3000. 1988–1999, 2017–present. Television Series. Seasons 1–13. USA: various networks.
Nosferatu. Directed by F. W. Murnau, Prana Film, 1922.
Orphans of the Storm. Directed by D. W. Griffith, D. W. Griffith Inc., 1921.
Passage à l'acte. Directed by Martin Arnold, 1993.
The Perils of Pauline. Film series. Directed by Louis J. Gasnier and Donald MacKenzie, General Film Company/Eclectic Film Company, 1914.
Rocky and His Friends. 1959–1961. Television Series. Seasons 1–2. USA: ABC.

The Running Jumping & Standing Still Film. Directed by Richard Lester and Peter Sellers, Peter Sellers Productions, 1959.
Shoes. Directed by Lois Weber, Universal, 1916.
Silents Please. 1960–1961. Television Series. Seasons 1–2. USA: ABC.
The Son of the Sheik. Directed by George Fitzmaurice, United Artists, 1926.
The Steve Allen Show. 1956–1964. Television Series. Seasons 1–6. USA: various networks and first-run syndication.
Tarzan of the Apes. Directed by Scott Sidney, National Film Corporation, 1918.
"Thrills of Yesterday." Vitaphone/Warner Bros., 1931.
To Kill a Mockingbird. Directed by Robert Mulligan, Brentwood/Pakula-Mulligan, 1962.
The Typhoon. Directed by Reginald Barker, Paramount, 1914.
"The Unshod Maiden." Directed by Albert DeMond, Universal, 1932.
Young April. Directed by Donald Crisp, Producers Distributing Corporation, 1926.

3
Wearing French Cuffs to a Gunfight

Camp and Violence in Hanna-Barbera's *Snagglepuss* (1961)

Emily Hoffman

In the opening scene of the 2018 DC Comics series *Exit Stage Left: The Snagglepuss Chronicles*, Snagglepuss, leaning into his camp persona as a Southern dandy while appearing before the House Un-American Activities Committee, declares his profession as "American cultural icon" (Russell and Feehan). That may be true within the comic book's unique world where Dorothy Parker, Marilyn Monroe, and Nikita Khrushchev interact with versions of Hanna-Barbera's anthropomorphic cartoon animals, but it is undoubtedly hyperbole in actual American culture. His stature, as animated character-cum-cultural icon, pales in comparison to Bugs Bunny, Bart Simpson, or even Yogi Bear. He is best known as the star of *Snagglepuss*, a series of cartoon shorts included in *The Yogi Bear Show* (1961–62, syndicated), that depicts him as a pastel pink mountain lion who dreams primarily of becoming a stage and screen star while also desiring some form of friendship and belonging. His efforts are undermined by a variety of antagonists, including a hunter in perpetual pursuit of Snagglepuss so he can add his head to an already impressive display of big game trophies. He has re-emerged periodically in animated specials like *Scooby's All-Star Laff-A-Lympics* (1977–78, ABC) or brief original series like *Yo Yogi!* (1991, NBC). It is *Exit Stage Left*, however, that reintroduces him as a character of substance and cultural relevance. It does this by confirming what many suspected: Snagglepuss is gay. The Snagglepuss of *Exit Stage Left* can claim to be an "American cultural icon" because writer Mark Russell has reimagined him as a Southern playwright challenging the limits of good taste on Broadway in the early 1950s. Basically, he is Tennessee Williams.[1] That is, until his blacklisting ruins his career, and he has little choice but to become a supporting actor in the low-culture medium of television. By embracing some viewers' assumptions of the character, *The Snagglepuss Chronicles* is an origin story for the protagonist of the 1960s cartoon shorts.

Exit Stage Left is not the first time, however, that Snagglepuss has been unambiguously depicted as gay. For instance, Bobby Moynihan plays Snagglepuss in a 2008 "Weekend Update" segment on *Saturday Night Live* (1975–present, NBC), commenting on California's passage of Proposition 8 that banned gay marriage. When Seth Meyers says Snagglepuss must be frustrated, he insists he is "straight as a line, a chorus line," but then admits his lover is the Great Gazoo, the green alien from *The Flintstones* (1960–66, ABC). *Saturday Night Live* is not produced by Hanna-Barbera, which contributes to the transgressive humor. The sketch voiced what had never been officially acknowledged. With the publication of *Exit Stage Left*, camp's essential multivalence disappears and speculation becomes canon.

Exit Stage Left overtly confronts controversial issues: blacklisting, homophobia, suicide, police brutality, fears of being outed, and the price of assimilating into the heterosexual mainstream. Surely unbeknownst to most of its original viewers, these same concerns occur throughout the two seasons of *Snagglepuss*. Cultural assumptions about animation and the multivalence of camp work in tandem to obscure them. As Paul Willis says in his contribution to *Prime Time Animation*, "the cartoon operates as a potentially non-regulatory or subversive space by virtue of its very artifice and the assured innocence that goes with it" (16). This assumed innocence serves as a perfect cover for issues of sex, desire, and gender. It is not only the innocence of the target audience as presumably reflected in the stories but the aesthetics of the cartoons that open them up to consideration. Sexual content exists in cartoons, but "the hypergraphic flatness of cartoons diverts the erotic gaze to the razed ground of flat-pained blocks of color devoid of depth" (Brophy 175). Through the thorough deployment of camp signifiers across the thirty-three cartoon shorts from *The Yogi Bear Show*, Snagglepuss's acting ambitions and his struggles to reconcile his sexuality with midcentury mainstream attitudes play out beneath rudimentary chase narratives. Those wild and violent chases can be dismissed (or embraced) as boys-will-be-boys mayhem. For those fluent in camp, however, Snagglepuss resembles Hollywood's closeted gay labor that feared exposure both in the industry and in a city committed to intimidation and violence against homosexuals. Constantly threatened with guns and constantly attempting to use disguises to fulfill his dreams but with little success, *Snagglepuss* is a cautionary tale about the pitfalls of the closeted gay man relying on same-sex drag, a close attention to "clothing and performance ... without actually donning the gender-coded garb of the other sex" (Williamson 6) to pass as straight.

To better understand how Snagglepuss embodies the harsh realities faced by Hollywood's midcentury gay labor, this chapter begins by presenting the confluence of influences and character traits that have enabled queer readings of Snagglepuss and reach their apotheosis in *The Yogi Bear Show* cartoon shorts. The second section explains how the cartoon shorts' occasionally dense intertextuality helps enhance the status of Snagglepuss as a queer character. Finally, the third section argues that the version of Snagglepuss present in *The Yogi Bear Show* shorts, which combined the "star is born" showbiz narrative with violent cartoon chases, recasts the perilous existence of gays in midcentury Los Angeles (Russell's comic book series ends before it can address this highly relevant historical reality) as harmless children's entertainment. For Snagglepuss, the cultivation of an exaggerated public masculinity that caters to heteronormative expectations is both essential to his professional success and personal safety because it masks his secret gay identity.

The Camp Origins of Snagglepuss

Queer representations and meanings in 1950s and 1960s television resided primarily in sitcom guest stars whose camp presence offered "situational humor about social norms and taste distinctions and in seemingly throwaway punchlines and bit performances" (4), Quinlan Miller argues. The guest stars "are, within and against the grain of the system, a central attraction" and "marked as eccentric" (5). Miller's analysis focuses exclusively on live-action prime-time sitcoms, but it applies to cartoon series of the era, such as Hanna-Barbera's *The Quick Draw McGraw Show* (1959–61, syndicated), which stars an anthropomorphic horse who, as a sheriff in the Old West, polices the frontier with his burro sidekick, Baba Looey. Here, Snagglepuss originates as just such an eccentric "guest star" figure who upstages the dim-witted Quick Draw by humorously violating social norms through flamboyant disregard for law and order.

On *Quick Draw*, Snagglepuss is a more heteronormative male figure than he becomes later. Orange in color and lacking his signature effete accessories, he operates as a villain intent on stealing sheep. He is cunning, clever, intimidating, and violent. In "The Lamb Chopped" (S1 E6, 1959), Snagglepuss enters the episode brazenly thieving an entire flock of sheep. He declares to Quick Draw that "stealin' sheep is my destiny." Snagglepuss reacts with disdain to the prospect of Quick Draw apprehending him, going so far as to casually lean against the long, phallic barrel of Quick Draw's pointed rifle. Snagglepuss gets the best of him, saying, "You can't shoot a lion with an elephant gun." Snagglepuss takes advantage of Quick Draw's bewilderment, seizes the gun, and proclaims, "But me, I'll shoot anything with an elephant gun." He then shoots Quick Draw in the face at point-blank range.

Although more heteronormative by comparison, this early iteration of Snagglepuss is already imbued with camp. He possesses his distinctive, exaggerated drawl and employs his catchphrase, "Heavens to Murgatroyd," said with a paw melodramatically lifted to his forehead. He displays his affection for a Shakespearean turn of phrase when Quick Draw conveniently tracks Snagglepuss to his cave. He tries to convince him that he really wants his brother Snaggletooth: "Stars above, are you mistakin' me for my scapegrace twin brother, Snaggletooth? If so, whom you are searching for to wit, three wit, languishes in yon cave." The episode even concludes with crossdressing of sorts that leads to queer humor when Quick Draw, to exploit Snagglepuss's desires, disguises himself as a sheep to lure Snagglepuss back into the open. Quick Draw, you could say, wants to stage a kind of seduction. The plan gets hijacked when an amorous mountain goat with a French accent suddenly appears with seduction plans of his own.

"El Kabong Meets El Kazing," the first episode of *The Quick Draw McGraw Show*'s second season (1960), cements the relationship between Snagglepuss and camp. Still a formidable outlaw, he appears on a WANTED poster with a menacing look in his eyes. His capture seems doubtful as the poster pessimistically reads, "No One Will Dare Take the Job." The only hope is Quick Draw's alter ego, the Zorro-inspired El Kabong, "champion of the good guys." When El Kabong—in black cape, black mask, and black hat—confronts a criminal, he bludgeons him with his "kabong," which is merely his guitar. When Quick Draw/El Kabong catches up to Snagglepuss, they stare each other down, nose to nose. Their proximity is startlingly intimate. A kiss or embrace seems imminently possible. Wise to Quick Draw's masquerade, Snagglepuss dashes off to get the "champion of the bad guys," a similar Zorro-inspired crusader, El Kazing. Rather than a guitar, he weaponizes a double bass, dubbed a Kazinger. In comparison to Quick Draw's guitar, Snagglepuss's huge double bass makes his impression of a Zorro-style avenger even campier. Once Quick Draw/El Kabong gets a look at the kazinger, this sexually charged exchange follows:

SNAGGLEPUSS/EL KAZING: "Would you like to see how it works?"
QUICK DRAW/EL KABONG: "I'd be much obliged for the trade secret."
SNAGGLEPUSS/EL KAZING: "Bend over, and I'll show ya."

Quick Draw promptly bends over.

QUICK DRAW/EL KABONG: "How's this?"
SNAGGLEPUSS/EL KAZING: "Very good."

A *Los Angeles Times* review of *Quick Draw* alludes to the show's multivalence: "Only the big kids understand it fully" (qtd. in Lenburg 89). But should it be "only the *gay* kids understand it fully"?

The camp playfulness of the encounter becomes clearer when Snagglepuss uses the strings on the bass as a bow to shoot arrows into Quick Draw's behind. The dialogue and actions are camp enough, but the intertextual presence of Zorro merits attention. Zorro brings queer meanings of his own to the scene. The 1940 version of *The Mark of Zorro* illustrates the queer sensibility at work in the character by foregrounding his "dependence on clothing and performance" in a way that helps solidify "the convention of the 'secret identity' as a form of same-sex drag" (Williamson 6). For this reason, Snagglepuss as El Kazing is a pivotal moment in the character's evolving identity. That Snagglepuss so willingly joins Quick Draw in Zorro cosplay foreshadows the same-sex drag and preoccupation with passing that dominates the *Snagglepuss* shorts on *The Yogi Bear Show*.

The elevated homoerotic tension between Quick Draw/El Kabong and Snagglepuss/El Kazing continues a pattern that persists across many of Hanna-Barbera's early television cartoons. It begins, in fact, with Hanna and Barbera's *Tom and Jerry* (1940–58) franchise made at MGM. Tom and Jerry, two male characters, repeatedly enact a simple (and literal) cat-and-mouse chase narrative, the opposite of the Classical Hollywood Cinema emphasis on the heterosexual couple.[2] Jeffrey P. Dennis sees the homosexual subtext in Hanna-Barbera cartoons escalating with their transition to television. Their first television cartoon, *Ruff and Reddy* (1957–60, NBC), centers on a cat and dog who are "companions rather than enemies" (132). It is this companionship that raises the question Dennis poses: "are they brothers, coworkers, roommates, buddies?" Because televised cartoon shorts cannot accommodate exposition or develop characters' private lives due to their brevity, Dennis contends, there exists "a space to subvert hegemonic heterosexuality and allow same-sex desire or identity into the reading" (132). Dennis identifies this ambiguous male pairing as "the trademark of Hanna-Barbera studio in the 1950s and 1960s" (133). In addition to Ruff and Reddy, there are Yogi Bear and Boo Boo as well as several other duos, like Quick Draw and Baba Looey. Dennis sees "erotic tension" as "inherent" (134) to these pairings. By comparison, the suggestive scene with Snagglepuss/El Kazing and his double bass leaves little room for interpretative guesswork. Perhaps this explains Baba Looey's intervention, announcing to viewers that "I think I better put a stop to all this Kazinging." The camp subtext has gotten too close to text.[3]

Snagglepuss as an avatar of camp begins not with *The Quick Draw McGraw Show* but *The Wizard of Oz* (1939) and the casting of vaudeville and Broadway performer Bert Lahr as the Cowardly Lion. Snagglepuss, who is a mountain lion and therefore does not embody the obvious irony of the king of the jungle as a self-described effeminate "dandy-lion," is "clearly derived" (Sennett 63) from Lahr's performance. Nevertheless, from Lahr, Hanna-Barbera borrows a highly distinctive voice as well as a cowardly demeanor that writer Michael Maltese does not fully exploit until *The Yogi Bear Show* shorts. More specifically, Daws Butler co-opts Lahr's "slurred words [and] not quite articulate diction" (Lahr 332).[4] *The Wizard of Oz*'s lyricist, E. Y. Harburg, suggested Lahr for the part (321), believing he projected both bravado and endearing sweetness, qualities he believed Lahr had perfected while honing his stage persona. That persona relies on the perpetuation of "Jewish immigrant traditions of masculinity that often countered the aggressively heterosexual 'all-American man'" (Bronski 115). Although Lahr was heterosexual, his reputation and stardom were grounded in camp elements, such as his "prissy crooning," garish costuming, physical comedy, and "over-the-top reactions, gestures, and noises" (Mordden 65; Scarfone and Stillman 94). The revised Snagglepuss of the cartoon shorts leans into garish camp through costuming (pink fur rather than orange), over-the-top reactions ("Heavens to Murgatroyd!" and "Exit, stage left!"), and his overall performative verbal excess that subverts the nonverbal stoicism of American masculinity.

The queer masculinity Snagglepuss inherits from the Cowardly Lion may not have emerged with such camp intensity without crucial script and costuming choices. Although not yet the head of the unit responsible for producing MGM's lavish musicals, Arthur Freed served as an uncredited producer on *The Wizard of Oz* and spearheaded the reshaping of the script, which resulted in "the gradual elimination of all heterosexual elements in the earlier script drafts" (Doty 52). These erasures only help to magnify the Cowardly Lion's non-heteronormative masculinity once he is shown with a mane of perfect ringlet curls topped with a girlish red bow.

If the voice and behavior of Snagglepuss originate with both Lahr's stage persona and the Cowardly Lion, then his sartorial style evokes Oscar Wilde, who has long since replaced Beau Brummel as the default image of dandyism. Wilde is textually present when the Cowardly Lion sings, "I'm just an awful dandy-lion." Whenever Snagglepuss is not masquerading in same-sex drag, his minimal wardrobe consists of a few evocative accessories: a pair of white French cuffs fastened with cuff links, a high, white Victorian collar, and a black tie knotted in a bow. Photos of Wilde often show him sporting just such a floppy bow or scarf around his neck, and though he consistently wears a coat, French cuffs frequently peek out from the sleeves. Through this resemblance to Wilde (see Plates 8 and 9), Snagglepuss projects an even more overdetermined campiness than if he had only appeared as a cotton-candy pink lion speaking in what sounds uncannily like Lahr's "cowardly" voice. To pinpoint the origins of camp, scholars often look back to Wilde and, in particular, his public indecency trial (Meyer). Snagglepuss's resemblance to Wilde evokes associations with the persecution and imprisonment he endured as a result of his homosexuality and opens up the *Snagglepuss* episodes to readings that cast the pink lion as a similar victim of homophobia.

Any examination of camp elements of *Snagglepuss* would be incomplete without acknowledging the full intersection of MGM/Freed Unit musicals and Hanna and Barbera's work at the studio. Regardless of whether they did so intentionally, Hanna and Barbera brought the visual spectacle of MGM's camp style (and, by association, the gay labor responsible for it) to television. Unsurprisingly, Steven Cohan sources the campification of MGM's musicals to the prominence of gay labor, which was most concentrated in the Freed Unit (46). Multiple departments, like those overseeing wardrobe and set decoration, employed majority gay personnel. Within Hollywood, the Freed Unit functioned as "something of a liminal space . . . where, regardless of the sexual partnering, queer and straight outlooks intermingled, influencing each other's work. Their meeting place was camp" (47–48). Although they never worked within the Freed Unit directly, by the time they left MGM for television Hanna and Barbera had significant opportunities—as a result of both MGM's house style and their proximity to the Unit's production culture—to absorb elements of camp into their aesthetic and narrative sensibilities.

In fact, they participated directly in the perpetuation of the MGM musical's camp style through their work on two Freed Unit musicals. Hanna and Barbera played a pivotal role in the production of the most famous song-and-dance number from *Anchors Aweigh* (1945). They created ten thousand frames of Jerry Mouse that would, with rotoscope technology, allow him to dance alongside Gene Kelly (Cohan 97–98). "The Worry Song" number works to answer the question that dogged Kelly throughout his career: "is he a sissy dancer or not?" (152). Against a typically camp backdrop of gaudy, saturated colors, including a purple-cushioned throne, heavy red curtains, and diaphanous lime green curtains puddling on the shiny teal floor, Kelly schools Jerry the Mouse King. The campy mise-en-scène plus Hanna and Barbera's animation on top of the excessive masculinity of Kelly's choreography results again in queer spectacle:

> [Kelly] bounces Jerry from bicep to bicep, sends the mouse down his leg, swings him in the air and under his legs, dances over him. The camp in the choreography derives from its eroticization of Kelly ... [T]he number's eroticization of the dancer's liberated and lawless body is not heterosexualized in its aim or energy; after all, Kelly is dancing with a male mouse and the number is being imagined by a boy. (Cohan 171)

The camp excess is furthered by Kelly's costuming for the number: a variation on a French sailor's uniform consisting of high-waisted white pants that hug his thighs and a tight blue and white-striped, short-sleeved Breton shirt that attracts attention to his biceps and chest. Even without the plot context Cohan references, the dance's physicality and Kelly's appearance while performing it create a camp spectacle that transgresses heterosexual norms.

Later, Hanna and Barbera would animate an underwater spectacle, the dream sequence in the musical *Dangerous When Wet* (1953). Tom and Jerry rescue Esther Williams from a "handsy" octopus, the cartoon incarnation of her love interest, played by Fernando Lamas. The lascivious bright blue octopus, with a jaunty yellow beret, red scarf, and a gurgling French accent courtesy of Lamas, is a camp take on continental masculinity. Hanna and Barbera's animated contributions to these musicals intensify the multivalent quality of camp. General (heterosexual) audiences will be entertained by the anthropomorphism of Jerry's mastery of complex choreography and the octopus as comic lover while other audiences will recognize the non-normative masculinity on display in both. Snagglepuss, on television less than a decade later, revives this blend of the animated, talking animal fond of performance and unafraid to deviate from traditional masculinities.

Snagglepuss as Camp TV: Intertextuality and Reflexivity

On the one hand, Snagglepuss is not unusual among other early television cartoon characters. He is just one of many "zany animals with obsessive or compulsive personalities in bizarre conflicts and pursuits" (Wells 21). What makes Snagglepuss unique is the instability of his appearance and characterization. Between *The Quick Draw McGraw Show* and *The Yogi Bear Show* he undergoes a radical revision, and all of the changes intensify his camp persona. By the time *The Yogi Bear Show* premieres in 1961 and Snagglepuss begins headlining his own shorts within the series, he is divested of all the traditionally masculine traits from his *Quick Draw McGraw* appearances while retaining the impulse to engage in suggestive banter with other males. He sexualizes past violent encounters with the big game hunter Major Minor in exchanges like this:

MAJOR MINOR: But didn't I shoot you in the Mato Grosso?
SNAGGLEPUSS: Negative. I believe you got me below the equator. Or was it the left clavicle? ("Major Operation," S1 E1, 1961)

Like the Cowardly Lion, he undergoes a feminizing makeover. He is now an over-the-top cotton candy pink. Phillips and Pinedo identify the emerging popularity of color television among both network programmers and consumers as vital to the advent of Camp TV. They link the influx of color programming to the mainstreaming of Andy Warhol and Roy Lichtenstein's Pop Art aesthetics. Hanna-Barbera's cartoons use a similar bold, flat color palette. The arresting pinkness of Snagglepuss in a world where everything else broadly adheres to a realistic relationship with color marks him as excessively non-normative. The camp pinkness of Snagglepuss would not have registered with the cartoon's original audience. Recognizing the switch to color television as an inevitability, Hanna-Barbera produced its early cartoons with great attention given to color, though they were initially broadcast in black and white. William Hanna and Joseph Barbera agreed that "ultimately the demand for color product would greatly extend the shelf life of what we were doing" (Barbera 123). In the more conservative, pre-counterculture early 1960s, the airing of *Snagglepuss* in black and white places the character in the televisual closet, suppressing questions about his sexuality. His dull monochrome appearance, preserved in his Kellogg's Cocoa Krispies commercials, appropriately situates him in a world of heterosexual gray flannel suit conformity. The growing interest in gay rights parallels the growing presence of color television sets in American homes so that, when seen in color in syndication over the ensuing decades, Snagglepuss, in his true pinkness, can come out of the closet to viewers.

As the protagonist of his eponymous series, Snagglepuss cannot be the criminal he was on *Quick Draw*. He must be sympathetic, someone the viewer will root for. Rather than the attacking hunter, now he is always the hunted victim and repeatedly flees danger with a harried, "Exit, stage left." At the heart of this new persona are his acting ambitions, a change that gives purpose to his previously unmotivated mimicking of Shakespeare and striking of melodramatic poses. As his catchphrase indicates, Snagglepuss sees all of life's moments as performative events and opportunities for him to display and hone his acting abilities. In Shakespearean terms, all the world is a stage.

Phillips and Pinedo outline four traits of Camp TV: (1) explicit satire and campification of aggressive political ideologies, (2) intertextuality and cross talk, (3) performativity and self-reflexivity, and (4) performativity and gender fluidity (27–34). With *Snagglepuss*, satisfying these four traits depends on the introduction of the title character's acting ambitions. The first and fourth traits are most significant for the reading that follows, and their relevance is developed in the next section, but the others are present and bear some discussion as well. In fact, all four are tightly woven together in many *Snagglepuss* episodes.

Snagglepuss excels at incorporating intertextuality. According to Phillips and Pinedo, Camp TV "nodded to viewers' familiarity with other TV programs of the period" (28). As seen in Video 3.1 ⓑ, Snagglepuss acts out the closing scene from an episode of *The Unbearables* in front of his television, a reference to the crime series *The Untouchables* (1959–63, ABC) about Eliot Ness and his pursuit of Al Capone in "The Gangsters All Here" (S1 E9, 1961). Another episode features a theater manager resembling Ed Sullivan. The most elaborate collection of intertextual references occurs in "Remember the Daze" (S1 E16, 1961), which casts Major Minor as the subject of a *This Is Your Life* (1952–61, NBC) parody titled *This Is Your Strife*. A Major Minor and Snagglepuss chase sequence traverses multiple TV show sets, interrupting a taping of *The Yogi Bear Show*. At one point, Snagglepuss even poses as Groucho Marx and asks, "What's the secret word?," an allusion to a running bit Marx did on *You Bet Your Life* (1950–61, NBC). Phillips and Pinedo focus only on Camp TV's intertextual relationships with other contemporaneous television shows, but cartoons have historically referenced contemporaneous films and film stars. *Looney Tunes* (1930–69), a Warner Brothers property, naturally invited intertextual play that brought Bugs Bunny face to face with animated versions of the studio's contract stars. "Racketeer Rabbit" (1946) pits Bugs against gangsters resembling Edward G. Robinson and Peter Lorre. Michael Maltese, who wrote "Racketeer Rabbit," also wrote every episode of Snagglepuss. Maltese brought his penchant for film allusions to *Snagglepuss*. For example, in "Paws for Applause" (S1 E7, 1961), a desperate director casts Snagglepuss as a lion in an unimpressive biblical epic starring an oafish Samson, a passing wink at a genre that was reaching its apex with 1959's *Ben Hur*.

As the interruption of a *Yogi Bear* "taping" demonstrates, self-reflexivity abounds in *Snagglepuss*. One representative example is again "Paws for Applause." A book on how to be a TV actor arrives in the mail, and Snagglepuss excitedly opens it to a full-page picture of Yogi Bear. He proceeds to do a flawless imitation of Yogi, turns the page to a picture of Quick Draw McGraw, and does another flawless imitation, which is possible because Daws Butler voices all three characters. The quality of his imitations convinces Snagglepuss that stardom awaits, and he needs an agent. This is also an episode in which Snagglepuss breaks the fourth wall to address the audience, a common Brechtian feature of Camp TV's performativity and self-reflexivity (Phillips and Pinedo 30). These intertextual moments can be read as instances of performativity, passing as someone else.

The Politics and Price of Passing

The political content of *Snagglepuss* derives from the intersection of the character's newfound acting goals and the combination of camp elements present in his *Quick Draw* appearances and those added for his *Yogi Bear* reboot. Together, they position Snagglepuss as a character that resembles Hollywood's closeted midcentury gay labor that feared exposure in the industry and in a city committed to violence and intimidation against homosexuals. Naturally, then, the political content of *Snagglepuss* relies on its emphasis of performativity and gender fluidity: the two remaining traits of Camp TV go hand in hand.

The cartoon's limited characterization of Snagglepuss's life has many of the hallmarks of a typical homosexual in midcentury America: isolation, alienation, a struggle to assimilate, a heightened concern for clothing and personal appearance, and a fear of targeted violence aimed at the body. He has no friends, no family, no neighbors. There is only one mention of Snagglepuss having any sort of ongoing relationship. In "Tail Wag Snag" (S2 E12, 1961), he greets the male dog Snuffles, a recurring character on *Quick Draw*, as "[m]y old canine companion." Whatever the nature of this same-sex relationship, it is in the past, and Snuffles never appears again. Overall, he lives a solitary existence in a cave. The narrative structure of the cartoons reinforces Snagglepuss's loneliness and alienation. Of the two Hanna-Barbera templates—the cat-and-mouse (predator/prey) chase of *Tom and Jerry* or the ambiguous male companionships—Snagglepuss most closely aligns with the former, but with significant differences. Snagglepuss has no consistent adversary to produce the predictable action that powers *Tom and Jerry*. The closest he comes is the recurring Major Minor. Despite his diminutive stature, Major Minor, with his arsenal of firearms and exotic animal heads mounted on his walls, exhibits a masculinity far closer to the hegemonic norm than Snagglepuss. Minor's obsession with Snagglepuss is arguably not just about adding another trophy to his collection. Perhaps he wants to eliminate a threatening non-normative presence.

Several episodes begin with the mailman making a delivery to the box outside Snagglepuss's cave and remarking on him being a lion in a way that foregrounds him as a dangerous other. "Delivering mail to everyday type people I don't mind," he says, "But when a lion starts getting mail, it's time I started thinking of that little bookstore business" ("Paws for Applause"). Normally, a mailman would have good reason to fear a lion. However, Snagglepuss always greets his arrival with excitement and a few lines of faux-Shakespearean monologue. He never does anything threatening. What is it, then, that bothers the mailman? Is it the pinkness of Snagglepuss? Is it his flamboyant theatricality? Is it that those monologues can parody *Romeo and Juliet* and cast the mailman in the role of Juliet during the balcony scene? "But, hark! What whistle through yon windward breaks? It is the east, and the mailman is the sun," Snagglepuss rhapsodizes ("Paws for Applause"). Is it the fawning adoration itself that discomfits him? The mailman and Major Minor serve as representatives of the era's mainstream homophobia. The chase and male companionship templates can both generate moments of visual comedy from size as a basic structure of difference. This is true for Tom and Jerry, Ruff and Reddy, Yogi and Boo Boo, and Quick Draw and Baba Looey. It is also true for Snagglepuss and Major Minor, whose name underlines his obvious Napoleon complex. Major Minor's bloodlust and the mailman's anxiety derive from an expected antagonism that fails to materialize because, despite his carnivore status, Snagglepuss is utterly benign. From this, a new structure of difference is born. The thrill of hunting and killing a lion, plus the masculine affirmation that comes with the kill, must derive in part from the animal's violent reputation. Snagglepuss is never the aggressor and only ever acts against the major in self-defense. It is the major's futile (and hypermasculine) efforts to kill a docile (and feminized) beast which helps sustain their chases as a satisfying running gag. Meanwhile, the mailman is repeatedly confronted with Snagglepuss's well-mannered refinement but interprets it as a dire threat to not just himself but the community.

No wonder, then, that many episodes feature Snagglepuss attempting to join a traditionally masculine homosocial group or pretending to be a member of such a group that situates much of that masculine identity in members' clothing. Specifically, he attempts to:

- join King Arthur's Knights of the Round Table;
- become Robin Hood, placing him at the center of a band of merry men;
- join the Three Musketeers;
- join a college football team as a halfback; and
- join the army, which he mistakes for the Boy Scouts.

He also pretends to be a number of figures who typically align with hegemonic masculinity:

- Ulysses J. Unbearable, an intimidating gangster;
- Memphis Mortimer, a swaggering riverboat gambler;
- a deputy circuit court judge in the Old West; and
- a sheriff.

Several of these groups and individuals relate to popular movie figures (Robin Hood and the Three Musketeers) or genres (the gangster film and the Western). We can see these efforts as a series of acting exercises, a broadening of his repertoire to hopefully ensure success at a future audition. Even more importantly, these are heterosexual performances as Snagglepuss tries to prove his ability to successfully pass in each of these contexts.

All of his attempts require extensive costuming. In each case, Snagglepuss's willingness to don an elaborate costume does not simply reinforce his show business aspirations. It strengthens his status as a gay man passing as straight. To quote the Cowardly Lion, he is trying to "[have] the nerve" to "show my powers" and "be a lion, not a mouse." His solitude predisposes him to others' suspicions of deviance. It also creates a desire for connection, especially connections that will integrate him into mainstream masculinity, which would then divert those suspicions about his sexuality and help make him a viable screen star. Crucially, as a homosexual male, he will have proven that he can play masculine male leads.

The emphasis on clothing and costuming on *Snagglepuss* mirrors the postwar reality that the gay population in Los Angeles had to take clothing very seriously, an issue that had to be carefully negotiated to ensure successful passing. To not dress in a way socially acceptable for your sex could lead to arrest (Faderman 93). "I take ruthless stock of myself in the mirror before going out," Noël Coward explained to Cecil Beaton after coming to Hollywood. "A polo jumper or unfortunate tie expose[s] one to danger" (qtd. in Faderman 56). (A male lion "wearing" bright pink fur could also seemingly expose Snagglepuss to danger.) Being seen in unambiguously masculine attire was, then, key to passing as heterosexual in a city where both the police and tabloids, like the notorious *Confidential* that "tapped into a whole world of pervasive homophobia and prurient fascination with homosexuality" (Kasher and McNair 18), seemed to literally hunt and entrap those suspected of being gay. Police officers carrying out "utterly terrifying" postwar bar raids relied on strategies that "seemed close to those brutal Gestapo tactics which America had recently been fighting" (Faderman 91). Homosexuals who succeeded in landing work either in front of or behind the camera enjoyed "at least a modicum of openness as long as they played the movie game and hid the fact of their flexibility from their fans" (48). In the cartoon, despite various brushes with film, television, and theater, Snagglepuss has yet to land his big break. He does not have a studio contract or the benefit of mentor relationships with the industry's "[o]lder men [who] considered it a social obligation to take in hand a youth new to the city . . . instructing him in passing" and "advising him how to evade the police" (Cohan 14). If arrested or caught in a compromising position, he could not count on the studio to pay off the media and the police so that his controversial true identity could be kept secret, as was common practice for Hollywood's contracted talent (Faderman 56–57). Nevertheless, Snagglepuss is committed to playing "the movie game," to demonstrating that he can pass as a member of various homosocial groups that have been deemed suitably masculine by the general public and the movie industry itself. We might, then, understand Snagglepuss as someone who fully understands the harsh reality that will accompany any fulfillment of his acting dreams, that "[i]f homosexuality was immoral in the mind of the general public, gay and lesbian actors needed to convince the public that they were straight" (61).

Despite his innocent and initially peaceful attempts at joining homosocial groups and appearing in same-sex drag, Snagglepuss invariably finds himself as the target of violence, in particular gun violence. He is "in a constant state of calamity" (Sennett 63). When considered in relation to Snagglepuss's apparent queer sexuality, the violence he suffers starts to become something other than the "rhetoric of harmlessness" (Snead 84) conferred on cartoons, which has allowed them to traffic in spurts of extreme violence with little public pushback. Instead, the violence functions as a reaction to his sexuality by the same traditionally masculine men he wishes to join. Major Minor shoots him from close range on several occasions, and multiple characters shoot at him in other episodes. When not threatened with gun violence, he faces extreme bodily harm in various and ridiculous forms, such as baseballs, spears, and cannons.[5] *Snagglepuss* cartoons dramatize the threats to and anxieties of the gay population just as the cultural revolution of the 1960s galvanizes America's youth with its insistence on equality. However, because the midcentury gay experience is presented in animated form from the perspective of an anthropomorphic, camp mountain lion, the cartoon shorts obscure political ideologies in the way Phillips and Pinedo argue is common in Camp TV (27–28). That obfuscation, though, does not make Snagglepuss any less sympathetic to the viewer as part of the camp excess resides in the supposedly comic taunts, harassments, and assaults he endures.

Snagglepuss episodes end in one of three ways: heavily qualified victory that proves to not be a victory at all, capture/imprisonment/subjugation, or flight. For instance, the king in "Royal Rodent" (S2 E16, 1961) makes him court jester, seemingly a chance for Snagglepuss to perform for an audience, but the king wears earmuffs to avoid hearing his bad jokes. In "Cloak and Stagger," even though they have tricked him, bullied him, and will not accept him, Snagglepuss chooses to remain with the Three Musketeers. The showbiz break Snagglepuss stumbles into gets undone in "Paws for Applause" after he accidentally blows himself up in an on-set shack stocked with dynamite. The laughing director informs him he will have to reshoot because the camera ran out of film. At this prospect, Snagglepuss exits, stage right. The first episode of *Snagglepuss* introduced the idea that his relationship with zoos and imprisonment ties directly to his sexuality. As he tells Major Minor, he ended up in a zoo because he was "captured in Cambodia while cavortin' with a Cambodian" ("Major Operation"). When his efforts at playing Robin Hood take a disastrous turn, he wants to be taken to a zoo for protection in "Arrow Error" (S1 E12, 1961). "The Roaring Lion" (S1 E6, 1961) ends with a contented Snagglepuss in a cage on a circus train. Although he may not be behind bars, some episodes conclude with him in humiliating subjugation. He becomes a queen's living rug in "Royal Ruckus" (S1 E5, 1961) and, with his head stuck through a hole in the wall for hours on end, agrees to play a taxidermized lion to boost Major Minor's male ego in "Major Operation." He pretends to be a hunting trophy again in "Twice Shy," lying on the ground so Major Minor can pose for a photo with his boot on Snagglepuss's back. Other episodes end with Snagglepuss in flight from unresolved danger.[6] These conclusions might also count as qualified victories. Any Snagglepuss victory is temporary because the cartoons are purely episodic. While *Snagglepuss*'s episodic structure aligns with other cartoons of this era, it also resembles more contemporary cartoons like *The Simpsons* (1989–present, Fox), which, according to Jason Mittell, "generally embraces an excessive and even parodic take on episodic form, rejecting continuity between episodes by returning to an everlasting present equilibrium state" (21). As a perpetually struggling actor always facing a violent pursuer, he is trapped in a futile cycle that cannot be broken, deepening his connection to the era's alienated gay population that found itself similarly trapped. The futility queers Snagglepuss further, aligning him with iconic female sitcom characters, such as Lucy Ricardo who is always "rebelliously incarcerated within situation comedy's domestic mise-en-scène, acutely frustrated, trying to escape via the 'comic movement' while cheerfully cracking jokes along the way to her own unmasking and capture" (Mellencamp 54).

Exit Stage Left reinforces this by providing an origin story for the character we meet in the cartoon shorts. It concludes with the blacklisted Snagglepuss needing work. His old friend Quick Draw offers him a guest-starring role on his cartoon show. The demand for television cartoons is so high anyone is a potential star, "even a blacklisted pink lion accused of being a red" (Russell and Feehan). Snagglepuss resists because "I'm a writer! I don't want to work on some stupid cartoon!" But he relents. Quick Draw then confirms passing and multivalence as foundational to the Snagglepuss TV persona. He suggests Snagglepuss be painted orange. "Everybody will know" it's Snagglepuss, he explains, "but if somebody squawks about it, the studio can claim they were fooled." He will pass as both a capitalist *and* a heterosexual. Eventually, once the scandal blows over, Quick Draw promises Snagglepuss can be his pink self on camera. For the moment, though, he is trapped, thanks to his politics and sexuality as well as Quick Draw's passing strategy, in a low-culture medium beneath his talents. The real *Snagglepuss* cartoon, despite never offering its protagonist an alternative to entrapment, passing, and violence, proves more progressive than the era's sitcoms. *Snagglepuss* upends Miller's queer guest star paradigm. It is the star of the show who occupies a queer space while representations of hegemonic masculinity—musketeers, a pair of gangsters, or a big game hunter—appear as fleeting guest stars. Snagglepuss himself may be marginalized in the world he inhabits, but Hanna-Barbera allows him, as an obviously non-normative character, the privileged status of camp protagonist. This is a bold, if not ground-breaking choice.

Notes

1. The comparison to Williams originates with the comic book's author, Mark Russell, who says he "envision[s] him like a tragic Tennessee Williams figure" (qtd. in Hughes).
2. Rather than a homoerotic pursuit, chases like those found in *Tom and Jerry* cartoons can also be understood as examples of narrative distillation, the removing of all extraneous action and details so that only the action remains, as in the tradition of "cutdowns" that condense films to their most exciting sequences.
3. As with Snagglepuss, Quick Draw's closeted homosexuality becomes canon in *Exit Stage Left*. In it, Quick Draw has a clandestine affair with Huckleberry Hound and ashamedly participates in the Stonewall raid to preserve his assumed heterosexuality within the police force.
4. Daws Butler was the prolific voice actor responsible for many of Hanna-Barbera's most well-known characters, including Yogi Bear, Quick Draw McGraw, Huckleberry Hound, Augie Doggie, and Elroy Jetson. Butler's voices are often obvious imitations of other stars and comedians. Examples include Huckleberry Hound (Andy Griffith), Hokey Wolf (Phil Silvers), and Wally Gator (Ed Wynn) (Lawson and Persons 77, 83). Lawson and Persons describe his Snagglepuss voice as only a "loose" interpretation of Lahr (83).
5. Among the episodes in which Major Minor shoots Snagglepuss are "Major Operation," "Twice Shy" (S1 E13, 1961), "Remember Your Lions" (S1 E15, 1961), and "Remember the Daze." He is also shot at by a zookeeper in "Express Trained Lion" (S2 E1, 1961),

hunters in "Feud for Thought" (S1 E2, 1961), the army in "Charge That Lion" (S2 E7, 1961), and a riverboat captain in "Cagey Lion" (S2 E6, 1961). He gets pelted in the face with baseballs in "Fight Fright" (S2 E4, 1961), has a barrage of spears hurled at him in "Jangled Jungle" (S2 E2, 1961), and has cannons fired at him in "Cloak and Stagger" (S1 E14, 1961).
6. These include "Remember the Daze," "Lion's Share Sheriff" (S2 E5, 1961), "Cagey Lion," and "Legal Eagle Lion" (S2 E10, 1961).

Bibliography

Barbera, Joseph. *My Life in Toons: From Flatbush to Bedrock in Under a Century*. Turner, 1994.

Bronski, Michael. *A Queer History of the United States*. Beacon, 2011.

Brophy, Philip. "Auralis Sexualis: How Cartoons Conduct Paraphilia." *Funny Pictures: Animation and Comedy in Studio-Era Hollywood*, edited by Charlie Keil and Daniel Goldmark, University of California Press, 2011, pp. 175–188.

Cohan, Steven. *Incongruous Entertainment: Camp, Cultural Value, and the MGM Musical*. Duke University Press, 2005.

Dennis, Jeffrey P. "The Same Thing We Do Every Night: Signifying Same-Sex Desire in Television Cartoons." *Journal of Popular Film and Television*, vol. 31, no. 3, 2003, pp. 132–140.

Doty, Alexander. *Flaming Classics: Queering the Film Canon*. Routledge, 2000.

Faderman, Lillian. *Gay L.A.: A History of Sexual Outlaws, Power Politics, and Lipstick Lesbians*. Basic Books, 2006.

Hughes, William. "New Comic Series Reimagines Snagglepuss as a Gay 1950s Playwright." *A.V. Club*, January 31, 2017, https://news.avclub.com/new-comic-series-reimagines-snagglepuss-as-a-gay-1950s-1798257072. Accessed February 7, 2021.

Kasher, Sam, and Jennifer MacNair. *The Bad and the Beautiful: Hollywood in the Fifties*. Norton, 2002.

Lahr, John. *Notes on a Cowardly Lion: The Biography of Bert Lahr*. Open Road Media, 2017.

Lawson, Tim, and Alisa Persons. *The Magic Behind the Voices: A Who's Who of Cartoon Voice Actors*. University of Mississippi Press, 2004.

Lenburg, Jeff. *Legends of Animation: William Hanna & Joseph Barbera*. Chelsea House, 2011.

Mellencamp, Patricia. "Situation Comedy, Feminism, and Freud: Discourses of Gracie and Lucy." *Critiquing the Sitcom: A Reader*, edited by Joanne Moreale, Syracuse University Press, 2003, pp. 41–55.

Meyer, Moe. "Under the Sign of Wilde: An Archaeology of Posing." *The Politics and Poetics of Camp*, edited by Moe Meyer, Routledge, 1994, pp. 75–109.

Miller, Quinlan. *Camp TV: Trans Gender Queer Sitcom History*. Duke University Press, 2019.

Mittell, Jason. *Complex TV: The Poetics of Contemporary Television Storytelling*. New York University Press, 2015.

Mordden, Ethan. *Broadway Babies: The People Who Made the American Musical*. Oxford University Press, 1988.

Phillips, W. D., and Isabel Pinedo. "Gilligan and Captain Kirk Have More in Common That You Think: 1960s Camp TV as an Alternative Genealogy for Cult TV." *Journal of Popular Television*, vol. 6, no. 1, 2018, pp. 19–40.
Russell, Mark, and Mike Feehan. *Exit Stage Left: The Snagglepuss Chronicles*. DC Comics, 2018.
Scarfone, Jay, and William Stillman. *The Road to Oz: The Evolution, Creation and Legacy of a Motion Picture Masterpiece*. Lyons Press, 2018.
Sennett, Ted. *The Art of Hanna-Barbera: Fifty Years of Creativity*. Studio, 1989.
Snead, James. *White Screens/Black Images: Hollywood from the Dark Side*. Routledge, 1994.
Wells, Paul. "'Smarter Than the Average Art Form': Animation in the Television Era." *Prime Time Animation: Television Animation and American Culture*, edited by Mark Harrison and Carol A. Stabile, Routledge, 2003, pp. 15–32.
Williamson, Catherine. "'Draped Crusaders': Disrobing Gender in *The Mark of Zorro*." *Cinema Journal*, vol. 36, no. 2, 1997, pp. 3–16.

Media

Anchors Aweigh. Directed by George Sidney, MGM, 1945.
Ben Hur. Directed by William Wyler, MGM, 1959.
Dangerous When Wet. Directed by Charles Walters, MGM, 1953.
Exit Stage Left: The Snagglepuss Chronicles. 2018. USA: DC Comics.
The Flintstones. 1960–1966. Television Series. Seasons 1–6. USA: ABC.
Looney Tunes. 1930–1969. Short Film Series. USA: Warner Brothers.
The Mark of Zorro. Directed by Rouben Mamoulian, 20th Century Fox, 1940.
The Quick Draw McGraw Show. 1959–1961. Television Series. Seasons 1–3. USA: Syndicated.
"Racketeer Rabbit." Short Film. Directed by Fritz Freleng, Warner Brothers, 1946.
Ruff and Reddy. 1957–1960. Television Series. Seasons 1–3. USA: NBC.
Saturday Night Live. 1975–present. Television Series. Seasons 1–48. USA: NBC.
Scooby's All-Star Laff-A-Lympics. 1977–1978. Television Series. Seasons 1–2. USA: ABC.
The Simpsons. 1989–present. Television Series. Seasons 1–34. USA: Fox.
This Is Your Life. 1952–1961. Television Series. Seasons 1–9. USA: NBC.
Tom and Jerry. 1940–1958. Short Film Series. USA: MGM.
The Untouchables. 1959–1963. Television Series. Seasons 1–4. USA: ABC.
The Wizard of Oz. Directed by Victor Fleming, MGM, 1939.
The Yogi Bear Show. 1961–1962. Television Series. Seasons 1–2. USA: Syndicated.
Yo Yogi! 1991. Television Series. Season 1. USA: NBC.
You Bet Your Life. 1950–1961. Television Series. Seasons 1–11. USA: NBC.

SECTION II
CAMP TV'S TENTPOLES

4
They're Creepy and They're Campy

Camping the American Family on 1960s Horror Television

Jamie Hook

With the release of Alfred Hitchcock's *Psycho* in the United States and Michael Powell's *Peeping Tom* in the United Kingdom, 1960 proved a watershed year that foreshadowed major changes for cinematic horror in the decade ahead. This was the time when, as Robin Wood memorably wrote, "The American family . . . moved into the genre where it had always rightly belonged," explaining that most renowned US horror films released in *Psycho*'s wake dealt explicitly with the family ("American Family Comedy" 11). While films that critiqued familial politics through horror indeed flourished on the big screen, a different configuration between domesticity and monstrosity emerges when our attention turns to television.

Two iconic situation comedies of the 1960s united family-centered narratives with horror through the representation of family units composed of literal monsters: *The Addams Family* (1964–66, ABC) and *The Munsters* (1964–66, CBS), both of which intentionally camped American mores and the generic tropes of the domestic sitcom itself.[1] These programs contributed to the liminal, tentative, and ambiguous representational practices of a decade that has since become shorthand for sweeping cultural change. Sitting at the crossroads between the mainstream (what with their enormous popularity and characters who became cultural icons) and the subcultural (what with the subversive pleasures they offered and their continuing legacies as cult media franchises in the twenty-first century), comedy and horror, and competing modes and meanings of camp, these shows offered two images of the American family—one blue-blooded, the other blue-collar—that were simultaneously monstrous and endearing during a cultural maelstrom that saw the institutional politics of the family reconsidered and renegotiated at domestic and national levels.

Jamie Hook, *They're Creepy and They're Campy* In: *Camp TV of the 1960s*. Edited by Isabel C. Pinedo and W. D. Phillips, Oxford University Press. © Oxford University Press 2023. DOI: 10.1093/oso/9780197650745.003.0005

Both *The Addams Family* and *The Munsters* premiered in 1964 (on September 18 and 24, respectively) and ran for two seasons, ending in 1966. Their debut is uncannily resonant with the publication of Susan Sontag's perennial "Notes on 'Camp,'" which was first published in the fall issue of the *Partisan Review* in 1964. Sontag's much discussed and debated attempt to "snare a sensibility [like camp] in words" (54) confirmed and concretized its arrival as a topic of public discourse. What was once a reading strategy and performative practice endemic to (largely) gay male communicative and physical spaces had by the mid-sixties permeated a wider culture that, as the existence of Sontag's notes attest, was now reflexively aware of its presence. Rather than "betraying" camp, as Sontag feared, more widespread acts of naming and defining only increased its heterogeneity during this time.[2] By 1966, the year in which the Addamses and Munsters went off the air (even if they refused to stay buried, returning as they did in syndication, made-for-TV movies, and future series), Harry Benshoff argues "camp was everywhere" ("1966" 153). While ubiquitous, a coherent meaning of the term remained evasive, given its tendency to "'bleed into' other popular textual forms such as parody, satire, black comedy, pop, mod, and kitsch" ("1966" 153). These cultural modes did indeed bleed into one another on both shows, which sat at the intersection of mainstream and countercultural ideologies and representational practices. This makes both programs exemplars of what W. D. Phillips and Isabel Pinedo have recently theorized as Camp TV, defined, among other things, through "the presence of textual features such as irony, satire and parody intended to foster interpretive practices specific to adult viewers capable of recognizing secondary meaning systems" (22). Unlike the number of significant camp series that debuted in the years immediately following, which "were either part of their respective network's transition to a full-colour prime-time line-up or were moved to colour as a part of that shift" (21), *The Addams Family* and *The Munsters* sported a black-and-white aesthetic that would no longer be the norm by the time they went off the air. These dark and shadowy mise-en-scènes also reflected those of the generic heritage they camped.

While the pervasiveness of the Addams and Munster families in the pop culture landscape (a visibility that continues to this day)[3] has perhaps led to a strange kind of normalization, it is important to keep in sight the subversively camp charge offered to audiences in the mid-sixties by the insertion of families composed of monstrous weirdoes into a form as familiar and hegemonic as the domestic sitcom. This was a time when, according to Mary

Beth Haralovich, "An ideal white and middle-class homelife was a primary means of reconstituting and resocializing the American family after World Word II" (61–62). Tellingly, the 1964 debut of *The Addams Family* and *The Munsters* put them on the air the year immediately following the disappearance from the small screen of the two programs most closely analyzed by Haralovich: the end of syndication for *Father Knows Best* (1954–55, CBS; 1955–58, NBC; 1958–60, CBS) and the cancellation of *Leave It to Beaver* (1957–58, CBS; 1958–63, ABC).[4]

If, as Wood has argued, horror dramatizes a return of the repressed,[5] it is difficult not to see the Addamses and the Munsters as the nightmarish others of the Andersons or the Cleavers. Still, in the middle of a period that saw a rapidly increasing divorce rate and cohabitation between unmarried partners become a subject of national moral debate, these nuclear families who lived together in stable homes might simultaneously have been seen as a bastion of tradition (however oddly styled) away from the tumult of the sexual revolution and other cultural upheavals brewing outside—and elsewhere on the television set.[6] As has been much observed, these two extended nuclear families mirrored one another to a considerable extent: households headed by two parents (Gomez and Morticia Addams/Herman and Lily Munster), each with two children or young adults (Wednesday and Pugsley Addams/Marilyn and Eddie Munster), elder or unattached relatives (Uncle Fester and Grandmama Addams/Grandpa Munster), and even family pets (Kitty Cat, a full-grown lion/Spot, a fire-breathing dragon) all living under the same roof.

This more normative side of these ghoulish families was suggested in media discourse that heralded their prime-time arrivals. A two-page *Variety* ad announcing the coming live-action adaptation of Charles Addams's *New Yorker* cartoons campily queried, "Can a typical suburban family make good on television?" (32–33). Similarly, the *New York Times* previewed the coming of their cross-network competitors with a headline that announced, "Monsters to Be Just Plain Folks on a CBS-TV Comedy Series" (Adams). To paraphrase the title of an iconic episode from a supremely influential program of the period, the monsters had arrived on Maple Street.[7]

The syntheses between the macabre and the moral, the frightful and the familial, and the creepy and the campy defined both programs and were themselves the result of larger cultural reappraisals and recontextualizations of earlier media objects as well as the horror genre at large. So from where did these domestic monstrosities emerge?

Camp Recycling: 1960s Monster Mania

> "It's your original blueprint! . . . a souvenir from Doctor Frankenstein."
> —Grandpa Munster to Herman ("Just Another Pretty Face," S2 E17, 1966)

In her groundbreaking work on feminist camp, Pamela Robertson describes camp "as a mode of productive anachronism, a form of recycling" (142). The Frankensteinian connotation of the word *recycle* makes it a perfect verb to conceptualize both programs' reanimations of the supernatural gothic à la Hollywood and their relation to the larger "monster culture" of the preceding decades.

Self-reflexive treatments of horror tropes and clichés were not unique to *The Addams Family* and *The Munsters* during this time; rather, they did for television sitcoms what other texts did for cinema (e.g., Hammer Film Productions' remakes of the Universal Studios monster franchises, starting with Terence Fisher's *The Curse of Frankenstein* in 1957), music (e.g., Bobby "Boris" Pickett's 1962 *Billboard* chart-topper "Monster Mash"), and magazines (e.g., *Famous Monsters of Filmland*, 1958–83), together constituting a sixties monster mania. These texts were especially popular among children and the growing youth culture of the time. In his pioneering cultural history of horror *The Monster Show*, David Skal cites a *Look* cover story that declared, "Toyland '64 looks like a charnel house with all its ghoulish delights. There are monster models and monster games, monster dolls and all manner of monstrous cards, rings, by-the-number paint sets, costumes and masks" (qtd. in Skal 284).

Appropriate to camp's penchant for hewing its reference points from across the cultural hierarchy, the recycled horror culture that was reassembled to form *The Addams Family* and *The Munsters* came from Hollywood films that had by this time achieved something of classic status (and could be widely seen on television)[8] as well as more contemporary, B-grade productions. Beyond her direct pen-and-ink ancestor, Morticia Addams as now embodied by Carolyn Jones resembled no one as much in both maquillage and apparel as Maila Nurmi's Vampira, the character Nurmi played on *The Vampira Show* (1954–55, KABC-TV) and in the cult film *ne plus ultra*, *Plan 9 from Outer Space* (Ed Wood, 1957). In an act of triangulated reincarnation, Nurmi credited Addams's original cartoons as an inspiration for her character but ultimately "decided to create her own unique persona, and the campier, sexier 'Vampira' took to the airwaves" (Greene) where Jones's "campier, sexier" television version of Morticia would follow just over a decade later. The Addamses' disembodied houseboy, Thing, seems like nothing so much as a literally domesticated version of the eponymous appendage of *The Hands of Orlac* (Robert Wiene, 1924), a silent classic that had recently been remade both as a British/French co-production of the same name (Edmond T. Gréville, 1960) and as a low-budget American film retitled *Hands of a Stranger* (Newt Arnold, 1962). For his part, the family's hulking butler, Lurch, had been understood "as a knock-off of the Boris Karloff Frankenstein monster as far back as 1939" in Addams's original cartoons (Van Hise 8), the 6'9" actor Ted Cassidy now camping Karloff's immortal embodiment of the creature through live performance.

Given that Universal Studios, whose name was synonymous with cinematic monsterdom, owned CBS, such recycling on *The Munsters* could be that much more direct, with Herman, even more so than Lurch, a veritable copy of Karloff's physical appearance in queer Hollywood auteur James Whale's *Frankenstein* (1931) and its sequel *Bride of Frankenstein* (1935), a film Benshoff has called "most explicit in its queer intentions" (*Monsters* 49).[9] Direct camp homages to iconic moments from these films recur throughout the series, such as the recreation of Whale's unforgettable creation sequence (in season two's "Just Another Pretty Face" when Grandpa must repair Herman's "good looks" after he is "normalized" by a lightning strike, an episode that ends with actor Fred Gwynne in literal monster drag) or replaying the Monster's fear of fire (when Herman lookalike Johann is driven into a hotel closet by Dr. Frankenstein IV in the season two episode "A Visit from Johann" [S2 E26, 1966]). Other monsters from the Universal stable made single-episode appearances in the personae of Cousin Lester (the Wolf Man) and Uncle Gilbert (the Gill-Man of 1954's *Creature from the Black Lagoon* [Jack Arnold]). To maintain the diegetic world in which the Munsters are just "plain folks," these characters are simply family relatives, not "famous monsters of filmland"; only the audience registers them as intertextual links to an earlier era of horror.[10]

Indeed, when intertextual references to horror media are made within the world of the show, they eschew citing Universal monster films by name and take other modalities of horror as reference points; for instance, when a couple of frat pledges sneak inside their home for an initiation rite, they describe the sleeping Lily and Herman as "a coupla rejects from an old Vincent Price movie," the exceedingly obvious reference remaining unspoken.[11]

Normal Monsters or Monstrous Normals?

"Lily, I go to the movies for escapism. I don't wanna see everyday people doing everyday things."
—Grandpa Munster ("Lily Munster—Girl Model," S1 E33, 1965)

In Wood's formula of horror "the relationship between normality and the Monster... constitutes the essential subject of the horror film" (*Hollywood* 79). Both *The Addams Family* and *The Munsters* were predicated on camping this primal structure of the genre through blurring the lines between normality and monstrosity, inflecting each with a patina of the other. Andrew Ross has described how camp is generated "when the products ... of a much earlier mode of production, which has lost its power to produce and dominate cultural meanings, become available, in the present, for redefinition according to contemporary codes of taste" (312). And, indeed, the sixties were marked by a "massive reorganization of cultural taste" (Ross 327). Camp recycling, as discussed in the previous section, might then be understood to foreshadow ideas that would develop later in the decade. These were discourses that intensely interrogated questions of normality as the hippie ethos and other countercultural formations started to offer new ways of being and the sexual revolution began to challenge repressive mores outright (the Monster, for Wood, being the embodiment "of all that our civilization represses or oppresses" [*Hollywood* 75]). Even if far from tolerated, especially in the earlier years of the decade, a broadly defined sense of social difference was starting to be recognized and conceded cultural and mediated visibility to a degree it simply had not been previously. As sociologist Erving Goffman declared in his pioneering study of social stigma, published the year before our shows debuted, "there is only one complete unblushing male in America: a young, married, white, urban, northern, heterosexual Protestant father of college education, fully employed, of good complexion, weight, and height, and a recent record in sports" (128).

Here Goffman offers a more panoramic understanding of difference—that is, as something outside the cultural ideal, yet that does not necessarily offer a direct challenge to the oppressive structures of patriarchy, white supremacy, heterosexism, and so forth. This more nuanced view of cultural nonconformity provides a helpful proscenium through which to view the proverbial stage on which the creepy, kooky antics of what were still heterosexually led, nuclear family units played out for sixties audiences. Much of the camp in both shows was produced through a reversal of normalcy within these traditionally drawn boundaries. This camp travesty of normality is established in the opening scene of the pilot episode of *The Munsters* ("Munster Masquerade" S1 E1, 1964) when Lily suggests with amazement that suitor Tom is willing to look past (blonde beauty) Marilyn's homely appearance.[12] This extends throughout the series to matters of quotidian domesticity, such as Lily's vacuum that spews out dust or Marilyn's tarnishing of a candelabrum. Such humor might well qualify as being "frivolous about the serious" (Sontag 62) in a decade that held the understanding, according to social historian Kristin Ross, that "If the woman is clean, the family is clean, the nation is clean" (78). For the Munsters, putrefaction instead of purification defines good housekeeping practice.

Beyond this displacement of cleansers for cobwebs and disinfectants for dust, truly macabre are certain home furnishings such as the Munsters' prominent electric chair. As Phillips and Pinedo note that camp and Pop Art "were applied in an intertwined and—to a degree—subversive form to American television in this period" (24), it is worth mentioning that only the year before *The Munsters* premiered, Pop Art exemplar Andy Warhol commenced his ongoing series of garishly colored silkscreen images of the execution device, effectively recontextualizing it through the Pop Art idiom "that make[s] sublime the cold horror of execution at the hands of an all-powerful State" (Halley 43). In the case of *The Munsters*, too, the macabre piece of furniture is given a new valance as it resides not in the death chamber but in its polar opposite, the living room. In a similar camp reversal, the Addamses' so-called playroom is a functional torture chamber, replete with rack, bed of nails, iron maiden, and other such devices.[13] The joke, of course, was that the goodhearted Addamses never tortured any of their unsuspecting guests with these implements; rather, the family availed themselves of them when they needed to relieve stress or a troublesome headache.

Of what was perhaps the decade's camp show par excellence, *Batman* (1966–68, ABC), Benshoff posits how "it was the [1966 film adaptation's] colorful villains that appealed to queer and countercultural audiences..." ("1966" 157). While far from villainous (except to some in the parade of "normals" who encountered them week after week), the Addamses and the Munsters were likewise simultaneously flamboyant and appealing to diverse audience demographics.[14]

While to audiences the families could appear both normative (in structure) and iconoclastic (in style), to the ordinary folk who shared their respective diegetic worlds they were purely abnormal, a narrative configuration that primed viewers to root for the Other often at the direct expense of the so-called normals, "those who do not depart negatively from the particular expectations" (5) of a given social context, in Goffman's formulation. On both shows the otherness of the titular families was often produced vis-à-vis the bewildered reactions of representatives from the normative communities in which they live. The social interactions between monstrously colorful others and domestically drab normals engender the narrative conflicts of more than a few episodes. Sometimes the latter are neighbors or other residents of the community, but much of the time they are also individuals vested with various forms of institutional authority: medical professionals; city officials, commissioners, or politicians; showbiz/entertainment industry insiders; and law enforcement personnel, among others. This trope led to a number of storylines that appear uncannily consonant between the two shows.[15] "Pike's Pique" (S1 E5, 1964), for instance, deals with the Munsters' conflict with gas department officials running a line beneath their home directly into Grandpa's basement laboratory while in "Progress and the Addams Family" (S1 E30, 1965), the Addamses face eviction after plans for a new highway route it directly through their home.

The American school system becomes a prime locus of institutional conflict as it is taken up as a satirical target both in *The Addams Family* pilot and the finale of *The Munsters*; a camping of educational values bookended their shared time on air. "The Addams Family Goes to School" (S1 E1, 1964) camps moral panic surrounding what children read in the classroom when Gomez and Morticia are as distraught as Wednesday, who comes home from school in tears after having heard a fairy tale in which a knight in shining armor slayed a defenseless dragon.[16] "A Visit from the Teacher" (S2 E32, 1966) depicts Eddie's teacher and principal coming to visit the Munsters in order to confirm that what they take to be flights of fantasy described in his essay "My Parents: An Average American Family" are exactly that, only to be petrified at their discovery that the document is in fact a work of vérité.

The variable degrees of otherness visited upon the families find their likely terminus when the Addamses are thought to literally be alien. Summoned to investigate missile launches set off by Pugsley, representatives of the Bureau of Mysterious Space Objects find the family enjoying a late-night picnic in their backyard and take them for a group of Martians. So secure are they in their own normality, the Addamses in turn misread these interlopers as otherworldly visitors who must be put at ease ("Well, whoever they are, we must be neighborly. We don't want them thinking we Earth people are snobs," directs Morticia).

This exchange illustrates one of the key narrative mechanisms driving the shows' camp pleasures and countercultural appeals: namely, how neither family seems to internalize the stigma directed against them and instead view themselves as the embodiment of—or even aristocratically superior to—the average, ordinary American. An earnest belief in their own normative physicality is humorously borne out when Lily, filing a missing persons report with the police, describes Herman as having no distinguishing characteristics ("You'd never even notice him if you met him on the street"). Likewise, when the family's photograph appears on the cover of *Event Magazine* with the caption "America's Average Family Celebrates Halloween," the Munsters reason the magazine has made a mistake but, as Herman concludes, "We're not just the plain old Munsters anymore, you know. We're *the* average American family and I think we owe it to our country to keep our sense of humor."

Even without regard to their monstrosity, neither family is "all-American" (the term itself, of course, a racist misnomer) in national origin. Gomez's ancestral Spain and Grandpa and Lily's Romanian old country are frequently invoked as sources of pride and nostalgia throughout both series.[17] Beyond their heritage, the Addamses in particular incorporate an appreciation of the "exotic" into their daily lives, from Gomez's Zen Yoga practices to Morticia's cultivation of Cleopatra, her African strangler plant. The show's mise-en-scène itself is defined through a camp version of exoticism. During the 1960s, an interest in other, particularly Eastern, cultures pervaded religious, philosophical, sexual, and musical spheres of the counterculture. Far from the resulting societal anxieties over teenagers and young adults who rejected their parents' values and WASPish upbringings for the new consciousness offered by the countercultural, however, "exoticism" for the Addamses was part and parcel of daily life in the family home.

Creepy, Kooky, Classy

> "This house is a tribute to generations of Addams taste. It took years to achieve its rare beauty."
> —Morticia Addams ("Morticia, the Decorator," S2 E23, 1966)

"The architect who designed this place must have been Frank Lloyd Wrong!"
—Fraternity brother appraising the Munster home
("Herman's Sorority Caper," S2 E30, 1966)

For all the similarities between the shows, their camp posturing diverges most sharply in terms of class and gender. Broadly, in terms of the former, the Addamses are upper class with a seemingly endless amount of disposable income, while the Munsters are lower-middle or working class such that money problems not infrequently initiate the narrative conflict of individual episodes. Their respective Victorian homes at 0001 Cemetery Lane and 1313 Mockingbird Lane concretize this class difference. The latter, occupied by the Munsters, has fallen into disrepair and its further, literal breaking down (of front door, front porch, ceiling, etc.) amounts to a running gag throughout the series. While following what Haralovich discusses as a comedic trope of working-class sitcoms such as *The Honeymooners* (1955–56, CBS), the Munsters' orientation toward their distressed domicile registers differently within the domain of camp. While dilapidated, their sprawling home is hardly cramped and not at all unpleasant in terms of the family's own tastes. The show's camp sensibility takes the mode of humor identified by Haralovich a step further; while the physical spectacle of the house falling in on itself is innately humorous, the way the Munsters accept the destruction as quite normal camps the entire gag through its subversion of the socially scripted response to major home damage. In contrast, the Addams family manse (cum "museum," as famously noted in the opening theme song) is defined by its camp view of "high art." As Sontag's note five sets out, "Clothes, furniture, all the elements of visual décor . . . make up a large part of Camp. For Camp art is often decorative art, emphasizing texture, sensuous surface, and style at the expense of content" (55).

Classic surrealist *objets d'art* such as Man Ray's *Cadeau* (1921), a clothes iron with protruding nails, or Méret Oppenheim's *Le Déjeuner en fourrure* (1936), a furry tea set,[18] would easily blend into *The Addams Family*'s mise-en-scène. Well-remembered items from the show's iconic living room set include, among all other manner of what would politely be termed "conversation pieces," a two-headed turtle, antique harpsichord, mounted swordfish with a human leg protruding from its mouth, and a curved settee impossible for two people to occupy side by side while still facing the same direction. Camp emerges in the space between this eccentric kitsch and the Addamses' belief that their high cultural taste for "rare beauty" manifests itself through these possessions. An editing trope that recurs throughout the series consists of eye-line matches that link point-of-view shots from visitors to whatever curio in the Addams home has arrested their gaze. This running gag becomes the explicit subject matter of the episode "Morticia, the Decorator," when Gomez takes a neighbor on a tour of their art gallery and, surrounded by such *objets* as a plant-wrapped foot extending from a vase, the stupefied visitor declares, "I can hardly wait to see that collection of artworks of yours," so illegible as art are the very pieces before him.

Such things furnish the domestic stage on which the Addamses play out their sybaritic lives. Another trope of the series involves episodes opening to find the family in the midst of some decadent or eccentric activity: fencing, smoking hookah, dancing to the harpsichord, or moonbathing, to give just a few. Like the family's décor, the camp here comes both from the absurdity, exoticism, or antiquated nature of many of these activities, as well as from how they at times hew away at the supposed line between so-called high and low cultures. This is encapsulated by two early episodes of the second season, one of which starts with Gomez practicing an outrageous balancing act (associated with the circus or vaudeville), as Video 4.1 shows ⏵; the other opens to find him composing a three-handed sonata for the harpsichord (surely a bourgeois pastime), which can be seen in Video 4.2 ⏵. On a narrative level, the placement of such activities at the beginnings of episodes—thereby dropping viewers *in medias res* to observe the Addamses' quotidian lives—begets a sense of perpetual leisure. It is as though these pastimes, pursued only for the pleasure they bring in and of themselves, are what fill the family's time whenever they are away from us off-screen; viewers have the privilege of joining in only when a new drama or conflict—a disruption of this more permanent state of dalliance—is about to erupt.

Gender Trouble

"Cara mía!"
—Gomez Addams to Morticia

"Herman, you goofed it again!"
—Lily Munster to Herman

The divergent representation of gender on both shows is most clearly seen in the relationship between each family's respective husband and wife. The repeated catchphrases used in the above epigraph clearly demarcate the affection that defines Gomez and Morticia's interplay as well as the matrimonial censure that frequently explodes between Herman and Lily. Much commented upon, and a central part of the Addamses' place in cultural memory, is the omnipresent sexual desire that runs between Gomez and Morticia. In a retrospective appraisal in the countercultural tome *The Psychotronic Video Guide to Film*, Michael Weldon declared Gomez and Morticia to be "the only 60s TV couple who seemed to have sex on their minds (24 hours a day)" (3). In an era when even real-life spouses Lucille Ball and Desi Arnaz infamously slept in separate beds as their television alter egos, the physical desire between Gomez and Morticia is striking in its palpability.

To this end, camp both made possible this prime-time eroticism *and* mitigated its potential threat. A particularly clear double entendre occurs in the series finale, "Ophelia's Career" (S2 E30, 1966); "Let's go to the playroom and read," Morticia suggests, to which Gomez takes her by the arm and rejoins, "I've got a better idea. Let's go to the playroom and *play*." The knowing look she gives confirms the unsayable meaning while the resulting pinwheel wipe[19] relocates them now preparing to play hockey with Uncle Fester overseeing as referee (see Figure 4.1). The libidinal release here is adolescent (playing sports indoors!), while firm in its redirection of the ostensible meaning (the phallic nature of the hockey sticks aside), and ultimately camp in the baldly unsubtle, exaggerated way in which the substitution is made.

Figure 4.1 Gomez (John Astin) invites Morticia (Carolyn Jones) to play. Uncle Fester (Jackie Coogan) referees. "Ophelia's Career" (S2 E30, 1966, *The Addams Family*, MGM Studios Inc.).

The marital relationships on the two programs are further characterized with respect to the aforementioned class distinction. As both Morticia and Gomez remain home all day, so the possibility of romance becomes yet another option on their menu of perpetual leisure activities discussed earlier. Even Morticia's ability to speak (and Gomez's predilection to arousal by) the French language carries a specifically high cultural valence. In contrast, Herman's view of himself as de facto head of the household and Lily's patronizing chastisement of him for his repeated failures to successfully occupy this role bespeak a more common marital dynamic of the domestic sitcom. Herman, of course, *is* incompetent and accident-prone, making him part of the representational lineage Richard Butsch has analyzed as the male working-class buffoon. These prime-time husbands, unlike their middle-class counterparts, "were dumb, immature, irresponsible, and lacking in common sense" (101). All of these descriptors are adjectively appropriate to Herman. The immaturity of the blue-collar father is especially exaggerated through camp on the show; the running gag of Herman's childlike naivety and behavior, including frequent tantrums, becomes momentarily literalized in a truly camp manner when in the episode "Eddie's Brother" (S2 E27, 1966) Lily and Marilyn discover him clad in a baby bonnet and holding his (appropriately enormous) old rattle and teether in an attempt to give "a subtle hint that Eddie wants a new baby brother to play with" (see Figure 4.2).

Beyond such traits outlined by Butsch, a clear ideological traditionalism also attends this characterization of the blue-collar father. What Herman lacks in aptitude, he is shown to possess in conservative morality. One episode finds him returning home high (on laughing gas mistakenly administered at the hospital), which leads Marilyn to lament, "Oh Uncle Herman, to see you now no one would ever think that you were a charter member of the Pat Boone fan club."[20] More disturbing is the misogyny inherent to much of the gendered humor on *The Munsters*, which confirms that, as Richard Dyer reminds, camp can be both "progressive and reactionary" (111), a point that becomes more pronounced when it is "taken over by straights" and "loses its cutting edge" (115). Such is the case when, for instance, Herman performs a magic act accompanied with sexist jokes; he prefaces his attempt to make Lily disappear as "a trick which any husband should appreciate." The lack of a reaction shot blurs the laughter emanating from his diegetic audience and the show's non-diegetic laugh track (a surrogate, of course, for the viewers at home).

Figure 4.2 Lily (Yvonne De Carlo) confronts an infantile Herman (Fred Gwynne). "Eddie's Brother" (S2 E27, 1966, *The Munsters*, Kayro-Vue Productions).

Even the more amorous marrieds of *The Addams Family* still featured in storylines that denotatively reinscribed certain sociosexual norms. The episode "Morticia, the Sculptress" (S2 E9, 1965) illustrates how the show's outré, camp style could still cover traditionally gendered sitcom tropes. Here, Morticia throws all her attention and energy into a new artistic pursuit of sculpting. Emotionally absent from home and family, Morticia only returns to her matriarchal role when she overhears Wednesday and Pugsley's plan to whip up some (gasp!) chocolate marshmallow fudge, which leads her to declare, "I'm going back to the most important role a woman can have!" "Lover?" the eager Gomez queries. "Mother," corrects Morticia. "*And* lover," she softens, touching Gomez's cheek. At a moment when the burgeoning second-wave feminist movement rigorously interrogated and "explored the politics of the bed, the nursery and the kitchen" (Garton 224), such a plotline performed mass media's traditional function of reinscribing hegemony, in this case by representing women's agency as socially disruptive through the metonym of home and family.

Camp, however, engenders another level of meaning in which the absurdity of the signifiers—giant boulders, the medium in which Morticia works (the signifier of her dereliction), and the fudge (the signifier of the children's corruptibility in her absence)—serves to unveil the constructed and predictable nature of such plots. This begs the question of how and to what degree the macabre, gothic, and campy aesthetics of *The Addams Family* and *The Munsters* fundamentally change their staging of conventional family sitcom narratives and their attendant ideologies. Underlying such a question is the ongoing debate over the locus of camp—whether it is intrinsic to its objects or requires activation by a clued-in gaze ("Camp depends on where as well as how you pitch it" [82], surmises Philip Core). Especially in a decade as complex and contradictory in its politics and representational practices as the sixties, it can be assumed that some contemporaneous viewers read *The Addams Family* and *The Munsters* as travestying the staid televisual conventions established in the preceding decade that were now replayed through a camp style predicated on the iconography of horror. Those more leery of social change—traditionalists who viewed the decade and its mutating social roles as a real-life horror show, as it were—could permissibly take comfort that conventionality reigned at the end of the day even in these most outlandish of television domiciles.

Otherness and/as Camp Performance

Paul Newmar: "Man, this is certainly a fascinating theater you got here."
Lily Munster: "Eh, this isn't a theater; this is our home."
—"The Sleeping Cutie," S1 E12, 1964

The relationship between camp and performativity is as complex as it is enduring. Countless scholars of camp have developed Sontag's initial note that "To perceive Camp in objects and persons is to understand Being-as-Playing-a-Role. It is the farthest extension, in sensibility, of the metaphor of life as theater" (56). Both the Addamses and the Munsters are highly theatrical families in several senses that run the gamut of the term from the metaphorical to the literal. First, they comport themselves theatrically even as they go about their quotidian lives. Second, there are numerous episodes across both series in which outsiders mistake the distance between these flamboyant versions of everyday living and prevailing social norms as theatrical practice (recall here the aforementioned *Event Magazine* cover). Third and finally, both series feature numerous episodes set in and around the actual worlds of showbiz and the entertainment industry.

A particularly clear example of how these categories can intermingle is found in *The Munsters* episode "The Sleeping Cutie." Here Grandpa has accidentally put Marilyn into a sleeping spell, after which the family places an ad in the paper seeking a prince whose kiss can wake her. The ad is answered by two actors (category three); the elder camps the erudite style of a Laurence Olivier, while the younger does the same for the newer Hollywood brand of "cool" masculinity, as reflected in his name, Paul Newmar. They have mistaken the ad for an audition notice and upon arrival take the Munster home for a stage set (category two). "Goodness, Newmar, these off-Broadway theaters get creepier and further out all the time," bemoans the elder to his compatriot. "Well, whatever they're doing, they're already in rehearsal," he adds, as Lily dramatically ascends through a trap door (category one), as seen in Video 4.3 ▶. Similarly, in the episode "Grandpa Leaves Home" (S1 E14, 1964), Grandpa mounts his magic act at a burlesque club (category three). After Herman and Lily have convinced him to return home, the owner looks after them as they leave and declares with approval, "Boy, there's a real showbiz family for you; they even go home with their makeup on" (category two).

The Addamses also find themselves drawn into the world of showbiz. Appropriately, in keeping with their lofty class position, many of these scenarios camp not only the entertainment industry at large but also the taste hierarchy separating so-called low from high cultural forms of performance. As suggested by its title, the opening episode of season two, "My Fair Cousin Itt" (1965), is a campy pastiche of Alan Jay Lerner and Frederick Loewe's Broadway hit *My Fair Lady*, the monumentally successful film adaptation of which (George Cukor, 1964) premiered near the beginning of the sitcom's previous season. In the episode, a washed-up Broadway director is engaged by Gomez to direct a play he has written in which Cousin Itt will star. Itt is given elocution lessons (Eliza Doolittle's famous exercise "The rain in Spain stays mainly in the plain" here becomes "The witch's ditch is mainly full of pitch") until not only has he tamed his gibbering, stratospherically pitched voice, but now speaks in the crooning, sonorous tones of a matinee idol. The taste-driven gag comes at the end of the episode when, after being scouted by a Hollywood producer for a feature film role, Itt's serious thespian ambitions are insulted when he learns the offer is for the title role in *The Hairy Beast from the Mars Canals*. A desire to enter the echelons of high art in fact drives the series finale, "Ophelia's Career." Here the family attempts to launch Morticia's twin sister (also played by Jones) into operatic stardom. At first put off by Ophelia's screeching coloratura, her Italian vocal coach (played by character actor Ralph J. Rose as a broad camp parody) is later stunned by the complex harmonies she can sing . . . by herself. The episode (and thus series) ends with Morticia declaring, "I have a lovely idea for her next record . . . the sextet from *Lucia*!" This joke leans into a more recognizably high cultural camp reference, the suggested travestying of Donizetti's 1835 bel canto masterwork momentarily resituating camp from its mass to queer provenance.[21]

In a different musical stratum, one highly visible arena of the emerging counterculture in the sixties was, of course, rock 'n' roll, a trend both shows camped with episodes in which their respective Frankensteinian characters find fleeting success as pop stars. Lurch's and Herman's questionable talents for such "monster mashing" are used to make digs at the new soundscape of popular music. Another episode, "Far Out Munsters" (S1 E26, 1965), guest-starred the garage rock band The Standells as themselves.[22] When the group is first introduced in the episode by way of a record Eddie plays on the phonograph, the family's distaste for the new sound is visceral: their black cat leaps from Lily's arms, Herman's jar of popcorn kernels begins to autonomously pop, and smoke billows out of Grandpa's ears.[23] After this initial othering of the counterculturally coded music, the episode concludes with an affinity formed between the band, their beatnik audience, and the Munsters, who, in a reversal of the theatrically based explanations for their eccentricity discussed earlier, are here welcomed as just "some cats from L.A.," thereby *also* forging a connection between "monsters" and "cats" alike as they would have been viewed by a middle-American audience "unhip" to their "far out" ways. As the band performs their rendition of The Beatles' first number-one hit on US charts, "I Want to Hold Your Hand," Lily concedes, "They do have a certain . . . *style*"; see Video 4.4 ▶. Later, surveying the motley crowd gathered in the family's living room, Grandpa declares, "I haven't seen so many good-looking people in one place since we closed down the Mausoleum back home." This episode's representation of The Standells performs in microcosm what the program itself did for monstrosity writ large: it acknowledges a perceived (countercultural) difference from the prevailing norm and then manages that difference, rendering it consumable to an appreciative audience, through strategies of camp.

Conclusion

Among the other upheavals and reversals of the sixties, the new monsters of cinema (from Norman Bates to George Romero's living dead) looked increasingly human even as they behaved otherwise, whereas these monsters of prime-time television retained their creepy visages while behaving as true family types. The transplantation of visual codes and the reversal of meanings have long been understood as the province of camp. *The Addams Family* and *The Munsters* recycled the gothic horrors of Hollywood's previous decades, reassembling them in accordance with the tropes and structures of the domestic family sitcom; the underlying narrative framework still resembled normality, only now with something just aslant: a creaking iron gate instead of a white picket fence. In so doing, these shows were able to offer both mainstream values and countercultural pleasures through the language of camp. As case studies, they give us a granular-level view of the processes by which "camp attitudes and artifacts were increasingly enshrined by the popular media in the 1960s and 1970s" (Klinger 137). The early- and mid-sixties mark the beginning of this transformation that would see the height of its cultural visibility and aesthetic freedom later in the decade, prior to the broader (and some would say flattening) mainstreaming that would carry over into the seventies. These programs, then, provide a vantage onto the origins of a period when camp was about to enter the throes of a cultural realignment and revaluation that would lead to the definitional and ontological skirmishes that have carried on throughout its academic study.[24]

In June 2020, as the United States continued to reel from only the latest intensification erupting from the country's history of xenophobia, racism, sexism, and police brutality, a twenty-five-second clip from the January 28, 1965, episode of *The Munsters*, "Eddie's Nickname," went viral after it was posted on Twitter by former NBA player Rex Chapman. In the clip (which was widely shared and reposted across mainstream and social media outlets), Herman tells his bullied son, "The lesson I want you to learn is it doesn't matter what you look like. You can be tall or short, or fat or thin, or ugly or handsome (like your father), or you can be black or yellow or white. It doesn't matter. What does matter is the size of your heart and the strength of your character." Amassing millions of views, this strikingly sincere moment clearly resonated with contemporary audiences (many of whom, in online comments, nostalgically recalled watching the program as children).[25]

This chapter demonstrates that the camp sensibilities and representational politics of these programs could rarely be distilled into so pat and tidy a message as Herman's. Indeed, on the whole, neither show was simplistic enough in its worldview for that. Nevertheless, their camping of horror by way of resituating it within a genre predicated on cultural ideals of normality opened a space where multivalent understandings and critiques of overly rigid investments in said normality could permeate homes through the small screen. Through the realignment of morality and monstrosity via a rapidly democratizing form of televisual camp, monsters were ushered out from under the proverbial bed and welcomed into the living room—both those of their own gothic abodes as well as the less remarkable spaces in which American families sat together to watch them and, in doing so, engaged through laughter with the shifting symbology of a horrifically volatile decade.

Notes

1. Television scholar Lynn Spigel includes both shows as part of a broader category she calls the fantastic family sitcom, made up of titles such as *I Dream of Jeannie* (1965–70, NBC), *The Jetsons* (1962–63, ABC), and *Lost in Space* (1965–68, CBS). She distinguishes *The Addams Family* and *The Munsters* in how they "engaged the fantastic by turning to horror rather than science fiction" (220).
2. Such new forms of camp, detached from its queer origins, have been theorized as het camp (Chuck Kleinhans), mass camp (Barbara Klinger), and pop camp (Andrew Ross), among others.
3. As of this writing, the most recent Addams family film was released in October 2021 and a Munsters television special, *Mockingbird Lane*, aired on NBC in 2012. Forthcoming are *Wednesday*, a Tim Burton-directed Netflix series centered on the Addams daughter, and *Rob Zombie's The Munsters*, a feature film written and directed by the controversial horror auteur. Both original series remain readily available in deluxe DVD sets and on various streaming platforms.
4. *The Munsters* was produced by *Leave It to Beaver*'s creator-producers Joe Connelly and Bob Mosher. Self-reflexively, *Leave It to Beaver* is referenced and acknowledged as a favorite of Herman's on the show.
5. See Wood's "The American Nightmare: Horror in the 70s" in his collected essays *Hollywood from Vietnam to Reagan*.
6. Even the Collinses of *Dark Shadows* (1966–71, ABC), another monstrous TV family of the period, constantly found themselves embroiled in such sordid things as murder, love triangles, blackmail, and revenge in keeping with generic tropes of the daytime soap opera that were all but anathema to the sitcom format.

7. Here, of course, I reference the "The Monsters Are Due on Maple Street" (S1 E22, 1960) of *The Twilight Zone* (1959–64, CBS), an episode that—along with "Eye of the Beholder" (S2 E6, 1960)—probably best exemplifies the program's investment in questioning social conformity and the construction of normality.
8. Notably, in 1957, fifty-two Universal horror movies—including monster heavyweights *Dracula* (Tod Browning, 1931), *Frankenstein* (James Whale, 1931), *The Mummy* (Karl Freund, 1932), *The Invisible Man* (James Whale, 1933), and *The Wolf Man* (George Waggner, 1941)—were packaged and distributed for syndication under the name *Shock Theater*.
9. Queer subtexts would become queer text in *Gods and Monsters*, Bill Condon's 1998 film about Whale (herein played by Ian McKellen). The title comes from the moment in *Bride of Frankenstein* when Dr. Pretorius, played by "the outrageously campy character actor" (Benshoff, *Monsters* 42) Ernest Thesiger, drinks a toast to his partnership with Henry Frankenstein (Colin Clive), declaring, "To a new world of gods and monsters!"
10. Later in the decade, satirized versions of Dracula, Frankenstein's Monster, the Mummy, and the Wolf Man would make an appearance on *The Monkees* (1966–68, NBC) episode "Monstrous Monkee Mash" (S2 E18, 1968), an obvious play on the title of Pickett's song, thereby confirming just how densely woven the web of intertextual recycling that sustained the era's monster culture had become. I am grateful to the editors for pointing me to this episode.
11. A running gag throughout the series involves stupefied individuals likening Herman's appearance to anything *but* the Karloff monster, surely the most camp of which is when a con artist-cum-dance instructor (played by insult comic Don Rickles) describes him as "a cross between Li'l Abner and Ramses II."
12. This particular reversal is anticipated by the famous twist of the aforementioned *Twilight Zone* episode "Eye of the Beholder." I thank Joan Hawkins for this observation.
13. This campy representation came at a moment when cinematic scenes of torture were being rendered with increasingly grisly special effects in films such as *The Pit and the Pendulum* (Roger Corman, 1961) and *Bloody Pit of Horror* (Massimo Pupillo, 1965).
14. In his pioneering work on queer reception practices, Alexander Doty cites lesbian humorist Gail Sausser who recalled having a crush on Morticia: "You've got to love a woman who has pet man-eating plants and only lets her husband kiss her hand" (qtd. in Doty 119n11).
15. Skal has observed additional examples of episodic parallelism, noting both "featured episodes in which the children were believed to have turned into chimpanzees, in which the families built robots, and parallel plots that turned on spacemen, beatniks, and amnesia" (284).
16. This plotline would itself be recycled the following season in "Morticia, the Writer" (S2 E8, 1965), when the Addams children are again upset by the unflattering representation of giants, goblins, and witches in their school curriculum, leading Morticia to take it upon herself to publish her own series of stories for children, the first of which is "Cinderella: The Teenage Delinquent."

17. There is, too, the Munsters' heavily coded Jewishness. That they never seek to downplay or "cover" their otherness (recall, for instance, the pride with which they frequently reminisce about their beloved "old country") evokes, especially in this period of rapid social change, Goffman's discussion of the stigmatized individual who "will give praise to the assumed special values and contributions of his [sic] kind. He may also flaunt some stereotypical attributes which he could easily cover ... The stigmatized individual may also openly question the half-concealed disapproval with which normals treat him" (113–114).
18. This particular piece is strongly evoked in the episode "Cousin Itt's Problem" (S2 E 6, 1965), in which it is presumed that Itt's hair is growing throughout the house and eventually covers a family portrait, Thing's box, and so on.
19. Baroque scene transitions were something of a hallmark of the series, such editorial flamboyance camp in itself.
20. The name of the Barry Goldwater–supporting gospel singer was invoked on more than one occasion during the show's run to signify homespun normality and its associated values.
21. While he doesn't address the sextet specifically, Wayne Koestenbaum includes *Lucia di Lammermoor*'s famous mad scene, which follows the events precipitating the sextet, in his "Pocket Guide to Queer Moments in Opera," the final chapter of his definitive study of opera and queer sensibilities, *The Queen's Throat: Opera, Homosexuality, and the Mystery of Desire*. His description of Lucia as "a body divided from itself" (225) is uncannily resonant with the very quality of Ophelia's voice that would make her solo version of the sextet possible within the absurd logic of the episode.
22. This same year on *Gilligan's Island* (1964–67, CBS), The Wellingtons (the folk group who performed the show's theme song) played the members of The Mosquitoes (a thinly veiled camp take on The Beatles) in the episode "Don't Bug the Mosquitoes" (S2 E12, 1965). These instances of musical groups performing as such within the diegetic worlds of the sitcom genre perhaps anticipate the premiere of *The Monkees* on NBC the following year in 1966. I am indebted to the editors for this observation.
23. A high/low cultural divide is prefigured here: before Eddie plays the record, Grandpa tells him, "Back in the old country, you couldn't keep me away from good music. Why, I used to haunt the opera house night and day."
24. Compare, for instance, writings on pop and mass camp with someone like Moe Meyer who maintains, "There are not different kinds of Camp. There is only one. And it is queer" (5).
25. *The Addams Family*, too, has continued to function in online expressions of social progressivism. Beyond the original television series, it has become something of a holiday tradition to see replayed across social media the scene from the feature film *Addams Family Values* (Barry Sonnenfeld, 1993) in which Wednesday (dressed in an indigenous costume) leads the sabotage of a racist Thanksgiving pageant in an exposure and reversal of the holiday's genocidal origins.

Bibliography

Adams, Val. "Monsters to Be Just Plain Folks On a CBS-TV Comedy Series." *New York Times*, February 15, 1964, p. 50.

Allyn, David. *Make Love, Not War: The Sexual Revolution: An Unfettered History*. Little, Brown and Company, 2000.

Benshoff, Harry M. "1966: Movies and Camp." *American Cinema of the 1960s: Themes and Variations*, edited by Barry Keith Grant, Rutgers University Press, 2008, pp. 150–171.

Benshoff, Harry M. *Monsters in the Closet: Homosexuality and the Horror Film*. Manchester University Press, 1997.

Butsch, Richard. "Ralph, Fred, Archie, Homer, and the King of Queens: Why Television Keeps Re-Creating the Male Working-Class Buffoon." *Gender, Race, and Class in Media: A Critical Reader*, third edition, edited by Gail Dines and Jean M. Humez, Sage Publications, 2011, pp. 101–109.

"Can a Typical Suburban Family Make Good on Television?" *Variety*, March 23, 1964, pp. 32–33.

Cleto, Fabio, editor. *Camp: Queer Aesthetics and the Performing Subject: A Reader*. University of Michigan Press, 1999.

Core, Philip. "From *Camp: The Lie That Tells the Truth*." Cleto, pp. 80–86.

Doty, Alexander. *Making Things Perfectly Queer: Interpreting Mass Culture*. University of Minnesota Press, 1993.

Dyer, Richard. "It's Being So Camp As Keeps Us Going." Cleto, pp. 110–116.

Garton, Stephen. *Histories of Sexuality: Antiquity to Sexual Revolution*. Routledge, 2004.

Goffman, Erving. *Stigma: Notes on the Management of Spoiled Identity*. Simon & Schuster, 1963.

Greene, Ray. "The Big Picture." *Boxoffice*, vol. 130, no. 4, 1994, p. 166.

Halley, Peter. "Fifteen Little Electric Chairs." *Andy Warhol: Electric Chair Paintings*. Stellan Holm Gallery, 2001, pp. 39–43.

Haralovich, Mary Beth. "Sitcoms and Suburbs: Positioning the 1950s Homemaker." *The Quarterly Review of Film and Video*, vol. 11, no. 1, 1989, pp. 61–83.

Kleinhans, Chuck. "Taking Out the Trash: Camp and the Politics of Parody." Meyer, pp. 182–201.

Klinger, Barbara. *Melodrama and Meaning: History, Culture, and the Films of Douglas Sirk*. Indiana University Press, 1994.

Koestenbaum, Wayne. *The Queen's Throat: Opera, Homosexuality, and the Mystery of Desire*. Poseidon Press, 1993.

Meyer, Moe, editor. *The Politics and Poetics of Camp*. Routledge, 1994.

Meyer, Moe. "Introduction: Reclaiming the Discourse of Camp." Meyer, pp. 1–22.

Phillips, W. D., and Isabel Pinedo. "Gilligan and Captain Kirk Have More in Common Than You Think: 1960s Camp TV as an Alternative Genealogy for Cult TV." *Journal of Popular Television*, vol. 6, no. 1, 2018, pp. 19–40.

Robertson, Pamela. *Guilty Pleasures: Feminist Camp from Mae West to Madonna*. Duke University Press, 1996.

Ross, Andrew. "Uses of Camp." Cleto, pp. 308–329.

Ross, Kristin. *Fast Cars, Clean Bodies: Decolonization and the Reordering of French Culture*. MIT Press, 1995.

Skal, David J. *The Monster Show: A Cultural History of Horror*. Farrar, Straus and Giroux, 2001.

Sontag, Susan. "Notes on 'Camp.'" Cleto, pp. 53–65.

Spigel, Lynn. "From Domestic Space to Outer Space: The 1960s Fantastic Family Sit-Com." *Close Encounters: Film, Feminism, and Science Fiction*, edited by Constance Penley et al., University of Minnesota Press, 1991, pp. 205–235.
Van Hise, James. *Addams Family Revealed: An Unauthorized Look at America's Spookiest Family*. Las Vegas: Pioneer Books, 1991.
Weldon, Michael J. *The Psychotronic Video Guide to Film*. St. Martin's Press, 1996.
Wood, Robin. "The American Family Comedy: From *Meet Me in St. Louis* to *The Texas Chainsaw Massacre*." *Wide Angle*, vol. 3, no. 2, 1979, pp. 5–11.
Wood, Robin. *Hollywood from Vietnam to Reagan*. Columbia University Press, 1986.

Media

The Addams Family. 1964–1966. Television Series. Seasons 1–2. USA: ABC.
The Addams Family 2. Directed by Greg Tiernan, Conrad Vernon, Laura Brousseau, and Kevin Pavlovic, United Artists Releasing, 2021.
Addams Family Values. Directed by Barry Sonnenfeld, Paramount Pictures, 1993.
Batman. 1966–1968. Television Series. Seasons 1–3. USA: ABC.
Il Boia Scarlatto (*Bloody Pit of Horror*). Directed by Domenico Massimo Pupillo, M.B.S. Cinematografica, 1965.
Bride of Frankenstein. Directed by James Whale, Universal Pictures, 1935.
Creature from the Black Lagoon. Directed by Jack Arnold, Universal Pictures, 1954.
The Curse of Frankenstein. Directed by Terence Fisher, Hammer Film Productions, 1957.
Dark Shadows. 1966–1971. Television Series. Seasons 1–6. USA: ABC.
Dracula. Directed by Tod Browning, Universal Pictures, 1933.
Father Knows Best. 1954–1960. Television Series. Seasons 1–6. USA: CBS and NBC.
Frankenstein. Directed by James Whale, Universal Pictures, 1931.
Gilligan's Island. 1964–1967. Television Series. Seasons 1–3. USA: CBS.
Gods and Monsters. Directed by Bill Condon, Lions Gate Films, 1998.
Hands of a Stranger. Directed by Newt Arnold, Allied Artists Pictures, 1962.
The Hands of Orlac. Directed by Robert Wiene, Pan Film, 1924.
The Honeymooners. 1955–1956. Television Series. Season 1. USA: CBS.
I Dream of Jeannie. 1965–1970. Television Series. Seasons 1–5. USA: NBC.
The Invisible Man. Directed by James Whale, Universal Pictures, 1933.
The Jetsons. 1962–1963. Television Series. Seasons 1–3. USA: ABC.
Leave It to Beaver. 1957–1963. Television Series. Seasons 1–6. USA: CBS and ABC.
Lost in Space. 1965–1968. Television Series. Seasons 1–3. USA: CBS.
Mockingbird Lane. Directed by Bryan Singer, Universal Television, 2012.
The Monkees. 1966–1968. Television Series. Seasons 1–2. USA: NBC.
The Mummy. Directed by Karl Freund, Universal Pictures, 1932.
The Munsters. 1964–1966. Television Series. Seasons 1–2. USA: CBS.
My Fair Lady. Directed by George Cukor, Warner Bros., 1964.
Peeping Tom. Directed by Michael Powell, Anglo-Amalgamated Film Distributors, 1960.
The Pit and the Pendulum. Directed by Roger Corman, American International Pictures, 1961.
Plan 9 from Outer Space. Directed by Ed Wood, Valiant Pictures, 1957/1959.
Psycho. Directed by Alfred Hitchcock, Paramount Pictures, 1960.
The Twilight Zone. 1959–1964. Television Series. Seasons 1–5. USA: CBS.
The Vampira Show. 1954–1955. Television Series. Season 1. USA: KABC-TV.
The Wolf Man. Directed by George Waggner. Universal Pictures, 1941.

5
Spellcasting Camp
Bewitched (1964–72)

Andrew J. Owens

On October 30, 1964, the *Baltimore Sun* celebrated the culmination of that year's Halloween season with a brief article detailing the fascinating, shadowy realms of one of the decade's most enchanting cultural phenomena: a rising interest in all things occult. "Man's fascination with the supernatural," the paper stated, "is an emotional balancing act between fear and fun. The hearty laugh of those who sneer at ghost stories frequently has an embarrassing resemblance to a nervous giggle" ("Of Ghosties and Things"). As I've detailed elsewhere, throughout the 1960s and early 1970s, American popular culture became "swept up in an occult revival the likes of which had not been witnessed in the West since the fin-de-siècle days of Russian mystic Helena Petrovna Blavatsky's Theosophical Society and Aleister Crowley's Hermetic Order of the Golden Dawn. From Los Angeles to Baltimore, nearly every national newspaper and magazine marveled at the resurgence of this phenomenon" (Owens 351–352). Astrological charts, crystal ball gazing, I Ching readings, palmistry, astral projection, witchcraft, and other "occultly marvelous" experiences increasingly became telltale signs of one's participation in the intensifying countercultural fervor of the 1960s; and American popular culture quickly took notice (Lachman 17). There is, as the *Sun* continued, "an irresistible appeal about the shadowy world of the occult that has attracted poets, playwrights, and authors for centuries. And, throughout the history of mankind, this appeal has spelled success in the entertainment business" ("Of Ghosties and Things").

As Paul E. Steiger of the *Los Angeles Times* echoed toward the end of the decade, "around the nation, the practitioners of the occult, the mysterious, and the mystical are enjoying a heyday unmatched since the Salem witch trials. What's more, the whole thing is growing into a substantial business" (Steiger). On bookstore shelves, Ray Bradbury's *Something Wicked This Way*

Comes (1962), Shirley Jackson's *We Have Always Lived in the Castle* (1962), Robert Bloch's *The Skull of the Marquis de Sade* (1965), and Ira Levin's *Rosemary's Baby* (1967) promised to enthrall horror-seeking readers. In film, *Black Sunday* (1960), *Black Sabbath* (1963), *The Crimson Cult* (1968), Roman Polanski's adaptation of *Rosemary's Baby* (1968), Roger Corman's cycle of Edgar Allan Poe adaptations at American International Pictures (AIP) between 1960 and 1964, and the gothic revival at England's Hammer Studios made occult storylines some of the most successful offerings in 1960s big screen horror.[1]

And indeed, if scholars were to place an awarded vintage on 1960s occult popular culture on broadcast television, 1964 stands out as an especially prominent year. With the cancellation of Rod Serling's atomic age sci-fi classic *The Twilight Zone* (1959–64, CBS), that year's fall TV lineup included three new series, what Lynn Spigel refers to as "fantastic family sitcoms," wherein more decidedly occult figures like vampires, witches, and warlocks became central to refiguring the white, heteronormative bliss of suburban Americana: *The Addams Family* (1964–66, ABC), *The Munsters* (1964–66, CBS), and *Bewitched* (1964–72, ABC).[2] The latter series, premiering on September 17, followed the life of an ordinary American man who just happens to be married to a witch, a real "broom-riding, house-haunting, cauldron-stirring witch" ("Of Ghosties and Things"). Yet the success of *Bewitched* was founded on a paradox, wherein witchcraft was "intended to produce laughs but the basic ingredients of the gags are found deep in man's tribal lore . . . and, presumably, there was nothing funny about the superstitious beliefs of those early times" ("Of Ghosties and Things"). How then did this socio-spiritual transition occur? How did ancient religious belief become risible postwar popular culture that embraced the revival of the occult "without the feeling of fear of the supernatural" (Harris)?

Using *Bewitched* as an especially apt case study, this chapter examines a transitional moment across both the industrial and programming landscape of 1960s American television and US occult media through the lens of what Susan Sontag and others have referred to as one of the most enigmatic sensibilities of popular culture: camp. As defined in Sontag's 1966 collection of essays *Against Interpretation*, and often reductively used as a colloquialism simply meaning ostentatious or tacky "bad" taste, camp is a "certain mode of aestheticism. It is one way of seeing the world as an aesthetic phenomenon. That way, the way of Camp, is not in terms of beauty, but in terms of the degree of artifice, of stylization" (Sontag 277). Looking through this affection for "the exaggerated, the 'off,' of things-being-what-they-are-not" (279), *Bewitched* refracted 1960s occultism through the lens of camp in order to produce one of the most successful TV series of the decade. Yet while Sontag denies any true political potentialities of approaching the world in a campy way, I argue that *Bewitched* nevertheless used its love of "artifice and exaggeration" (275) to assemble a generative ideological ground for analysis of American television's ability to engage in social critique during the 1960s, especially surrounding changing midcentury mores of gender and sexuality (Metz 13).

Camp Appeals of the Occult

Camp, as Sontag and others have argued, is especially difficult to define, given the dual valences through which it operates. "Not only is there a Camp vision, a Camp way of looking at things," Sontag contends, but camp is simultaneously a quality "discoverable in objects and the behavior of persons. There are 'campy' movies, clothes, furniture, popular songs, novels, people, buildings . . . But not everything can be seen as Camp. It's not *all* in the eye of the beholder . . . the Camp sensibility is one that is alive to a double sense in which some things can be taken" (Sontag 277, 281). As a way of approaching popular culture wrapped up in hierarchical values of aesthetics, discrimination, and taste, particularly "bad" taste, camp on 1960s TV dynamically blended eclectic borrowings from the high and the low. Indeed, camp afforded even the most avowed consumers of high culture, as Andrew Ross maintains, the ability to "pass" as subscribers to supposedly "throwaway Pop aesthetics, and thus as patrons of the attractive world of immediacy and disposability created by the culture industries in the postwar boom years" (Ross 54).

Yet perhaps the most critical element in discerning camp aesthetics on 1960s American television is the crucial distinction Sontag makes between pure/naïve and deliberate camp: "Pure Camp is always naïve. Camp which knows itself to be Camp ('camping') is usually less satisfying. The pure examples of Camp are unintentional; they are dead serious . . . in naïve, or pure, Camp, the essential element is seriousness, a seriousness that fails" (282–283). This distinction is, I submit, at the heart of how the earlier-cited article from the *Baltimore Sun* articulates television's relationship to the occult ("presumably, there was nothing funny about the superstitious beliefs of those early times") the same year as *Bewitched*'s premiere and one way in which the series itself approached the potentially campy appeals of the supernatural.

To be sure, there are many ways in which occultism of the 1960s could be read as deliberate camp. Take, for example, the cult of personality surrounding Church of Satan founder Anton LaVey. Having purchased a large Victorian home in San Francisco's Richmond district in 1956 that he proceeded to paint entirely in black and shelter a pet lion named Togare in the backyard, LaVey began holding high-profile Friday evening occult lectures in the early 1960s on topics ranging from the teachings of Crowlean Thelema to contemporary incarnations of the Satanic Black Mass. Magick really works, LaVey told *McCall's* columnist Judith Rascoe in a March 1970 issue dedicated entirely to the explosion of countercultural occultism in America: "You can call it alpha, beta, delta, or gamma wave energy or whatever scientists are dabbling in now, but I've been practicing it for years." Nevertheless, it was precisely the campy spectacle of "narcissism, radical chic, [and] carnivalesque conflict" (Ross 54) that made LaVey and his church a cornerstone of American counterculture. "It's showmanship," LaVey confessed to *Los Angeles Times* reporter Dave Smith in July 1970, "calling it a church enabled me to follow the magic formula of nine parts outrage and one part social respectability that is needed for success."

For some countercultural enthusiasts, however, behind its showy spectacles, professed belief in midcentury occultism was no laughing matter. "The new lifestyle of the young is not merely a matter of marijuana versus martini," Penny Kolsrud of the *Baltimore Sun* reported: "It's an unconventional way of looking at the self, the world, and the universe. Part of this different way of life is a burgeoning interest in ESP, Eastern religions, and the occult—astrology, witchcraft, numerology, [and] tarot." Using the example of astrology, for instance, *Time* reported in 1969 that there were certainly those who had found the practice "fun, or fascinating, or *campy* [emphasis mine]" but also those who found it "worthy of serious study, or a source of substitute faith." "Isn't astrology just a fad, and a rather absurd one at that?" the magazine asked. "Certainly. But it is also something more," it answered, leading to the conclusion that:

> It is one of the stranger facts about the contemporary US that Babylon's mystic conceptions of the universe are being taken up seriously and semiseriously by the most scientifically sophisticated generation of

young adults in history. Even the more occult arts of palmistry, numerology, fortunetelling and witchcraft—traditionally the twilight zone of the undereducated and overanxious—are catching on with youngsters. ("Astrology: Fad and Phenomenon" 47)

For many skeptical observers across the popular press, interest in occultism amounted to what could only be described as communal practices of naïve camp on a nationwide scale. "Interest in the occult, once restricted to the poor and the uneducated," William A. Davis of the *Boston Globe* wrote in November 1969, "is now high almost everywhere . . . the occult, in fact, is becoming big business—and respectable." It was precisely this final point, the newfound, enigmatic legitimacy of astrology, witchcraft, and other occultly marvelous phenomena, that reporters like Davis found especially "odd" and Marilyn Goldstein of the *Washington Post* could only describe as "strange": "While most of the rest of the world still shrugs off horoscopes, tarot cards, ESP, palmistry and the netherworld as celestial hogwash, right here under our unmystical atomic-age eyes, strange things are beginning to turn up in the most respectable places." According to many, among this "most scientifically sophisticated generation of young adults in history," sincere interest in the occult could only be a feigned seriousness fated to fail.

Yet as demonstrated in the case of *Bewitched*, one of the most intriguing elements of approaching popular media culture of the 1960s with a camp sensibility is its ability to refashion the very foundation of what it means to succeed or fail in the eyes of audiences, consumers, and critics. As Quinlan Miller instructively argues, American sitcoms of this period "rehearsed the confusion of social change through camp" (Q. Miller 40). Indeed, the whole point of camp, as Sontag suggests, is to "dethrone the serious. Camp is playful, antiserious. More precisely, Camp involves a new, more complex relation to 'the serious.' One can be serious about the frivolous, frivolous about the serious" (Sontag 288).

Your Witch Is Showing: *Bewitched*'s Deliberate Camp

When *Bewitched* premiered on ABC in the fall of 1964, American network TV was in the midst of a transitional identity crisis. Still reeling from the loss of audience/consumer confidence prompted by the quiz show scandals of the late 1950s, the decision to broadcast more explicitly fictional/fantastic/

far-out programming, sometimes literally out of this world in the case of *The Jetsons* (1962–63, ABC) and *My Favorite Martian* (1963–66, CBS), made quite a bit of sense. Indeed, the industrial landscape of 1960s American television provided ample latitude for witches, warlocks, and other occultly marvelous figures to begin camping things up across domestic screens. As Jane Feuer, Paul Kerr, and Tise Vahimagi note, the crucial change that began to occur across industry boardrooms toward the end of the decade was a sudden "de-emphasis on numbers and a greater emphasis on 'demo-graphics,' i.e., directing television shows toward specific audience groups, [whereas previously] . . . the emphasis in ratings was on numbers alone" (Feuer et al. 3). As Mark Alvey concurs, explicit concern on the part of network executives for "composition and indeed 'quality' of audience rather than sheer size" traces its origins precisely to this moment (Alvey 44). Significantly, during the height of 1960s counterculture, US television's fictional programming caught up (albeit often in the vein of campy situation comedy) with the topicality of its news reporting, dramatizing the various social revolutions of the decade, including the civil rights movement, black radicalism, youth unrest, women's and gay liberation, and opposition to the Vietnam War (43–44). This shift in fictional programming was intended to catalyze an attendant realignment in audience demographics, with the increasingly solidified youth market seen as the most lucrative of all. And nowhere was the targeting of youth counterculture more emphatic than at ABC.

As Elana Levine details in *Wallowing in Sex: The New Sexual Culture of 1970s American Television*, the industrial image of ABC during this period was one of "an impetuous adolescent, quick to jump into bed with whatever attractive offer came by, unconcerned with how it looked to the others . . . ABC not only trailed in ratings but also in respectability, at least in the eyes of its fellow networks" (20). While witches, warlocks, and other occultly marvelous figures seemed poised only to underscore Newton Minow's vast wasteland of escapist television during the 1960s, *Bewitched* actually found an opportune match with the kind of "wild-ass programming" directed toward American youth counterculture that was being promoted by then-Vice President of ABC Daytime Programming Harve Bennett (qtd. in Wheatley 128). As Aniko Bodroghkozy observes, between 1960 and 1970, "the population between the ages of eighteen and twenty-four increased by a spectacular and unprecedented 53 percent. Never had so much of the population been at the turbulent years of youth all at the same time" (6). And as the television industry quickly realized, the values of this coming-of-age demographic would soon push American popular culture into untried territories. Indeed, these new bohemians were "deeply critical of and disengaged from the values of white, middle-class, suburban family life [and] embraced philosophies and worldviews associated with Eastern mysticism . . . these new bohemians would bring into being the most widespread and influential counterculture ever to appear on the American sociocultural landscape" (61).

Enter here *Bewitched*. Created by industry veteran Sol Saks, *Bewitched* starred Elizabeth Montgomery and Dick York (later replaced by Dick Sargent) as Samantha and Darrin Stephens, would-be poster couple of postwar marital bliss. As Walter Metz points out, *Bewitched*'s parade of "assorted magical characters, animals, and the special effects associated with the portrayal of witchcraft" bridged youth affections for the fantastic and far-out with a decidedly adult "strong-willed critique of discrimination of those who cannot or will not abide by conventional social mores" (4–6), turning American suburbia into both a deliberate and naïve camp playground over an eight-year, 254-episode run. And to be sure, commentary on the campiness of *Bewitched* heavily favors its deliberate representations, especially vis-à-vis the portrayals of Samantha's meddling mother Endora (Agnes Moorehead) and prankster uncle Arthur (Paul Lynde).

Camp, Miller argues, is "a critically queer mode of production attuned—even in highly appropriative commercialized mass culture contexts—to everyday theatricality, [and it] gains incredible momentum from casting, especially those cases when multiple camp actors perform together" (Q. Miller 27). Toward the end of an extensive, well-respected acting career in Hollywood, Agnes Moorehead's portrayal of Endora mixed a hyper-exaggerated femininity (purple eyeshadow and green chiffon kaftans spectacularly in tow—an "inspiration to drag queens everywhere" [T. Miller]) with a staunchly pro-feminist and pro-outsider sensibility, all delivered with tongue firmly in cheek and eye habitually winking (at least metaphorically) toward the audience (see Plate 10). Yet Endora was a screen witch unlike many who came before her. As Tanice Foltz observes, prior to the emerging legitimation of witchcraft as a spiritual practice in the 1960s, witches in popular culture were generally portrayed in two stereotypical ways:

> Either they were ugly, old hags who used their powers for evil, or those portrayed as beautiful covertly used their magical powers to "catch" or keep a man or to maintain the peace (as well as traditional gender roles) within their homes. Since the religion's importation, however, which coincides

with the women's movement, witches frequently appear in books, films, and television programs . . . as attractive, youthful, strong, and independent females who openly use their magical powers to fight against evil for the greater good. (137)

Although Endora may not be as young and conventionally beautiful as her daughter, her fierce individuality, boisterous personality, and magically campy antics served as foils to Samantha's tentative tightrope walk between her supernatural heritage and her desire to live the serious life of a "typical" American housewife. As Moorehead once said of her character, "On this series I'm not at all wicked. I'm quite a sophisticated gal. Endora is a very attractive and charming witch with a supernatural philosophy all her own. The humans in the script do plenty of very foolish things and she loves showing up their foolishness" (qtd. in T. Miller).

And indeed, she does. Take, for example, the first season episode "Driving Is the Only Way to Fly" (S1 E26, 1965). After an exasperated Samantha refuses to allow an impatient and patronizing Darrin to teach her how to drive, the Stephenses hire local agency Reliable Driving School to take over the task. As Endora teleports in and out of the backseat of the instructor's car while taunting him and Samantha with disembodied cackles of laughter, the lesson ends abruptly as the anxious, nerve-shot tutor flees the scene. After chastising Samantha for attempting to learn how to drive when all witches can travel anywhere by flying, Endora gleefully raises her arms with a dramatic flourish as the car vanishes in a puff of smoke. "You should be ashamed," Samantha reprimands her mother: "You have that poor dear man talking to himself." "I know," Endora sarcastically counters: "And I'm sure it's a fascinating conversation."

Tracing the etymology of camp, Andrew Ross points to the French "*se camper* (to posture or to flaunt)" (55) and this is precisely how Endora approaches her mischievous magical relationships with those humans on *Bewitched* who do plenty of very foolish things, not insignificantly a majority of whom are men. As Susan Douglas argues in *Where the Girls Are: Growing Up Female with the Mass Media*, gender politics in the 1960s were largely defined by "political rumblings about women's second-class status, and their desire for more opportunities and choices, [which] now registered on America's media seismographs" (123). Within what *Harper's* termed the "crypto-feminist" environment of the early sixties, witches turned out to be just what the televisual doctor ordered:

All of a sudden, female characters in TV sitcoms were capable of magic. They had fantastic supernatural powers . . . whenever women used these powers outside the home, in the public sphere, the male world was turned completely upside down . . . Men were made impotent by these powers, and the husbands (or husband figures) of such women were stripped of their male authority and made to look foolish and incompetent in front of their male superiors. (Douglas 126–127)

Indeed, if we "put these TV shows and the impulses behind them on the shrink's couch for a minute, we see that a significant portion of the pop culture moguls were trying to acknowledge the impending release of female sexual and political energy" (126). Powder kegs always threatening to explode with disruptive vigor, witches are, according to Margot Adler, "changer[s] of definitions and relationships" (42), especially within the turbulent realm of 1960s gender politics insofar as their alleged abilities to cause impotence embodied "fears which men would rather forget" (Russell 121). And although Endora, with her "overly bouffant, bright red hairdos, two-inch-long false eyelashes, and thick eyeliner that shot up at a forty-five-degree angle to her eyes" exaggeratedly camped up femininity "like a Mardi Gras mask," it was precisely her defiance in the face of postwar patriarchy that "gave her power, and made her such a liberatory character" (Douglas 132).

Not to be outdone by the series' bombastic matriarch, Paul Lynde's portrayal of Samantha's prankster uncle Arthur is perhaps even more infamous in shoring up *Bewitched*'s deliberate camp legacy. Indeed, practically everything for Arthur was fodder for his own personal amusement, and no one was more tickled than him at his unique brand of magical physical comedy mixed with punchy one-liners. At the beginning of the second season episode "The Joker Is a Card" (S2 E5, 1965), Arthur's head appears under the dome lid of a silver serving platter: "Forgive me for not rising but I'm up to my neck in work" (Plate 11). Later in the same episode, a cow suddenly appears in the Stephenses' living room: "Forgive me," Arthur quips, "I just can't help milking a joke."

Notorious for his affective, flamboyant, and often fey delivery, Lynde's portrayal of Uncle Arthur introduced a decidedly queer brand of camp into the normative middle-class American home at 1164 Morning Glory Circle. As Metz observes, Arthur's "delight in playing practical jokes . . . coupled with his genuine love for Sam, caused playful chaos to reign in the Stephenses' household" (11). This kind of mischievous commotion is partially why, according to Sontag, there is a "peculiar relation between Camp taste and homosexuality... there is no doubt a particular affinity and overlap" (290). One potential explanation is that camp often serves as a solvent of morality and moral relevance, one that "neutralizes moral indignation, sponsors playfulness" (290). Indeed, in an era that saw everything from "civil rights struggles and the rise of second wave feminism to free love and landing on the moon," some of those Americans most interested in neutralizing moral indignation were undoubtedly gay men and women, whose increasingly visible "born this way" ethos mounted a potent political campaign that often intentionally camped up their supposedly perverse deviance in order to accomplish precisely what Sontag suggests: being serious about the frivolous and frivolous about the serious (Metz 77). For instance, after Arthur offers to teach Darrin witchcraft as a way of getting revenge on Endora for turning her son-in-law's hair into a mop-top in "The Joker Is a Card," Darrin steadfastly sticks to his sober, normative guns: "No, Arthur, you see Sam and I have an agreement. No witchcraft. We're going to live like normal people." Ever the jesting neutralizer of moral indignation, Arthur responds: "Your mother-in-law just turned you into Prince Valiant. That's normal living?"

While there's nothing gay, at least in the purely sexual sense, about Arthur, rumors surrounding Lynde's sexuality combined with his own affinity for gay innuendo as a star on NBC's *Hollywood Squares* made his queerness highly legible to American viewers who read popular culture through a camp sensibility. It may be true that camp's affinity for artifice and playful stylization has been historically celebrated by gay individuals (mostly men) as a kind of aesthetic dandyism in the style of Oscar Wilde and others, but perhaps camp as a sensibility and way of seeing the world is more congruent with the ways in which critics like Alexander Doty have specifically theorized what it means to be queer. In *Making Things Perfectly Queer: Interpreting Mass Culture*, Doty marks a crucial distinction: "'queer' or 'queerness'... suggest a range of nonstraight expression in, or in response to, mass culture. This range includes specifically gay, lesbian, and bisexual expressions; but it also includes other potential (and potentially unclassifiable) nonstraight positions," marking a "flexible space for the expression of all aspects of non (anti, contra) straight cultural production and reception" (xvi). As Annamarie Jagose concurs, queerness's "definitional indeterminacy, its elasticity, is one of its constituent characteristics" (1).

The indeterminate, flexible features of queerness combined with the playful, imaginative characteristics of camp merged in the way Uncle Arthur flamboyantly approached his use of magic on *Bewitched*. As Miller argues of camp's deliberately queer mode vis-à-vis sitcoms like *Bewitched*, "you really can't miss the parody of gender conventions, even if you don't appreciate the eccentric details, because the actor delivers the dialogue idiosyncratically, punctuating trans gender queer lines with iconic nonnormative bodily and facial accent" (Q. Miller 30). What's more, queerly camp characters like Endora and Arthur anticipated the ways in which queer Wiccan Michael G. Lloyd once articulated his own supernatural style: "Shake it up and shake it out . . . Be hermetic, be mercurial, react, reject, rebel, look outside the bone box, look up the Goddess' skirt, be more than they'll let you be, breathe the free air, fight the good fight, seize the day, brave the elements, bust a nut, and live! All magick is an act of rebellion against the status quo" (qtd. in Adler 370).

What Fools These Mortals Be: *Bewitched*'s Naïve Camp

In Act III, Scene II of Shakespeare's *A Midsummer Night's Dream*, the magical, mischievous Puck famously declares: "Lord, what fools these mortals be!" Nearly four hundred years later, this line perfectly encapsulates a vast majority of the naïve style of camp that pervades *Bewitched*. To reiterate the fundamental distinction Sontag makes between deliberate and naïve camp, the essential element in the latter is "seriousness, a seriousness that fails" (283). Yet not all failed seriousness can be "redeemed" as camp: "only that which has the proper mixture of the exaggerated, the fantastic, the passionate, and the naïve" (283). To create a rough analogy, deliberate camp might be the equivalent of laughing *with* someone: characters/actors are "in" on the artifice of "Being-as-Playing-a-Role," of life as theater, as much as the audience (280). In naïve camp, however, it is more often the case that we, as an audience, are laughing *at* someone. Yet our amusement with naïve camp is not necessarily motivated by malice or cruelty. Rather, as the name suggests, we laugh at this kind of camp precisely because the naivety of the person(s) involved places them in those exaggerated and/or fantastic situations wherein they have little choice but to become the butt of the joke.

In the previously discussed episode "Driving Is the Only Way to Fly," it just so happens that Harold Harold, the Reliable Driving School instructor tasked with teaching Samantha how to drive, is none other than Paul Lynde, hired in a first season guest spot before being cast as Uncle Arthur in *Bewitched*'s second season. Caught in a constant pattern of being hired and fired by his brothers-in-law, the reason "I tend to be insecure," Harold is the ultimate personification of a nervous nelly. Arming himself with a crash helmet before leaving for his appointment with Samantha, Harold's brother-in-law Basil, the owner of Reliable Driving School, asks Harold why he's bringing a cookie with him. With all seriousness, Harold responds: "Basil, this isn't a cookie. It's a tranquilizer. I need such a big one the doctor prescribes it in the form of a wafer." While there's nothing ostensibly funny about Harold's nervous condition that verges on paranoiac cautiousness, the exaggeratedness of a wafer-size tranquilizer, a crash helmet for a suburban driving lesson, and so many other objects/situations on *Bewitched* are heightened through the use of one of the oldest staples of the television sitcom: the laugh track. An initial reaction to Harold might be one of pity, yet the insertion of the laugh track invites us to refashion our reception to find something he takes very seriously—his anxiety and its impact upon his life—as funny.

Assessing the seemingly ageless dichotomy between success and failure, Jack Halberstam argues that "under certain circumstances failing, losing, forgetting, unmaking, unbecoming, not knowing may in fact offer more creative, more cooperative, more surprising ways of being in the world" (2). Failure, in Halberstam's words, can be conceptualized as a queer art and style. There is, to be sure, certainly the temptation to retroactively read Harold as queer in light of Lynde's deliberately campy portrayal of Uncle Arthur later in the series. Yet the unsuccessful middle-aged driving instructor raised entirely by women, a mother and four sisters, has a queer style all his own predicated upon failure: both his acute emotional sensitivity and revolving door of botched careers are anathema to the image of the successful postwar businessman and breadwinner. While failure is, as Halberstam suggests, often accompanied by a "host of negative effects, such as disappointment, disillusionment, and despair, it also provides the opportunity to use these negative affects to poke holes in the toxic positivity of contemporary life" (3). Indeed, in the final scene of "Driving Is the Only Way to Fly," Harold shows up to the Stephenses' home as a changed man, largely due to enrolling in the same basket weaving class as Samantha: "It's done wonders for him," she asserts, "He's given up wafers. He stands up to his brother-in-law. And there's even talk of making him a partner in the company!" The near-saccharine positivity of Harold's newfound "success" combined with the absence of the laugh track suddenly evacuates any naïve camp from his character, allowing the aforementioned can-do "toxic positivity" of American suburbia to reestablish itself as the status quo.

If characters on *Bewitched* are constantly placed in naively camp situations that exaggerate the "very foolish things" that mortals do, no one is more prone to such experiences than Darrin. For instance, after initially refusing Arthur's offer to help him learn witchcraft early in "The Joker Is a Card," Darrin eventually acquiesces to Arthur's badgering when Endora's antics simply become too frustrating to bear. As Video 5.1 shows, armed with a cowbell, duck call, and the staunch conviction that five minutes of "training" has given him the ability to make his mother-in-law vanish in a puff of smoke, Darrin approaches Endora with the promise that she's victimized him for the last time. "Be careful, Tinkerbelle," Endora warns, recalling Douglas's observation (127) that witches often threatened to strip men of their male authority and make them look foolish and incompetent. And of course, that is precisely how Darrin ends up looking, persisting with an outlandishly choreographed incantation intercut with shots of Arthur doubled over in laughter in the hallway and mirrored by the almost deafening laugh track. At the conclusion of the spell, Darrin slowly lowers the duck call from his lips in stupefied disbelief that his seriousness has in fact failed, as Endora remains right in front of him:

SAMANTHA: Darrin, what's wrong?
DARRIN: You're supposed to vanish.
ENDORA: But I don't want to vanish! I want to stay and see what you're going to do for your next number.

Faced with the crushing realization that he has indeed been taken for a fool by someone he should have known better than to trust, Darrin slowly walks away mumbling his regret at believing Arthur's promises. Immediately after, hearing her uncle's cackling from the den, Samantha approaches Arthur inquiring whether he had anything to do with Darrin's behavior. Hardly believing the ease with which he could manipulate Darrin's naivety, Arthur responds between fits of laughter: "Best . . . best joke I ever pulled . . . he went for it all the way!" What begins as Darrin's earnest pursuit of revenge quickly becomes an ostentatious spectacle of humiliation engineered for Arthur's and Endora's amusement ⏵.

As Metz argues, because *Bewitched* witnessed "so much cultural change in the time it was written and filmed [1964–72], it provides a particularly fertile ground for understanding the cultural currents that flowed through 1960s U.S. society" (77). One of those currents, the changing nature of gender roles and shifting relationships between men and women in both the public and private spheres, became the target at which so many of *Bewitched*'s naïvely camp critiques were often aimed. Yet critique does not equate to annihilation, and those mortals who do end up the butt of *Bewitched*'s jokes are almost always redeemed by the episode's conclusion as the series recenters the clichéd normativity of postwar American life. Indeed, toward the end of "The Joker Is a Card," Darrin conspires with Samantha and Endora to teach Arthur a lesson. As Darrin reenacts the same incantation that he now knows is simply a jumble of nonsense words, Endora turns herself into a parrot, convincing Arthur that Darrin has miraculously made magic that might doom his mother-in-law forever:

ARTHUR: Darrin, you don't realize what you've done. Endora can stay inside that parrot forever unless you bring her back immediately.
DARRIN: So what, I don't see what you're so concerned about. You don't like her either.
ARTHUR: Of course I like her! I love her!
DARRIN: I don't get it. You said it yourself. She's an interfering . . .
ARTHUR: Never mind what I said. She's family. Now please bring her back . . . Hold tight, Endora. I won't let this happen to you . . . now bring her back!

As Endora returns to her usual form, taunting Arthur that she didn't know how much he really cared, Arthur realizes that the joke is now quite literally on him: "It was all a joke. Well, it's not very funny!," to which Samantha simply replies, "That's the point."

Conclusion: Double, Double, Toil, and Trouble

Tapping into the occult zeitgeist that defined so much of American counterculture in the 1960s, *Bewitched* used both deliberate and naïve camp to effectively put midcentury American social mores under a microscope. As Miller argues, sitcom actors of this period became expert at camping up gender and sexuality "in all kinds of sacrilegious and intertextually charged ways, combining the unruly antics of screwball film comedy with traditions of stage and radio performance transferred to TV" (Q. Miller 35). Shrugging off the disbelief that postwar scientific rationality, technology, and the supernatural were mutually exclusive, famed Canadian media theorist Marshall McLuhan told *Time* in 1969 why broadcasting occultism on television seemed perfectly logical:

> The current interest of youth in astrology, clairvoyance, and the occult is no coincidence... Psychic communal integration, made possible at last by the electronic media, could create the universality of consciousness foreseen by Dante when he predicted that men would continue as no more than broken fragments until they were unified into an inclusive consciousness. Mysticism is just tomorrow's science dreamed today. ("Astrology: Fad and Phenomenon" 48)

And while interest in all things occultly marvelous continued well into the 1970s, American television largely left both occultism and camp behind, as the social unrest of the era spurred US broadcasting's new "turn toward 'relevance'" (Gitlin 205).

Notes

1. For more on the midcentury rise in American horror entertainment, see Benshoff, Heffernan, Newman, and Skal.
2. For a consideration of *The Addams Family* and *The Munsters* within the context of 1960s Camp TV, see Jamie Hook's chapter (Chapter 4) in this collection.

Bibliography

Adler, Margot. *Drawing Down the Moon: Witches, Druids, Goddess-Worshippers and Other Pagans in America*. Penguin Books, 2006.
Alvey, Mark. "'Too Many Kids and Old Ladies': Quality Demographics and 1960s US Television." *Screen*, vol. 45, no. 1, 2004, pp. 40–62.
"Astrology: Fad and Phenomenon." *Time*, vol. 93, no. 12, March 1969, pp. 47–48, 53–54, 56.
Benshoff, Harry M. *Monsters in the Closet: Homosexuality and the Horror Film*. Manchester University Press, 1997.
Bodroghkozy, Aniko. *Groove Tube: Sixties Television and the Youth Rebellion*. Duke University Press, 2001.

Davis, William A. "Occult: Oddly Enough, It's Thriving." *Boston Globe*, November 23, 1969, p. 33.
Doty, Alexander. *Making Things Perfectly Queer: Interpreting Mass Culture*. University of Minnesota Press, 1993.
Douglas, Susan J. *Where the Girls Are: Growing Up Female with the Mass Media*. Times Books, 1994.
Feuer, Jane, et al., editors. *MTM: "Quality Television."* British Film Institute, 1984.
Foltz, Tanice. "The Commodification of Witchcraft." *Witchcraft and Magic: Contemporary North America*, edited by Helen Berger, University of Pennsylvania Press, 2005, pp. 137–168.
Gitlin, Todd. *Inside Prime Time*. Pantheon, 1983.
Goldstein, Marilyn. "Strange Things Are Happening in the Occult." *The Washington Post*, July 25, 1971, p. G2.
Halberstam, Jack. *The Queer Art of Failure*. Duke University Press, 2011.
Harris, Joann. "Occult Goes Modern with Charms, Churches, TV: A Soap Opera Vampire Even Has a Fan Club." *The Baltimore Sun*, April 26, 1970, p. C1.
Heffernan, Kevin. *Ghouls, Gimmicks, and Gold: Horror Films and the American Movie Business, 1953–1968*. Duke University Press, 2004.
Jagose, Annamarie. *Queer Theory: An Introduction*. New York University Press, 1996.
Kolsrud, Penny. "Aquarian Alternatives: Search for the Self Leads Youth to Witchcraft, the Occult." *The Baltimore Sun*, February 25, 1971, p. B1.
Lachman, Gary. *Turn Off Your Mind: The Mystic Sixties and the Dark Side of the Age of Aquarius*. Sidgwick & Jackson, 2001.
Levine, Elana. *Wallowing in Sex: The New Sexual Culture of 1970s American Television*. Duke University Press, 2007.
Metz, Walter. *Bewitched*. Wayne State University Press, 2007.
Miller, Quinlan. *Camp TV: Trans Gender Queer Sitcom History*. Duke University Press, 2019.
Miller, Taylor Cole. "Remembering Elizabeth Montgomery: 9 Queerest Moments of Bewitched." *The Huffington Post*, December 6, 2017, https://www.huffpost.com/entry/remembering-elizabeth-mon_b_7289652.
Newman, Kim. *Nightmare Movies: Horror on Screen Since the 1960s*. Bloomsbury, 2011.
"Of Ghosties and Things: Shadowy World of the Occult Fascinating." *The Baltimore Sun*, October 30, 1964, p. 14.
Owens, Andrew. "Coming Out of the Coffin: Queer Historicity and Occult Sexualities on ABC's *Dark Shadows*." *Television & New Media*, vol. 17, no. 4, 2016, pp. 350–365.
Rascoe, Judith. "San Francisco's Church of Satan." *McCall's*, March 1970, pp. 74–75, 133–136.
Ross, Andrew. "Uses of Camp." *The Cult Film Reader*, edited by Ernest Mathijs and Xavier Mendik, Open University Press, 2008, pp. 53–66.
Russell, Sharon. "The Witch in Film: Myth and Reality." *Planks of Reason: Essays on the Horror Film*, edited by Barry Keith Grant, The Scarecrow Press, 1984, pp. 113–125.
Skal, David J. *The Monster Show: A Cultural History of Horror*. Farrar, Straus and Giroux, 2001.
Smith, Dave. "Satanist Speaks to Set Record Straight." *Los Angeles Times*, July 17, 1970, p. 1.
Sontag, Susan. "Notes on 'Camp.'" 1964. *Against Interpretation and Other Essays*. 1966. New York, Picador, 2001, pp. 275–292.

Spigel, Lynn. "From Domestic Space to Outer Space: The 1960s Fantastic Family Sitcom." *Welcome to the Dreamhouse: Popular Media and Postwar Suburbs*, Duke University Press, 2001, pp. 107–140.

Steiger, Paul E. "Big Business: Practitioners of Occult Enjoy a Rich Heyday." *Los Angeles Times*, May 28, 1969, p. A1.

Wheatley, Helen. *Gothic Television*. Manchester University Press, 2006.

Media

The Addams Family. 1964–1966. Television Series. Seasons 1–2. USA: ABC.
Bewitched. 1964–1972. Television Series. Seasons 1–8. USA: ABC.
Black Sabbath. Directed by Mario Bava, Galatea Film—Emmepi/ Lyre Film, 1963.
Black Sunday. Directed by Mario Bava, Galatea-Jolly Film, 1960.
The Crimson Cult. Directed by Vernon Sewell, Tigon British Film Productions, 1968.
Hollywood Squares. 1966–1981. Television Series. Seasons 1–14. NBC.
The Jetsons. 1962–1963. Television Series. Seasons 1–3. USA: ABC.
The Munsters. 1964–1966. Television Series. Seasons 1–2. USA: CBS.
My Favorite Martian. 1963–1966. Television Series. Seasons 1–3. USA: CBS.
Rosemary's Baby. Directed by Roman Polanski, Paramount Pictures, 1968.
The Twilight Zone. 1959–1964. Television Series. Seasons 1–5. USA: CBS.

6

How the West Was Fun

F Troop (1965–67) and the American Frontier

Cynthia J. Miller

For two years in the mid-1960s, the American frontier was the site of accidental heroism, pratfalls, and gender role subversion. It was a time when cavalrymen impersonated officers . . . and women . . . and clergy . . . while the local tribe made whiskey for the town's saloon and conspired to make soldiers look heroic. These were the original years of the ABC series *F Troop* (1965–67); a sitcom set in the Wild West, at the fictitious Fort Courage, featuring a cast of characters that parodied iconic frontier figures, from soldiers to Indigenous people and townspeople to renegades.

The show offered its audiences mildly "lowbrow" vaudeville-esque humor designed to elicit easy laughs, with characters written to subvert classic Western stereotypes, displaying the "unmistakably modern" humorous and often ironic sensibility that Susan Sontag has noted as characterizing camp (515). The series' competing discourses focused on the American West are self-consciously designed to exploit the space between portrayal and pretense (see Cohan 1) as cultural commentary. In each episode, the over-the-top parody and exaggerated physical comedy send up interwoven stereotypes of the frontier and the characters that animate it, calling into question assumptions about not only long-cherished histories but classic portrayals of gender—and masculinity in particular—as well.[1]

However, rather than overtly queering the frontier in ways that characterize later camp television efforts (see Malinowska for a discussion of these), *F Troop* offers a range of portrayals and styles that playfully extend and subvert prevailing images and identities. Captain Wilton Parmenter (Ken Berry) is inept, gullible, and clumsy—the antithesis of frontier masculinity—and known to the Indigenous people as "the Great White Pigeon." He is supported

Cynthia J. Miller, *How the West Was Fun* In: *Camp TV of the 1960s*. Edited by Isabel C. Pinedo and W. D. Phillips, Oxford University Press. © Oxford University Press 2023. DOI: 10.1093/oso/9780197650745.003.0007 by a cast of rough-and-tumble comic military figures (Larry Storch, Forrest Tucker, James Hampton) who, while more masculine, play fast and loose with hierarchy and rules of conduct. They are "old school," mocking military rules much like their counterparts in the more successful *McHale's Navy* (1962–66, ABC), where the establishment is challenged by characters who try to circumvent the rules for their own benefit. These characters stand as the "everyman," pursuing benign self-interest with comic results in the face of rules and regulations that would curtail their behaviors. They are joined in their antics by Parmenter's rowdy, tomboyish girlfriend, the buckskin-clad Wrangler Jane (Melody Patterson), who can out-rope, out-wrassle, and out-shoot any man in the fort.

Their Indigenous counterparts, members of the Hekawi tribe, are likewise played for laughs, drawing heavily on Borscht Belt humor. Dialogue that mirrors stand-up comedy of the era abounds, such as when the origin of the tribe's self-identification, "We're the Hekawi," is revealed to have its roots in a story of ancestors wandering aimlessly in the wilderness, exclaiming "Where the heck are we?" Chief Wild Eagle (Frank DeKova) is a shrewd businessman rather than a warrior, who frequently provides sage advice for the main characters, though he admits he has no clue what his "old Indian sayings" mean. Featured tribesmen, such as the rotund Happy Bear (Ben Frommer) and medicine man Roaring Chicken (Edward Everett Horton), son of Sitting Duck, extend the comic interpretation of the West's Indigenous people delivered by non-Indigenous actors.

The series' comedy is visual and visceral, leaving little to interpretation. This chapter, however, will dig below these surface laughs, situating the series in the sociopolitical context of the 1960s and examining the ways in which *F Troop* and its characters both mirror and grapple with the era's uneasy and incomplete shifts in American notions of masculinity, from rugged archetypes to those that privilege intellect and business savvy. Situated firmly in the camp aesthetic, the series uses comedy to move beyond traditional narratives about "civilizing" the West to serve as a well-timed parody of the clash between two American masculine archetypes: the "soft" Eastern upper-class intellectual and the frontier soldier. This chapter will also illustrate how, as part of this shifting constellation of ideologies, the series engages with long-held notions about the gendering of the wilderness, Anglo–Indigenous relationships, and frontier (and military) nobility and, in so doing, both mocks and reinforces Manifest Destiny and the Myth of the Frontier.

The End of the Civil War Was Near

American situation comedy has featured a wide range of circumstances and settings in which characters struggle to follow—or circumvent—social norms. Comic ne'er-do-wells abound in 1960s television programming, in particular, from the military (as in *F Troop*, *McHale's Navy*, and *The Phil Silvers Show* [1955–59, CBS]) to high society (as in *The Beverly Hillbillies* [1962–71, CBS], *Green Acres* [1965–71, CBS], and *Gilligan's Island* [1963–67, CBS]) to crime-fighting (as in *Get Smart* [1965–70, NBC, CBS], *Batman* [1966–68, ABC], and *Car 54, Where Are You?* [1961–63, NBC]). In each of these cases, hapless, inept, or otherwise out-of-step characters evoke laughs while poking fun at a corner of everyday life. The characters of *F Troop* are no exception: Wilton Parmenter, a private in charge of officers' laundry, is established in the opening credits as the one incompetent member of his family—lacking in leadership qualities, gravitas, and even stature, as we see him in Figure 6.1, standing at inspection, a foot shorter than various heroic male relatives named Hercules, Achilles, Zeus, and Jupiter. When a fortunately timed sneeze during his laundry ride is mistaken as a command to

Figure 6.1 Parmenter and his heroic male relatives in "Scourge of the West" (S1 E1, 1965, *F Troop*, Warner Bros.).

charge that turns the tide of battle, and results in victory for the Northern troops, Parmenter accidentally achieves the honor, status, and regard that his ancestors clearly earned. As he receives a medal for his unwitting valor, the pin draws blood, and he receives yet another for his "wound." Parmenter is then assigned to Fort Courage—a problematic frontier post where commanders have either deserted or had nervous breakdowns as a result of being stationed there.

His assignment, however, turns out to be a blessing in disguise, not only for him, but for the misfits under his command and the nearby Hekawi tribe, all of whom recognize that his incompetence will allow their shady dealings and shortcomings to continue without repercussion. Parmenter routinely trips over his own sabre, fumbles with his gun, and falls over (or into, or out of) furniture, remarking "I fall down a lot. My father used to say that I had more left feet than any kid in Philadelphia." His soft masculinity, in contrast with the cast of roughnecks surrounding him, provides the series' viewers with ongoing laughs as he repeatedly fails tests of traditional manhood, but is shorn up by those who do.

The cast of characters residing at Fort Courage serve as Parmenter's comic counterparts and foils and provide many of the series' misadventures through their own ineptitude. While some, such as the decidedly tone-deaf bugler Private Dobbs (James Hampton), nearly blind lookout Trooper Vanderbilt (Joe Brooks), and the aged Trooper Duffy (Bob Steele), who claimed to be a veteran of the Battle of the Alamo thirty years prior, all provide pratfalls and sight gags worthy of vaudeville, the narrative focus typically rests on Sergeant O'Rourke (Forrest Tucker) and Corporal Agarn (Larry Storch). Together, they not only run the fort's saloon but also head the clandestine O'Rourke Enterprises, which buys and sells Indigenous trinkets, souvenirs, and whiskey made by the Hekawi. The series' "dilemma of the week" often pivots on the pair's cover-ups and get-rich-quick schemes, along with attempts to keep the Hekawi safe from government interference. A narrative thread of romance-chasing rounds out the comic fare, as Wrangler Jane alternately pursues and protects the Captain, hoping to land the dimwit as a husband. Together, they all take gentle aim at the social norms of the day amid laughs at each other's expense.

The brainchild of Warner Bros. screenwriter Richard Bluel, *F Troop* was ultimately created by writers Seaman Jacobs, Ed James, and James Barnett.[2] Like many early television sitcoms, the series' concept, development, and story creation were the product of the studio's stable of writers, and its exact origins have proven contentious, but its formula of endearingly flawed characters, comic mishaps, and celebrity guest appearances sustained the series' success across sixty-five episodes. An article in *TV Guide* in December 1965 noted that out of a survey of forty newspaper columnists, 80 percent recommended *F Troop*, making it the most critically acclaimed of the thirty-five new shows to debut in the 1965–66 season (Youman 22). After its premiere on ABC on September 14, 1965, the series' first season ran for a now almost-unimaginable thirty-four black-and-white episodes, while the second season, of similar length (thirty-one episodes), was aired in color. Despite the change in format—and a shift in time slots—the series was ABC's second highest rated situation comedy after *Bewitched* (1964–72). It was so highly regarded, in fact, that in 1967, series co-star Larry Storch received a nomination for the Emmy for Outstanding Continued Performance by an Actor in a Leading Role in a Comedy Series, alongside stars Bob Crane (*Hogan's Heroes* [1965–71, CBS]), Don Adams (*Get Smart*), and Brian Keith (*Family Affair* [1966–71, CBS]).

F Troop's success, however, came at a cost. While it was a worthwhile endeavor for third-rated ABC, the series proved to be a significant financial drain for Warner Bros. Studios. Despite promotional materials' claims that the series was set in Kansas, its primary setting—Fort Courage, a nineteenth-century cavalry fort—was constructed on Warner Bros.' "Tatum Ranch," an area adjacent to the studio's famous "Laramie Street" on its backlot (Bingen 185). Fort Courage, including its famous watchtower (which crashed to the ground at least once in nearly every episode), was patterned as closely as possible after the eponymous fort in the cavalry Western *Fort Dobbs* (1958) (Canote). This allowed the producers to insert stock footage from the film into the series' first season whenever there was a fight with the "Indians." It also made *F Troop* the first sitcom to utilize feature-film-sized sets—not a small expense for the studio. As Terence Towles Canote relates, a significant number of Warner Bros. executives, including Jack Warner himself, were none too happy with the amount of money spent on a half-hour television sitcom, and were likewise concerned by the space Fort Courage occupied on the Warner backlot. Warner, who had a reputation for being tightfisted, had never before approved such a substantial amount of construction for television (Bingen 185).

Like many other series of its era, *F Troop* proved to be a hit in syndication, as well, continuing to air in reruns beyond its fiftieth anniversary, as well as on full-season DVD releases. The show was part of a significant cluster of programming in the 1960s that relied on satire, parody, and farce, such as *The Beverly Hillbillies*, *Get Smart*, *McHale's Navy*, *Gilligan's Island*, *Green Acres*, and *Petticoat Junction* (1963–70, CBS), and shared comic elements and plot points with several of these. A closer look, however, will explore what set *F Troop* apart from its contemporaries—many of which also have developed "cult" status in the decades after their release.

Gee, Sarge!

The inhabitants of Fort Courage were most definitely products of their media era, drawing archetypes, narratives, and gags from a range of contemporary programming, as well as the comedies of radio and stage. Likewise, they were also products—and reflections—of their wider social era and were, in many ways, just as complex. Just below the surface of the series' affable irreverence, we find significant social response and cultural commentary on issues of the day, as well as on taken-for-granted notions about American life embedded in the characters' ongoing comic exchanges. Various scholars, such as Aaron Barlow, Laura Westengard, Martin Kich, and David Pierson, have examined the dynamic relationship between sitcoms that arose in the "uneasy '60s" and the period of rapid social change in which they emerged and evolved, alternately reinforcing and questioning traditions, values, and norms. They note that the laughs offered by mid-century sitcoms such as *F Troop* not only reassured and grounded viewers caught up in the confusion of change but also gently nudged them forward (Verschuure 92).

Through its use of exaggerated clichés and camp satire, the series shines a comic spotlight on long-cherished notions of American manhood at a time when it was increasingly contested, complicating and interrogating deeply rooted archetypes of masculinity and heroism that have traditionally animated tales of both the frontier West and the military.[3] Both of these archetypes have had far-reaching impacts on characterizations of manhood, both in fictional narratives and in our lived realities. While the actual traits most highly prized in American men—bravery, loyalty, integrity, and resourcefulness—changed little over time, their interrelationship with constructions of national identity and political economy led to ongoing shifts in the ways in which they were expressed, emphasized, and encouraged. As we shall see, the series' narratives respond to these shifts in a variety of ways, from quietly continuing to valorize traditional notions of masculinity to lampooning them, while at the same time creating space for a multiplicity of masculinities that grant success, acceptance, belonging, and romance to those characters for whom traditional archetypes are an uncomfortable fit.

From the early days of westward expansion through the Golden Age of the Cowboy, the frontier provided challenges that shaped notions of rugged American manhood, individualism, and ingenuity. Mythic tales of heroic pioneers who pushed the borders of the nation westward to establish "civilization" in the wilderness set the stage for tales of moral triumph. Cultural critic Tom Engelhardt observes, "As every child learned in school, our history was an inclusive saga of expanding liberties and rights that started in a vast, fertile, nearly empty land" in order to expand "the boundaries of that space within which freedom might 'ring'" (4). Easterners and immigrants alike traveled west to make their future in territories where hard work (and a bit of luck), rather than background or breeding, was the determiner of success. These tales conveyed a particular archetype of masculinity: that of a capable pioneer who innovated and conquered in order to build a prosperous, ordered future in a land that first resisted and then yielded to his efforts.

As our engagement with the West deepened, grand tales of lone heroic figures emerged—cowboys, lawmen, rough riders, and of course, cavalrymen—competent, brave, and often violent men who could ride, rope, brawl, and shoot, bending men and nature to their will, and enacting what would come to be viewed as a nation-defining conflict between civilization and savagery. These masculine heroes of the West were charged with taming the wilderness, so that it might be drawn into the scope of civilization, although, as M. Elise Marubbio observes, these masculine icons straddled a difficult line, balancing their allegiance to the spirit of the West and their moral commitment to "civilization," maintaining a "tenuous existence on the edge of both" (113). Narratives of these hardy individuals were a staple of motion pictures from silent films through the 1950s, featuring cowboy stars that ranged from Tom Mix to Gene Autry, and again (in a more complex fashion) from the mid-1960s into the 1970s with revisionist Westerns. Television series and serials, taking their cue and often their plots from movie house stars and successes, brought tales of cowboy heroes to the small screen, in action and drama series such as *Bat Masterson* (1958–61, NBC), *Bonanza* (1959–73, NBC), *Rawhide* (1959–65, CBS), *The Rifleman* (1958–63, ABC), *Wagon Train* (1957–65, NBC, ABC), and countless others. While motion pictures frequently featured tongue-in-cheek frontier comedy, few small-screen Westerns prior to *F Troop* took a consistently comedic turn. In fact, only *Maverick* (1957–62, ABC), which featured a trio of witty gamblers, the genre-bashing hybrid *The Wild Wild West* (1965–69, CBS), and the short-lived *Pistols 'n' Petticoats* (1966–67, CBS) featured significant comic elements regularly across episodes. So, although domestic and rural comedy programming thrived in the early years of television, the West, it seemed, was serious business. For the characters of *F Troop*, a tale set near the end of the Civil War, however, it was anything but, and the interweaving of irony, satire, and parody within the series' narratives offered secondary meaning systems that undercut the prevailing template of televised Western melodrama, along with the myths and mythos that informed them.

In the midst of this multilayered presentation of the frontier tradition, the hypermasculine environment of the military is also continually a focus of *F Troop*'s characters' comic send-ups. The United States Cavalry, formed in 1861, fought in nearly every campaign of the Civil War and played a significant role in Western expansion—particularly in battles with Indigenous people, such as the Battle of Little Bighorn. Cavalrymen, stationed at forts throughout the frontier, were the main "peacekeeping" forces and were tasked with occupying the territory and protecting settlements, wagon trains, railroads, and businesses west of the Mississippi River from "Indian" attacks. As Robert Marlin describes, finding recruits for this "hazardous and sometimes fatal duty" was difficult, but it offered those who enlisted "a new start in life with few questions asked," and the ranks were often filled with immigrants, adventurers, and criminals. Thus, while the popular culture imaginary celebrates the hardships, challenges, and bravery of iconic frontier military peacekeepers, in tandem with the independence and ingenuity associated with life in the wilderness, the realities of those who served might be closer to *F Troop*'s ragtag characterizations than viewers realize.

Reception of the series' messages of masculinity plays a significant role here in other ways as well. Long after the lone cowboy hero had been replaced or overlaid by other masculine ideals, these archetypal popular culture images would persist in the minds of the series' audiences, who added their own contemporary imaginings of military masculinity to their estimations of *F Troop*'s cavalrymen. For some, these images were derived from World War II—the event that defined the men of what journalist Tom Brokaw would later term the "Greatest Generation." During the war, the cowboy ethos that had shaped earlier images of masculinity and heroism was, in large measure, replaced by a new group-centered model.

Virtually every unit was a mélange of soldiers from different states, different ethnic backgrounds, and different peacetime occupations... Cast into a sea of strangers, GIs reached out to those closest to them for support and reassurance: men of the same barracks, or the same squad. The career soldiers who supervised their training encouraged such bonds, knowing that—in combat—men fought and died not for their country or the ideals it represented by for the buddies on either side of them. (Jacobs 57)

This merging of hardscrabble working-class individuals—"rich and poor, white and colored, native and immigrant, urban and rural"—into a successful combat unit is, as Jeanine Basinger has argued, the *ur*-narrative of the American World War II combat film (46–58). For other segments of the series' audience, however, the "band of brothers" masculine archetype was joined by yet another, even more contemporary image: that of the Cold War hero. Educated, refined, and bureaucratic, icons of Cold War masculinity privileged intellectual over physical prowess; ideology over independence; discipline over ingenuity. None of these masculine archetypes could succeed without the heroic masculine figures of earlier eras, and each occupied a privileged space of their own that resonated with various segments of viewers of the mid-1960s, who were living through a war in their own time, in Vietnam, a conflict that historian Robert O. Self argues disrupted traditional American concepts of masculinity (17–43). As Self observes, the nobility of soldiering came squarely under attack as the fiction of the "mythic American soldier" was revealed and the morality of enduring and committing violence was openly and vigorously challenged (48).

Within the narrative space of *F Troop*, we see a genteel, educated man of privilege failing epically at the valued traits and behaviors of both the frontier cowboy and working-class archetypes as Parmenter pratfalls his way through episode after episode, constantly consulting manuals and history texts for solutions that should come from his gut. Similarly, the bravest and most independent member of the troop, Sergeant O'Rourke, straddles the line between civilization and wildness as he resorts to black-market commerce to get ahead, choosing to outwit and circumvent authority, rather than play by government rules. The scruffy, blue-collar Corporal Agarn, meanwhile, is exploited time and again by O'Rourke's wiles, bearing the brunt of the labor (and the consequences) out of loyalty to his friend.

The Pidgeon We've Been Waiting for

The complexity of these multiple masculinities highlights the extent of the effectiveness of the series' use of comedy. Parody, satire, burlesque, irony, black humor, absurdity, farce . . . all shine a spotlight on the human condition. The laughter they evoke, as John Morreall points out, is one of the most basic—and in many ways, difficult to control—physical and emotional experiences (2). We "double over" with laughter; it "overtakes" us. It is, as Henri Bergson contends, a vital force—not only a manifestation of personal energy, but a force that we can't live together without (124). Still, as theorists have observed for centuries, humor (and its functions for both the individual and society) is a very complicated and contentious thing: it can be both an expression of aggression and a means of building rapport; anarchic as well as a symbol of community; a sign of discomfort and a form of release; social medicine and social critique. Humor can be irrational, and it can do significant social work.

As an intentional elicitation of laughter, comedy makes use of all of these. It seizes elements of everyday life—from the socially awkward to the politically charged—and uses them, as *New Yorker* columnist Robert Mankoff observes, "as material within the larger context of dramatic form." The comedy of *F Troop* gently, but persistently, does exactly this, as it holds up both archetypes and stereotypes, points a finger, and laughs. Following philosopher Thomas Nagel, the series' humor points to the need to examine facets of social life and the human condition in a larger context, from a distance—in this case, both mediated and historical—in order to recognize their absurdity and incongruity, and then laugh.

The various performances—or mis-performances—of gender in the series provide continual platforms for such examination, particularly as they relate to heterosexual male physical prowess, economic success, assertions of power, and gender relationships (or "Can you fight?" "Are you rich?" "Are you in charge?" "Can you get the girl?"). Often, these are overlapping issues in the series and are questions that should be—but are not—made simpler by virtue of the series' regimented military setting. And therein lies the comedy.

It is a well-established fact that military personnel in the United States have not been well-paid in any era. Robert Marlin notes of the Plains Cavalry—men who enlisted at *F Troop*'s historical moment—that "A trooper started off at the pay of $13 per month. By the time he finished his first hitch and re-enlisted this was raised to $15. By now the trooper was a '50-cent-a-day professional.'" Little wonder, then, that cavalrymen O'Rourke and Agarn, created in the 1960s, would have secret revenue streams to pad their pockets (although it is unclear if Agarn ever sees much of those funds). Their ownership of the town's saloon, along with the wheelings and dealings of O'Rourke Enterprises, is a lucrative way to supplement a miniscule military paycheck and establish a form of masculine power not shared by the rest of the troop, in addition to serving as a major source of comic tension. In this, they are direct descendants of the "anti-organization man" figure featured in the character of Sergeant Bilko, of the *Phil Silvers Show*, where Bilko spent most of his time trying to make money through various get-rich-quick scams and promotions, and Quinton McHale, of *McHale's Navy*, whose moonshine and fraternizing with the locals are echoed by O'Rourke and Agarn. This theme would continue in Corporal Newkirk of *Hogan's Heroes* and reach its peak as political commentary in 1970 with the release of the films *Kelly's Heroes* and *M*A*S*H*. While these economic antics carried a significant amount of social cache in their narrative worlds—as well as in the worlds of their audiences, whose faith in government was at an increasingly low ebb—they were never quite enough to resuscitate the masculinity of the characters who played fast and loose with rules followed by others.

With the exception of the rough-and-tumble Sergeant O'Rourke, the misfits assigned to Fort Courage are also dismal failures as fighting men. Aches, pains, fears, inabilities, and disabilities seemed to plague many of the fort's denizens. Each of the featured characters is singularly unsuited to their roles, and skirmishes with both "Indians" and outlaws are only accidentally won. Vanderbilt, the nearly blind lookout, sounds the alarm and fires at turkeys and the plumage on women's hats, mistakenly believing that he has spotted "Indian feathers." Bugler Dobbs blows an unrecognizable Reveille and is frequently caught blowing dirt, feathers, and occasionally food out of his bugle when needed to blow a call to arms or Charge. Agarn, a hypochondriac, is routinely convinced that he is about to die; and Parmenter trips over his sword, his desk, hitching posts, reins, stairs, and occasionally, nothing at all. His men help him avert indignity time and again, untangling his attire, catching his falls, or racing after him as he is dragged through the dirt by a running horse. When Parmenter's doppelgänger, an outlaw called Kid Vicious, terrorizes the fort, the Captain prepares for a confrontation ("Wilton the Kid," S2 E13, 1966). Practicing alone in his quarters, he adopts a "shootout" stance, muttering "Kid Vicious, huh?" He then unfastens his sidearm holster, calls out "Alright, draw!," misses his gun, and draws an umbrella in its place (see Plate 12). Parmenter's clumsiness saves the day, however, when the outlaw attempts to escape, holding Wrangler Jane hostage. Stumbling over a door frame, he falls to the ground, accidentally discharging his gun. In good Rube Goldberg fashion, the shot hits the cannon wheel, causing it to collapse and fire, sending a cannonball into the water tower, and the jet of escaping water hits Kid Vicious, knocking him to the ground, making Parmenter a (still clueless) hero:

JANE: I'm so proud of you... You risked *your* life to save *my* life!
PARMENTER: Well, I suppose that was part of it. Also, I didn't want a civilian to get away with my uniform.
JANE: I've never seen anything like it. Wilton fell down, and the bullet hit the cannon, and the cannon hit the water tower, and the water hit Kid Vicious.
KID VICIOUS: Parmenter?
PARMENTER: Yes, Vicious?
KID VICIOUS: Lucky shot!

So Parmenter accidentally gets his man—and the girl—but all through no agency of his own. As was the case with his battle-winning sneeze, he is merely carried forward on a wave of happenstance.

Relationships with women are a constant challenge for not only Parmenter, but also the rest of the regiment's struggling men, who are either overwhelmed by beauty or browbeaten into compliance. Their attempts to assert masculine power are nearly always utter failures, unless the women involved grant them success (with a wink and a knowing smile to the viewers). Exotic immigrant travelers from Romania, Italy, and elsewhere are occasionally introduced to life at the fort, along with beautiful women from "back East," but all either take advantage of *F Troop*'s hapless soldiers or enlist their aid in snaring the *true* love of their lives. Maternal interference is also an issue: In "A Fort's Best Friend Is Not a Mother" (S1 E31, 1965), Parmenter's overbearing "cavalry mother"—and the wife of General Thor X. Parmenter—arrives at the fort and proves to be a far more exacting commander than her easygoing son. As she shadows him during inspection, she berates the men about their appearance, and chides her son: "I made an officer out of your father, and I'll make an officer out of you!," making clear where the true power in the Parmenter lineage is located.

The troops' power is subverted in other, larger ways, as well. While the canonical history of the frontier is an ongoing story of Anglo domination over

Indigenous people, the history of Fort Courage reads a bit differently. The Hekawi are peaceful, covert allies—and partners in O'Rourke Enterprises—who would rather exploit the white men than conquer them ("Hekawi lovers; not fighters!" Chief Wild Eagle asserts in a running gag). Together with O'Rourke and Agarn, the chief helps conspire to keep the fort just successful enough for Parmenter to remain in his post, staging periodic fake attacks so that the soldiers can report victories in their efforts to control the local tribes. While the cavalrymen provided the physical gags, much of the series' verbal humor is provided by the Hekawi, who frequently set up jokes lampooning Indigenous stereotypes, such as this exchange between O'Rourke, Agarn, and Wild Eagle:

O'ROURKE: Wild Eagle, my brother.
WILD EAGLE: You some brother. The still is still busted. How you expect Hekawi make firewater?
AGARN: We'll get you a new coil and when we do, stop holding out liquor for the tribe. Indians aren't supposed to drink alcohol.
WILD EAGLE: Who says so?
AGARN: Everybody.
WILD EAGLE: That's just nasty rumor spread by sister-in-law Sparkling Water! She one big blue-nosed red skin!

Other humorous moments spoke even more directly to audiences, with send-ups of their own 1960s culture, such as when Wild Eagle's free-spirited, beatnik son Crazy Cat (Don Diamond) frustrated his father by spending too much time at the Playbrave Club, or this moment, when Wild Eagle attempts to renege on a treaty:

COMMANDER: But you made that treaty in good faith. I was even told you smoked a peace pipe.
WILD EAGLE: I didn't inhale.

The tribe's vaudeville-esque camp was not only delivered by cast regulars but also guest "Indians" straight from the Borscht Belt, such as Don Rickles (Bald Eagle), Milton Berle (Wise Owl), and Phil Silvers (Flaming Arrow), subverting yet another Western archetype of masculinity: that of Indigenous people as embodiments of wild, untamed nature. As cast member Larry Storch relates: "We had all manner of Indians. All the actors may have been white, but we had Mexican Indians, Hawaiian Indians, Italian Indians. Anybody who could put on a pair of moccasins and some feathers was certainly welcome" (qtd. in Pegg 331). Together, the series' comic cast of Indigenous people successfully undermined military authority, along with the hypermasculine image of cavalry "peacekeepers" and "Indian fighters," magnifying the aura of ineffectual masculinity that already surrounded the fort's misfit soldiers.

Conclusion: Laughs That Last

Given that the ways in which we "do" and receive humor vary according to historical era, subject position, and a host of other elements, the persistence in popularity of *F Troop*'s humor is particularly interesting. Phillips and Pinedo have situated the series in a set of "pre-cult" programming—influential texts that possess a set of "mutually informing textual features, reception practices, and differentiation from the mainstream"—citing their humor and secondary meanings as signaling the beginning of television's cultivation of "interpretive" audiences that are now more the norm (21–22). A strong case can be made for capturing, in *F Troop*, a significant moment in reception, when television viewers learned higher-order interpretive skills. As a product of its era, it was transgressive—mocking authority, questioning history, cracking jokes involving racial and gendered stereotypes, and calling cherished institutions into question—and has, in several ways, become even more transgressive in the over half a century that has passed. The series, like many of its contemporaries, simply would not be produced today; and yet viewers continue to watch and laugh—but from a historical and developmental vantage point that further complicates those laughs. As Chiaro and Baccolini observe, a central aspect of humor is its social function, and one possible answer to the series' persistence in popular culture, then, is that it joins viewers in easy laughter about issues that are anything but easy (2). Over half a century later, lampooning authority retains a significant appeal, romantic relationships are still comically awkward, and the social construction and negotiation of gender roles is still complicated.

Another possible answer is that in capturing a moment in time when notions of masculinity are beginning to unhinge from American national identity and become increasingly contested, we get to observe the renegotiations, set to a comedic track designed to free viewers from experiencing the discomfort of drama. Classic Western narratives colored by the Myth of the Frontier are heavy-laden with binary oppositions, from civilization versus wilderness to simplistic notions of masculinity versus femininity. Blurred boundaries, as Jeffrey Cohen argues, create the discomfort of liminality—betwixt and betweenness—that we strive to resolve. Embedded in the comedic reimaginings of *F Troop*'s narratives, all of these complex notions become less uncomfortable and anxiety-provoking—because we laugh. And finally, as John Morreall suggests (56), humor is liberating, freeing us from what Robert Mankoff calls "the hegemony of reason," and allowing us to take not only norms, values, and authority less seriously, but everyday life itself. And so we continue to laugh.

Notes

1. Representations of race also figure significantly in the series' lampooning of masculine archetypes and in its larger camp framework, as well. For an in-depth analysis of race and camp representations, see Ken Feil's chapter (Chapter 12) in this collection.
2. Original screen credits cite Richard Bluel, but later arbitration gives full credit to Seaman, James, and Barnett.
3. For more on how satire and camp are related in 1960s TV, see Phillips and Pinedo 27–28.

Bibliography

Barlow, Aaron, and Laura Westengard. *The 25 Sitcoms That Changed Television: Turning Points in American Culture*. ABC-Clio, 2018.
Basinger, Jeanine C. *The World War II Combat Film: Anatomy of a Genre*. Wesleyan University Press, 2003.
Bergson, Henri. *Laughter: An Essay on the Meaning of the* Comic. Translated by Cloudesley Brereton and Fred Rothwell, Macmillan, 1913.
Bingen, Steven. *Warner Bros.: Hollywood's Ultimate Backlot*. Rowman & Littlefield, 2014.
Brokaw, Tom. *The Greatest Generation*. Random House, 1998.
Canote, Terence Towles. "*F Troop* Turns 50." *A Shroud of Thought*, September 14, 2015, http://mercurie.blogspot.com/2015/09/f-troop-turns-50.html.
Chiaro, Delia, and Raffaella Baccolini. "Humor: A Many-Gendered Thing." *Gender and Humor: Interdisciplinary and International Perspectives*. Routledge, 2014, pp. 15–24.
Cohan, Steven. *Incongruous Entertainment: Camp, Cultural Value, and the MGM Musical*. Duke University Press, 2005.
Cohen, Jeffrey J. "Monster Culture: Seven Theses." *Monster Theory: Reading Culture*, edited by Jeffrey J. Cohen, University of Minnesota Press, 1996, pp. 3–25.
Engelhardt, Tom. *The End of Victory Culture*. University of Massachusetts Press, 1995.

Jacobs, Robert. "Boy's Wonder: Male Teenage Assistants in 1950s Science Fiction Serials and Cold War Masculinity." *1950s "Rocketman" TV Series and Their Fans: Cadets, Rangers, and Junior Space Men*, edited by Cynthia J. Miller and A. Bowdoin Van Riper, Palgrave MacMillan, 2012, pp. 53–66.

Kich, Martin. *Pop Goes the Decade: The Sixties*. Greenwood, 2020.

Malinowska, Ania. "Camp TV." *The International Encyclopedia of Gender, Media, and Communication*, edited by Karen Ross et al., John Wiley & Sons, 2020, pp. 1–6.

Mankoff, Robert. "Untitled." *The New Yorker*, January 27, 2014, http://www.newyorker.com/cartoons/bob-mankoff/untitled.

Marlin, Robert W. "The US Cavalry." *History Magazine*, http://www.history-magazine.com/cavalry.html.

Marubbio, M. Elise. *Killing the Indian Maiden: Images of Native American Women on Film*. University Press of Kentucky, 2006.

Morreall, John. *Comic Relief: A Comprehensive Philosophy of Humor*. Wiley-Blackwell, 2009.

Nagel, Thomas. "The Absurd." *Journal of Philosophy*, vol. 68, no. 20, 1971, pp. 716–727.

Pegg, Robert. *Comical Co-Stars of Television*. McFarland, 2002.

Phillips, W. D., and Isabel Pinedo. "Gilligan and Captain Kirk Have More in Common Than You Think: 1960s Camp as an Alternative Genealogy for Camp TV." *Journal of Popular Television*, vol. 6, no. 1, 2018, pp. 19–40.

Pierson, David. "The American Situation Comedy and the Modern Comedy of Manners." *The Sitcom Reader*, edited by Mary M. Dalton and Laura R. Linder, SUNY Press, 2005, pp. 35–46.

Self, Robert O. *All In the Family: The Realignment of American Democracy Since the 1960s*. Hill and Wang, 2012.

Sontag, Susan. "Notes on 'Camp.'" *Partisan Review*, vol. 31, no. 4, 1964, pp. 515–530.

Verschuure, Eric Peter. "Stumble, Bumble, Mumble: TV's Image of the South." *Journal of Popular Culture*, vol. 116, no. 3, 1982, pp. 92–96.

Youman, Roger. "The Critics Speak." *TV Guide*. December 25, 1965, pp. 22–25.

Media

Bat Masterson. 1958–1961. Television Series. Seasons 1–3. USA: NBC.
Batman. 1966–1968. Television Series. Seasons 1–3. USA: ABC.
The Beverly Hillbillies. 1962–1971. Television Series. Seasons 1–9. USA: CBS.
Bewitched. 1964–1972. Television Series. Seasons 1–8. USA: ABC.
Bonanza. 1959–1973. Television Series. Seasons 1–14. USA: NBC.
Car 54, Where Are You? 1961–1963. Television Series. Seasons 1–2. USA: NBC.
F Troop. 1965–1967. Television Series. Seasons 1–2. USA: ABC.
Family Affair. 1966–1971. Television Series. Seasons 1–5. USA: CBS.
Get Smart. 1965–1970. Television Series. Seasons 1–5. USA: NBC, CBS.
Gilligan's Island. 1963–1967. Television Series. Seasons 1–3. USA: CBS.
Green Acres. 1965–1971. Television Series. Seasons 1–6. USA: CBS.
Hogan's Heroes. 1965–1971. Television Series. Seasons 1–6. USA: CBS.
Kelly's Heroes. Directed by Brian Hutton, Metro–Goldwyn–Mayer, 1970.
M*A*S*H. Directed by Robert Altman, 20th Century Fox, 1970.

Maverick. 1957–1962. Television Series. Seasons 1–5. USA: ABC.
McHale's Navy. 1962–1966. Television Series. Seasons 1–4. USA: ABC.
Petticoat Junction. 1963–1970. Television Series. Seasons 1–7. USA: CBS.
The Phil Silvers Show. 1955–1959. Television Series. Seasons 1–4. USA: CBS.
Pistols 'n' Petticoats. 1966–1967. Television Series. Season 1. USA: CBS.
Rawhide. 1959–1965. Television Series. Seasons 1–8. USA: CBS.
The Rifleman. 1958–1963. Television Series. Seasons 1–5. USA: ABC.
Wagon Train. 1957–1965. Television Series. Seasons 1–8. USA: NBC, ABC.
The Wild Wild West. 1965–1969. Television Series. Seasons 1–4. USA: CBS.

7
"Holy Fruit Salad, Batman!"

Unmasking Queer Conceits of ABC's Late-1960s Branding

Benjamin Kruger-Robbins

A first season episode of the television adaptation of *Batman* (1966–68, ABC), winkingly titled "The Penguin Goes Straight" (S1 E21, 1966), opens with the seemingly "reformed" supervillain emerging from a matinee stage production. The Penguin (leeringly played by Burgess Meredith) responds to his sophisticated and elegantly attired companion that the play was, indeed, "so superior to the thing one usually sees . . . a penetrating documentary of our times, a mirror of our cliched minds, of our sadly weakened moral fiber!" This dialogue, of course, echoes critiques of *Batman* as vacuous, commercially exploitative entertainment and mocks the types of educationally enriching programs that former Federal Communications Commission (FCC) Chairman Newton Minow championed during his tenure (1961–63). It positions "documentary realist" series as the province of "straightness," a boring and rigid masquerade from which the Penguin, *Batman*, and its "bat channel," the American Broadcasting Company (ABC), will surely break by episode's end. Regardless, Robin (Burt Ward) ponders in a relatively serious tone: "I had a terrible thought, Batman, what if the Penguin really has gone straight?" In line with the Boy Wonder's reasoning, the caped crusader's well-documented formal excesses, immature indulgences, and queer overtones ironically abetted ABC's quest for respectability in the mid-1960s. *Batman*'s well-documented queer/camp positioning, evident in the self-aware exchange above, contradictorily reaffirmed ABC's historical penchant for scrappy irreverence while also signaling the network's transition toward more mature, "social realist" fare.

This chapter discusses how *Batman* functioned as a part of ABC's competitive drive against the other two major "classic" broadcast-era networks, the National Broadcasting Company (NBC) and the Columbia Broadcasting

System (CBS), to push boundaries of acceptable denotative and connotative queer visibility in prime time. While academics and popular critics frequently cite William Dozier's TV adaptation of Bob Kane's comic series as a canonically camp anomaly, I analyze reception, production, and distribution artifacts surrounding *Batman* in conjunction with those relating to explicitly gay-themed episodes of the short-lived detective procedural *N.Y.P.D.* (1967–69, ABC). Such comparison reveals a dual marketing strategy that positioned ABC as an emerging venue for "quality" adult gay content while tightening the network's grip on "adolescent" entertainment for young families. Letters housed at the University of Southern California's Cinematic Arts Library illuminate some viewers' frustrations with both shows' social address to children and the perceived "insincerity" of the programs' queer/camp frameworks. Production memos from William Dozier's Greenway Productions collected at the University of Wyoming's American Heritage Center affirm ABC's "way-out" programming strategies meant to rebrand the network as risqué. In analyzing these resources, I seek to complicate and build upon television histories that locate class-driven appeals to consumers via "edgy" gay content as principally a 1990s phenomenon.[1] The chapter's first section employs viewer letters to relocate *Batman*'s queer "threat" to kids from the show's historically understood sexual suggestiveness to concerns about its juvenile "frivolity." Next, I address producer William Dozier's contradictory attempts to "legitimize" *Batman* as a quality production in official correspondence while basking in the production's campy "unseriousness" through exchanges with fans and colleagues. Ultimately, I link ABC's marketing of its superhero production with the more "serious" and "socially relevant" *N.Y.P.D.*, one of the first network television programs that denotatively engaged gay storylines, to forefront a cohesive strategy tying the struggling network's brand to "mature" queer content. In doing so, I maintain that the "niche" fragmentation more emblematic of contemporary television became an emergent force in the 1960s, one that sought to capitalize on sexual difference to foment taste cultures among presumably straight viewers.

Bat-Threats to Kids: A Reconsideration of "Deviance"

Much academic discourse on *Batman* draws on the show's unmistakable camp coding and queer overtures to historicize fears about its "corrupting" effects and gay influence on young people. Naturally, these writings, including Andy Medhurst's "Batman, Deviance and Camp" and Sasha Torres's "The Caped Crusader of Camp: Pop, Camp and the Batman Television Series" invoke psychiatrist Fredric Wertham's 1954 *Seduction of the Innocent*, which positioned Kane's comic book as a passageway through homosocial retreat into "deviant" sexual arrangements and juvenile delinquency. Academic treatments of *Batman* also consider how producer William Dozier and writer Lorenzo Semple Jr. bolstered the character's gay reputation through aesthetic and narrative stylization. Such analyses provide rich points of entry for grappling with *Batman*'s enduring queer influence but rarely account for the program's network positioning. Concerned parents and letter writers in the 1960s who viewed themselves as socially accepting New Frontier liberals may have accepted "boundary-pushing" homosexual representations in prime time but also regarded *Batman* as a "danger," albeit because of the show's presumed frivolity and commercial exploitation of children. In protesting *Batman*, many trained their vitriol on ABC's nakedly commercial appeals to young people.

    Scholars have appropriately tangled with *Batman*'s genre construction, aesthetic logics, and flamboyant characterizations to simultaneously analyze the show's appeal to children and its "subversive" qualities. Medhurst's influential essay begins explicitly with a reading of *Seduction of the Innocent* that seeks to reclaim *Batman* using Wertham's own derogatory language about queer coding. Medhurst positions himself as a gay child under the crusader's sway from the onset, explaining that "Batman hasn't been important to me since I was seven years old" (237) before later describing the TV program's "knowing" appeal. He writes that "[*Batman*] employed the codes of camp in an unusually public and heavy-signaled way" that rendered its gay qualities almost denotative, and he determines, "it was as if Wertham's fears had been vindicated at last" (244). Torres cites Medhurst's arguments in "The Caped Crusader of Camp" to underscore that, "*Batman* ... has been read by fans and producers alike, as a major setback in Batman's redemptive heterosexualization" (332) but fleshes out the program's marketing contexts. She recognizes an industrial strategy in *Batman*'s promotion that oscillates between disavowal of gay pretenses, most recognizable in Dozier's assertion that he hates the word camp ("which sounds so faggy and funzies") and tongue-in-cheek nods toward *Batman*'s ironic tactics of subversion, best encapsulated in writer Lorenzo Semple's quote that "on a very sophisticated level, the show is highly immoral because crime seems to be fun" (334). Indeed, the show delights in the deviant criminality of its recurrent villains, portrayed with flamboyant excess by queer-tinged actors, including closeted Cesar Romero as the Joker (Plate 13), antiwar activist/cabaret icon Eartha Kitt as Catwoman, and self-described "ambisextrous" (Stern 39) Tallulah Bankhead as Black Widow (Plate 14). While certain program personnel, notably Dozier and Burt Ward, attempted to downplay the show's queer tropes and amenability to gay reception, Torres cites others such as Semple and Adam West who recognized and economically exploited *Batman*'s non-straight valences. She quotes West as quipping in a 1966 interview, "with the number of homosexuals in this country, if we get that audience, fine, just add 'em to the Nielsen ratings" (339), a comment that underscores *Batman*'s simultaneous hailing of children and queer viewers, and one which brings Medhurst's textual reading into the realm of production.

These observations about "queer" excess and "childish" frivolity, however, are not exclusive to *Batman* but rather extend to ABC's 1960s branding strategies more generally. As Elana Levine recognizes in *Wallowing in Sex*, paraphrasing a joke among TV insiders, "ABC was the impetuous adolescent, quick to jump into bed with whatever attractive offer came by, unconcerned with how it looked to the others [NBC and CBS]" (20). As a result, Levine notes, the network profited off what one-time Vice President for Daytime Programming, Harve Bennett, referred to as "wild-ass" programs with exceptionally fantastical plotlines, over-the-top characterizations, and candied visual palettes ready-made for color television sets. Lynn Spigel refers to a prominent subset of these shows as "fantastic family sitcoms," and, while she discusses such programs as permeating the schedules of all three networks in the 1960s, some of her most counter-heteronormative examples are reserved for ABC fare. In describing *Bewitched* (1964–72, ABC), for instance, Spigel writes that the premise and weekly antics "inverted the conventional power dynamics between masculinity and femininity and, in the process, made viewers laugh at their own assumptions about gender" (225). Andrew Owens, whose study of *Bewitched* occupies a preceding chapter in this collection, has previously tied ABC's branding strategy to "occult" and "sensual" soap operas like *Dark Shadows* (1966–71, ABC), extending Spigel's claims to other television genres. In that earlier article, Owens emphasizes how the network, in its "attempt to move out of its longtime location in the basement of the Big Three, realized that corralling the interests of a more youth-oriented audience steeped in the sexy, supernatural fascinations of 1960s counterculture was absolutely critical to survival" (357). He recognizes in ABC's address a tendency to flout "seriousness" and "maturity" in a move toward adolescent appeal but also illuminates the network's efficacious queer overtures.

Selectively archived correspondence housed in the Leonard Goldenson Collection at the University of Southern California's Cinematic Arts Library reveals numerous predominantly white, married, and self-described middle- to upper-middle-income detractors who correlated *Batman*'s address with childhood delinquency. Letters from concerned parents certainly admonished ABC's "uncouth" positioning and expressed concern with the show's difficult-to-define "inappropriateness" but ran the gamut of political perspectives and geographic orientations. Mrs. James R. Wells of Omaha, Nebraska, for instance, expressed disgust with the program and prompted a "return" to wholesome comedy routines, writing that "when I think that the refreshing humor of *O.K. Crackerby!* [a rural sitcom] has been done away with for this sort of trash, I can only feel sorry for ABC Stockholders; you make me sick."[2] Mrs. Wells's critiques illuminated unease with perceived threats to social normativity bound to a countercultural "takeover" of network TV. Aniko Bodroghkozy observes in *Groove Tube: Sixties Television and the Youth Rebellion* that during the late 1960s and early 1970s, "primetime turned into an arena of cultural clash, political controversy, generational battle and ideological upheaval" (5) as networks attempted to lure profitable youth audiences to "edgier" fare. *Batman* remains somewhat ill at ease within Bodroghkozy's "groove-tube" paradigm, though, because of its polysemic (and indeterminate) address, which Matt Yockey refers to as a complicated "bat civics." Yockey writes that, unlike discourses of the more explicitly political and counterculturally aestheticized programs such as *The Monkees* (1966–68, NBC), *The Smothers Brothers Comedy Hour* (1967–69, CBS), and *The Mod Squad* (1968–73, ABC), "Bruce/Batman's tutelage of Dick/Robin stands in for a paternalistic relationship between state and citizens, reinforcing it for young viewers, lampooning it for adults" (18). Nonetheless, letters unfavorably comparing *Batman* with increasingly diminished "rural-coms" appropriately recognized the show's "fantastic and silly nature" as "reflecting ambivalence about the salience of particular national myths" (18). *Batman*'s adult cheekiness, for respondents like Mrs. Wells, eroded the clarity of law and order for children and rose to the level of social danger.

Other exchanges between viewers and the network, however, highlighted aggravation with *Batman*'s anti-intellectualism and overt commercialism as the dominant menace to kids. While Mrs. Wells's note pined for a revival of rural family sitcoms and more traditional family structures, correspondence between Nelson R. Kerr Jr., an attorney from Towson, Maryland, and Alfred Schneider of ABC raised concerns about the capitalist exploitation of kids viewing *Batman* and advances a declension narrative regarding educational TV. Mr. Kerr expressed alarm with ABC's legal skirting of an FCC advertising rule to air four minutes of commercials during the broadcast of *Batman*'s pilot episode (which Schneider justified using the excuse of color television's high costs[3]) to profit on a young audience. The letter condemned ABC for "prostituting the voluntary regulations all the other networks promptly followed," but unlike Mrs. Wells's laments, chastised the network for not living up to former FCC chairman Minow's "New Frontier" ideals. Mr. Kerr wrote regarding ABC's prime-time spate that "the area of desolation is still more vast, and the intellectual content so dry that the wasteland (which presumably supported some vegetative life) is now an arid desert." Mrs. Robert A. Thode of Wayne, New Jersey, reiterated Mr. Kerr's complaint in observing that *Batman*'s airing eclipsed news coverage of "two astronauts' safe recovery"[4] and a "decent 20-year-old's life snuffed out in Vietnam." The writer here positioned herself as an advocate for socially cognizant programming who ties *Batman* to delinquency. She presented the show's popular standing as a moral failure and "a dreadful reflection of our times." To similar but more personal effect, a fan note from seven-year-old Laurie Zucker of Babson Park, Massachusetts, to Leonard Goldenson offered an internalization of her parents' disaffection with *Batman*. She first mentioned "liking *Batman* very much" but then appears distraught at how her parents "laugh at it." Subsequently, the young girl requested that the writers "don't make Batman say stupid things like 'Watch Out [sic] Robin when you're crossing the street'" both because of her frustration with the dialogue's hammy "bat civics" ("mothers and fathers already say that and I don't want to hear it over again") but more importantly because of her parents' projections about the show's unseriousness and their derisive reactions. Zucker's enjoyment fell victim to legitimating tendencies to the extent that she contacted the network's head executive to try and change *Batman*'s "quality" standing.

Nonetheless, these diverse letters all tangentially engaged the queerness central to ABC's brand identity in the late 1960s and linked the network to childhood threat. Zucker, likely channeling her parents' qualms, begged Goldenson to "please make a straight picture on Batman," unwittingly using the same double entendre that marks "The Penguin Goes Straight." Moreover, the letters from Mrs. Thode, Mrs. Wells, and Mr. Kerr each positioned ABC unfavorably against its network competitors, with Mrs. Wells indicating that ABC's airing of *Batman* in place of Gemini VIII coverage would only help to "build an audience for CBS and NBC," a strategy that "worked for me." Mrs. Thode indicated that the other two networks provided "serious" breaking news bulletins during *Batman*'s 7:30 pm timeslot and, like her fellow letter writers, singled out kids as most amenable to ABC's social disruptiveness. All correspondents, apart from Laurie Zucker, refused to recognize the program's dual address and focused on what theorist Lee Edelman terms the "symbolic child," "a figure that alone embodies the citizen as an ideal, entitled to claim full rights to its future share in the nation's good, though always at the expense of the rights 'real' citizens are allowed" (11). The responses are complicated, though, by the authors' different relationships with countercultural politics, for instance Mrs. Thode's and Mr. Kerr's hunger for socially evocative television content. Alongside such viewer responses, Dozier's company (Greenway Productions, Inc.) forcefully sought to contest press discourses about *Batman*'s illegitimacy while winking toward its youthful fan base. Concurrently, ABC developed and marketed denotatively gay content to entice "quality" audiences dismissive of the network's more juvenile (though queerly coded) shows.

Bat-Bids for Quality

While *Batman*'s production personnel rarely exerted energy to contest their program's queer positioning, William Dozier and Greenway Productions did adamantly challenge discourses that presented the show as an example of a "wasteland" product. Their responses to unfavorable popular press articles chastised "elitist" considerations of escapist television shows but, unlike the more dismissive perspectives of 1960s showrunners like Sherwood Schwartz (who infamously named the sinking ship on *Gilligan's Island* after Newton Minow), Greenway also sought to reframe *Batman* as quality-TV-adjacent. Many of these efforts to disavow its "camp" or "cartoon" associations appeared half-hearted and designed around courting an audience for the show but, nonetheless, spoke to ABC's measured 1960s rebranding as a site for "edgy" but relevant adult dramatic fare.

Popular press outlets typically characterized *Batman* as dumb, escapist entertainment but grappled with its camp excesses as a potentially redemptive element. Uniformly, though, critics negatively contrasted the show against a purportedly lost era of intellectual TV drama. *Los Angeles Times* columnist Hal Humphrey drew explicit attention to the marketing prerogatives of Dozier and ABC, writing in a 1967 article that "Batman runs around in a mask but the producer William Dozier at least had the good sense to make it into a comedy of sorts ... high camp, low camp, burlesque, or whatever one may want to call it, Batman and Robin don't ask to be taken seriously" ("Justice Will Out on Batman, Green Hornet"). Humphrey posited in an earlier piece, however, that the show "stops short of real comedy" and suggested that it reveals "a come-on for junk TV" ("Batman and Robin: An Insidious Plot?"), leading into unsavory prime-time spates that included fare like *My Mother the Car* (1965–66, NBC). Alongside his contemporaries like Jack Gould of the *New York Times* and Lawrence Laurent of the *Washington Post*, Humphrey aggressively advocated for programming more akin to "Golden Age" teleplays and for the realization of Minow's early 1960s television-based prescriptions. In a 1966 article, for example, Humphrey mourned programs that he cherished as "memorable," even though "those of us who remember the 'Golden Age' with respect and longing are told by Madison Avenue soap-sellers that our memories are playing tricks on us" ("TV Golden Age Still Untarnished"). His list of notable television "authors" who were "lured away from television with more money and the promise that their work would not be blue-penciled by some ad agency man" included Rod Serling, Paddy Cheyefsky, and Gore Vidal; Dozier, with whom Humphrey seemed to have a contentious rapport but grudging respect, is absent from the discussion. Given the journalist's torrent of articles obsessing over *Batman*, however, Gotham's dark knight remained an antagonistic presence haunting the landscape of mid-to-late-1960s American television.

Numerous academics have provided social context for such laments about TV's deteriorating "quality" in the 1960s and uncovered crucial (but hidden) contradictions in such discourses. Michael Curtin, in describing how NBC promoted television news documentaries as socially responsible maladies to "popular entertainment," notes that trade publications framed telefilm productions, and action-adventure serials in particular, as "purveyors of blood, murder, mayhem and sex" (181). His account recognizes "socially conscious" programs like *The Huntley-Brinkley Report* (1956–70, NBC) and *NBC White Paper* (1960–89), however, less as examples of networks honoring public service mandates and more as marketing prerogatives. Regarding NBC, he writes that "news leadership had the potential to calm restless station managers" who were concerned about dismal ratings for the network's entertainment fare (182). Nonetheless, "NBC responded to ABC's [campaign to lure VHF affiliates away] by distinguishing itself as a network with 'balanced programming'" as opposed to "ABC's narrow gauge" (182). This public relations strategy resonated in the popular press where *New York Times Magazine* ran a 1966 cover story titled "At War with Batman," arguing that what reads as camp coding for adults produces deleterious effects in children. The author and psychologist Eda LeShan, referring to the same viewing situation as the letter-writer Mrs. Thode, derided *Batman* fans for calling into their local ABC affiliate stations and complaining that the program had been overshadowed by Gemini VIII coverage.[5] LeShan's first paragraph, though, presented the news decision as unusual for a network profiting off action-adventure serials, and the remainder of her piece contested *Batman*'s overtures toward social satire. In line with media scholar Victoria E. Johnson's determination that "responses to FCC Chairman Newton Minow's 'Vast Wasteland' speech also broadly indicate alliance with critical or regulatory discourses that questioned 'mass taste' in television viewing" (Johnson 91), LeShan advocated for deferring to teachers concerned with guarding civic principles rather than siding with parents who "don't see that it's having any bad effect" (115). LeShan's perspective, though, like that of Humphrey, still grappled with the possibility that *Batman* prompted adult-level social critique before ultimately disavowing its intentions as both commercial and juvenile.

Moreover, Dozier consistently engaged both press critics and producers of "quality television" in playful correspondence, indicating his desire to walk the line between winking camp and "legitimate" art. In an exchange with *Washington Post* writer Lawrence Laurent (casually addressed as "Larry"), Dozier chided the journalist for neglecting details of *Batman*'s diegetic world and teased him about not carefully watching a show "liked by the millions to whom it is intended to appeal" (Dozier, Letter to Lawrence Laurent). Nonetheless, the producer promised an amplification of the show's excessive features in the theatrically released film (1966), guaranteeing Laurent "four villains, a batcopter, a batcycle, a bat boat" but, correcting Laurent's earlier misidentifications, "the same Gotham City, the same police commissioner, and the same Catwoman!" Laurent's response reiterated the show's hit status, especially among adult viewers, and, like Humphreys's articles, conveyed a guilty respect for its pleasures, although with the broader caveat that "my companionship at the color set is dwindling . . . once I had a dozen kinds of children watching the color set with me; now I am down to one five-year old" (Laurent, Letter to William Dozier). He indicated, in league with his contemporaries, the status of TV programming as increasingly spectacularized and intellectually diminished but reciprocated Dozier's humor, indicating that the *Batman* film would be "[film critic] Dick Coe's problem, not mine" and signing off with a list of intentional misrepresentations as he bid his pal "Bill" "good luck with Burgess Meredith's Goose, Romero's Jokester, Gorshin's Puzzler, and someone's female civet." Letters between Dozier and Rod Serling featured a similar tone, as *The Twilight Zone* creator greeted his colleague as "Uncle Bill" and, in response to positive fan letters and requests for tapes forwarded by Dozier, sarcastically exclaimed, "Heartened my ass! Why couldn't *I* have thought of Batman?" (Serling, emphasis in original). The back and forth reveals camaraderie and fandom between television producers placed on opposite sides of the "quality" divide, as well as the capitalist imperatives bound to the network system's "prestige" programming but unrecognized (or elided) in popular press. As Mike Mashon underscores in "NBC, J. Walter Thompson, and the Struggle for Control of Television Programming, 1946–58," the teleplay dramas (some written by Serling) that Humphrey and others cherished were the consequence of the anthology programs' "ability to move product" for a corporate sponsor like Kraft Foods. Certainly, Dozier's self-aware correspondence with journalists and colleagues demonstrates that he (and usually they) was in on the corporate joke.

Still, Dozier and Greenway remained ardent defenders of *Batman*'s prestige in the press and positioned themselves as (perhaps fickle) proponents of New Frontier ideology, this despite official marketing materials that placed Greenway programs in league with ABC's "wasteland" staples. The producer's concerns about his shows' "seriousness" reverberated in a Humphrey column which quoted Dozier as worrying that "it may be because we turned [Batman] into a camp character that people refuse to buy *Green Hornet* [1966–67, ABC] or any other character in a mask who isn't treated the same way" ("Justice Will Out on Batman, Green Hornet"). These laments from 1967 followed an official ABC memorandum authored by Dozier called "The Facts on *Batman*," which stated, "we have heard to our horror that we are preparing a cartoon for juvenile audiences . . . when the fact is that it is very much attuned to millions of adults who can appreciate the humor and nostalgia of these incredible feats of daring" (Dozier, "The Facts on *Batman*"). Such official documents consistently reframed the program as civically minded, mature, and *intelligent*, a descriptor that Dozier seemed particularly enamored with. In one of his few archived responses to a fan, Ann Riopelle of Los Angeles, he commended her searing letter to the *Los Angeles Times* editorial board haranguing Hal Humphrey for negative coverage. Riopelle had rhetorically asked, "Is it possible that people enjoy watching *Batman* because they are intelligent?" before answering that "intelligence requires and enjoys variety as relaxation and because their [sic] thinking and imagination can cover a larger scope." Dozier replied directly to Riopelle that "yours is one of the most intelligent letters I have seen on the subject of *Batman*, and I have seen a great many" (Dozier, Letter to Ann Riopelle). Considering that Riopelle's correspondence also defended ABC and mocked Humphrey's selective disdain of commercial outlets, Dozier's response positioned the network and Greenway as covert proponents of intellectual TV programming, albeit unpretentious and unhypocritical advocates for shows that were also *fun*.

Certainly, despite Dozier's bat-bids for quality, ABC's principal marketing strategies and the producer's own rhetoric reinforced *Batman* first and foremost as a "fun" outlet for kids. A *Los Angeles Times* advertisement from 1966 pictured the dark knight surrounded by the bold-lettered, Pop Art onomatopoeia that appear abruptly during fight sequences: "Pow," "Bam," "Wham," "Zap." Most tellingly, though, the copy read, "Orbiting with *Lost in Space*" ("TV Times"), a family-driven adventure serial that cultural critics placed squarely within the realm of frivolous entertainment. *Batman*'s early-evening timeslot on the 1966–67 schedule, which overlapped with what Dozier himself referred to as "way-out" shows like *Lost in Space* (1965–68, CBS), emerged as a point of defense in Riopelle's letter. Despite her initial argument for *Batman*'s covert intelligence, Riopelle swatted at Humphrey for his lumping the serial program thematically in with "adult" prime-time entertainment and concluded, "let's take it at face value that *Batman* was put on as 'a fun thing'" that "young and old could enjoy as they once did family reading" (Riopelle). The statement implicitly absolved ABC, Greenway, and *Batman* of social responsibility *because of* the program's status as a commercial product scheduled for "family hour" entertainment. Dozier himself conceded in a memorandum about the future of television, written for *Variety* editor Thomas M. Pryor, that "television is *primarily* a merchandizing medium... it exists to sell product, [and] deplore it as we might, we must understand and accept it" ("William Dozier Statement"). This resigned stance, however, included minimal nostalgia for "Golden Age" programming and instead championed "good way-out shows" that would break imitative genre cycles. *Batman* could then function, in his estimation, as the best possible form of television within an exploitative system, a "conspicuous breakthrough in demonstrating that something fresh and unique can succeed on television and achieve high ratings" ("William Dozier Statement"). Dozier implored TV producers in his memo, though, to stop replicating *Batman*'s camp narrative/stylistic approach, this despite *Batman*'s financial reliance on ABC's "way-out" (or "wild-ass") branding and its proximity to similarly conceptualized action-adventure serials.

All this industry correspondence reveals contradiction and indeterminacy, leading back to *Batman*'s adolescent disposition and queer predicament. Jack Halberstam in *The Queer Art of Failure* advocates for productions catering to young audiences where "repetition is privileged over sequence . . . [and] mythic space forms the fantastical backdrop for properly adolescent or childish and very often patently queer ways of life" (119), a description that captures *Batman*'s aesthetic and narrative sensibility. Moreover, these imperatives punctuate many of Dozier's cheeky writings, only to be reined in by "mature" ambitions that eliminate in-between spaces of enjoyment and interpretation. The either/or proposition of selling, critiquing, and enculturating *Batman* as either a grown-up or child property recenters "adults [as] the viewers who demand sentiment progress and closure" (119), a project that ABC and Greenway flirted with to render the dark knight both "legitimate" and "straight." Dozier's conflicted correspondence and unwillingness to fully embrace *Batman*'s "way-out" orientation indicated an uneasiness with the "immature" queerness his program propagated. Indeed, this queasiness with camp address proved contagious; as the 1960s progressed, ABC continued its strategy to "evolve" as an outlet for grown-up gay programming while grappling uncomfortably with its adolescent identity vis-à-vis NBC and CBS.

N.Y.P.D. and ABC's "Quality" Productions

During the 1967–68 television season, ABC also aired one of the first primetime fiction programs to feature overtly gay characters, *N.Y.P.D.* In contrast to *Batman*, the short-lived police procedural appeared more akin to the types of programming that Minow, press critics, and other TV reformers in the 1960s championed. The socially aware but largely forgotten series tackled numerous fraught topics, including sexual assault, political violence, and, on more than one occasion, homosexual discrimination. Its liberal predisposition and semi-anthology format, wherein two lead crime fighters engaged a different case each week with a rotating cast of supporting characters, most closely resembled critical darlings of the genre like CBS's lauded and quickly cancelled *East Side/West Side* (1963–64). Moreover, *N.Y.P.D.*'s 9:30 p.m. timeslot signaled a more "mature" prime-time presentation, separating the crime drama from ABC's early-evening content. Nonetheless, the network engaged shock-based tactics to court controversy and hail "niche" viewers in ways that reflected *Batman*'s conflicted promotional discourse. The program's adult masquerade played into ABC's desire to maintain a dual address to young people and "quality audiences" while it rebranded as an "edgier" alternative to its competitors.

N.Y.P.D.'s pilot, "Shakedown" (S1 E1, 1967), aired to vitriolic response among some affiliates and viewers while simultaneously recruiting new "enlightened" fans for ABC. The episode used an unorthodox blackmail storyline to introduce its protagonists, Lieutenant Mike Haines (Jack Warden) and Detective Jeff Ward (Robert Hooks), as sympathetic and ethically motivated opponents of bigotry and social injustice who convince a closeted construction worker (James Broderick) to risk outing himself as gay to expose a gang of extortionists preying on homosexual men. In response to this framing device, James Brown, the General Manager of ABC's San Antonio affiliate station KONO-TV Channel 12, accused the show's writers of "reaching way out to try the shock treatment with a highly distasteful subject." In his letter to the network's president, Leonard Goldenson, Brown invoked his own children to lament, "I sincerely hope that you did not have to try to explain a homosexual to an 11, 12, or 14 year old, as I did," thereby reviving fears of queer influence that also surrounded *Batman*. Another letter from David Chapman of Los Angeles similarly described "Shakedown" as "filth," though principally because of the show's portrayal of police officers and its elevation of "East Coast" politics. Chapman unfavorably cited the gay plotline and its dangers to children but most emphatically claimed that "this was not a program dedicated to New York's Finest but to the degradation of them, and the supposed mire that New York lives in—New York being a mirror of the country." His letter called out "inept" and "childish" depictions of the police, critiques in line with Eda LeShan's earlier *New York Times* examination of how "bat civics" corrupted kids' understanding of law and order. Both Brown's and Chapman's letters, though, placed blame on ABC and its sponsors (companies that Chapman carbon copied on his letter to Goldenson) for explicitly marketing gay politics to an unsuspecting public.

Unlike much of the correspondence around *Batman*, however, *N.Y.P.D.* attracted favorable commentary from self-described "enlightened" viewers who considered the program a step toward "realist," socially aware TV. Michael Timchek of San Diego wrote, for instance, "I have, in the past, found the industry waning in the field of quality of production" and gushed that "it has been a long time since I have enjoyed so fine a show on television as your presentation of *N.Y.P.D.*" His letter to Goldenson intuited controversy but applauded ABC's audacious programming decision, noting that "Shakedown" would "receive a lot of criticism from the *unsophisticated* viewer who does not accept life as it is and dares not involve himself [sic] in such taboo subjects as [homosexuality]" (emphasis mine). Timchek here aligned himself with Minow's aspirational views on television and recognized an opportunity for the medium to "pull itself out of the rut it was getting into" despite the supposedly prudish tastes of "mass" viewers who preferred their programming "clean" and politically disengaged.

Moreover, ABC reiterated Timchek's line of reasoning in official correspondence, vigorously defending homosexuality as an appropriately *mature* subject for "educational" prime-time dramas. The network's director of the Department of Standards and Priorities, Grace Johnsen, maintained in her response to Brown's letter that:

> *N.Y.P.D.* is an adult show dealing with topical, adult themes of which homosexuality is one. The blackmailing of homosexuals is a distasteful subject, to be sure. However, the majority of problems encountered by police departments are distasteful. Yet they exist. It is our responsibility as broadcasters to not only entertain but to acquaint the adult viewer with his responsibility to society and in this particular show to *educate* him as to the function of the New York Police Department. (emphasis mine)

Her reply framed ABC as a pedagogue rather than a commercial entity and insisted that *N.Y.P.D.* offered a "factual" account of police activities, thereby departing from the network's "way-out" and "wild-ass" branding. Johnsen's rhetoric also hinted at an ethos of public service that Timchek advocated in stating, "I feel the industry is under too much pressure from the sponsors to conform to the not too sophisticated middle-class mind . . . it is a shame that those of us who enjoy a particular show have to be denied our pleasure because of ratings and statistics." Johnsen's "quality" defense of *N.Y.P.D.* differed substantially from Dozier's "The Future of Television" memorandum, thereby allowing ABC to court viewers like Timchek (who also cited the network's crime dramas *The Avengers* [US: 1966–69, UK: 1961–69] and *Hawk* [1966] as among his favorite programs) while profiting primarily off the sitcoms and serials that such audiences would have disavowed.

Amusingly, Brown's and Chapman's letters also indicated frustrations with the network's financial imperatives and charged that ABC used homosexuality as a "shock" tactic to bolster ratings. Chapman implored a boycott of the program's "profiteers" including Bristol Meyers's products Clairol and Bufferin and Liggett's Lark brand cigarettes, while Brown indicated that the "many, many very irate telephone calls from extremely angry parents" would invalidate ABC's marketing gambit. Despite the vitriol and homophobia inherent in their responses, both men illuminated ABC's marketing of *N.Y.P.D.* as "edgy" rather than simply "realist." A 1967 promotional spot for the police procedural emphasized aspects of visual spectacle over narrative coherence and prompted comparison with trailers for American International Pictures (AIP) films such as *The Wild Angels* (1966) and *Riot on the Sunset Strip* (1967) that were meant to entice youth audiences with anti-establishment stories and graphic depictions of sex and violence. Indeed, Bodroghkozy emphasizes in *Groove Tube* that, by 1967, the major networks were concerned about losing the youth market, which granted producers more leverage to develop series like *The Mod Squad* that "attempted to work through the moral panic about rebellious, anti-authoritarian, wild-in-the-streets youths" (164). The *N.Y.P.D.* ad, in line with Bodroghkozy's cultural observations, featured a gritty neo-noir voice-over from Jack Warden and languished in chaotic depictions of social strife, employing abrupt zooms and quick, disorienting edits to conjure a frantic, urban landscape. This teaser reified Johnsen's allusions to the "topical, adult themes" with which *N.Y.P.D.* sought identification but also negated her coy insinuation that "this show was factual, in good taste, and in no way attempted to shock." Rather, the show banked on a pseudo-subversive address meant to interpolate both a "quality" viewership disinvested in TV escapism *and* young viewers with a penchant for risqué material in prime time.

Notably, however, *N.Y.P.D.* received a lukewarm critical response, limiting the show's reach for relevance while bolstering its network's quirky, queer bona fides. Grace Johnsen's letter ended not with the public service conceits detailed through the bulk of the correspondence but rather by prompting

Brown to investigate middling "reviews, which, although mixed, [do not] criticize the aspect [of homosexual depiction]." As historian Stephen Tropiano notes in *The Prime-Time Closet*, the *New York Times* and other popular press publications commented unfavorably on the "Shakedown" episode's appeals to quality and realism. Tropiano writes that *New York Times* reviewer George Gent was critical of the episode and especially an exchange between the African American Detective Ward and the closeted victim Gaffer. Gent surmised that "the use of a Negro officer to persuade a homosexual that life is easier if one concedes being different from others was a very embarrassing grafting of different sociological concerns" (Tropiano 59). Johnsen's invocation of such press reviews in her response to the San Antonio affiliate station's General Manager, articles which she herself describes as unflattering, ironically undercut ABC's claims to verisimilitude and substantiated Brown's allegations regarding the program's shock intent. At the same time, though, the show's investment in delegitimated gay themes, stemming primarily from ABC's marginalized status rather than Johnson's allusions to respectability and realism, bolstered *N.Y.P.D.*'s and its network's queer resonance. ABC's flaunting of convention stood out particularly in relation to the late-1960s conservatism of CBS, nicknamed the Tiffany Network, which proceeded to cancel its counterculture-inflected *The Smothers Brothers Comedy Hour* in 1969 amid its hosts' on-air political interventions, and NBC, content to tread water with long-running Westerns such as *Bonanza* (1959–73) and *The Virginian* (1962–71) along with tired repackaging of 1950s episodic police procedurals like *Dragnet* (revival: 1967–70). Levine discusses such programming difference as born out of economic necessity, writing that "ABC had long been the butt of jokes among industry insiders . . . said to stand for the 'Almost Broadcasting Company'; its rapid turnover in series, which were quickly cancelled if they failed to perform, prompted the quip 'if President Nixon put the Vietnam War on ABC, it would be cancelled in thirteen weeks'" (19–20). The network's financial failure and necessarily "way-out" corrections compelled odd, short-lived series populated by characters that Chapman excoriated as "deranged, sick, vicious people"—Bat-villains in gritty drag.

Repositioning Chapman's and Brown's remarks in a more queer-affirmative manner, ABC's "trailing in respectability" demanded experimentation with fraught, unruly subject matter and provided counterpoints to normative considerations of sexuality. Tropiano, for instance, argues that "Shakedown" overtly "points out the hypocrisy in condemning homosexuality, while at the same time engaging in sexual practices outside the so-called 'norm' of heterosexual monogamy" (59). He cites an excerpt of dialogue that the character of Charles Spad, a liaison to the New York gay community, imparts to Lieutenant Haines and Detective Ward: "[you need] information about an area of human activity feared and abominated by our pluralistic, moralistic, straighter than thou—forgive the expression—body politic, so dedicated to hypocrisy that they do their own secret things and call it having a little fun and what someone else does they call perversion" (59). Such bluntness regarding heteronormative double standards applied not only to this episode but to a later installment of *N.Y.P.D.*, "Everybody Loved Him" (S2 E22, 1969), and, to more negotiated effect, a 1968 episode of ABC's *Judd, for the Defense* (1967–69), "Weep the Hunter Home" (S2 E7). The latter show similarly employed a grisly crime plotline wherein a presumably gay teenager is framed for shooting (without killing) his lover's father. The episode mirrored the convoluted narrative premise and "shock-based" use of homosexuality in "Shakedown" but also compelled the "victim," Lawrence Corning Sr. (Harold Gould), to confront his internalized homophobia while on the stand. Attorney Clinton Judd (Carl Betz) prods Corning Sr. to admit "closing his mind" to the reality that his son, Larry Corning (Richard Dreyfuss), pulled the trigger while defending his "friend" Don from the older man's violence. Despite its sensationalized and potentially exploitative elements, the program illuminated an activist angle that explicitly contrasted with specials like CBS's derisive, fear-tinged 1967 news documentary "The Homosexuals," which crassly reiterated social myths surrounding gay men. Moreover, *N.Y.P.D.* and *Judd, for the Defense* both positioned gay life within "everyday" contexts rather than reserving the subject for a singular TV "event." In these regards, ABC's marketing through narrative "shock" coincided with empathetic treatment of gay storylines on numerous series a year prior to the Stonewall uprisings (June 28–July 3, 1969), albeit as a financial ploy rather than a civil rights stance.

    These imperatives, I maintain, reached across boundaries of genre and breached binaries between quality and frivolity, fantastical and "real." Consequently, discourses undergirding *N.Y.P.D.*'s narrative and marketing conceits also revolved around queer threats emanating from an "adolescent" network, this despite the program's clear distinctions from *Batman*'s camp framing. Herein, *N.Y.P.D.* proved a comfortable fit with Dozier's enthusiasm for "way-out" broadcasting, substantiating his claim that "within the establishment of television . . . we can still do something original now and then, and even something thought-provoking now and then" ("William Dozier Statement"). Bromides aside, Dozier recognized ABC's corporate model as allowing, briefly, for queer ways of thinking to pervade mainstream television and disrupt long-standing correlations between reform, progress, and quality.

Conclusion: Mature Ambitions

Batman, *N.Y.P.D.*, and their industrial discourses, I maintain, worked to counter narratives of programming homogeneity and ideological heteronormativity across the three major networks during the 1960s. Indeed, ABC's marginalized standing prompted experimentation with queer-attuned programming and countercultural marketing conceits that positioned the network as simultaneously "edgy" and, in Dozier's parlance, "way out." This strategy, as I have argued, relied on ironic sensibilities and shock tactics to bolster ABC's adolescent standing while subtly reframing its gay-affirmative offerings as increasingly "mature." Even *N.Y.P.D.*'s more grown-up disposition, though, still reflected what Jack Babuscio identifies as "camp and the serious," wherein "the camp aspect of the work emerges in the calculated use of melodrama . . . [to accentuate] complex and interrelated themes" (129). ABC explicitly marketed the police procedural as hyperstylized escapism while engaging public relations rhetoric that elevated the show's public pedagogical ethos.

Still, it would be foolish to dismiss the seeming paradox that the network and its programming had "gone straight" using the cudgel of gay programming to carve an adult identity. Bodroghkozy explains that "by the 1970/1971 season, CBS, NBC, and ABC all touted their relevant 'with it programming'" (204), and she notes that ABC remained in a uniquely strong position for advancing youth-oriented political programming, given its 1960s strides. Nonetheless, she writes that such relevant "dramatic" fare faded by the end of 1971 as "it became obvious that the new shows were proving Nielsen duds" (225). While CBS went on to build a "quality" reputation via its Tandem Productions and MTM Enterprises' "relevance sitcoms," ABC's legitimacy in the early 1970s remained contingent on one-off "adult" productions like the 1972 movie of the week, *That Certain Summer*. Notably, that gay-themed film's marketing and press framing reinforced Grace Johnsen's earlier defense of *N.Y.P.D.*, with its Peabody Awards submission entry form describing "a unique departure from sensationalism . . . portrayed with restraint, honesty, clarity, directness, and startling sensitivity" ("*That Certain Summer*: Entry Form"). *That Certain Summer*'s critical success arrived amid and further anticipated a glut of "sensitively" handled homosexual storylines on episodes of ABC dramas such as *Owen Marshall: Counsellor at Law* (1971–74), *Room 222* (1969–74), *The Streets of San Francisco* (1972–77), and *Family* (1976–80). These programs adhered more stringently to the standards of "respectability" that Dozier paid lip service to during the 1960s but largely eschewed in favor of camp excess. Whether or not ABC's efforts at mature reinvention (at the expense of queer indulgence) were sincere, the Boy Wonder's fears about a straight masquerade taking hold proved entirely prescient.

Notes

1. Scholars including Ron Becker and Amanda Lotz have produced rich accounts that detail network television's (and particularly NBC's) appeal to a "niche" demographic of what Becker refers to as the Slumpy (socially liberal urban-minded professional) class amid increased competition in the mid-1990s. I contend that ABC forged a similar, though more covertly targeted, strategy as early as 1966.
2. The elimination of programs like *O.K. Crackerby!* (1965–66, ABC) from prime-time schedules to court more upscale, urbane audiences foreshadowed CBS's "rural purge" of popular country-themed shows during its 1970–71 season. The network abruptly cancelled long-running hits, including *The Beverly Hillbillies* (1962–71), *Green Acres* (1965–71), *Mayberry R.F.D.* (1968–71), and *Petticoat Junction* (1963–70).
3. Schneider's response first (confusingly) justified the extra commercial time permission by explaining that "the *Batman* format has already eliminated commercial billboards, certain promotional announcements, and reduced the color symbol and network identification [which commercial material in prime time customarily includes]" before rationalizing that "there was also an economic consideration involved, i.e. [*sic*] the high cost of color programming in early time periods as against the revenue that can be expected from the sale of same" (Schneider, letter to Nelson R. Kerr Jr.).
4. A reference to Neil Armstrong and David Scott's successful docking of the Gemini VIII spacecraft with the Agena target vehicle in March 1966.
5. Local stations could make their own choices about programming and, in Mrs. Thode's market, the ABC affiliate preempted Gemini VIII coverage with the "regularly-scheduled" *Batman* episode while the CBS and NBC affiliates aired special coverage of this breaking news. In certain other markets, such as those to which LeShan refers, ABC affiliates instead displaced *Batman*.

Bibliography

Babuscio, Jack. "The Cinema of Camp (*aka* Camp and the Gay Sensibility)." Cleto, pp. 117–135.
Becker, Ron. *Gay TV and Straight America*. Rutgers University Press, 2006.
Bodroghkozy, Aniko. *Groove Tube: Sixties Television and the Youth Rebellion*. Duke University Press, 2001.
Brown, James M. Letter to Leonard H. Goldenson, September 6, 1967, Box 37, Folder 1, Leonard Goldenson Collection, Collection no. 2242, Cinematic Arts Library, USC Libraries, University of Southern California.
Chapman, Robert J. Letter to Leonard H. Goldenson, September 13, 1967, Box 37, Folder 1, Leonard Goldenson Collection, Collection no. 2242, Cinematic Arts Library, USC Libraries, University of Southern California.
Cleto, Fabio, editor. *Camp: Queer Aesthetics and the Performing Subject: A Reader*. University of Michigan Press and Edinburgh University Press, 1999.
Curtin, Michael. "NBC News Documentary: 'Intelligent Interpretation' in a Cold War Context." *NBC: America's Network*, edited by Michele Hilmes, University of California Press, 2007, pp. 175–191.
Dozier, William. "The Facts on *Batman*." December 13, 1965, Box 5, "Batman" folder, Hal Humphrey Collection, Cinematic Arts Library, USC Libraries, University of Southern California.
Dozier, William. Letter to Ann Riopelle, June 16, 1966, William Dozier Papers, Box 8, Coll. 06851, American Heritage Center, University of Wyoming.
Dozier, William. Letter to Lawerence Laurent, June 2, 1966, William Dozier Papers, Box 8, Coll. 06851, American Heritage Center, University of Wyoming.
Dozier, William. "William Dozier Statement," n.d. 1966, William Dozier Papers, Box 12, Folder 3, Coll. 06851, American Heritage Center, University of Wyoming.
Edelman, Lee. *No Future: Queer Theory and the Death Drive*. Duke University Press, 2004.
Halberstam, Jack. *The Queer Art of Failure*. Duke University Press, 2011.
Humphrey, Hal. "Batman and Robin: An Insidious Plot?" *Los Angeles Times*, January 24, 1966, p. 22 (Part V), Box 5, "Batman" folder, Hal Humphrey Collection, Cinematic Arts Library, USC Libraries, University of Southern California.
Humphrey, Hal. "Justice Will Out on Batman, Green Hornet." *Los Angeles Times*, March 19, 1967, n.p., Box 5, "Batman" folder, Hal Humphrey Collection, Cinematic Arts Library, USC Libraries, University of Southern California.
Humphrey, Hal. "TV Golden Age Still Untarnished." *Los Angeles Times*, May 5, 1966, p. 18 (Part V).
Johnsen, Grace M. Letter to James M. Brown, September 14, 1967, Box 37, Folder 1, Leonard Goldenson Collection, Collection no. 2242, Cinematic Arts Library, USC Libraries, University of Southern California.
Johnson, Victoria E. *Heartland TV: Prime Time Television and the Struggle for U.S. Identity*. New York University Press, 2008.
Kerr, Nelson R., Jr. Letter to the President of the American Broadcasting Company, January 5, 1965, Box 54, Folder 6, Leonard Goldenson Collection, Collection no. 2242, Cinematic Arts Library, USC Libraries, University of Southern California.
Laurent, Lawrence. Letter to William Dozier, June 2, 1966, William Dozier Papers, Box 8, Coll. 06851, American Heritage Center, University of Wyoming.

LeShan, Eda J. "At War with Batman." *New York Times Magazine*, May 15, 1966, pp. 112–117.
Levine, Elana. *Wallowing in Sex: The New Sexual Subculture of 1970s American Television*. Duke University Press, 2007.
Lotz, Amanda. "Must See TV: America's Dominant Decades." *NBC: America's Network*, edited by Michele Hilmes, University of California Press, 2007, pp. 261–274.
Mashon, Mike. "NBC, J. Walter Thompson, and the Struggle for Control of Television Programming." *NBC: America's Network*, edited by Michele Hilmes, University of California Press, 2007, pp. 135–152.
Medhurst, Andy. "Batman, Deviance and Camp." *The Superhero Reader*, edited by Charles Hatfield et al., University of Mississippi Press, 2013, pp. 237–251.
Owens, Andrew J. "Coming Out of the Coffin: Queer Historicity and Occult Sexualities on ABC's *Dark Shadows*." *Television & New Media*, vol. 17, no. 4, 2015, pp. 350–365.
Riopelle, Ann. Letter to Nick B. Williams, March 14, 1966, William Dozier Papers, Box 6, Coll. 06851, American Heritage Center, University of Wyoming.
Schneider, Alfred. Response Letter to Nelson R. Kerr Jr., January 12, 1965, Box 54, Folder 6, Leonard Goldenson Collection, Collection no. 2242, Cinematic Arts Library, USC Libraries, University of Southern California.
Serling, Rod. Letter to William Dozier, May 6, 1966, William Dozier Papers, Box 7, Coll. 06851, American Heritage Center, University of Wyoming.
Spigel, Lynn. "From Domestic Space to Outer Space: The 1960s Fantastic Family Sit-Com." *Close Encounters: Film, Feminism, and Science Fiction*, edited by Constance Penley et al., University of Minnesota Press, 1991, pp. 205–236.
Stern, Keith. *Queers in History: The Comprehensive Encyclopedia of Historical Gays, Lesbians and Bisexuals*. Shoreham House, 2009.
Stone, Judy. "Caped Crusader of Camp." *New York Times*, January 9, 1966, p. 75.
"*That Certain Summer*: Entry Form," February 14, 1973. Box 83, Folder 72003 ENT, George Foster Peabody Awards Collection, Series 2. Television Entries, ms 3000, Hargrett Rare Book and Manuscript Library, The University of Georgia Libraries.
Thode, Mrs. Robert. Letter to the Executives of the American Broadcasting Company, March 18, 1966, Box 54, Folder 6, Leonard Goldenson Collection, Collection no. 2242, Cinematic Arts Library, USC Libraries, University of Southern California.
Timchek, Michael L. Letter to Leonard Goldenson, September 5, 1967, Box 37, Folder 1, Leonard Goldenson Collection, Collection no. 2242, Cinematic Arts Library, USC Libraries, University of Southern California.
Torres, Sasha. "The Caped Crusader of Camp: Pop, Camp, and the *Batman* Television Series." Cleto, pp. 330–343.
Tropiano, Stephen. *The Prime Time Closet: A History of Gays and Lesbians on TV*. Applause Books, 2002.
"TV Times: Orbiting with *Lost in Space*," *Los Angeles Times*, March 13, 1966, n.p., Box 5, "Batman" folder, Hal Humphrey Collection, Cinematic Arts Library, USC Libraries, University of Southern California.
Wells, Mrs. James R. Letter to Mr. Leonard Goldenson of the American Broadcasting Company, January 12, 1966, Box 54, Folder 6, Leonard Goldenson Collection, Collection no. 2242, Cinematic Arts Library, USC Libraries, University of Southern California.
Yockey, Matt. *Batman*. Wayne State University Press, 2014.

Zucker, Laurie. Letter to the President of the American Broadcasting Company, May 19, 1966, Box 54, Folder 6, Leonard Goldenson Collection, Collection no. 2242, Cinematic Arts Library, USC Libraries, University of Southern California.

Media

The Avengers. 1961–1969. Television Series. Seasons 1–6. UK: Associated British Corporation and USA: ABC.
Batman. 1966–1968. Television Series. Seasons 1–3. USA: ABC.
The Beverly Hillbillies. 1962–1971. Television Series. Seasons 1–9. USA: CBS.
Bewitched. 1964–1972. Television Series. Seasons 1–8. USA: ABC.
Bonanza. 1959–1973. Television Series. Seasons 1–14. USA: NBC.
Dark Shadows. 1966–1971. Television Series. Seasons 1–6. USA: ABC.
Dragnet (Revival). 1967–1970. Television Series. Seasons 1–4. USA: NBC.
East Side/West Side. 1963–1964. Television Series. Season 1. USA: CBS.
Family. 1976–1980. Television Series: Seasons 1–5. USA: ABC.
Green Acres. 1965–1971. Television Series. Seasons 1–6. USA: CBS.
The Green Hornet. 1966–1967. Television Series. Season 1. USA: ABC.
Hawk. 1966. Television Series. Season 1. USA: ABC.
The Huntley-Brinkley Report. 1956–1970. Television News Program. USA: NBC.
Judd, for the Defense. 1967–1969. Television Series. Seasons 1–2. USA: ABC.
Lost in Space. 1965–1968. Television Series. Seasons 1–3. USA: CBS.
Mayberry R.F.D. 1968–1971. Television Series. Seasons 1–3. USA: CBS.
The Mod Squad. 1968–1973. Television Series. Seasons 1–5. USA: ABC.
The Monkees. 1966–1968. Television Series. Seasons 1–2. USA: NBC.
My Mother the Car. 1965–1966. Television Series. Season 1. USA: NBC.
NBC White Paper. 1960–1989. Television News Program. USA: NBC.
N.Y.P.D. 1967–1969. Television Series. Seasons 1–2. USA: ABC.
O.K. Crackerby! 1965–1966. Television Series. Season 1. USA: ABC.
Owen Marshall: Counsellor at Law. 1971–1974. Television Series. Seasons 1–3. USA: ABC.
Petticoat Junction. 1963–1970. Television Series. Seasons 1–7. USA: CBS.
Riot on the Sunset Strip. Directed by Arthur Dreifuss, American International Pictures, 1967.
Room 222. 1969–1974. Television Series. Seasons 1–5. USA: ABC.
The Smothers Brothers Comedy Hour. 1967–1969. Television Series. Seasons 1–3. USA: CBS.
The Streets of San Francisco. 1972–1977. Television Series. Seasons 1–5. USA: ABC.
That Certain Summer. Directed by Lamont Johnson, Universal Television/ABC, 1972.
The Virginian. 1962–1971. Television Series. Seasons 1–9. USA: NBC.
The Wild Angels. Directed by Roger Corman, American International Pictures, 1966.

8

"We're Being Passed off as Something We Aren't"

Authenticity versus Camp on *The Monkees* (1966–68)

Dan Amernick

By January 1967, Mike Nesmith had reached his breaking point with *The Monkees* (1966–68, NBC), the sitcom that transformed him from an actor playing a rock musician into a real-life pop star. Speaking to *The Saturday Evening Post*, Nesmith addressed the lingering issue of the group's musical legitimacy head on: "The music has nothing to do with us. It is totally dishonest" (Sanders 539). The upshot of Nesmith and the rest of the Monkees' pushback against their producers and music director was that the four principals were ultimately granted additional creative control in the music studio. Consequentially, this took place at a time when such authenticity, measured by an artist's involvement in writing, creating, and performing their work, was becoming a prerequisite for serious standing in the music community (Lefcowitz 61; Stahl 322; Marshall 161). As a result of this (momentary) success, much of the Monkees' story has been whittled down to "the Pre-Fab Four" and their quest to be received as an authentic band.

The Monkees as a prime-time television sitcom, however, grappled with different ideas of authenticity than the Monkees, the musical act.[1] This is compounded by the fact that little has been written about *The Monkees* in the context of televisual authenticity and, more generally, scholarship on the band has overshadowed academic study of the TV show. For instance, the ways in which the group utilized the television series in their quest for authenticity, a revolutionary approach to television for that time, has largely been ignored. Moreover, in comparison to the scholarship on rock music, there is little consensus within television studies around what constitutes "authenticity." Issues of authorship and the presence of a laugh track, as significant pieces of those debates, are relevant of course to a study of *The*

Monkees (Bore 24; Becker 25; Mills 133). Yet as the group's simultaneous struggles with authenticity as musicians makes clear, there are other issues as well worth considering. A deeper examination of *The Monkees* sitcom in tandem with the group's musical output and ambitions provides an opportunity to reexamine the Monkees' personal narrative through the prism of their eponymous television series.

Over the course of two seasons on NBC, the four members of the Monkees used their prime-time platform to address their behind-the-scenes battles for control, incorporating several markers of televisual authenticity in the process. The general consensus is that the second season of the series initiated the Monkees' attempts to directly address their detractors. A closer examination, however, reveals earlier efforts, beginning in the middle of season one, to forge a metanarrative surrounding the group's experience in the entertainment industry. The band also used several episodes of their series to present themselves as authentic members of the developing youth counterculture. In addition, *The Monkees* sitcom sought a degree of authenticity by regularly positioning itself against the "inauthentic other" of prime-time television— the domestic sitcoms, TV Westerns, spy stories, and other genres that they deconstructed over the course of fifty-eight episodes.

The various ways in which the Monkees used their television series to demonstrate their authenticity as musical artists are worth further exploration. The resulting tension between fabrication and authenticity which these practices and strategies necessarily produced and that has been previously recognized in the latter part of the series' run should, as I will establish in this essay, rather be considered as a key aspect of the entire series. To that end, *The Monkees*' position within and contribution to Camp TV of the late 1960s can provide here a germane framework for my analysis.

History

In 1965, producer Bob Rafelson teamed up with Bert Schneider to create a potential sitcom about a fictional rock and roll band, buoyed by the success of The Beatles' 1964 film *A Hard Day's Night* (Sanders 530). Pitching the series to Columbia Pictures, where Schneider's father Abe served as president, the duo got the green light to produce the pilot (Lefcowitz 8). Out of the hundreds of applicants to star in the series, the final four were two former child actors, Davy Jones, best known for his role as the Artful Dodger from 1960 to 1964 in the stage musical *Oliver!*, and Micky Dolenz, former star of *Circus Boy* (1956–58, NBC, ABC). Rounding out the group were Michael Nesmith and Peter Tork, struggling musicians hailing from Texas and Connecticut, respectively.

Although all four were hired specifically as actors to portray members of a fictional rock and roll band, all had varying degrees of musical experience and ambitions. At the outset, Dolenz, Jones, Nesmith, and Tork were informed that their musical contributions were limited to vocals only (Sanders 533). Producers Rafelson and Schneider enlisted professional musicians and songwriters to handle the demands of churning out the musical output required, while the four actors focused on the TV series. This arrangement eventually rankled both Nesmith and Tork, who were lobbying for more creative input.

This desire for creative independence was further exacerbated when Rafelson and Schneider agreed that the Monkees needed to go on tour, in order to promote *The Monkees* sitcom, as well as their eponymously titled debut album, which had climbed to the top of the Billboard charts (Lefcowitz 54–55). Beyond simple promotion, however, was an added attempt to silence critics who were questioning the Monkees' legitimacy as a real band for not playing their own instruments (Watts 50). During a production hiatus in December 1966, the group performed their first concert in Honolulu (Sanders 536; Watts 50). The early tour was a huge success, but new conflicts arose when the Monkees' music supervisor Don Kirshner released the second album, *More of the Monkees*, in early 1967. The foursome was blindsided by the musical selections on the record, handpicked by Kirshner without their input (Lefcowitz 76; Sanders 538).

Nesmith had a heated exchange with Kirshner, leading to Kirshner's eventual dismissal from his position as musical director for both the Monkees and *The Monkees* TV series (Austen 60; Sanders 538; Stahl 322).[2] Following the confrontation, Nesmith held a press conference, where he famously announced: "We're being passed off as something we aren't. We all play instruments but we haven't on any of our records. Furthermore, our company doesn't want us to and won't let us" (Sanders 539). The Monkees achieved their goal of creative control on the group's third album, *Headquarters*, writing most of the music and playing all their own instruments. As a result, it was perceived as a watershed moment in the band's pursuit of authenticity (Austen 60; DiBlasi para. 7; Sanders 540). However, unlike their first two albums, *Headquarters* was not a runaway success, and subsequent musical efforts reverted to a compromise of sorts—the next two Monkees albums would once again utilize experienced studio musicians and songwriters (Austen 61).

Alongside their quest for musical creative control, the Monkees began another battle, focused on the creative direction of *The Monkees*. Although the changes to the TV series were more apparent between season one and season two, there was already an attempt during season one to address their critics while simultaneously deconstructing the whole "Monkees" enterprise. As the battle lines were drawn with Kirshner, subsequent episodes in the first season of *The Monkees* featured the boys being fleeced by unscrupulous music publishers ("I've Got a Little Song Here," S1 E12, 1966), unscrupulous TV producers ("Captain Crocodile," S1 E23, 1967), and unscrupulous teen magazine editors ("Monkees a la Mode," S1 E24, 1967). The Monkees themselves had not seized control of the scripts at that point, although the series' producers were aware of the growing tension, as demonstrated in these and other episodes from the latter part of the first season (Lefcowitz 91).

During the second season of *The Monkees*, Dolenz, Jones, Nesmith, and Tork used their newfound creative control to create an air of authenticity within the boundaries of the TV sitcom format. Most salient was the slow abandonment of the season-one "uniform" look of the group, in favor of more individualized hair and wardrobe, reflecting the styles and tastes of each band member (Bodroghkozy 68, 74; Sanders 537). In addition, Dolenz and Tork were both granted opportunities to write and direct episodes later that season (Sanders 537). *The Monkees* also began to incorporate more experimental aspects in both the aesthetic style and approach to storytelling as the season progressed. This chapter reads this change in the television program in relation to the group's efforts to achieve musical authenticity and argues the transition from season one to season two in *The Monkees* marked an attempt by the band to move away from the trappings of Camp TV toward televisual authenticity. However, a complete transformation was not attainable due, in varying degrees, to the conventions of the American sitcom and the success of the first season, and an inherent tension and even tug-of-war between the two concepts would remain throughout the series' run.

Camp

Fittingly, Susan Sontag's 1964 "Notes on 'Camp' " essay was reprinted in 1966, a year in which camp entered the national lexicon, largely fueled by ABC's weekly *Batman* television series (1966–68). As *Batman* made its January 1966 debut, early reviews and publicity made sure to trumpet the show's camp bona fides (Phillips and Pinedo 20, 25; Torres 333–334). Notably, Sontag's parameters for camp are at odds with the monolithic "So bad it's good" definition used to describe much of *Batman*'s output. Digging deeper into this area, scholars Phillips and Pinedo have developed criteria for Camp TV that goes beyond *Batman*'s pop art exaggeration, such as satire and intertextuality, among others (27–28). A particular challenge to television shows that wear the camp label as a badge of honor is Sontag's assertion that "Camp which knows itself to be Camp ('camping') is usually less satisfying" (Sontag 521). In the case of *Batman*, the series was far more "camping" than "Pure Camp," which Sontag categorizes as "naïve" and "unintentional" (521). Everyone involved in the production, from the executive producers to the prop masters, was in on the joke.

The Monkees arrived on the pop-culture landscape in fall 1966, right as "Batmania" was starting to fade, with a decrease in ratings following the disappointing performance by the *Batman* feature film in the summer of 1966 (Garcia 57–58). While *Batman*'s ratings were starting to flatten, it did have some stylistic influence on *The Monkees*' aesthetic. Both shows strived to be more visually interesting than standard TV fare, with *The Monkees* utilizing camera tricks, sped-up or slowed-down film, and unusual camera angles. Both shows were loaded with intertextuality, frequently referencing various contemporary TV series, and both took full advantage of television's merchandising opportunities. Aside from the platinum-selling records, millions of dollars' worth of Monkees toys, bubblegum cards, bracelets, comic books, and other ephemera were sold (Lefcowitz 80).

At the same time, while much of Sontag's criteria for "camp" were at odds with the artistic goals of Dolenz, Jones, Nesmith, and Tork, they were on full display in the first season of *The Monkees*. According to Sontag, "the essence of Camp is its love of the unnatural: of artifice and exaggeration" (Sontag 515). In line with this, the first season of *The Monkees* reveled in exaggeration, with the foursome "turning themselves into living cartoons by means of their broad, goofy humor" (Austen 58). The very nature of the Monkees' existence was artifice by design, with four actors simulating an American version of The Beatles. On camera, the boys pretended to play instruments as they lip-synced to music performed by top session musicians (Lefcowitz 73). Even early press conferences were staged, with the Monkees answering questions from Screen Gems and NBC representatives (69). This performative aspect of *The Monkees*, then, firmly landed the series in the realm of Camp TV, whether or not the participants were willing.

Authenticity

The dual nature of the Monkees and their existential struggle between TV sitcom characters and rock-and-roll band members leads to an interesting schism when discussing authenticity. Both the Monkees and *The Monkees* were painted with the same broad stroke of "artificiality," forcing them to grapple with the label of inauthenticity on two fronts.

There is no final consensus over what constitutes authenticity in the television sitcom. For example, David Marc describes "presentational" versus "representational" as one such marker of television comedy's levels of "realism" (Marc 17). *The Monkees* TV series was largely "representational" in this regard. The actors played their parts in a scripted narrative, a representation of the day-to-day existence of a struggling rock-and-roll band living in a Southern California beach house. More recent scholarship has focused on other aspects of sitcom production, such as the inclusion of the laugh track (Bore 24) or filming in front of a live studio audience (Becker 1; Mills 54–55). This particular research is underscored by disagreement over authenticity. Inger-Lise Bore found that viewers saw the laugh track as inauthentic, but were more charitable toward the inclusion of laughter generated by a live studio audience (Bore 25). Christine Becker, on the other hand, reported conflicting views over the authenticity of the live studio audience. Some production professionals defended the live audience as authentic. Performers such as *How I Met Your Mother*'s (2005–14, CBS) Neil Patrick Harris, in contrast, felt that multiple takes of the same material for a live audience violated the notion of authenticity (Becker 5). Critics, on one hand, strongly consider the single camera approach as authentic, yet many industry professionals continue to defend the multi-camera, live audience sitcom for its authenticity (6).

The Monkees as musical act has a more straightforward relationship with the concept of authenticity, as applied to rock culture. Philip Auslander, citing Lawrence Grossberg, distills the essence of the authenticity/inauthenticity divide to a distinction between the artistic goals of rock versus the crass, slick commercialism of pop (Auslander 4). From this perspective, the Monkees as musical group could never be considered authentic. Even if Jake Austen makes the counterargument that "millions of people saw them, heard them, were moved by them" and thus they were not a "fake" band (Austen 52), Auslander's idea of pop as "inauthentic other" (Auslander 4) automatically excludes the Monkees. Austen makes an earnest case for the Monkees as a real band, but his argument is diminished by his central thesis that any "documented band" cannot be considered fake, even a fictitious one appearing on a television program. Thus, along with the Monkees, other "real bands" according to Austen include the Partridge Family, the Archies, and even *The Muppet Show*'s (1976–81, syndicated) house band, Dr. Teeth and the Electric Mayhem (52). Much of Austen's argument rests on the notion that real musicians such as Elvis Presley and Motown's roster of singing groups did not write their own music and his case ultimately does less to build up the authenticity of the Monkees than to simply point out the manufactured nature of other, more respected artists. Auslander, on the other hand, more forcefully argues that "The Monkees could never be considered authentic, no matter how many live concerts they gave, because they were known to have originated as a synthetic, television group, not as musicians with an 'organically' developed history of live performance" (11). Many shared this view that the Monkees were a band by committee, the embodiment of Grossberg's definition of a co-opted art form (Lefcowitz 51). Other scholars such as P. David Marshall emphasize the role of creating one's own music as a definitive marker of authenticity in rock culture, a movement he claims began in the early to mid-1960s, not long before the Monkees' arrival. "The largest and most enduring transformation," Marshall writes, "took the form of a move toward performers' writing their own material and the related celebration of the singer-songwriter" (161). The Monkees as a music act once again meet the criteria of inauthenticity here, as the songwriters were clearly credited on the group's first two musical albums, even if the actual musicians remained anonymous.

As a hybrid product of television and the music world, the Monkees, a band created for a television sitcom, were directly at odds with authenticity. Auslander, again citing Grossman, discusses television as automatically "inauthentic," since television was viewed as part of the mainstream that rock culture, by definition, opposed and rebelled against (17). Through the prism of rock culture, any televisual attempt to narratively portray the music world would automatically, by nature of its highly performative artificiality, be viewed as camp. Despite the dual burden of inauthenticity as both a television sitcom and a manufactured band, the Monkees would ultimately attempt to prove their authenticity in both frameworks. As discussed later in this chapter, even during the camp first season, the Monkees, steeped in representational performance, were disrupting the schism between fictional characters and real-life actors. The ending "tag" segment (when episodes ran short) generally employed a more presentational style, with cast members giving interviews and the four Monkees allowed to address topics of the day as themselves, not their fictional sitcom analogs (Lefcowitz 52; Welch 37). In addition, the meta-narrative of Dolenz, Jones, Nesmith, and Tork's struggle for authenticity emerged during the course of the television show's first season when, as previously noted, a number of episodes dramatized the tensions between the foursome and the real-life entertainment moguls attempting to exploit them and forcing them to play their prescribed roles. The parody in these episodes was easy to read yet also occasionally crossed into an authenticity anchored in the actual experiences of the performers.

The Monkees Season One—Camp or Authentic?

The general perception of *The Monkees* first season is that of Camp TV, clearly legible in relation to the conventions set forth by Phillips and Pinedo: "explicit satire and the campification of aggressive political ideologies," "intertextuality and cross talk," "performativity and self-reflexivity," and "performativity and gender fluidity" (27–32). Episodes such as "The Spy Who Came in from the Cool" (S1 E5, 1966) are prime examples of the Camp TV genre, with all four traits readily on display. Along with their description of Camp TV, Sontag's emphasis on "artifice and exaggeration" (Sontag 515) is lucidly manifest throughout the majority of *The Monkees*' first season. Dolenz, Jones, Nesmith, and Tork willingly portrayed the artificial, fictionalized versions of themselves during these episodes. Although Micky's clownish mugging, Mike's wry deadpan humor, and Davy's song-and-dance man personas were exaggerated extensions of their real-life identities, Peter's dizzy naïf was at odds with reality. Scholars such as Goostree have noted Tork's real-life personality, which was more "articulate and intellectual" than what was ever displayed on the series (52). This schism between the Monkees in real life versus *The Monkees* sitcom characters places these episodes squarely in the category of camp, with exaggeration (Micky, Davy, Mike) and stark artifice (Peter) dominating the on-screen characterizations.

Beyond the personas, however, a number of season-one's other trademarks bolstered the show's camp image, including, but not limited to, the laugh track and the narrative-based musical "romps" that punctuated the episodes (Welch 107, 113). Furthermore, *The Monkees* did not waste any time employing familiar camp traits, as demonstrated by the third episode to air, "Monkee vs. Machine" (S1 E3, 1966). Notably, three of the four Monkees appear in drag, as well as dressing up like small children, part of a plot to sabotage a toy company's focus group. This is not the only time that the Monkees dress up like women, but this particular sequence sets the stage for the type of exaggerated "camping" that their disguises yield. First, Peter enters dressed as Davy's "mother"—adding to the camp artifice, a comic book–style bubble appears on the screen reading "Do You Believe This?!" as the two enter. Davy, as an overgrown small toddler, wears a beanie and shorts as he kicks their adversary, a heartless toy company executive, in the shins. After the pair wreaks havoc, their "replacement" arrives—Davy in drag, with Micky as the overgrown child. Yet another comic book overlay appears on-screen, "Possessive Mother," surrounded by a heart outline. Once again, the camp comedy is derived from the overly exaggerated antics of Davy clad in a wig and dress, and an adult Micky, dressed in the trappings of a young child, spouting lines in a childish "baby talk" tone. Finally, after the duo is removed, Micky returns, now in drag as the mother, with Peter assuming the role of the young boy, clad in a beanie and shorts. Completing the comedy trifecta, another title appears on the screen when the pair enters, reading "Send This Boy to Camp!"—playing obviously on the dual meaning of the word in this context (Plate 15). Given the cultural impact and mainstreaming of camp during the 1966–67 television season, it is no coincidence for the writers to acknowledge that in terms of going to "camp," Peter is already there.

The over-the-top mugging of the disguises encapsulates the first-season camping of *The Monkees*. The initial season routinely features the foursome playing dress-up in some form. Examples include Micky's drag act in "The Chaperone" (S1 E9, 1966), or the Monkees posing as little kids in "Captain Crocodile" (S1 E23, 1967). *The Monkees'* reliance on drag to denote itself as Camp TV reads as a logical continuation of *Batman*'s cross-dressing from the premiere "Hi Diddle Riddle/Smack in the Middle" episodes. In this instance, instead of antagonists being fooled by unrealistic disguises, Burt Ward plays henchwoman Molly disguised as Robin, jutting his hand on his hip to signify the gender swap (Phillips and Pinedo 33; see also Plate 6 and Video 1.3) ▶.

"The Spy Who Came in from the Cool," the fifth episode to air (S1 E5, 1966), is truly the standard-bearer for the camp first season of *The Monkees*. Here, *The Monkees* takes on the spy genre, as the boys are unwittingly thrust into a Cold War caper. A pair of bungling Russian spies, Boris and Madame, mistakenly pass along a stolen microfilm to Davy. Right off the bat, the episode incorporates explicit satire and campification of aggressive political ideologies. As in *Get Smart* (1965–69, NBC; 1969–70, CBS), there is a battle between the incompetent foreign spies pitted against the barely competent American "C.I.S." organization. Immediately, C.I.S. Agent Honeywell blows his cover in front of Mike while disguised as an ice cream man. Likewise, the episode is loaded with intertextuality and cross talk. In this instance, the foreign spies are portrayed as live-action analogs of *The Bullwinkle Show*'s (1961–64, NBC) Boris Badenov and Natasha Fatale. Later in the episode, as Video 8.1 shows, when the Monkees are called in to assist the C.I.S., Micky picks up the phone and calls "The Chief," while performing his best Maxwell Smart impression ▶. The intertextuality continues with a James Bond–esque cutaway sequence, with the boys getting their spy gear, followed by a martial arts lesson at a spy training camp straight out of *From Russia with Love* (1963). Later, Davy rubs a small table lamp, and out of a puff of smoke springs a blonde, harem-costumed genie (see Video 8.2). The Barbara Eden lookalike offers to help her "master," prompting a fourth-wall break as Davy utters, "Imagine that. Wrong show," a nod to *I Dream of Jeannie* (1965–70, NBC), which followed *The Monkees* on NBC's Monday night schedule ▶.

Performativity and self-reflexivity also feature prominently in the episode. Like many season-one episodes of *The Monkees*, the group performs for an audience of frugging teenagers at a discotheque. Near the episode's climax, after repeated failed attempts to record a confession from Boris and Madame, an exasperated Micky pulls out a director's clapboard and yells, "Spy confession, take four!" Lastly, performativity and gender fluidity are on display when Boris and Madame go undercover in hippie garb. Boris, clad in a mod, Beatles-esque wig, comments that "A teenager just stopped me and wanted a date." After Madam remarks that "teenage girls are very aggressive in this country," Boris sadly retorts, "It wasn't a girl."

The Monkees and Authenticity—Season One

As much as the first season of *The Monkees* was clearly marked by its camp trappings, the show exhibited an interesting tension between camp and authenticity even in early episodes of the series. A handful of interview "tags" aired at the end of several episodes, with the boys fielding questions from an off-camera

Rafelson, speaking as their authentic selves, detached from their sitcom personas. That said, the interview tags were initially motivated by the exigencies of television production, rather than an immediate response to questions of authenticity; these tags were tacked on when the episodes were running short and needed filler material (Welch 122). Moreover, the inclusion of Jones's and Nesmith's screen tests in the pilot episode "Here Come the Monkees" (S1 E10, 1966) was similarly a utilitarian move, as they were used to mitigate the negative reaction from test audiences (Austen 58; Goostree 52; Welch 28).

Nevertheless, as the series progressed, the interviews, initially devised as a functional device, allowed Dolenz, Jones, Nesmith, and Tork to speak candidly on a variety of topics relevant to the emergent counterculture.[3] In "Success Story" (S1 E6, 1966), Davy recounts an incident where he visited family back in Manchester, and his father refused to let him inside the house until he got a haircut. In "Find the Monkees" (S1 E19, 1967), Micky and Mike diplomatically voice their support for the Sunset Strip demonstrations, with Mike likening a 10 p.m. curfew to teens being told that they had to cut their hair. In "Monkees at the Movies" (S1 E31, 1967), Mike talks about a run-in with a reporter backstage at one of their concerts who questioned whether they played their own instruments. Mike defiantly responded that he was about to go onstage in front of 15,000 people, adding, "If I didn't play my own instruments, I'm in a lot of trouble!" These tags in particular work as a multilevel attempt at authenticity. On one level, they allow the Monkees to be themselves, unscripted and off the cuff. On another, the segments showcase the Monkees attempting to express solidarity with the counterculture movement, as well as tackling the issue of playing their own music. As much as the interview tags offer a window into the quest for authenticity, a handful of episodes address this theme as well, mirroring the Monkees' real-world power struggles in the storyworld of the series.

"Captain Crocodile" (S1 E23, 1967) was the first on-air acknowledgment within the show's narrative of a behind-the-scenes battle for independence. Here, the Monkees are hired to appear on a TV show, the (fictional) popular children's series *Captain Crocodile*. When the jealous host hears that the Monkees want to sing on his show, he sabotages their efforts to play their music, instead pelting Micky, Davy, Mike, and Peter with pies. As in real life, the group's musical ambitions were overshadowed by their roles as slapstick comedians. The thinly veiled commentary continues when the Monkees go to meet the TV executive in charge of *Captain Crocodile*, a ten-year-old child named Junior Pinter (see Video 8.3) ▶. Pointedly, Junior's father is the network president, an obvious nod to the relationship between *The Monkees* executive producer Bert Schneider, and his father Abe, president of Columbia Pictures (Lefcowitz 8). Just as Bert Schneider, along with Bob Rafelson, paved the way for the Monkees' creative autonomy, so it was with the fictional Junior Pinter, who promises the Monkees that that they will be allowed to sing on the show. In the end, Micky wins over Crocodile's young fan base by reading an improvised fairy tale about "The Land of Kirshner," another explicit reference to the behind-the-scenes power struggles.

However, the final episode of season one, "Monkees on Tour" (S1 E32, 1967), which was shot on 16mm film—a signifier of documentary realism at the time, was the most unabashed attempt at authenticity presented in the series to that point. Eschewing the usual sitcom format, "Monkees on Tour" instead went full-on "direct cinema" for a half-hour, showing a documentary of the Monkees arriving in Phoenix for one of their early live concert appearances. Aside from a pre-credit teaser sequence with Davy introducing the season finale and briefly clowning around with his fellow Monkees, the episode showcases the musician personas of Dolenz, Jones, Nesmith, and Tork; shorn of their sitcom personas, they engaged instead another form of performativity.

Beginning with a very "Beatlemania"-style arrival at the airport, with screaming girls awaiting their appearance, "Monkees on Tour" follows the group as they go through their paces during this stop on their live concert tour, complete with downtime at the hotel, promotional appearances at a local radio station, and some moments of quiet introspection from all four members of the group. As opposed to the artificial camp of the previous episodes, where the stories focus on the fictional, struggling Monkees, this episode offers the authentic perspective of a chart-topping phenomenon trying to grapple with their overnight success. There is a short sequence of the foursome briefly acting out their TV sitcom personas during an interview at a Phoenix radio station to promote the concert tour. However, this is only a small fragment of "Monkees on Tour." The final episode of the first season is significant for showcasing the authentic Dolenz, Jones, Nesmith, and Tork, intercut with preparing for the concert, and just as importantly, playing their own instruments in concert. Notable moments include Mike quoting Peter about life on the road (see Video 8.4): "Your life when you go out on the road turns into an endless tunnel of limousines and airplanes and hotel rooms, and all of the sudden there's one brief period of light, and that's when you walk out on the stage. And it all seems worthwhile" ⏵. In this instance, viewers of the show are given several opportunities to see this introspective side of Tork, at odds with the naïve, Harpo Marx–esque character previously portrayed. The focus on authenticity continues during the solo sequences at the concert. Consequentially here in relation to their quest for musical authenticity, each member performs a song of their own choosing, with three of the four Monkees playing non-Monkees songs.[4] Intercut with these individual musical numbers are solo interviews, where the boys open up and each reveal a side to themselves not seen in a typical episode of *The Monkees*. Tork goes on a contemplative walk (Video 8.5), admitting to the camera that he needs some quiet after all of the noise of the concert ▶. Nesmith reminisces about his childhood dreams of becoming a big star. Jones describes how disorienting life can be on the road, discussing how he woke up at 11 a.m. and proceeded to play with a swan for an hour (recalling a scene shown earlier in the episode). Finally, Dolenz is seen visiting the remains of a house that a man had built by himself, prompting him to reveal that he also wants to "make something that will last, something important, something I can say is my own" (Video 8.6) ▶.

Dolenz's attempt at authenticity here seems however to push the boundaries of performativity to the point where it becomes nearly as exaggerated as his camp sitcom persona and his child actor pedigree lends credence to the idea that this on-camera confessional was just another role to be played. At the same time, it is significant that the vignettes promoting authenticity—Tork's quiet, contemplative walk, in particular—consciously reflect a certain counterculture idealism. The Monkees were fully taking advantage of the formal and tonal shift in this episode to present something more attuned to counterculture sensibilities.

From start to finish, the behind-the-scenes look at the phenomenon of the Monkees in episode is a departure from the rest of the camp first season. Although "Monkees on Tour" as season finale did not usher in a new era of authenticity on the TV series any more than *Headquarters* allowed the Monkees to be fully accepted as authentic musicians, the episode telegraphs some of the compromise—and continued struggle between camp and authenticity—that would transpire throughout season two.

The Monkees Season Two—Authentic or Camp?

Just as the first season of *The Monkees* displays a subtle yet evident tension between camp and authenticity, the show's sophomore outing reflects a similar struggle, albeit from a different angle. Throughout the course of season one, the foursome fought—and won—their battle for musical independence, with this conflict playing out in specific episodes during the latter half of the season. If *Headquarters* was the apotheosis of the Monkees proving their authenticity as a musical entity, then "Monkees on Tour," the season-one finale, was a similar milestone in relation to the television series.

However, the freedoms afforded by *Headquarters* were short-lived. After a week as the number-one-selling album, *Headquarters* was knocked off of Billboard's top spot by The Beatles' *Sgt. Pepper's Lonely Hearts Club Band* (Austen 60; Lefcowitz 108; Sanders 540). Combined with the grind of the weekly sitcom production schedule, the Monkees were forced to take a step back from the driver's seat in terms of their musical output. Subsequent LPs such as *Pisces, Aquarius, Capricorn & Jones, Ltd.* and *The Birds, The Bees and The Monkees* were hybrid efforts, allowing for some musical independence but also reverting to the Kirshner formula. *The Monkees'* second season displays a similar compromise, where the Monkees were allowed more freedom to be their authentic selves, but only within the boundaries of Camp TV.

Some of the liberties granted were more focused on the group's appearance, for example. Commenters from both a scholarly perspective as well as the mainstream press emphasized the jarring transition from the group's season-one aesthetics to their season-two look. This appearance shift was most apparent in the season-two musical romps, which often featured the foursome in a straight musical performance, taking place on a set with a rainbow-colored backdrop. In these sequences, Nesmith resembled a budding country rocker, with tinted sunglasses, shirt and tie, and his long sideburns no longer obscured by his first season's wool hat. Dolenz's hair went from a straight Beatles style into a natural, wild and wiggy afro, and his wardrobe consisted of paisley ponchos. Tork was clad in love beads and moccasin boots, while Jones wore trendy Nehru jackets (Lefcowitz 103; Sanders 537; Welch 26–27, 104, 124).

However, the first-season uniforms never completely vanished, but rather shared the stage with the season-two countercultural looks. Early in season two, the Monkees' more individual styles were relegated to the aforementioned standalone musical tags, tacked onto either the beginning or end of the episode. For all intents and purposes, the "authentic Monkees" were kept as a separate entity from the narrative, at least during the first half of season two. Other cosmetic changes were the abandonment of the laugh track toward the end of the season and replacing the band's end theme song, "(Theme from) *The Monkees*," with "For Pete's Sake," a track from *Headquarters* written by Peter Tork with a stronger counterculture message (Sanders 527). Despite a shift toward authenticity during season two, the promise held by "Monkees on Tour" to showcase the real personalities of the group never fully materialized, just as the camp aspect—its Janus-like partner—never fully disappeared.

As mentioned above, season two of *The Monkees* attempts to distance itself from the camp image largely during the second half of the season, with the removal of the laugh track—at the insistence of the four Monkees themselves—as the demarcation point (Welch 103). As referenced earlier, scholars often point to the laugh track, fake laughter inserted as cues to prompt the audience when they should laugh, as an obvious instance of artificiality in television. For the actors on the show, the decision to excise the canned laughs was a combination of the continued desire for authenticity, along with their insistence that their audience, the "TV Generation," knew the syntax of sitcoms and thus already knew instinctively when to laugh (103).

Aside from audiovisual markers of authenticity, the late-season episodes make several attempts to step away from the camp Monkees formula. Although not the only season-two example, "The Devil and Peter Tork" (S2 E20, 1968) is the strongest instance of the Monkees working their personal metanarrative into the scripts. This episode is the logical successor to such season-one episodes as "Monkees a la Mode," "I've Got a Little Song Here," and "Captain Crocodile." In "The Devil and Peter Tork," Peter's desire to purchase and play a harp he sees at a pawn shop comes with the ultimate price—his soul. In the episode's climactic trial over Peter's soul, Mike makes an impassioned plea (see Video 8.7) ▶, using language that could have easily been adapted from the real-life battles between the Monkees and Don Kirshner:

> You didn't give him the ability to play the harp. You see, Peter loved the harp, and he loved the music that came from the harp. And that was inside of him. And it came ... it was ... the power of that love was inside of Peter. It was inside of him from the first. And it was that kind of power that made Peter able to play that harp. You didn't have anything to do with it at all.

The earnest, authentic nature of Mike's speech is underscored by his raw delivery, complete with stammering and pauses, redolent of cinematic method

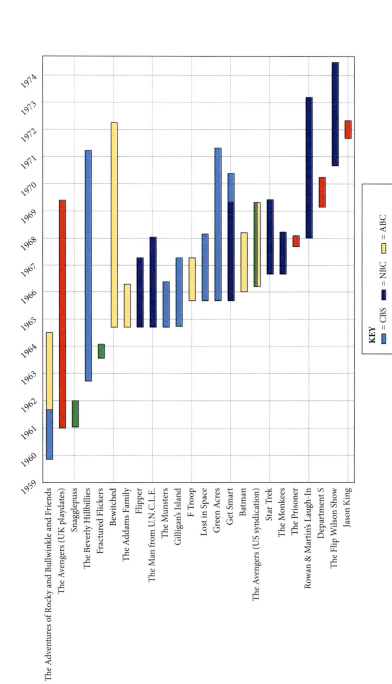

Plate 1 This Gantt chart represents the programming runs of the principal Camp TV shows addressed in this volume. The horizontal bar indicates the first run of the series, from initial air date to the last air date of an original episode (reruns played prior to cancellation are not included in this periodization). (Dates sourced from imdb.com. Compiled and illustrated by W. D. Phillips with assistance from Sumaita Hasan.)

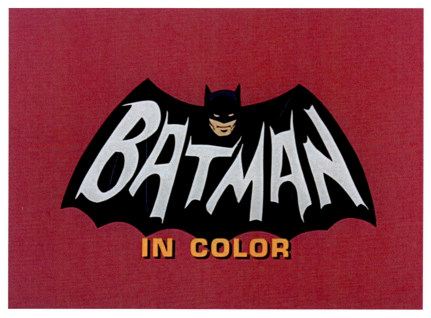

Plate 2 Advertising *Batman*'s color—even when the viewer's television was black and white. "Smack in the Middle" (S1 E2, 1966, *Batman*, DC Comics, Warner Bros. Entertainment, Inc.).

Plate 3 The campiness of the colors in the original image (upper left) is clearly lost in the black-and-white version (lower right). "Fine Feathered Finks" (S1 E3, 1966, *Batman*, DC Comics, Warner Bros. Entertainment, Inc.).

Plate 4 Peter Tork and Davy Jones of The Monkees as Frogman and Tadpole. "Captain Crocodile" (S1 E23, 1967, *The Monkees*, Screen Gems, Rhino Entertainment Co.).

Plate 5 Mike's masculine sideburns show clearly through his feminine costume. "Fairy Tale" (S2 E16, 1968, *The Monkees*, Screen Gems, Rhino Entertainment Co.).

Plate 6 Without mask (left): Jill St. John's Molly in Robin's costume. With mask (right): Burt Ward performs Jill St. John/Molly performing Robin. "Smack in the Middle" (S1 E2, 1966, *Batman*, DC Comics, Warner Bros. Entertainment, Inc.).

Plate 7 Cross-dressing on *Gilligan's Island*—and Camp TV generally—though effective within the diegesis, was rendered highly visible as performance to the viewing audience. "Gilligan the Goddess" (S3 E30, 1967, *Gilligan's Island*, WB and Turner Entertainment Co.).

Plate 8 Oscar Wilde. Sarony, Napoleon. *Oscar Wilde, Number 24*. 1882. Oscar Wilde in America, https://www.oscarwildeinamerica.org/sarony/sarony-photographs-of-oscar-wilde-1882.html.

Plate 9 Snagglepuss in his Oscar Wilde–inspired accessories. "Major Operation" (S1 E1, 1961, *The Yogi Bear Show*, Screen Gems).

Plate 10 Endora's (Agnes Moorehead) camp femininity in *Bewitched*. "A Very Special Delivery" (S2 E2, 1965, CPT Holdings, Inc.).

Plate 11 *Bewitched*'s practical joker, Uncle Arthur's (Paul Lynde) head appears under the dome lid of a silver serving platter: "Forgive me for not rising but I'm up to my neck in work." "The Joker Is a Card" (S2 E5, 1965, CPT Holdings, Inc.).

Plate 12 A bumbling Parmenter draws an umbrella instead of his gun in "Wilton the Kid" (S2 E13, 1966, *F Troop*, Warner Bros.).

Plate 13 Cesar Romero strikes a grinning pose in "The Joker's Epitaph" (S2 E48, 1967, *Batman*, DC Comics, Warner Bros. Entertainment, Inc.).

Plate 14 Tallulah Bankhead's Black Widow, flanked by her adversaries—Adam West's Batman and Burt Ward's Robin—basks in her own reflection. "Caught in the Spider's Den" (S2 E56, 1967, *Batman*, DC Comics, Warner Bros. Entertainment, Inc.).

Plate 15 As Mike Nesmith looks on, Micky Dolenz and Peter Tork try to pass themselves off as mother and son in a season-one embrace of camp. "Monkee vs. Machine" (S1 E3, 1966, *The Monkees*, Screen Gems, Rhino Entertainment Co.).

Plate 16 The hypnotic Frodis trance coming from the Monkees' TV set—looking eerily similar to rival network CBS's eye logo. "The Frodis Caper aka Mijacogeo" (S2 E26, 1968, *The Monkees*, Screen Gems, Rhino Entertainment Co.).

Plate 17 Number Six (Patrick McGoohan) looks on at the kitsch and camp mise-en-scène of The Village. "Arrival" (S1 E1, 1967, *The Prisoner*, ITC, Granada International Media Limited).

Plate 18 Steed (Patrick McNee) and Mrs. Peel (Diana Rigg) drink champagne as part of *The Avengers* Season 5 opening titles (S5, 1967, *The Avengers*, Associated British Corporation).

Plate 19 Peter Wyngarde demonstrates the performance of masculinity and "macho drag." "The Shift That Never Was" (S1 E15, 1969, *Department S*, ITC).

Plate 20 As the tribbles fall and bury Captain Kirk, the comedic value of the scene is heightened by Fielding's musical representation of the tribbles. "The Trouble with Tribbles" (S2 E15, 1967, *Star Trek*, ViacomCBS).

Plate 21 "Nice lookin' boy you got there." "Dolphin in Pursuit: Part Two" (S2 E3, 1965, *Flipper*, MGM Television in association with Ivan Tors Films, Inc.).

Plate 22 Flipper is able to track down the speedy lobster and return the bracelet. "The Most Expensive Sardine in the World" (S3 E16, 1967, *Flipper*, MGM Television in association with Ivan Tors Films, Inc.).

Plate 23 The gem-clad turtle owned by Des Esseintes, protagonist of Joris-Karl Huysmans's novel *À rebours* (1884). Auguste Lepère, wood engraving in Joris-Karl Huysmans, *À rebours: Deux-cent-vignt Gravures sur bois en Couleurs d'Auguste Lepère*. Paris, Le Cent Bibliophiles, 1903.

Plate 24 Flip Wilson guesting on *Rowan & Martin's Laugh-In*. Wilson's camp style overcomes that of Alan Sues (the show's resident "sissy") in a brief sketch that skewers the racist assumptions of Hollywood (S2 E6, 1968, *Rowan & Martin's Laugh-In*, Time Life).

Plate 25 A notoriously untelegenic politician, Nixon made a cameo appearance on *Rowan & Martin's Laugh-In*, where he stiltedly uttered, "Sock it to me?" (S2 E1, 1968, *Rowan & Martin's Laugh-In*, Time Life).

acting, giving it an authenticity that contrasted with most of season-one's output as well as most of the sitcom product of the era.

The final episode to air, "The Frodis Caper aka Mijacogeo" (S2 E26, 1968), is the zenith of the Monkees' on-air creative freedom, bookending the attempts at authenticity explicitly depicted in "Monkees on Tour." Although some of the goofier antics would have fit in during season one, "The Frodis Caper," written and directed by Micky Dolenz, ultimately surrenders the camp trappings to the framework of authenticity. The episode is notable for its lack of laugh track, as well as its use again of 16mm film as opposed to the 35mm of the rest of the series (aside from "Monkees on Tour"). Although the episode resorts to the series' usual film tricks and has the Monkees facing off against a typical "villain of the week," Dolenz as the episode's director-cum-auteur manages to include more pointed commentary about *The Monkees* and the television industry while also incorporating blatant nods to the counterculture. In the episode, Peter, along with everyone else in the neighborhood, has been put into a trance by a strange signal coming from the TV set (Video 8.8) ▶. In a none-too-subtle jab at their rival network, the signal on the set is a clear reference to the CBS "eye" logo (Plate 16). The Monkees attempt to find out the cause of the trance, facing off against the campy Wizard Glick, played by Rip Taylor in a performance that lands somewhere between a season-three *Batman* villain and a character from the world of Sid and Marty Krofft.

This motif of authenticity existing within *The Monkees* formula continues with the climactic chase scene, a "Typical Monkees Romp" (as the title card reads), which is anything but typical. Although the Monkees run around in a slow-motion chase evocative of their first-season romps, instead of the usual commercial top-40 fare playing in the background, we hear the anti-war ballad "Zor and Zam." Hammering home this last-ditch effort at authenticity on the series' part, the episode tag continues a late-series tradition of allowing a member of the group to showcase another musician. Previous tags featured Davy with composer Charlie Smalls, and Mike with musician Frank Zappa.[5] In "The Frodis Caper," an off-camera Micky introduces progressive rocker Timothy Buckley, who performs "Song to the Siren" on acoustic guitar. Concluding *The Monkees*, a series created to sell the records of a "manufactured band," with an acoustic performance by a respected member of the counterculture was a fitting send-off for a group that struggled to prove its authenticity. Like "Monkees on Tour," the series' final moments once again attempted to show the world that there was more to the Monkees—and *The*

Monkees—than the music and image concocted by Rafelson, Schneider, Kirshner, and the rest.

Conclusion

Like the Monkees' musical legacy, the television legacy of *The Monkees* sitcom is complex and worthy of close analysis. Although there is a clear delineation between the camp season one and the more authentic season two, what this chapter has argued is that the tension between these two modes was never fully resolved, with the first season making several bold attempts to incorporate authentic aspects of the Monkees' real lives and the second season never fully abandoning the show's connections to Camp TV. The surface elements of season two such as the revamped wardrobe, the removal of the laugh track, and the Tork-penned closing song help perpetuate the notion that the series made an abrupt shift, but closer analysis reveals far more nuance. Just as the musical Monkees struggled with artistic compromise for their albums, *The Monkees* as a show, to the very end, reflected a strained coexistence between the over-the-top artifice of camp and the quest for authenticity.

Notes

1. This practice of italicizing the television program but not the band follows convention and will be employed throughout this chapter.
2. Despite the success of *More of the Monkees*, Kirshner sealed his fate by ignoring Rafelson and Schneider's demand to put Nesmith's "The Girl I Knew Somewhere" on the B-side of the single "A Little Bit Me, A Little Bit You." Kirshner's actions placed him in violation of his contract, and he was summarily fired from *The Monkees* and Columbia–Screen Gems (Lefcowitz 93, 95).
3. These tags, which spoke to events of the moment, were excised from syndicated reruns, most likely due to a combination of the time constraints of longer commercial pods, along with the tags' dated topicality.
4. Tork performs the bluegrass standard "Cripple Creek" on banjo, Nesmith—without his signature Monkees' wool hat—performs Bo Diddley's "You Can't Judge a Book by the Cover," and Dolenz sings Ray Charles' "I Got a Woman" while performing an homage to James Brown, complete with cape. Notably, Jones is the one member of the group who maintains his TV show image, singing "I Wanna Be Free" from their debut album.

5. Smalls appears in "Some Like It Lukewarm" (S2 E24, 1968) and Zappa appears in "The Monkees Blow Their Minds" (S2 E25, 1968).

Bibliography

Auslander, Peter. "Seeing Is Believing: Live Performance and the Discourse of Authenticity in Rock Culture." *Literature and Psychology*, vol. 44, no. 4, 1998, pp. 1–26.

Austen, Jake. *TV-a-Go-Go Rock on TV from American Bandstand to American Idol*. Chicago Review Press, 2005.

Becker, Christine. "Acting for the Cameras: Performance in the Multi-Camera Sitcom." *Mediascape*, Spring 2008, 1–11.

Bodroghkozy, Aniko. *Groove Tube: Sixties Television and the Youth Rebellion*. Duke University Press, 2001.

Bore, Inger-Lise K. "Laughing Together? TV Comedy Audiences and the Laugh Track." *Velvet Light Trap*, no. 68, 2011, pp. 24–34.

Coates, Norma. "Filling in Holes: Television Music as a Recuperation of Popular Music on Television." *Music, Sound and the Moving Image*, vol. 1, no. 1, 2007, pp. 21–25.

Eisner, Joel. *The Official Batman Batbook: The Revised Edition*. AuthorHouse, 2008.

Garcia, Bob. "Camping Up the Comics: Batman." *Cinefantastique*, vol. 24, no. 6/vol. 25, no. 1, 1994, pp. 8–63.

Garcia, Bob, and Joe Desris. *Batman: A Celebration of the Classic TV Series*. Titan Books, 2016.

Goostree, Laura. "The Monkees and the Deconstruction of Television Realism." *Journal of Popular Film & Television*, vol. 16, no. 2, 1988, pp. 50–58.

Kitch, Carolyn. "Anniversary Journalism, Collective Memory, and the Cultural Authority to Tell the Story of the American Past." *Journal of Popular Culture*, vol. 36, no. 1, 2002, pp. 44–67.

Lefcowitz, Eric. *Monkee Business: The Revolutionary Made-for-TV Band*. Retrofuture Products, 2013.

Lury, Karen. "Chewing Gum for the Ears: Children's Television and Popular Music." *Popular Music*, vol. 21, no. 3, 2002, pp. 291–305.

Marc, David. *Comic Visions: Television Comedy and American Culture*. Unwin Hyman, 1989.

Marshall, P. David. *Celebrity and Power: Fame in Contemporary Culture*. University of Minnesota Press, 1997.

Mills, Brett. *The Sitcom*. Edinburgh University Press, 2009.

Phillips, W. D., and Isabel Pinedo. "Gilligan and Captain Kirk Have More in Common Than You Think: 1960s Camp TV as an Alternative Genealogy for Cult Television." *Journal of Popular Television*, vol. 6, no. 1, 2018, pp. 19–40.

Raesch, Monika. "'Let Me Put It This Way: It Works for Me': An Interview with Bob Rafelson." *Journal of Film and Video*, vol. 65, no. 3, 2013, pp. 49–55.

Robinson, Michael, and Timothy Winkle. "The Innocents Abroad: S Club 7's America." *Popular Music and Society*, vol. 27, no. 3, 2004, pp. 291–305.

Sanders, Maria. "Singing Machines: Boy Bands and the Struggle for Artistic Legitimacy." *Cardozo Arts & Entertainment Law Journal*, vol. 20, no. 3, 2002, pp. 525–587.

Scheurer, Timothy. "The Beatles, the Brill Building, and the Persistence of Tin Pan Alley in the Age of Rock." *Popular Music and Society*, vol. 20, no. 4, 1996, pp. 89–102.
Smith, Jacob. "The Frenzy of the Audible: Pleasure, Authenticity and Recorded Laughter." *Television & New Media*, vol. 6, no. 1, 2005, pp. 23–47.
Sontag, Susan. "Notes on 'Camp,'" *Partisan Review*, vol. 31, no. 4, 1964, pp. 515–530. Reprinted in *Against Interpretation, and Other Essays*, Farrar, Straus & Giroux, 1966, pp. 275–292.
Stahl, Matthew. "Authentic Boy Bands on TV? Performers and Impresarios in *The Monkees* and *Making the Band*." *Popular Music*, vol. 21, no. 3, 2002, pp. 307–329.
Torres, Sasha. "Caped Crusader of Camp: Pop, Camp, and the Batman Television Series." *Camp: Queer Aesthetics and the Performing Subject—A Reader*, edited by Fabio Cleto, Edinburgh University Press, 1999, pp. 330–343.
Watts, Peter. "Do I Have to Do This All Over Again?" *Uncut*, no. 229, 2016, pp. 46–51.
Welch, Rosanne. *Why The Monkees Matter: Teenagers, Television and American Pop Culture*. McFarland & Company, 2016.

Media

Batman. 1966–1968. Television Series. Seasons 1–3. USA: ABC.
The Birds, The Bees and The Monkees. 1968. The Monkees. LP record. Colgems Records.
The Bullwinkle Show. 1961–1964. Television Series. Seasons 1–5. USA: NBC.
Circus Boy. 1956–1958. Television Series. Seasons 1–2. USA: NBC, ABC.
From Russia with Love. Directed by Terence Young, Eon Productions, 1963.
Get Smart. 1965–1969. Television Series. Seasons 1–5. USA: NBC, CBS.
A Hard Day's Night. Directed by Richard Lester, United Artists, 1964.
Headquarters. 1967. The Monkees. LP record. Colgems Records.
How I Met Your Mother. 2005–2014. Television Series. Seasons 1–9. USA: CBS.
I Dream of Jeannie. 1965–1970. Television Series. Seasons 1–5. USA: NBC.
The Monkees. 1966–1968. Television Series. Seasons 1–2. USA: NBC.
The Monkees. 1966. The Monkees. LP record. Colgems Records.
More of the Monkees. 1967. LP record. Colgems Records
The Muppet Show. 1976–1981. Television Series. Seasons 1–5. USA: syndicated.
Pisces, Aquarius, Capricorn & Jones, Ltd. 1967. The Monkees. LP record. Colgems Records.

9
Straight Male Spies, Queer Camp Vistas

The Evolution of Non-Normative Masculinities in *The Avengers* (1961–69) and 1960s British Spy-fi TV

Craig Haslop and Douglas McNaughton

Introduction

"It is as camp as a row of tents, which is how we like it nowadays."
—Julian Critchley, *The Times* (UK) TV critic, writing about
The Avengers, October 10, 1968

The review above demonstrates a contemporaneous appreciation of a camp sensibility in 1960s television. This chapter explores a broad shift, from straight masculinist espionage to camp parody, in "spy-fi" television drama across the decade. It focuses on three significant series which featured a camp sensibility in different ways. *The Avengers* (1961–69, ABC [Associated British Corporation]) offered a stylized pop art parody of the crime and spy genres (Miller, *The Avengers*) and emblematized the emergence of the spy-fi subgenre in the United Kingdom (Sexton, "Celluloid Television"). *The Prisoner* (1967–68, ITC [Incorporated Television Company])—in some ways a continuation of the more conventional spy series *Danger Man* (1960–61, 1964–67, ITC)—allegorically *detourned* the television spy by trapping him in the architectural pastiche village of Portmeirion. *Department S* (1969–70, ITC) featured womanizing novelist Jason King, who glided through crime-fighting adventures in a range of flamboyantly trendy outfits. Camp features in all three series narratively and visually through ironically counterpointing the serious business of government conspiracies, killer spies, and megalomaniacs, against frivolous, playful, and exaggerated surroundings. While these series have already received considerable critical attention (Chapman; Short; Medhurst; Miller, *The Avengers*), less attention has

Craig Haslop and Douglas McNaughton, *Straight Male Spies, Queer Camp Vistas* In: *Camp TV of the 1960s*.
Edited by Isabel C. Pinedo and W. D. Phillips, Oxford University Press. © Oxford University Press 2023.
DOI: 10.1093/oso/9780197650745.003.0010

been paid to their use of camp as part of changing representations of masculinity across the 1960s.

In this chapter then, we consider how the development of early 1960s British spy drama TV into its spy-fi version of the later 1960s is interconnected to shifts in the portrayal of masculinity and the "pop camp" movement of the 1960s. To do this, we first survey the late 1950s and 1960s as a period of immense social and cultural change for masculinity and its subsequent portrayal in British crime and spy TV dramas. Then, we focus on our case studies. In the first, we look at camp in *The Prisoner* and consider its connections to its much straighter predecessor *Danger Man*, and in the second we look at *The Avengers*. Both case studies span the 1960s and allow us to trace changing representations of masculinity in the emerging spy-fi genre and the importance of camp as part of those changes. In the third and final case study, we analyze *Department S*, a lesser-known spy-fi series. Produced late in the 1960s, it represents a peak in production company ITC's interest in zany spy-fi.[1] In addition, it marks a high point in pop camp's role in the representation of masculinity in flux. These shows all playfully subvert genre conventions and deconstruct hegemonic masculinity by demonstrating the performative nature of gender. Thus, we argue these UK series make a significant contribution to the development of what Phillips and Pinedo call "Camp TV" of the 1960s and that pop camp left a lasting legacy on the representation of masculinity in telefantasy as part of the template for later industrialized forms of cult TV.

The Sixties: A Cultural Revolution

The sixties were a time of significant social, cultural, and political change for Britain. Between the late 1950s and early 1970s, attitudes to race relations, marriage, divorce, and homosexuality all became more liberal. The latter part of the era is often referred to as the "Swinging Sixties," in part due to the rapid expansion of the pop music scene and the sexual liberation of the period. The era also saw the explosion into mainstream culture of what Ross has termed "pop camp," which he argues enabled the pop movement—the legitimization of mass-produced goods, art, and music as "culture"—to be accepted by a range of audiences "as subscribers to the throwaway aesthetic" (309).[2] As Marwick notes of the sixties, "[c]ultural revolution seems not a bad description" (18). These and other changes challenged the dominant British model of white hegemonic masculinity of the period. Hegemonic masculinity is produced through a "configuration of gender practice" (Connell and Messerschmidt 77), and these configurations act to create and recreate gendered hierarchies as seen through social norms and media representations. Specific forms of masculinity are reified and become dominant, and usually work to devalue what is seen as feminine in relation to masculinity (Schrock and Schwalbe). Therefore, to analyze how British hegemonic masculinity was challenged during the 1960s, it is necessary to understand the social norms for men and influential representations of masculinity in the 1950s and early 1960s.

Masculinity in Crisis?

The notion of a "crisis of masculinity" might be in danger of losing its value, given its application to several periods in recent history (Malin 14), but the late 1950s and early 1960s was certainly a time of great change for men. Although men were trying to adjust to life post World War II, in many ways the masculinity of the period was still defined by the legacy of the war. In the United Kingdom, men had to complete a period of national service until 1963 and a steady stream of nostalgic war films often depicted men as solid, professional war heroes (Jordan), including *The Dam Busters* (1955), *Reach for the Sky* (1956), and *Dunkirk* (1958).

Other aspects of popular culture in the period reflected a masculinity that was trying to reassert its place in postwar society, albeit through the lens of the tough war hero image. For example, as American culture became more influential in the United Kingdom, masculine swagger was promoted through the emerging rock-and-roll scene. Moreover, advertising targeting young men in the 1950s insisted they should be striving for power away from the domestic sphere (Feasey, "Spray More" 360). For the most part, the norms and representations of men centered on the image of men as anything but feminine, as physically and emotionally in control, and powerful. British crime TV at the end of the 1950s and the early 1960s did little to challenge these assumptions.

In the late 1950s and early 1960s, male-dominated police procedural series were common on British TV, including *Fabian of the Yard* (1954–56, BBC), *Dixon of Dock Green* (1955–76, BBC), and *Z-Cars* (1962–78, BBC) (Feasey, *Masculinity* 83). Within the spy genre, Cold War anxieties were explored through the "existential" spy thriller, which, in contrast with the swinging sixties, reflected a nation grappling with issues of traumatic social change, postimperial decline, and paranoid anxieties over national identity (Barton; Willmetts and Moran) and included shows such as ITC's *Interpol Calling* (1959) and *Danger Man*. *Interpol Calling* followed the investigations of Paris-based Interpol detectives. With its international focus, it can be seen as a precursor to ITC's first British espionage series of the 1960s—*Danger Man*, which starred Patrick McGoohan as a secret agent who "freelances" for NATO. Both series were heavily masculinized, reflecting the heroic postwar version of masculinity. Indeed, McGoohan, who reportedly had a good deal of control over his on-screen character in *Danger Man*, wanted his spy Drake to be of the "heroic mould . . . which means he has to be a good man" (Sellers 43). The same can be said of McGoohan's next espionage role as Number Six in *The Prisoner*—a role for which, as the show's creator, he had almost complete control. McGoohan again plays an agent with integrity; a man who resigns from his role because he is focused on doing the right thing. Despite this commonality, with two runs of *Danger Man* (1960–61 and 1964–67) and his time as showrunner and star of *The Prisoner* spanning nearly the entirety of the 1960s, there are important differences in the portrayal of masculinity across the two series. These are reflective of the shifting cultural and social landscapes during the period and the important role of camp in foregrounding those changes. These shifts make these series worthy of close analysis as the first of our case studies for this chapter.

From *Danger Man* to *The Prisoner*: An Allegory for Changing 1960s Masculinities

The Prisoner follows the story of Number Six, an agent who attempts to resign but is instead involuntarily "retired" to the diegetically unknown location of "The Village." Filmed in Portmeirion in Wales, its isolated coastal setting created an idyllic yet sinister backdrop for what was, in effect, a prison for spies who no longer follow orders. The narrative of the series follows Number Six's subsequent attempts to escape his captors. It has been suggested that *The Prisoner* continues Drake's story after he resigns from his post as a NATO secret agent, although McGoohan himself denies this (Barrington). When McGoohan persuaded head of ITC Lew Grade to make the series, some material intended for *Danger Man* was certainly adapted for *The Prisoner* (White and Ali 145). However, there is little written evidence that *The Prisoner* was a follow-up story (Chapman 49). Nevertheless, for many *Danger Man* fans, as the next espionage series starring Patrick McGoohan, there was some sense of continuity between the two series (Britton and Barker 100).

Despite this sense of continuity, *The Prisoner* breaks from *Danger Man* in important ways. Unlike the straighter realism of *Danger Man*, which tells the stories of Drake's missions as an agent, *The Prisoner* hybridizes the espionage format with fantasy and science-fiction elements. In this way, the show was part of the emergence of the spy-fi subgenre in the mid to late 1960s (Sexton, "Celluloid Television"), driven by the success of the Bond films and further parodying its format through pop-fantasy elements (Oldham 21). The trend toward spy-fi is emblematized by shifts from realism to fantasy in espionage TV on both sides of the Atlantic, seen through shows such as *The Avengers*, which was produced in the United Kingdom but also distributed in America in the latter part of its run, and evident in the US TV series *The Man from U.N.C.L.E.* (1964–68).

There are also differences between *Danger Man* and *The Prisoner* in terms of their portrayal of masculinity. McGoohan's characters in both series can be read as misogynistic, in terms of the recurring use of the *femme fatale* trope and the distrust that both Drake and Number Six seem to have for women. However, in *Danger Man*, despite McGoohan's own insistence to the producers that Drake should not be sexualized (Reeder 37), there are suggestions in its third season that Drake was more heterosexually active. In "The Black Book" (S3 E1, 1965) he flirts with Simone (Georgina Ward) to try and persuade her to give him the Black Book being used to blackmail a British general's brother-in-law, and in the later season-three episode, "You're Not in Any Trouble Are You?" (S3 E4, 1965), Drake has a pseudo-romantic relationship with Lena (Susan Hampshire). In contrast, *The Prisoner's* Number Six is portrayed as even more distant from women than *Danger Man's* Drake. The audience could even assume the character is gay (Short 24), or more specifically asexual, based on his lack of romantic interest in any character in *The Prisoner*. Perhaps most significantly, Number Six's lack of overt heterosexuality contrasts with the most well-known filmic secret agent of the era, James Bond. By the time McGoohan played Number Six in *The Prisoner* in 1967, Sean Connery had starred in five Bond films. In contrast to Number Six, Bond was a philanderer, heavily defined by his encounters with women and sexual prowess—attributes closely aligned to the dominant model of hegemonic masculinity of the time. In this way, Number Six's masculinity was both more ambiguous than his previous role as Drake and much softer than that of the most well-known secret agent of the era—Bond. However, while McGoohan's masculinity is certainly softer, it is camp that foregrounds the conditions of masculinity in flux at that time.

"Arrival" into Kitsch and Camp

In *The Prisoner*'s first episode, "Arrival" (S1 E1, 1967), Number Six is gassed in his London flat, his last memory a view of skyscrapers from his window. He awakens to find himself with quite a different view: that of the quaint and rural surrounds of The Village, signaling a transition from the modernity of London to an ostensibly slower moving and less industrialized landscape. However, it is also a transition from the realism of Number Six's previous life as an agent and McGoohan's more serious espionage role as Drake, into the playful (if sinister), kitsch and camp surroundings of The Village. The real-life setting for the series—Portmeirion—is an Italianate folly, built by Sir Clough Williams-Ellis in North Wales. Portmeirion is characterized by its bright multicolored buildings and unusual architecture, a bricolage of styles including several neo-baroque buildings often featured in *The Prisoner*, such as "The Dome." With its rejection of utility, garish qualities, and interest in architectural imitation, a folly on Portmeirion's scale certainly qualifies as kitsch (Bould 98). However, we suggest that in the context of *The Prisoner*, The Village is more than just kitsch; it is also camp. Kitsch objects are often admired in an ironic way—they're so bad, they're good; it is that ironic aspect which makes kitsch such a close relation to camp (Kleinhans). However, while camp is often ironic, it is more than that; it is a performance, "one way of seeing the world"—a sensibility (Meyer 5; Sontag 54). Dyer argues that "camp has a radical/progressive potential" (49) which is supported by Medhurst for whom camp is political, "rooted in the space of social marginalization" (185). In *The Prisoner*, the kitsch architecture of Portmeirion is an exaggerated artifice constituting part of an overall narrative which raises political questions about identity, surveillance, the state, and gender—thus qualifying its status as camp. The Village and its accessories, including brightly colored costumes, twee "golf buggy" style taxis, and the use of a penny farthing as a logo symbolizing The Village, are part of the performed irony of the series (see Plate 17). For example, the invocation of Victoriana through the "penny farthing" bicycle as a logo is camp on several levels. It is a nostalgic relic representing a bygone era of slow transport, utilized as a symbol for an unknown organization that is clearly technologically advanced. As a piece of Victoriana, it also represents a time when the United Kingdom ruled over an empire. The sense of a United Kingdom still caught in its colonial past is further reflected through the presentation of The Village's citizens as retired aristocrats in capes and hats, drinking tea, mindlessly whiling away their captivity, while the modern world beyond continues, denoted by the underground command center and the inclusion of footage of a robot arm in the weekly opening titles, filing Number Six's resignation. As Sontag notes, "camp is the consistently aesthetic experience of the world. It incarnates a victory of 'style' over 'content,' 'aesthetics' over 'morality,' of irony over tragedy" (62). Thus, the passive ex-spies are seduced by The Village's aesthetics, in a camp televisual analogy, which highlights the artifice of a Britain still caught up in the nostalgia of its Imperial past, while the world changes around it.

While the camp juxtaposition of twee nostalgia against technological modernity is a commentary on national identity and shifting geopolitics, gender politics are also implicated. There is considerable commentary arguing that *The Prisoner* can be read as an individual's search for identity in a world experiencing rapid change (Britten and Barker; Miller, *Spyscreen*). However, Number Six's clarion call "I am not a number, I am a free *man*" (our italics), highlights the gendered aspect of Number Six's struggle to find meaning. Although the use of pop camp by McGoohan and his production team might well be caught up in creating a relevant TV aesthetic based on the wider popularization of the camp aesthetic in the 1960s, intentionally or not it also invokes camp's heritage as part of gay culture. Much of gay camp rests on sending up heteronormative notions of a gendered hierarchy using camp humor to undercut and undermine hegemonic masculinity. This was particularly important for gay men trying to survive the pressures of assumed hetero-masculinity before the legalization of homosexuality in the United Kingdom in 1967. As the website Chortle notes of the period, quoting Medhurst: "When seriousness was defined by male heterosexuality, one way in which queers and queens responded was to make fun of that seriousness, of the certainties of heterosexual masculinity" ("Carry on Camping").

McGoohan certainly plays Number Six as a serious man, desperate to find out who he is, but he must conduct this search in the frivolous, exaggerated, and artificial surroundings of The Village. This seriousness against such a backdrop of camp is highlighted by Number Six's reaction to his new environment when he is given an introductory tour of The Village (see Video

9.1). Thus, Number Six's seriousness (masculinity) stands in contrast to the camp (feminized) surroundings of The Village ▶. In this way, the use of camp in the series also allegorizes the shifting gender politics of the era. The previous generations' hegemonic masculinity was in flux in the hedonism of the 1960s, as the slow process of dismantling a patriarchal gendered hierarchy was gaining new confidence through second-wave feminism and more positive attitudes to homosexuality started to change assumptions about hetero-masculinity.

So far, we have traced masculinity across *Danger Man* and *The Prisoner* to highlight the way pop camp subtly subverted gender in espionage TV across the two series. In our next case study, we analyze another cult spy-fi series which was produced in the United Kingdom during the sixties—*The Avengers*—to highlight camp's role in deconstructing masculinity in a more overt and playful way.

The Vengeance of Pop Camp on 1960s Masculinities

The Avengers, as a series that spanned the sixties (1961–69), is a good cultural barometer in terms of the rise of pop camp, changing masculinities, and their interconnections. It started life as a straight spy show, featuring two leading men—Dr. David Keel (Ian Hendry) and John Steed (Patrick Macnee)—avenging the death of Keel's fiancée. Initially the show was heavily steeped in masculinity. While it was uncertain who employed Keel and Steed, the narrative suggested they were in the espionage business. However, in their trench coats, they aped the iconography of the hard-nosed private eye that had been fashionable since Humphrey Bogart's Phillip Marlow in *The Big Sleep* (1946) (Chapman 59). Indeed, ABC's Howard Thomas reportedly suggested basing the show on the 1930s detective novel/film noir, *The Thin Man* (1934) (Thomas). The show also had similarities with the traditional cop show in its narrative style. As Chapman notes of early episode "The Frighteners" (S1 E15, 1961), it explored the seedy world of underground crime and extortion rackets with studio production giving it a claustrophobic feel, suggestive of the urban thriller (59). These darker, more masculine episodes were a far cry from what the show would become in its later seasons. By its fourth season (1965–66), *The Avengers* became a celebration of modern London pop culture, parading the fashionability of its leading ladies and the garish and bold interior design of the period. Extensive academic analysis has focused on the show's introduction of female partners Dr. Cathy Gale (Honor Blackman) and Emma Peel (Diana Rigg) and the role that cross-dressing played in deconstructing stereotypical notions of femininity, regularly depicted elsewhere in 1960s TV fiction (Andrae; Karpovich). However, the series' cross-dressing was not confined to its female leads, and the effects of that, and its preoccupation with camp on Steed's masculinity, warrant close analysis.

The portrayal of Steed's masculinity began to change in seasons two and three, when he started wearing Pierre Cardin suits and regularly carrying his signature bowler hat and umbrella (although he is seen with the hat and umbrella in "The Frighteners"). He transformed from the trench coat–wearing moody agent he originally played, into a champagne-sipping, fashion-conscious dandy. Steed's new style was curated by Macnee with ABC's Head of Wardrobe, Audrey Liddle, and his tailors. Britton and Barker note Macnee's reflections on the look: "I thought of Regency days—the most flamboyant, sartorially, for men—and imagined Steed in waisted jackets and embroidered waistcoats. I was stuck with Steed as a name and it stayed. Underneath he was steel.... An old Etonian whose most lethal weapon was the hallmark of the English gentleman—a furled umbrella" (46). While this still firmly places Steed within a discourse of acceptable masculinity at that time—the English gentleman (Chapman 62)—it is a version of masculinity which has been associated with the feminine through style and the softer, more domesticated lifestyle, linked to a wealthy background. Narratively, the show also began to change. In season two, female partners were introduced, Venus (Julie Stevens) and Gale, with the latter appearing more frequently and eventually becoming Steed's regular associate in season three (1963–64). While Steed's fashion-conscious English gentleman image feminized him, Gale was masculinized through her active role in fight scenes and her armor-like leather catsuits. In 1993, Macnee commented on the gender subversion of seasons two and three, noting "I was the woman, and she was the man" (Britton and Barker 45).

While the series' quirky spy-fi narratives emerged in season four, the show did start to become more camp during its third season. For example, although the series' writers never suggested that Steed and Gale were an item, the writers did create sexual tension between the characters. The sense that the show did not completely take itself seriously even before its well-documented transformation in season four (Britton and Barker; Chapman) is highlighted by the production and release of a song about Cathy Gale's leather boots sung by Blackman and Macnee—campily titled "Kinky Boots" (1964). By season four, and with the introduction of new female partner Emma Peel, the series began to introduce science fiction and fantasy elements. "The Cybernauts" (S4 E3, 1965) features Steed and Peel trying to stop the Cybernauts, deadly robotic assassins programmed to kill leading industrialists. Throughout these bizarre but life-threatening situations, Steed and Peel never seem to take these incidents seriously. Instead, the series morphs into a parody of the espionage series, camping it up by knowingly sending up its own format and foregrounding style, fashion, and champagne-sipping frippery over serious content (see Plate 18). In this way, and to be crude in gendered terms, across its first four seasons the show shifted its center of gravity from masculinity to femininity, from hard-nosed storylines featuring macho detectives based in realism, to enigmatic fantasy-orientated narratives, played out in a diegetic universe steeped with camp and feminine sensibilities of the era.

The Avengers portrays Steed as more than comfortable with the series' transformation into a celebration of camp. The evolution of the opening titles across the life of the series gives a good indication of the way the series changed to depict Steed's part in its camp. Season two's (1962–63) opening titles feature moody monochrome portraits of Steed and Gale. By the time the series opens its fourth season, the titles feature Peel affixing a carnation to Steed's lapel, highlighting the show's move toward fashion, the surface, and the feminine, and Steed's immersion in the show's campier style. Season five's (1967) titles, now in color, take this one step further.[3] The intention to foreground decadence and style is emblematized through the opening shot of a gun next to a red rose, followed immediately by a shot of two champagne glasses close to camera, with Steed seen in the background of the shot, walking behind the glasses. Steed is carrying a champagne bottle which Emma shoots, popping the cork. Emma turns to Steed with a wry smile; he returns the look. Thus, whereas *The Prisoner* seems to highlight Number Six's serious masculinity within the camp surroundings of The Village, pointing to the disruptive nature of pop camp for sixties' masculinities, *The Avengers* revels in deconstructing masculinity through camp and its gender-subverting effects. Camp's influence on spy-fi and its role in deconstructing masculinity arguably reach a crescendo at the end of the sixties, in ITC's *Department S*.

Jason King: The "Queen" of *Department S*

Department S partly reworks ITC's *Interpol Calling*. The series involves an Interpol department which investigates baffling cases. Based in Paris and

London, its globe-trotting team comprises American former FBI agent Stewart Sullivan (Joel Fabiani), computer analyst Annabel Hurst (Rosemary Nicols), and sybaritic, womanizing crime novelist Jason King (Peter Wyngarde). Wyngarde gets first billing in the titles and went on to star in his own spinoff series, *Jason King* (1971–72).

Scholarship on the series generally centers on the King character and the sequel series rather than *Department S* itself (Hunt; Medhurst). But as the source of the King character, *Department S* deserves closer attention. The character was originally envisaged as a tweedy Oxford don named Roger Cullingford (Shelley); Wyngarde claimed to have devised King's name and chosen his Bentley and wardrobe, emulating McGoohan's influence on *The Prisoner* (Sellers 155). Chapman notes that King is another Steed-like dandy but argues: "Wyngarde's performance is the very definition of 'camp' in that it takes every opportunity to foreground the excessive and ostentatious characteristics of the role" (192).

Much has been made of King's flamboyance, often coded as homosexuality. Wyngarde claimed that he was almost dropped from the series after Lew Grade arranged a screening for potential buyers. Grade is quoted as saying: "I mean those clothes and that hair. The Americans won't like that, they'll think he's a faggot" (Sellers 158). Despite King's relentless Bondian womanizing, Medhurst notes, "the paradox [is] that while King's sexual narratives were entirely heterosexual, his appearances, mannerisms and speech were saturated with elements of camp and queerness" (169).

Richard Dyer comments that camp involves "mastery of style and wit" and camp gay men are characterized as "decadent, marginal, frivolous" (52). In *Department S*, the stylish, witty, decadent King frequently oscillates between trivial and serious. King regularly references author Oscar Wilde—"the queer par excellence" (Dyer 6)—paraphrasing Wilde in declaring, "The only thing to do with an impulse is to give into it" ("Black Out," S1 E9, 1969). Staking out a suspect in "The Trojan Tanker" (S1 E2, 1969), he tells Sullivan, "I'd offer you a glass of champagne, but it's very bad for you in small doses." In "The Pied Piper of Hambledown" (S1 E4, 1969), when interviewing a witness to a mystery, he drawls, "Oh do get to the point, it's nearly lunchtime." Shot in the leg, he complains, "Agony, and it's ruined my trousers" ("Who Plays the Dummy," S1 E11, 1969).

This flippancy, constantly jumping between the serious and the trivial, is camp in Dyer's sense of "anything deep or problematic or heavy is shimmied away from in a flurry of chic" (59). It could be argued that this allows its radical potential (Dyer 49). One of the strengths of Wyngarde's performance is his ability to switch between these modes; when necessary, his voice cracks like a whip. In this sense, not only does King's flippancy undermine the genre conventions of the adventure series, it also deconstructs the action hero archetype beloved of ITC by demonstrating the performative nature of hegemonic masculinity.

Jason King frequently adopts a kind of "macho drag" involving dressing up in a variety of action-man outfits. Healey notes that if all gender is performance, then overcompensatory performance of masculinity "overindulges in macho signifiers" (86). A regular gag in the series involves confusion around King's whereabouts; the episode then cuts to Jason taking part in athletic pursuits such as bobsleighing, fencing, skiing, or mountaineering. This allows King to "drag up" in the appropriate outfits. But the obvious artifice of stock footage, back-projection, and fake mountains draws attention to the performativity of these scenes. His attempts to engage in adventure sports frequently end in failure. For example, in "The Man Who Got a New Face" (S1 E13, 1969), he has a skiing accident which results in an excessively bandaged foot and much mockery of his age by Sullivan. As Video 9.2 shows, when he goes skydiving in "The Duplicated Man" (S1 E19, 1969), he ends up hanging upside down in a tree ⏵. Despite his athletic credentials, King's ineptitude at fighting means he frequently ends up unconscious.

This reflexive deconstruction of hypermasculinity draws attention to the performative quality of hegemonic masculinity. In "The Shift That Never Was" (S1 E15, 1969), the "where's Jason" segment opens with King sweating his way through an unconvincing studio jungle, wearing pith helmet and safari jacket (open to the waist, naturally). The camera pulls back to reveal that it actually *is* an unconvincing studio jungle, erected for publicity photos for his novels (see Plate 19). King complains "is this necessary, look at these ridiculous pants and these boots are killing me!"

As Video 9.3 shows, the scene deconstructs King's performance of action-man masculinity and highlights the fact that it *is* a performance ⏵. King is then joined by a female model in a fur bikini:

PHOTOGRAPHER: "Bare your chest."
(She poses obligingly.)
PHOTOGRAPHER: "No—Jason!"

While the camera in *Department S* regularly dissects women into body parts, notably legs under miniskirts, the scene draws attention to the constructedness of masculinity, foregrounding how costumes and props frame Jason as an action man. As Healey argues, the overcompensatory nature of hypermasculinity threatens to expose anxieties around men as spectacle (88), and King's Mulveyan "to-be-looked-at-ness" queers the camera's normatively male gaze, complicating conventions of hegemonic masculinity and identity.

Film sets, faked locations, counterfeits, and doppelgangers are central to *Department S*. In many ITC series, and particularly *Department S*, action takes place in "an often bewildering liminal zone" (Freeman 55) combining stock footage, "foreign" studio sets, and UK locations. This "visual and imaginative instability" (58) extends to the King character himself. Just as place is made strange by production practices (Bignell; Sexton, "Exotic Locales"), this instability extends to identity through the duplicates and facsimiles in the plots. This involves slippages between Wyngarde/King and the hero of King's novels, Mark Caine, drawing attention to the contingency of identity. King refers to Caine in the third person; plots under investigation resemble Mark Caine books; and parallels between King, Caine, and Wyngarde were encouraged by ITC publicity and Wyngarde himself (Hunt 72). Furthermore, the tensions between Wyngarde/King's flamboyant manner and dress and his lechery over women adds to the reflexive nature of the series. While this reflexivity has sometimes been read as postmodern (Bould), it can also be read as camp.

The King character is camp because of the way in which it draws attention to the constructedness of masculinity, and camp's "emphasis on artifice and parody gives rise to . . . its lack of depth and emphasis on surface" (Andrae 124). King's flippancy and focus on trivia engage with camp in this way; in addition, camp also appeals to the knowing viewer, where the pleasure is down to its "failure to convince" and style is more important than plausibility (123). This applies to the foregrounding of masculine performativity demonstrated above. Jason's relentless womanizing could be seen as a strenuous disavowal of anxieties about his/Wyngarde's sexuality. Noting Wyngarde's willingness to play queer characters on television as early as 1950, Medhurst suggests that Wyngarde's sexuality "facilitates a reading of the series as an extended camp jest" (182). While our other case studies destabilize gender, *Department S* goes further in its deconstruction of hegemonic masculinity through the inherent tensions in the King character. "Macho camp" emerges in the friction between Wyngarde's performance and outfits, and the character's hysterical overperformance of the male sexual predator, an exaggerated version of the camp drag attributed to Steed by Haslop. While the series made King/Wyngarde into heartthrobs for a large and demonstrative female audience, the King persona "seemed to exist on the nexus of heterosexual and homosexual codifications" (Collins). In its self-conscious play with *surfaces* in its performance of manliness, it thus uses camp to draw attention to the anxiously constructed nature of hegemonic masculinity.

Chapman finds the rest of the *Department S* team dull in comparison with King, but this arguably enables the King character to function as effectively as he does. Sullivan's robustly heterosexual, stock hero provides the heteronormative standard as a foil for King's performative and sartorial excesses. Sullivan grounds traditional representations of hegemonic masculinity and thus offers an effective counterpoint to the overperformance of masculinity represented by King. Series creator Dennis Spooner comments that King "worked very well because you saw him in small doses and he never dominated the show" (Chapman 192). It is the contrast between King's flamboyance and the relatively straight (in various ways) performances of Sullivan and Hurst which highlights King's performativity. *Department S* thus articulates a potentially queer challenge to the hegemonic logics of the spy-fi series. In its broader cultural context, it explores shifting tensions around expressions of male identity available within the changing social landscape in the late 1960s.

Conclusions

This chapter has traced the emergence of the spy-fi genre and the various ways camp deconstructed hegemonic masculinities in the 1960s. *The Prisoner* juxtaposed the seriousness of Number Six's masculinity against the camp vista of Portmeirion and a plethora of twee and nostalgic costumes, props, and iconography, highlighting a masculinity coming to terms with its new conditions in a changing cultural landscape. Number Six's search for identity is one that, through camp, questions fixed gender identities. *The Avengers*' camp went further in its deconstruction of masculinity, hamming up the delicious business of queering Steed into a feminized regency relic and, through this, challenging the norms of espionage TV. The culmination of the destabilization of hegemonic masculinity through pop camp in the 1960s spy-fi genre can be seen in *Department S*'s Jason King. In King, camp's love of irony and artifice took the deconstruction of gender identity to new extremes. The series played with the boundaries among King, the Mark Caine of his novels, and the actor Peter Wyngarde, purposefully mixing versions of masculinity. Some were more aligned to hegemonic versions, while others challenged this through camp mannerisms, thus highlighting the constructedness of masculinity.

While Medhurst argues that Jason King marked the last time such a quasi-queer leading man could "innocently" appear on television, elements of the King persona persisted into 1970s television. Barnes, for example, notes the similarity between *Department S* and the revamped format of *Doctor Who* (1963–89, 2005–present), which started shooting in autumn 1969 with a spy-fi flavor and Jon Pertwee as the flamboyant Third Doctor. Moreover, Barnes highlights the similarity between this "ruffle-shirted, fancy car-owning Third Doctor" and Jason King (20). Tracing the further development of a camp sensibility through 1970s spy-fi television would therefore continue the work begun by this chapter.

Goddard and Hogg have recently argued that contemporary shifts in television industries are linked to transformations in representation which amount to "a queering of television itself" (430) and that this process can be traced back to the cult spy-fi series of the 1960s. Phillips and Pinedo argue that 1960s camp has a major influence on cult television of the TVII and TVIII eras, identifying a generic cycle of Camp TV that involved "playful theatricality, deconstructive tendencies and satire," including the subversion of gender norms (35). Indeed, examples of television in the TVII era, including texts often cited as early examples of industrialized cult TV such as *Twin Peaks* (1990–91) and *The X-Files* (1993–2002), frequently engage in the kind of parody, irony, and gender play we have explored in this chapter. We have argued that 1960s British spy-fi, which was often a transatlantic export, is part of the 1960s Camp TV generic cycle and, as such, we should better acknowledge the influence of 1960s camp in the British spy-fi series on later industrialized models of cult TV.

Notes

1. ITC was a subsidiary of Lew Grade's ATV, set up to provide filmed series for overseas distribution (Bignell; Mann).
2. In this chapter we focus on the influence of "pop camp" in the sixties on British TV and masculinity, and its subsequent legacy for cult TV. However, pop camp has continued to influence mainstream culture and TV—for example, camp's presence in many later

mainstream sitcoms, including *Are You Being Served?* (1972–85, BBC) and *Hi-De-Hi!* (1980–88, BBC).
3. Color was not available on ITV—the UK channel which broadcast *The Avengers*—until 1969 (Bignell 57). However, ABC (Associated British Corporation) produced season five (1967) of *The Avengers* in color for the US market, which had shifted to full-color prime-time programming a year earlier (Phillips and Pinedo 23).

Bibliography

Andrae, Thomas. "Television's First Feminist: *The Avengers* and Female Spectatorship." *Discourse*, vol. 18, no. 3, 1996, pp. 112–136.

Barnes, Alan. "A Near Death Experience." *Doctor Who Magazine*, no. 555, 2020, pp. 18–22.

Barrington, Calia. "Talking with McGoohan." *New Video Magazine*, Summer/Fall 1985, no page.

Barton, Ruth. "When the Chickens Came Home to Roost: British Thrillers of the 1970s." *Seventies British Cinema*, edited by Robert Shail, BFI/Palgrave Macmillan, 2008, pp. 46–55.

Bignell, Jonathan. "Transatlantic Spaces: Production, Location and Style in 1960s–1970s Action-Adventure TV Series." *Media History*, vol. 16, no. 1, 2010, pp. 53–65.

Bould, M. "This Is the Modern World: *The Prisoner*, Authorship and Allegory." *Popular Television Drama: Critical Perspectives*, edited by Jonathan Bignell and Stephen Lacey, Manchester University Press, 2005, pp. 93–110.

Britton, Piers D., and Simon J. Barker. *Reading Between Designs: Visual Imagery and the Generation of Meaning in* The Avengers, The Prisoner, *and* Doctor Who. University of Texas Press, 2003.

"Carry on Camping." *Chortle*, January 19, 2011, https://www.chortle.co.uk/news/2011/01/19/12578/carry_on_camping%3f. Accessed August 12, 2020.

Chapman, James. *Saints and Avengers: British Adventure Series of the 1960s*. I.B. Tauris, 2002.

Collins, Frank. "Coppers and Spies Revisited—We Want Information: ITC and *The Prisoner*." *Cathode Ray Tube*, 2015, https://www.cathoderaytube.co.uk/2015/04/coppers-spies-revisited-we-want.html. Accessed April 4, 2021.

Connell, R. W., and James W. Messerschmidt. "Hegemonic Masculinity: Rethinking the Concept." *Gender and Society*, vol. 19, no. 6, 2005, pp. 829–859.

Critchley, J. "Still Good with Miss Thorson." *The Times*, October 10, 1968.

Dyer, Richard. *The Culture of Queers*. Routledge, 2002.

Feasey, Rebecca. *Masculinity and Popular Television*. Edinburgh University Press, 2019.

Feasey, Rebecca. "Spray More, Get More: Masculinity, Television Advertising and the Lynx Effect." *Journal of Gender Studies*, vol. 18, no. 4, 2009, pp. 357–368.

Freeman, Nick. "See Europe with ITC: Stock Footage and the Construction of Geographical Identity." *Alien Identities: Exploring Difference in Film and Fiction*, edited by Deborah Cartmell et al. Pluto Press, 1999, pp. 49–65.

Goddard, Michael, and Christopher Hogg. "Streaming Intersectionality: Queer and Trans Television Aesthetics in Post-Medium Transformation." *Critical Studies in Television*, vol. 14, no. 4, 2019, pp. 429–434.

Haslop, Craig. "Steed as a Drag Queen and the Asexual Number Six: Notes on Cult Telefantasy's Queer Roots." *Critical Studies in Television*, vol. 14, no. 4, 2019, pp. 456–461.

Healey, Murray. "The Mark of a Man: Masculine Identities and the Art of Macho Drag." *Critical Quarterly*, vol. 36, no. 1, 1994, pp. 86–93.

Hunt, Leon. *British Low Culture: From Safari Suits to Sexploitation*. Routledge, 1998.

Jordan, Peter E. R. "Repressing the Male Gaze? Sidney J. Furie's *The Leather Boys* and the Growing Pains of Post-War British Masculinity." *Film Criticism*, vol. 43, no. 1, 2019, https://doi.org/10.3998/fc.13761232.0043.101

Karpovich, Angelina. "The Avengers." *The Cult TV Book*, edited by David Lavery, University Press of Kentucky, 2015, pp. 36–43.

Kleinhans, Chuck. "Taking out the Trash: Camp and the Politics of Parody." Meyer, pp. 182–201.

Malin, Brenton J. *American Masculinity under Clinton: Popular Media and the Nineties "Crisis of Masculinity."* Peter Lang, 2005.

Mann, Dave. "From Minor Misdemeanours to Ill-Gotten Gains: The Emergence of Britain's First TV/Film Crime Series." *Journal of British Cinema and Television*, vol. 5, no. 1, 2008, pp. 19–37.

Marwick, Arthur. "The 1960s." *Contemporary Record*, vol. 2, no. 3, pp. 18–20, 1988.

Mason, Francis. "Nostalgia for the Future: The End of History and Postmodern 'Pop' T.V." *Journal of Popular Culture*, vol. 29, no. 4, 1996, pp. 27–40.

Medhurst, Andy. "King and Queen: Interpreting Sexual Identity in 'Jason King.'" *Action TV: Tough-Guys, Smooth Operators and Foxy Chicks*, edited by Anna Gough-Yates and Bill Osbergy. Routledge, 2001, pp. 169–187.

Meyer, Moe. "Introduction: Reclaiming the Discourse of Camp." Meyer, pp. 1–22.

Meyer, Moe, editor. *The Politics and Poetics of Camp*. Routledge, 1994.

Miller, Toby. *The Avengers*. British Film Institute, 1997.

Miller, Toby. *Spyscreen: Espionage on Film and TV from the 1930s to the 1960s*. Oxford University Press, 2003.

Mulvey, Laura. "Visual Pleasure and Narrative Cinema." *Screen*, vol. 16, no. 3, 1975, pp. 6–18.

Oldham, Joseph. *Paranoid Visions: Spies, Conspiracies and the Secret State in British Television Drama*. Manchester University Press, 2017.

Phillips, W. D., and Isabel Pinedo. "Gilligan and Captain Kirk Have More in Common than You Think: 1960s Camp TV as an Alternative Genealogy for Cult TV." *Journal of Popular Television*, vol. 6, no. 1, 2018, pp. 19–40.

Reeder, J. "No Girls or Guns for Danger Man." *Woman*, October 30, 1965, p. 69.

Schrock, Douglas, and Michael Schwalbe. "Men, Masculinity, and Manhood Acts." *Annual Review of Sociology*, vol. 35, 2009, pp. 277–295.

Sellers, Robert. *Cult TV: The Golden Age of ITC*. Plexus, 2006.

Sexton, Max. "Celluloid Television: The Action Adventure Genre of the 1960s." *Dandelion: Postgraduate Arts Journal & Research Network*, vol. 1, no. 1, 2010, pp. 1–18.

Sexton, Max. "Exotic Locales: Representations of Place and the Use of Colour in the Transatlantic Telefilm." *Journal of British Cinema and Television*, vol. 16, no. 4, 2019, pp. 444–461.

Shelley, Garry. "Peter Wyngarde—an Incurable Romantic." *Sydney Morning Herald*, May 8, 1972, p. 9.

Short, Sue. *Cult Telefantasy Series: A Critical Analysis of* The Prisoner, Twin Peaks, The X-Files, Buffy the Vampire Slayer, Lost, Heroes, Doctor Who *and* Star Trek. McFarland, 2010.

Sontag, Susan. "Notes on 'Camp.'" *Camp: Queer Aesthetics and the Performing Subject: A Reader*, edited by Fabio Cleto, Edinburgh University Press, 1999, pp. 53–65.

Thomas, Howard. "The Birth of The Avengers." *The Times*, April 2, 1977.

White, Matthew, and Jaffer Ali. *The Official* Prisoner *Companion*. Warner Books, 1988.

Willmetts, Simon, and Christopher Moran. "Filming Treachery: British Cinema and Television's Fascination with the Cambridge Five." *Journal of British Cinema and Television*, vol. 10, no. 1, 2013, pp. 49–70.

Media

Are You Being Served? 1972–1985. Television Series. Seasons 1–10. UK: BBC.
The Avengers. 1961–1969. Television Series. Seasons 1–6. UK: ABC (Associated British Corporation).
The Baron. 1966. Television Series. Season 1. UK: ITC.
The Big Sleep. Directed by Howard Hawks, Warner Brothers, 1946.
The Dam Busters. Directed by Michael Anderson, Associated British Picture Corporation, 1955.
Danger Man. 1960–1967. Television Series. Seasons 1–4. UK: ITC.
Department S. 1969–1970. Television Series. Season 1. UK: ITC.
Dixon of Dock Green. 1955–1976. Television Series. Seasons 1–22. UK: BBC.
Doctor Who. 1963–1989, 2005–present. Television Series. Seasons 1–39. UK: BBC
Dunkirk. Directed by Leslie Norman, Ealing Studios, 1958.
Fabian of the Yard. 1954–1956. Television Series. Season 1. UK: BBC.
Hi-De-Hi! 1980–1988. Television Series. Seasons 1–9. UK: BBC.
Interpol Calling. 1959–1960. Television Series. Season 1. UK: ITC.
"Kinky Boots." 1964. Patrick Macnee and Honor Blackman. SP record. Decca Record Co.
The Man from U.N.C.L.E. 1964–1968. Television Series. Seasons 1–4. US: Metro-Goldwyn-Mayer Television.
The Prisoner. 1967. Television Series. Season 1. UK: ITC.
Reach for the Sky. Directed by Leslie Gilbert, Lewis Gilbert Production Company, 1956.
The Thin Man. Directed by W. S. Van Dyke, Metro-Goldwyn-Mayer, 1934.
Twin Peaks. 1990–1991. Television Series. Seasons 1–2. US: ABC.
The X-Files. 1993–2018. Television Series. Seasons 1–11. US: Fox.
Z-Cars. 1962–1978. Television Series. Seasons 1–12. UK: BBC.

SECTION III
OTHER CAMP(TV)SITES

10
Can TV Music Be Camp?
Notes from the 1960s

Reba A. Wissner

Camp is no stranger to television and other arts, especially pop culture, given its pervasiveness and ubiquity (Miller 157). Often equated with the excessive, unusual, and flamboyant, camp is easily identifiable. In music, however, identifying camp characteristics can be difficult. In her oft-cited essay on camp, Susan Sontag writes that:

> Camp taste has an affinity for certain arts rather than others. Clothes, furniture, all the elements of visual décor, for instance, make up a large part of Camp. For Camp art is often decorative art, emphasizing texture, sensuous surface, and style at the expense of content. Concert music, though, because it is contentless, is rarely Camp. It offers no opportunity, say, for a contrast between silly or extravagant content and rich form. (56)

Sontag posits that the operas of composers such as Richard Strauss (1864–1949), genres such as Tin Pan Alley, and popular music can be camp, while the music dramas of Richard Wagner (1813–83) and jazz cannot (Sontag 56). Where, then, does television music fall, if anywhere, on the camp spectrum? And what would it mean for television music to be camp?

A close examination of the musical scores of 1960s television programs in genres such as space operas and spy shows reveals that they have certain camp aesthetic qualities: exaggerated style, hyperbolic sound, unique instrumentation and instrumental combinations, unexpected appearances, and outlandish musical vocabularies. Many of these musical techniques derive from styles that are equated with comedy and excess. The television episodes that are underscored with this music reveal that the music is as crucial to the interpretive framework applied by viewers as the visuals and can be just as camp as the episodes they underscore.

Reba A. Wissner, *Can TV Music Be Camp?* In: *Camp TV of the 1960s*. Edited by Isabel C. Pinedo and W. D. Phillips, Oxford University Press. © Oxford University Press 2023. DOI: 10.1093/oso/9780197650745.003.0011

This chapter investigates camp music in four 1960s television series—*Star Trek: The Original Series* (1966–69, NBC) and *Lost in Space* (1965–68, CBS), both space operas, and *The Man from U.N.C.L.E.* (1964–68, NBC) and *Get Smart* (1965–69, NBC; 1969–70, CBS), both spy shows—and its contribution to each series' camp aesthetics. To contextualize this analysis, I consider the earliest constructions of music to be considered camp, beginning in the eighteenth century and ending in the twentieth century, before moving to 1960s television music. Through examining the musical constructions common to these series to define and understand the role of camp in 1960s television music, I work to answer the question posed in this chapter's title: Can TV music be camp?

A Short History of Music and Camp

It is important to step back and examine what camp music generally has been understood to be. While many equate camp with homosexuality and/or queerness in music, it has a longer history, which appeared before the 1960s. In music, camp also has a long history dating back to eighteenth-century Europe. For example, composers in the Western art music tradition such as Joseph Haydn (1732–1809) and Francis Poulenc (1899–1963), the latter of whom died during the early 1960s, are equated with camp for their excessive and overly humorous musical gestures (Knapp 162; Moore 301). Although these composers did not consider their work camp, we can see their work fitting into camp style.

While discussions of camp often do not date back to the eighteenth century, there are some characteristics of Haydn's music that Raymond Knapp defines as camp. Haydn sometimes has a "preoccupation with triviality" (Knapp 89). One of the most striking is the ability of Haydn's music to "make light of serious art even when taking that art seriously" (xiii) in a very similar way to musical theater, achieved through overt musical humor. In his symphonies, Haydn features two distinct camp elements: "accommodation of eccentricity and what is often seen as an overly comic tone" (55). This eccentricity to which Knapp refers sometimes comes in the form of a "dramatic enactment of individuation," whereby an individual instrument (or small group of them) exaggeratedly breaks from the rest of the ensemble (37). He also borrows musical material from non-eccentric works in a notably exaggerated way (96). By tone, Knapp means "the manner in which movements treat their themes, affects, or referential narratives" (56). Haydn's symphonies create a sense of exaggerated complacency where all audience expectations of what comes next are shattered; quiet passages, for example, set up unexpected overly loud ones and vice versa (77).

Poulenc's music has also recently been acknowledged to contain overt camp elements that express his homosexuality, especially in his ballets (Moore 309), through what he called "adorable bad music" (303). This often took the guise of unexpected modulations, or unprepared key changes, which he used to represent a character's sexual ambiguity, as we see in his ballet, *Les Biches* (1924); like a character's deviant sexuality, the key changes were unexpected and unclear through an "elaborate musical makeup" (309). Poulenc also musically depicted camp through his departure from tonality (deemed "tonal obsolescence") and his "earnest approach to the representation of frivolity" (303).

Camp is also a feature of musical theater, featuring exaggerated musical numbers, flashy costumes, and abrupt demarcations between speech and song. These characteristics notably found their way into the classic MGM film musicals of the 1930s–1960s, which were generally intended as escapist entertainment from contemporary events (Cohan 2).[1] As Knapp writes, camp is "a hallmark of popular musical theater" (xiii), generally focusing on the exaggerated and containing artifice, often through the action of bursting into song at sometimes unprepared moments. The music of all these genres can be understood, in varying degrees, as predecessors to camp music in television.

Discussions of musical camp have been fraught with a variety of descriptions but no easy categorization: "Indeed, one need not listen terribly far to hear combinations of extravagance, excess, frivolity, theatricality, incongruity, artifice, the carnivalesque, and the epicene (all viewed as aesthetic gateways into full-fledged camp) throughout a large swath of music and musical performances" (Moore and Purvis ix). According to Moore and Purvis, therefore, anything that is musically excessive is often labeled camp. One problem with this labeling comes from Sontag's essay, where she discusses musical campiness without stating outright what makes it camp besides stating that camp privileges "style over content" (63). Therefore, when determining what makes camp, we must consider style over content, though content such as music and televisual plot devices still matter.

Camp on 1960s Television

Television in the 1960s was best known as FCC Chairman Newton Minow's "vast wasteland" where "people would more often prefer to be entertained than stimulated or informed" (Minow). Camp, with its exaggerated and hyperbolic aesthetics, did not help television's case. Camp was ubiquitous during the 1960s, especially on American television screens with sitcoms, though they are not explicitly recognized as camp (Miller 3). The production of camp television series began to escalate by the early 1960s with the production increase a response, in part, to Cold War nuclear anxiety (Miller 113; Drushel 95).

Camp also appeared in this Cold War context within more broadly satirical and comedic cultural products, especially those like spy shows that called American politics and international relations into question (Jenkins 16). Thus, camp took the political and social climate of the 1960s and, through television, "turn[ed] the terrible into something grotesquely amusing" (Benshoff 151). Despite networks' efforts to suppress television camp just a decade earlier, by 1966, the response was the production of more camp television shows (Miller 35). Television producers could do this by using material from other media, such as comics (49).

Because of camp's availability and ubiquity across multiple media, it has been assigned a range of definitions. For this essay, I employ Harry M. Benshoff's definition. For Benshoff, camp is "a means of textual production. A film may be called deliberately campy if its makers have purposefully encouraged outlandish plotting, baroque visual design, corny dialogue, and wooden acting" (150). In its original meaning, the word *baroque* referred to a misshapen pearl, and this definition was extended to anything that was exaggerated or in bad taste. Thus, according to this definition, camp film, and by extension, camp television, is visually in bad taste and exaggerated. Likewise, David Galef and Harold Galef (11–12) note that camp exhibits anxiety about the natural and embraces the artificial, emphasizing exaggeratedness.

Further, camp television requires a suspension of disbelief and portrays the impossible as possible, "manifesting itself by means of the 'super-unnatural,' hyper-real, bold, overly-shaped, material and vulgar. Using its excessiveness, camp creates alternative interpretations; it does not create alternative worlds but new meanings of the old senses of reality," thereby decorating, but not beautifying, the natural (Malinowska 18, 20). Film can be susceptible to camp through "those filmic techniques that often serve as intensifiers, such as close-ups (whether faces or objects), camera movement and montage, color saturation, or the use of music, especially or when following well-worn (and perhaps now-outmoded) expressive tropes" (Knapp 162). Indeed, "music brought color (as discourse and present absence), into black-and-white shows, through [. . .] scores, and performance, including in ads and interstitial material" (Miller 113).

Color television is one of the technological innovations most synonymous with the 1960s (Murray 145). The 1960s pop aesthetic, featuring vivid, bold, and exaggerated colors, was one of the hallmarks of the era's camp television (Phillips and Pinedo 26). However, many households were not watching these color television shows on color TV sets. At the beginning of 1966, less than 10 percent of American households with at least one television set had a color receiver in part because owners would retain their original black-and-white receivers as long as possible until they could afford to upgrade to color ("Over 5 Million"; Wissner, "I *Am* Big" 78). So, while these shows use bright, pop-art inspired colors and visuals, their creators also knew that not every viewer could experience these shows in the manner they were produced. One key result was the addition of a pop-art-like colorful audio component in the music and sound effects, creating the camp sonic style. As a result, then, music supplanted the visual color to convey the series' camp meanings in a medium that everyone did have relatively equal access to: sound.

As I discuss elsewhere, television sets' sound quality during the late 1950s was relatively uniform with specific but limited sound capabilities (Wissner, "I *Am* Big" 80–81). Although there were minor variations among receivers, certain instrument families such as brass and woodwinds came over speakers more clearly than others, which is why a specific musical style for television shows of that era was necessary and early television composers drew on these instruments so often (86–87). Unsurprisingly, these were the same instrument families that were maximally used in camp television shows during the 1960s, when sets and their sonic capabilities were only slightly more varied than before.

Musical Comedy through Contradiction

In general, camp creates comedy through contradiction, and camp television scores are no exception, especially regarding their creators' use of sonic and visual excess: "Television technology," Miller notes, "allowed consumers to differently privilege sound and image (such as vacuuming, doing laundry, entertaining, or napping). Producers tailored image, dialogue, and scores for a commercial market in which television-recording devices were unavailable and camp could potentially circulate out of range of censors, in spite of script approvals, rehearsals, and surveillance" (49). From its inception, television producers considered how to best convey sonic portrayals (or disguising) of camp. Even 1960s print publicity accounted for camp shows' typical sound style and production practices (Miller 60). Music was not haphazardly considered; in film, for example, it was sometimes subject to censorial scrutiny because of its style, with one 1960 film, *Private Property*, which features a closeted homosexual character cited for its "highly suggestive sequences, dialogue, and music" by the National Legion of Decency (NLD), a Catholic film reviewing organization and interest group (National Legion of Decency). For these three components, including its music, the NLD rated the film "Condemned" and not suitable for viewing by anyone (Kastner 226). Therefore, music could convey as much if not more meaning than the dialogue or the visual field on-screen.

Camp draws attention to itself through its exaggerated gestures, and its music is no exception (Booth 71). Much of the camp aesthetic in television music results from its incongruity between the on-screen events and the sound emanating from the television set. Since there is yet to be a distinct definition of musical camp, let alone camp in general, "camp [music] is best identified, analyzed, and understood when placed in relationship to specific musical practices, historical contexts, and performance traditions" (Moore and Purvis x). I define musical camp in 1960s television as scores that rely heavily on winds and brass, musical clichés, exaggerated and hyperbolic musical gestures like descending trombone glissandi (a rapid sliding motion through a series of notes, in this case down the scale) and the "wah-wah" mute on the trumpet, and altered timbres. Commensurate with Galef and Galef's (11–12) assertion that camp embraces the artificial, it is appropriate that musical instruments in camp television scores are manipulated with devices such as mutes, use extended techniques to create unusual timbres placed in unexpected places, and rely on exaggerated and repetitive music.

Though Benshoff does not specify it in his description, to his "baroque visual design" I would add "sound design and music," especially since the music purposefully contains unnatural timbres and sounds such as muting and manipulation of the instrument sound through recording techniques.

Mutes not only muffle the volume of the instrument but also can change its timbre depending on the type, shape, and construction of the mute used.[2] Often, sitcoms used muted trumpets to highlight especially funny moments. These attributes contributed to the parodic nature of camp television and emphasize the on-screen excessiveness.

But it is only fair that my definition and categorization of camp in 1960s television music apply to that specific genre and time. What may be musical camp in 1960s television is likely not musical camp in 1980s television or even 1960s film. Television producers did copy film conventions, particularly for genres such as comedy that are critical to camp television. However, 1960s television music conventions were primarily the result of following established television conventions coming from the 1950s than copying film conventions. Much of this was because there was very little overlap between film and television production personnel. Thus, camp television music is largely an outgrowth of the musical techniques associated with 1950s television comedy.

In camp television, the music, compared to that of contemporary non-camp shows, is bold, excessive, and exaggerated primarily through musical techniques, orchestration, and musical clichés; one of the most common of these clichés is the use of romantic strings to represent a beautiful woman. As film music scholar Claudia Gorbman writes, "A film of the forties is airing on television. Even though you're in the next room, you are likely to find that a certain kind of music will cue you in correctly to the presence of Woman [sic] on screen. It is as if the emotional excess of this presence must find its outlet in the euphony of a string orchestra" (80). Thus, this music had become so pervasive that it is immediately recognizable. Since these clichés tend to border on the excessive to illustrate what the music is meant to signify, they function especially well in camp television. Although the camp television sound is consistent, I confine my argument in this essay only to the colorful scores of specific camp television series and episodes where the camp sound is most prominent.

Some of the clearest iterations of musical camp were found in *Batman* (1966–68, ABC) and for many, the *Batman* television series and camp have become synonymous with each other (Richardson 74). James Van Hise (n.p.) has commented that, for television, *Batman* "didn't look or sound like anything else being done at the time," partially because of the financial resources put into both the sound and visual effects (Eisner 10). The series' camp sensibility is present immediately from Neal Hefti's theme. According to Randall Larson, Hefti struggled for weeks to write the theme as a direct result of his desire to sonically mirror the series' overt campiness (396). The recognizable jazz theme features brass punctuations and singers singing the word "Batman." The brass players mimic the singers and the music features the recognizable "wah-wah" sound, created with the movement of a "wah-wah" mute (often a rubber toilet plunger) to cover and uncover the brass instrument's bell as the musician plays, that would come to pervade camp television music throughout the mid- to late 1960s. Even the use of a rubber plunger as a mute is excessive and humorous. The theme is paired with the title sequence's bold colors and textures, though these would have not been visible in their true form unless viewed on a color television set. The sound, however, would remain uncompromised regardless of the nature of the on-screen image.

The underscoring for the first two seasons, however, was composed by Nelson Riddle, who drew on the ostinato (repeated bassline) in Hefti's theme to represent the Batmobile. But Riddle also composed themes that would heighten the camp aesthetic, typically for individual characters, especially the villains: "shrill, laughing brass for the Riddler; waddling woodwinds for the Penguin; a darker, cackling musical laughter for the Joker" (Burlingame 215). Generally, *Batman*'s underscoring contains brass punctuations that coincide with comic-book-like illustrations, or "music to be punched by" (215). In scenes where Batman engages in a scuffle with the episode's villains, we not only hear these punctuations but we also see graphics that similarly punctuate the action, often containing words such as "bang" and "pow," highlighting the campiness both aurally and visually. Riddle chose to use woodwinds and/or brass instruments to highlight these comic-book-like punctuations sonically (Garcia 37), and the graphics then were reflected and heightened by Riddle's music to enhance the exaggerated effect (Levinson 215). For those who could see the color on-screen, both the sound and the image come across as vivid and colorful (Levitt 182). The result was more than simply additive, as sound and image reinforced and amplified the camp meaning carried individually. The series' music was aided by brass, woodwind, and percussion-heavy orchestras (with strings rarely used) of typically twenty to twenty-five musicians (Garcia 37), an orchestration that would become relatively standard in camp television of the era. The sound effects, too, were pop, or what Will Brooker describes as "animated" (193). The music, therefore, is meant to be technicolor and striking.

One striking example of camp musical underscoring in *Batman* can be found in "Nora Clavicle and the Ladies' Crime Club" (S3 E19, 1968). In this episode, its eponymous character, Nora Clavicle (Barbara Rush), is an activist who ousts the current male police commissioner and police officers in Gotham City and replaces them with herself and other women. The episode not only is a commentary on the women's rights movement but also positions itself as a commentary on perceptions of feminism. We can *hear* this position, even if we do not directly analyze it as we watch; for example, exaggerated and excessive music and sound effects are used to poke fun at gendered perceptions of voice. In one prominent moment, Mayor Linseed's wife and her shrill voice are underscored with overexaggerated, comic music that mimics her physical actions such as walking to drumbeats through Mickey Mousing, or demonstrably syncing the sound effects to the on-screen action (Yockey 57). As Video 10.1 shows, Mrs. Linseed (Jean Byron) is given a playful theme while Nora Clavicle is given a march, emphasizing one woman—Clavicle—who is strong and powerful and another—Mrs. Linseed—who is not ▶. In Video 10.2, we can hear that the mechanical mice containing bombs intended to destroy Gotham City are heavily underscored with an ostinato (repeated bass line) as they circle the room, with the policewomen's frightened responses equally exaggerated. In traditional television scoring, ostinatos and tremolos (a rapid moving back and forth between two notes) are used to represent fear and danger. In the context of the scene here, it becomes camp ▶.

With *Batman*'s premiere, camp began to move from the periphery of queer culture to the center of mainstream culture (Levitt 171). With *Batman*'s popularity, more television series began to follow in its footsteps, especially sonically. For the rest of this chapter, I confine my argument to two genres of 1960s television frequently aligned with camp—the spy show[3] and the space opera—to illustrate how the musical language of camp television established in *Batman* influenced composers of later camp shows. My discussion of each genre focuses on two representative television series to make this distinction clear.

Spy Shows

Espionage television shows were popular during the 1960s with the rise in popularity of the James Bond films. Much of this concerned the desire for escapism that spy series could provide (Kackman 78). But how television used the Bond films as a launch point—satirical or not—lent itself well to small-screen camp portrayals of spies and spy organizations This is especially clear in satirical spy series such as *Get Smart*, which parodies the genre through the use of an incompetent, sometimes bumbling spy as a protagonist, and *The Man from U.N.C.L.E.*, which features exaggerated portrayals of espionage missions. Unsurprisingly, then, the music in these spy genres is consistent with the adventure and crime genres and uses television camp's musical vocabulary to heighten the camp element.

The Man from U.N.C.L.E.

Considered the James Bond of television, *The Man from U.N.C.L.E.* was part of the 1960s television spy craze and generated the production of later spy television series such as *Get Smart* (Kackman 70). As in many spy films and television shows, *The Man from U.N.C.L.E.* uses a secret organizational acronym; in this case, United Network Command for Law and Enforcement. They seek to destroy a nemesis organization, THRUSH, a reference to James Bond's nemesis, SPECTRE (Britton 39). It was not until shows such as *Batman* aired that *The Man from U.N.C.L.E.* took a turn toward camp, notably in the latter's second and third season, but then drifted away from camp in its fourth season (Walker 6). However, two cues from the series pilot composed by Jerry Goldsmith would become a core part of the music and its camp aesthetic: "a secondary four-bar action cue with a core melody first stated by brass, then repeated by unison flutes; and the bossa nova romantic theme designed for Solo's come-hither encounters with the 'civilian assistant of the week' (usually an attractive young woman)" (Bang 132). By the time the third season was in preparation, camp was especially popular and its creators decided to emphasize that element in the show, making it closer to *Batman* than Bond (Heitland 175). This included the music which, by its second season, began to mirror the pop elements on-screen through music and sound by incorporating instruments such as harpsichord, bongo, organ, and saxophone and heightening the use of brass and percussion (Larson 417).

In "The Super-Colossal Affair" (S3 E4, 1966), Cold War nuclear anxiety was juxtaposed with the spy genre. Here, a mobster attempts to please his mistress by getting her cast in a movie. However, the movie is nothing more than a front for the mob to detonate a nuclear weapon in Los Angeles. Two plot aspects make this episode camp: exaggerated portrayals of gender and the satirical treatment of nuclear attack. While the composer of this episode is uncredited, the music heightens these camp aspects. As in *Batman*, this episode, and many of the series' other scores, rely heavily on brass, woodwinds, and percussion rather than strings, which (as previously noted) were often absent from these scores (Burlingame 201).

In this episode, the trumpets play with "wah-wah" mutes to create the camp "wah-wah" sound as we meet an attractive female character named Ginger LaVeer (Carol Wayne); we can see this in Video 10.3. The camera tilts up from her feet to her face in an implied point of view shot from the perspective of agent Ilya Kuryakin (David McCallum). This is an example of the male gaze as purported by Laura Mulvey, and the music here renders the moment as camp; this kind of shot is used in later television, such as the introduction to *Police Woman* (1974–78, NBC), but the lack of this musical cue there does not signify the camp intention. This is followed by a guitar playing a pitch bend and the sound effect of a bouncing spring, exaggeratedly representing Kuryakin's attraction. It also represents a sort of G-rated-version of a sonic erection, a camp musical cliché ▶. This exaggerated portrayal of gender is an example of conservative use of camp, given its reinforcement of the male gaze to fetishize a female character in the years before the T&A, or Jiggle, television era during the mid-1970s to early 1980s when women were more frequently portrayed as sex objects (D'Acci 15). Later in the episode, when we see Ginger at the movie studio, her entrance is exaggerated and underscored with a twanging electric guitar passage. Each time that we see Ginger do something to emphasize her feminine wiles, such as rapidly blinking her eyes, we hear things such as vibraphone melodies and the rapid hitting of tin cans for sound effects.

In "The Pop Art Affair" (S3 E6, 1966), THRUSH agents attempt to obtain the components for a container holding gas that makes people hiccup to death (an overtly campy narrative device on its own). Kuryakin and Napoleon Solo (Robert Vaughn) infiltrate Beatnik culture to prevent the components from falling into the wrong hands. The episode contains a lot of source music of the type found in jazz and Beat clubs, but the underscoring features instruments that are frequently used in camp episodes such as electric guitar, double bass played pizzicato (or plucked), trumpets that play downward pitch bends, and vibraphones—instruments that feature an almost technicolor sound when combined. We can see this underscoring occurs at moments of heightened comedy, as in Video 10.4, when THRUSH agent Mark Olé (Robert H. Harris) holds Kuryakin hostage and attempts to drown him using soap suds ⏵. And we hear an ostinato again as Kuryakin and Sylvia (Sherry Alberoni) are shot out of the sky in their hot air balloon. As if this wasn't all obvious enough, this episode mentions camp directly. When Solo asks model Mari (Sabrina Scharf) about why she is holding a comic book during a photo shoot, she responds: "Comic books are camp, and camp is the last word." This notion of camp as the new, hip thing allows us to make sense of why other spy series approached camp later in their runs.

Get Smart

One of the most familiar camp television spy series is *Get Smart*, which featured its protagonist, Agent 86, Maxwell Smart (Don Adams), and his partner, later turned wife, Agent 99 (Barbara Feldon). The duo work for CONTROL, a secret US counterintelligence organization whose goal is to defeat an international organization of evil called KAOS (both acronyms are meaningless). The spy films of the day are parodied at their most extreme, including the fancy gadgets Bond uses; Smart uses a shoe phone, which often outs him as a spy, and the cone of silence that, despite its purpose to ensure no one can eavesdrop on his conversations with the Chief (Edward Platt), also ensures neither Smart nor the Chief can hear each other.

Series composer Irving Szathmary was conscious of the series' campiness when writing both the theme and the underscoring. The playful theme is not what one would expect for a spy series. It is a jazzy theme, similar in some ways to those more traditionally used in spy shows, but here it has uneven phrase lengths and accents on unexpected beats and is heightened through the twanging guitar. The end of the first phrase of the melody culminates with a sustained note that resolves upward rather than downward as one might expect. It finally resolves downward in the repeat of the phrase immediately afterward. The theme culminates with a two-note brass-heavy orchestral punctuation as the ground opens up under Smart. Thus, the on-screen action exaggerates the campiness of the theme, showing that we cannot take Smart seriously (Bang 148).

Throughout the series, far less music is used than in other contemporary camp programs; here, the music is mainly relegated to comic punctuations and scenic bridges. In episodes such as "Island of the Darned" (S2 E11, 1966), Maxwell and Agent 99 are trapped on a KAOS-controlled Caribbean Island.

As the situation goes awry, the music continues to sonically represent its absurdity, using electric guitars and bongos over an ostinato. The campiness is heightened through the trumpets' use of "wah-wah" mutes (e.g., as Smart and Agent 99 are chased by a pack of dogs on an island in Video 10.5) and descending trombone glissandi to illustrate the episode's tension but especially its absurdity, such as when Smart and Agent 99 are trying to outsmart the episode's villain ▶.

Another camp episode is the double episode, "The Not-So-Great Escape" (Part 1: S4 E25, Part 2: S4 E26, 1969), which focuses on the imprisonment of high-ranking CONTROL agents in a KAOS-controlled POW camp in New Jersey. The narrative set-up is a play on Nazi concentration camps (or at least their representation in films such as *The Great Escape* [1963]) and the music here (heard in Video 10.6) uses marches and drumbeats to heighten the military element, incorporating them at moments where the KAOS officers (and Smart disguised as a KAOS officer) should be taken "seriously." The effect is overdone and intentionally exaggerated, as we find in most spy camp music ▶. But if spy shows were becoming increasingly campy, they had nothing on what was occurring in space operas.

Space Operas

During the 1960s, television saw an increase in science fiction series. Shows such as *Star Trek*, which was billed as "*Wagon Train* to the stars," coincided with the Western's popularity. While it may seem incongruous, the Western was just as popular as camp and science fiction on television. Two science fiction television series of the 1960s became associated with camp: *Lost in Space* and *Star Trek*. Both of these series ask viewers to suspend their disbelief that space travel could occur, despite John Glenn's highly publicized 1962 sojourn into space. Often, the situations in which the characters find themselves are outlandish and unbelievable. Thus, the musical style used for the scores heightens this effect.

Lost in Space

In his original scores for *Lost in Space*, John Williams (billed as Johnny Williams) created a unique sound that aligned with the series' camp aesthetic.

The bold colors and satirical treatment found in camp television series were channeled through Williams's large orchestras—unusual for television at the time (e.g., the orchestra for *The Man from U.N.C.L.E.* only contained fifteen players for each score [Burlingame 201]), dissonant harmonies, and exaggerated timbres. From the beginning of the series' run, the theme music was overly humorous (Rodman 40), with a playful opening melody reminiscent of Modest Mussorgsky's (1839–81) "Ballet of the Unhatched Chickens" from *Pictures at an Exhibition* (1874) with trumpets and computer-like blips (the trumpets would be replaced by French horns in season two). Williams's season-three theme was jaunty, quirky, and funny in a different way than his original theme, reflecting the camp turn the series had taken. His episode scores relied on mostly brass with some woodwinds and percussion and, as with other camp TV scoring, there were rarely any strings in his orchestras for the series. Brass played a pivotal role in the series, used for the "Danger" motif and the robot's music (Burlingame 114). Williams also used an electro-theremin in some of his scores, originally developed for and used in *My Favorite Martian* (1963–66, CBS) to provide a campy and otherworldly sound (Larson 376). For these reasons, Williams's music for the series, which often "exaggerated events on the screen to an unfathomable degree" (Rodman 25) through sonic enhancement, is generally considered hyperbolic, the definition of camp.

One episode of the series, "The Space Vikings" (S2 E20, 1967), contains particularly campy elements. The episode is based on the premise that the Robinson family meets the Norse god, Thor (Bern Hoffman). In fact, at the beginning of the episode, right after the title theme, Richard Wagner's "Ride of the Valkyries" from *Die Walküre* (1870) (an easily recognizable piece of music in popular culture) is played deliberately slow to sonically portray the evocation of the Norse gods. As one might imagine, the typical musical underscoring used in the epic film genre to represent heroism, such as brass and heavy note articulations, is used here to emphasize the plot (Meyer 95). We hear this in Video 10.7 when Dr. Smith (Jonathan Harris) tries, and fails, to be heroic when he finds himself needing to use Thor's hammer to defend himself against a (poorly costumed) furry creature. Other *Die Walküre* references appear as well, such as when Brynhilda (Sheila Allen, credited as Sheila Mathews) emerges on a horse in a decidedly Wagnerian costume, complete with a horned helmet, singing in Wagnerian soprano style, which here sounds like feigned singing ▶.

While Sontag notes in her essay on camp that Wagner's music cannot be camp, this episode plays with his music in a way that exaggerates it so that it becomes unexpectedly humorous. This type of musical parody and quotation that helps the viewer recall a pre-existing and well-known musical composition appears frequently in *Lost in Space*. Often, these musical appearances are hyperbolic (Rodman 48). This music also functions as Haydn's exaggerated music does, overemphasizing the serious in unexpected ways at unexpected moments.

Even this episode is not exempt from the brass slides found in other camp episodes, here used as punctuations to draw in the audience's attention. One example is when Brynhilda says that she is giving Dr. Smith dried dragonflies after he states that they are delicious. Once again, the brass slides heighten the comedy, illustrate the episode's absurdity, and sonically represent the camp element. This kind of aural parallelism is distinct here from simple Mickey Mousing because it is not merely sonically replicating the on-screen movement; rather, the sound works to create a framework for interpretation so that viewers are cued to receive these moments of action through a camp-like lens that flags the second-level meaning the creators intended viewers to recognize.

"Castles in Space" (S3 E14, 1967) is another of the series' campiest episodes. With a score composed by Gerald Fried, the episode focuses on the accidental discovery of an ice princess (Corinna Tsopei) suspended in frozen fluid and an alien villain named Chavo (Alberto Monte) who wants to kidnap her for ransom. Here, several camp musical techniques found in Haydn's and Poulenc's music emerge: unexpected changes of instrumentation, typically from a cacophonous, dissonant music that sounds almost electronic to a lyrical solo melody, often played by flute. This dissonant music is amplified by the combination of instruments that do not sound like they go together. This happens often when we move from scenes with Chavo to scenes without him, with the cacophonous music representing him. It also features tremolos, which, as mentioned above, historically connote danger, used here when the camera pans to the ice princess's melted footprints. Chromatic trumpet ostinatos create the illusion of danger when the princess's identity is still unknown.

The episode also uses conventional techniques and instruments in unconventional ways. For instance, the harpsichord, a predecessor of the piano, is used in this episode, sometimes combined with electric guitar, to represent danger; this is most prominent when we see the ice princess after being set free from her frozen capsule. Brass instruments are also used here to represent the ice princess, and they typically play music that is meant to sound regal but here contains elements that make it sound less than regal, such as

230   CAMP TV OF THE 1960S

playing with accented notes. An oddly accented waltz, played by a clarinet and later joined by a trumpet, underscores humor in Chavo's scenes when he and the Robot become intoxicated. These two episodes' camp elements were also found in one of the campiest space operas in 1960s television, both visually and sonically: *Star Trek*.

Star Trek

Like many 1960s camp television series, *Star Trek* was a disguised anthology with diverse, unrelated narratives, unified in only a set of basic characters and scenarios but with new characters and locations each week (Anderson 4). *Star Trek* is one of the clearest examples of 1960s television that plays with camp aesthetics in purposeful ways, straddling multiple boundaries. As one 1967 viewer in a letter to *TV Guide* wrote, "the show is the newest kind of CAMP!" (Baker 52). One of the series' campiest episodes is "The Trouble with Tribbles" (S2 E15, 1967). Like many 1960s television episodes, this episode uses library music, or music that was pre-composed for another episode or series and then placed into a library for reuse (Wissner, *Dimension* 10). These libraries were mostly specific to networks but could also be specific to production companies. These library cues were generally used in similar contexts as the original use and, if a network tended to produce several shows of the same type—in this case, camp—it was likely that these cues would be used similarly across multiple episodes. This is one reason why there can be a common sound for specific genres or types of television such as camp; this use of library music can also be found in the other series discussed in this chapter.

In "The Trouble with Tribbles," Cyrano Jones (Stanley Adams) arrives on the Deep Space Station K7, to which the Enterprise crew has been summoned. He brings with him creatures called tribbles: round furry balls that make soothing cooing noises but also prolifically procreate and then die because they are eating a type of grain, quadrotriticale, stored on the ship. Soon, the crew discovers that the tribbles do not like Klingons and can alert the Enterprise crew to their presence. As if these outlandish plot points were not enough, their portrayal—both sonically and visually—was exaggerated as well.

There were three types of scores for *Star Trek*: original scores that could contain a few library cues, partial scores that were comprised partially of

CAN TV MUSIC BE CAMP? 231

original cues and partially of library cues, and wholly canned or tracked scores (Steiner 10). Jerry Fielding's score for "The Trouble with Tribbles" falls into the first category, as he composed most of the cues specifically for this episode and added some library music to it, creating a composite score of new music and music from earlier episodes of the series. The episode uses one cue with an appropriately comedic quality that plays when we see that the tribbles have multiplied to an extreme number in the cafeteria, as Captain Kirk (William Shatner) finds them in his sandwich and coffee and Scotty (James Doohan) enters the room with an armful of them, as Video 10.8 shows. This scene is underscored using slides played on the violin strings to emphasize the exaggeratedness of having an infestation of tribbles ▶.

In another scene, shown in Video 10.9, Captain Kirk opens the compartment housing the quadrotriticale and is engulfed by thousands of falling tribbles who have gorged themselves on the grain (Plate 20). As the tribbles fall, burying Kirk, we hear upward and downward sliding trombone glissandi that are punctuated with brass. Shortly after, we hear more brass slides as Kirk emerges from the pile of tribbles. The comedic element of the music is heightened in Fielding's musical representation of the tribbles, created by halving the recording speed of the trombones to create the high-pitched sliding sound when played back at normal speed (Bond 28) ▶. All of these musical techniques amplify the comedy of the situation—its outlandishness and excessiveness—to create a musical scoring that accentuates the campiness of the episode's premise.

Another camp episode is "The Way to Eden" (S3 E20, 1969). As in "The Pop Art Affair," this episode features another group from the 1960s counterculture—hippies. Like that *U.N.C.L.E.* episode, this *Star Trek* episode contains more source music than usual. It also features music common to the late-'60s hippie counterculture as "The Pop Art Affair" did with Beat culture a few years earlier. Electric guitars are used here as sonic surrogates for the space instruments that the hippies play, giving the score an otherworldly sound. We most notably hear this in Video 10.10 during the duet between Mr. Spock (Leonard Nimoy) and one of the space hippies (Deborah Downey) when she plays her alien instrument while Spock plays his Vulcan harp. This duet occurs as her friends immobilize the Enterprise crew who respond to their alien touch by letting out a contented, orgasmic moan as they faint ▶. The overstated nature of both the action/acting and the music illustrates another way that the series sonically and visually portrays camp with, yet again, the exaggeratedness of music and sound contributing to the series' camp aesthetic.

Conclusion

Returning to the question posed in this title about whether TV music can be camp, the answer, it seems, is complicated. On the surface, the answer is yes; however, the answer here has ultimately been determined by how well the choices made in the audio score fit with and built on the visual aesthetic. The better question, then, would be: Can TV music be camp without TV? Camp cannot be camp without an audience to receive it (Galef and Galef 18). But when the visual and sonic effects are paired, there is a synergistic effect that strengthens the work's camp association. The particular sound of these television scores portrays comedy, parody, and sonic excess, all of which reflect the notion of exaggeratedness and bad taste associated with camp (Horn 6).

Camp television style is relatively consistent, and its components determine whether or not it is camp. The audio and visual experiences, or picture and sound, were crucial to establishing and maintaining camp style. While viewers may not have watched 1960s camp television shows with their intended colors, they nonetheless heard their intended sounds, making aural camp a surrogate for visual camp.

We can credit 1960s television shows with the creation of a camp television sound. Although some of the sounds that we associate with camp television, such as bright and thick orchestrations, musical clichés, ostinatos, instruments such as electric guitars, comic punctuations, and techniques such as brass "wah-wah" sounds, came from earlier eras, their use in those genres was not to elicit audience attention and laughter. However, in television, its use in unexpected moments or in an exaggerated way, paired with the on-screen action and visuals, made it especially camp. This music, though sometimes incongruous, is well-suited to sonically portray camp and creates a sound just as bright as the era's technicolor television.

Notes

1. Hoffman's chapter on *Snagglepuss* (1961, syndication) in this collection (Chapter 3) also draws attention to the camp nature of the MGM musicals, particularly those made

by the Freed Unit, emphasizing there the role of gay labor in the development of a house style and production culture.
2. For an example of the sound of a muted versus an unmuted trumpet, see https://www.summersong.net/music-teacher/trumpet-lessons/brass-instrument-mutes/.
3. Phillips and Pinedo also address *The Man from U.N.C.L.E.* and *Get Smart* in their 2018 article, reprinted here as Chapter 1. Haslop and McNaughton's chapter in this collection (Chapter 9) directly considers a number of British "spy-fi" television programs of the 1960s, including *The Avengers* (UK: 1961–69, US: 1966–69).

Bibliography

Anderson, Christopher. *Hollywood TV: The Studio System in the Fifties*. University of Texas Press, 1994.
Baker, Djoymi. *To Boldly Go: Marketing the Myth of Star Trek*. I. B. Taurus and Co., 2018.
Bang, Derrick. *Crime and Spy Jazz on Screen, 1950–1970: A History and Discography*. McFarland and Co., 2020.
Benshoff, Harry M. "1966 Movies and Camp." *American Cinema of the 1960s: Themes and Variations*, edited by Barry Keith Grant, Rutgers University Press, 2008, pp. 150–171.
Bond, Jeff. *The Music of Star Trek: Profiles in Style*. Los Angeles: Lone Eagle Press, 1999.
Booth, Mark. "*Campe-Toi!* On the Origins and Definitions of Camp." Cleto, pp. 66–79.
Britton, Wesley Alan. *Spy Television*. Praeger, 2004.
Brooker, Will. *Batman Unmasked: Analyzing a Cultural Icon*. Continuum, 2001.
Burlingame, Jon. *TV's Biggest Hits: The Story of Television Themes from Dragnet to Friends*. Schirmer Books, 1996.
Cleto, Fabio, editor. *Camp: Queer Aesthetics and the Performing Subject: A Reader*. University of Michigan Press, 1999.
Cohan, Steven. *Incongruous Entertainment: Camp, Cultural Value, and the MGM Musical*. Duke University Press, 2005.
D'Acci, Julie. *Defining Women: Television and the Case of Cagney and Lacey*. University of North Carolina Press, 1994.
Drushel, Bruce E. "*Vicious* Camp: Performance, Artifice, and Incongruity." Drushel and Peters, pp. 93–129.
Drushel, Bruce E., and Brian M. Peters, editors. *Sontag and the Camp Aesthetic: Advancing New Perspectives*. Lexington Books, 2017.
Eisner, Joel. *The Official Batman Batbook*. Contemporary Books, 1986.
Galef, David, and Harold Galef. "What Was Camp?" *Studies in Popular Culture*, vol. 13, no. 2, 1991, pp. 11–25.
Garcia, Bob. "Batman Batmusic." *Cinefantastique*, vol. 24, no. 6/vol. 25, no. 1, 1994, pp. 37, 125.
Gorbman, Claudia. *Unheard Melodies: Narrative Film Music*. Indiana University Press, 1987.
Heitland, Jon. *The Man from U.N.C.L.E. Book: The Behind the Scenes Story of a Television Classic*. St. Martin's Press, 1987.
Horn, Katrin. *Women, Camp, and Popular Culture: Serious Excess*. Palgrave Macmillan, 2017.

Jenkins, Tricia. "Feminism, Nationalism, and the 1960s' Slender Spies: A Look at *Get Smart* and *The Girl from U.N.C.L.E.*" *Journal of Popular Film and Television*, vol. 43, no. 1, 2015, pp. 14–27.

Kackman, Michael. *Citizen Spy: Television, Espionage, and Cold War Culture*. University of Minnesota Press, 2005.

Kastner, James W. *Where the Movies Played in Downtown Pittsburg(h): 100 Years of "Going to the Show": 1896–1996*. RoseDog Books, 2011.

Knapp, Raymond. *Making Light: Haydn, Musical Camp, and the Long Shadow of German Idealism*. Duke University Press, 2018.

Larson, Randall D. *Musique Fantastique: 100 Years of Fantasy, Science Fiction, & Horror Film Music: A Historical Appreciation and Overview*. Book One. Creature Features, 2012.

Levinson, Peter J. *September in the Rain: The Life of Nelson Riddle*. Taylor Trade Publishing, 2005.

Levitt, Lauren. "*Batman* and the Aesthetics of Camp." Drushel and Peters, pp. 171–187.

Malinowska, Ania. "Bad Romance: Pop and Camp in Light of Evolutionary Confusion." *Redefining Kitsch and Camp in Literature and Culture*, edited by Justyna Stępień, Cambridge Scholars Publishing, 2014, pp. 9–22.

Meyer, Stephen C. "The Politics of Authenticity in Miklós Rózsa's Score to *El Cid*." *Music in Epic Film: Listening to Spectacle*, edited by Stephen C. Meyer, Routledge, 2017, pp. 86–102.

Miller, Quinlan. *Camp TV: Trans Gender Queer Sitcom History*. Duke University Press, 2019.

Minow, Newton N. "Television and the Public Interest." National Association of Broadcasters Convention, May 9, 1961, Washington, DC. Speech. *American Rhetoric Online Speech Bank*, www.americanrhetoric.com/speeches/newtonminow.htm.

Moore, Christopher. "Camp in Francis Poulenc's Early Ballets." *The Musical Quarterly*, vol. 95, no. 2/3, 2012, pp. 299–342.

Moore, Christopher, and Philip Purvis. "Introduction." *Music & Camp*, edited by Christopher Moore and Philip Purvis, Wesleyan University Press, 2018, pp. ix–xvi.

Mulvey, Laura. "Visual Pleasure and Narrative Cinema." 1975. *Film Theory and Criticism: Introductory Readings*, edited by Leo Braudy and Marshall Cohen, Oxford University Press, 1999, pp. 833–844.

Murray, Susan. *Bright Signals: A History of Color Television*. Duke University Press, 2018.

National Legion of Decency. *Motion Pictures Classified by the National Legion of Decency*. 1960 Edition. New York: National Legion of Decency, 1960.

"Over 5 Million Color Homes, According to NBC." *Broadcasting*, February 7, 1966, p. 50.

Phillips, W. D., and Isabel Pinedo. "Gilligan and Captain Kirk Have More in Common Than You Think: 1960s Camp TV as an Alternative Genealogy for Cult TV." *Journal of Popular Television*, vol. 6, no. 1, 2018, pp. 19–40.

Richardson, Chris. *Batman and the Joker: Contested Sexuality in Popular Culture*. Routledge, 2020.

Rodman, Ron. "John Williams's Music to *Lost in Space*: The Monumental, the Profound, and the Hyperbolic." *Music in Television: Channels of Listening*, edited by James Deaville, Routledge, 2010, pp. 34–51.

Sontag, Susan. "Notes on 'Camp.'" Cleto, pp. 53–65.

Steiner, Fred. "Keeping Score of the Scores: Music for *Star Trek*." *The Quarterly Journal of the Library of Congress*, vol. 40, no. 1, 1983, pp. 4–15.

Van Hise, James. *Batmania II*. Pioneer Books, 1992.
Walker, Cynthia W. *Work/Text: Investigating the Man from U.N.C.L.E.* Hampton Press, 2013.
Wissner, Reba. *A Dimension of Sound: Music in the Twilight Zone*. Pendragon Press, 2013.
Wissner, Reba. "'I *Am* Big, It's the *Pictures* That Got Small': Sound Technologies and Franz Waxman's Scores for *Sunset Boulevard* (1950) and *The Twilight Zone*'s 'The Sixteen-Millimeter Shrine' (1959)." *Journal of Film Music*, vol. 7, no. 1, 2017, pp. 79–95.
Yockey, Matt. *Batman*. Wayne State University Press, 2014.

Media

The Avengers. 1961–1969. Television Series. Seasons 1–6. UK: Associated British Corporation; USA: ABC.
Batman. 1966–1968. Television Series. Seasons 1–3. USA: ABC.
Les Biches. Ballet. By Francis Poulenc. 1924.
Get Smart. 1965–1970. Television Series. Seasons 1–5. USA: NBC, CBS.
The Great Escape. Directed by John Sturges, The Mirisch Company, 1963
Lost in Space. 1965–1968. Television Series. Seasons 1–3. USA: CBS.
The Man from U.N.C.L.E. 1964–1968. Television Series. Seasons 1–4. USA: NBC.
Police Woman. 1974–1978. Television Series. Seasons 1–4. USA: NBC.
Private Property. Directed by Leslie Stevens, Citation Films, 1960.
Star Trek. 1966–1969. Television Series. Seasons 1–3. USA: NBC, CBS.
Die Walküre. Music Drama. By Richard Wagner. 1870.
Wagon Train. 1957–1965. Television Series. Seasons 1–8. USA: NBC, ABC.

11

Flipper's (1964–67) Dark Camp

Nicholas C. Morgan

Flipper, a half-hour long program broadcast on NBC for three seasons beginning in 1964, portrays the adventures and family life of teenaged Sandy, his little brother Bud, and their father Porter, as well as the creature they often refer to as their "pet" dolphin, the eponymous Flipper, who has a knack for solving crimes and helping the boys out of scrapes. *Flipper* has an unusual place in a volume dedicated to camp television of the 1960s, as it largely trades the irony that is central to many definitions of camp for a deep earnestness. Any camp discernible in the show is "naïve," to use Susan Sontag's terms, rather than an intentionally arch "Camp that knows itself to be Camp" (294). Brian Kelly, who played Porter Ricks, implied as much in *Variety* when distinguishing "superbly produced" shows of its type from the "instant hit" of ABC's trendily self-conscious *Batman* (1966–68; Kaufman, "'Flipper' Butters Kelly's Bread"). Critics praised *Flipper* for its technically superb underwater cinematography while noting that for younger viewers—its target audience—the *Lassie*-like plots and delight in watching an intelligent dolphin would be a huge draw (Kaufman, "Flipper"). But reading it against the grain, as camp, allows for a reconsideration of camp's connection to non-normative sexuality in tension with what Sasha Torres identified in 1996 as the "de-gaying" of the category that accompanied the commercialized camp of 1960s television programs such as *Batman*. This process, Torres writes, rendered camp "a perfectly condensed marker for the simultaneous admission and denial of Batman's queerness" (250). More recent scholarship, including this volume, has expanded on the subversive potential that continued to adhere to camp even in the wake of its mid-1960s mainstreaming. For the purposes of this chapter, however, I follow Torres's model, in order to show how an account of naïve camp in 1960s television both supplements and differs from the histories that emerge from more arch, knowing programs such as *Batman*.

Flipper demonstrates the persistence of naïve camp in the mid-1960s. Further, *Flipper*'s attempt to restrain the camp proliferating in

Nicholas C. Morgan, *Flipper's (1964–67) Dark Camp* In: *Camp TV of the 1960s*. Edited by Isabel C. Pinedo and W. D. Phillips, Oxford University Press. © Oxford University Press 2023. DOI: 10.1093/oso/9780197650745.003.0012 contemporaneous shows overcompensated, producing space for accidental and unknowing camp, one which audiences would have been primed—by other shows like *Batman*—to perceive and appreciate. That *Flipper* warrants a place in genealogies of camp television is particularly suggested by the show's reception in fandom, artwork, and literature from the 1990s and 2000s. In the final section of this chapter, I examine several such works in which Sandy operates much as, say, the memory of the "Queen of Technicolor" Maria Montez did in relation to Jack Smith's *Flaming Creatures* (1963). The distance between Montez's output and Smith's—somewhat more than twenty years—is analogous to that separating *Flipper* and its 1990s receptions. By the 1990s, the objects artists appropriated as camp had shifted, and the form of the resulting works had shifted, too. Such works include the embrace of mass cultural detritus and heightened affect typical of 1960s camp, but fused with an emphasis on criminality, violence, and even horror. The evidence of such later artworks and fan responses invites a reading of the show in relation to what Kathryn Bond Stockton calls "dark camp," meaning a mode "that keeps the violent edge of debasement visibly wedded to camp caprice" (205). For some of its early theorists, camp was always dark in the sense that it reacted to a homophobic society by appropriating its cultural output (Babuscio 33–35). For other early critics its imbrication with stigma voided any radicality in camp (Britton 14). Stockton suggests instead a dialectical framework in which stigma and joy or pleasure coexist and inflect each other. In what follows, I argue for *Flipper* as an alternative, even subversive cultural site in which this dark camp dynamic was accessible to queer viewers within the broader mediasphere of 1960s television.

Queer Plots, Camp Villains

Camp viewings of *Flipper* respond not to the explicit invitation offered by *Batman* and others, but to an implicit, albeit nonetheless legible, dual address. In this section, I follow the lead of *Flipper*'s later reception in tracking some of the camp and queer interpretations that would have been available at the time. Some are counterintuitive, but the evidence of the receptions I trace at the end of the chapter suggests that criminality, surface, and a camp eroticism were all central to the engagement of a certain subset of the show's viewers. Gay readings would have been facilitated by *Flipper*'s homosocial structure: the show centers on the all-male Ricks family and, as such, is essentially devoid of women. When they do appear, they are treated as novel. This all-male sphere is regularly policed: in "Dolphin for Ransom" (S3 E20, 1967), for example, Bud—the younger son—chides, "Why is it that every time I'm looking for you guys, there's some girl involved in it?" Gay readings were also encouraged by the way the camera often lingers on the male body, both Sandy's toned swimmer's physique and Porter's buff, beefcake body. As Sandy, Luke Halpin is shirtless for large portions of most episodes, usually clad in little more than form-fitting denim cut-offs. As Porter, Kelly is regularly bare-chested.

Flipper's plots revolve around a limited set of problems: frequently a human outsider arrives in Coral Key and, out of various motivations ranging from profit (Flipper would make a great circus animal) to scientific inquiry (his brilliant mind could be studied) to pleasure (he makes a great pet), attempts to make off with the dolphin. Often the drama is tied to the incursion of an animal outsider or invasive species, with Flipper saving the boys from, say, a surprise pack of sharks. This exogamy plot central to so many episodes frequently hinges on gender, with the sometimes explicitly unwelcome arrival of the feminine within the Ricks' otherwise undisturbed homosocial arena. In "Aunt Martha" (S3 E19, 1967) Porter's recently widowed sister arrives unannounced, planning to stay for an unspecified amount of time. Noticing Flipper, she exclaims "What a horrible fish." Mistaking dolphins for fish recurs as a sign of outsider status in many episodes, marking the speaker as ignorant of animal life and lacking the affection for the natural world central to the Ricks' life. Either Sandy or Bud always disabuses the outside/villain of their misidentification, here noting "He's a mammal, like us, and he's our pet." Martha is an actively feminizing or effeminizing force: she buys matching clothes for the boys, preppy outfits more formal than their usual garb. Martha's poodle Fifi is, unlike Flipper, pretentiously groomed and, in some shots, dyed bright pink. Martha urges the Ricks to rearrange their furniture, to buy guest towels and candles, and to take vitamins. Accustomed to going on safari with her late husband, excursions on which "nothing ever went wrong," she aspires to introduce a tame, humanized nature into the Ricks' life, in part by banishing Flipper. Sandy and Bud—and even Porter—do not want to be acculturated, as Martha eventually ascertains: "You don't want me here . . . you just think I'm a meddling female."

Between the matching technicolor outfits, Martha's exaggerated performance of upper-middle-class femininity, and Fifi's hairdo, "Aunt Martha" is the episode in *Flipper*'s run that most self-consciously engages visual and thematic signifiers of camp. Despite *Flipper*'s explicit rejection of the overt camp increasingly popular in television, the proliferation of that knowing camp in contemporaneous programs had the distinct potential to train viewers to read across two meaning levels, leaving them attuned to these signifiers which were thus legible as camp. Crucially, this legible campiness coincides here with the incursion of the feminine. The narrative threat produced by Martha's difference hinges on both artificiality and gender: she threatens the purity of Coral Key's raw naturalness and its fraternal dynamic. Self-aware signs of camp emerge in service to demarcating this otherness.

Flipper thus sets up a system in which camp is both coded as effeminate and artificial and set off as opposed to the baseline homosocial masculinity and naturalness the show overtly celebrates. However, the unselfconscious camp of the show—unlike the *Batman*-esque knowing camp strategically deployed in "Aunt Martha"—disturbs this system. These moments of rupture often revolve around the overtly butch antagonists figured as criminals who regularly invade, like Aunt Martha, the paradise of Coral Key. These villains are often queerly coded, evoking a familiar topos from the writing of, say, Jean Genet and the wide-ranging currents in queer theory that the conflation of homosexuality and criminality (rooted in sodomy's historical illegality) has occasioned (Bersani). In *Flipper*, these queerly coded criminals are often bearers of a subterranean or unknowing camp. A dose of homoeroticism underpins their interactions with Porter and Sandy. Consider, for example, the counterfeiter in "Dolphin in Pursuit: Part Two" (S2 E3, 1965). On the run, he holds up Sandy and Porter at gunpoint, as seen in Plate 21. Training his weapon particularly on shirtless Sandy, who stands passively by with hands in pockets, the villain remarks: "Nice lookin' boy you got there." Mid-1960s cinema often featured such "sexually ambiguous" villains, whom Mark Booth identifies as figures of camp (105). Another example arrives in the two-part "Flipper and the Fugitive" (S3 E14–15, 1967). Here, a handsome bandit, Steve, has washed ashore from Miami, dressed like a city slicker. Steve's status as an object of male beauty is figured as artificial, polluted by urban life, in contrast to Sandy and Porter's rural, unstudied handsomeness. His brother and partner in crime, Chuck, looks nothing like him; they could as easily be outlaw lovers as brothers. Steve's hyperbolic speech—as when he assures Porter he does not need privacy—is shot through with melodrama. His amplified performance of working-class masculinity reveals, as in much classic camp, the performative dimension of normative gender.

Incommensurable worlds collide when such urbanites arrive in the wholesome Keys, occasioning pleasurably violent conflict with queerly erotic overtones. In "City Boy" (S1 E5, 1964), Mike, whose father has died, is left in Porter's care for a long weekend by his mother and despised stepfather. When he first appears, Mike approaches Sandy from behind, on the dock. Sandy does not notice because he is busy talking to Flipper, framing Mike as interloper and voyeur. Sandy and Mike contrast in every way: Mike is pale, sallow, and sporting a tie, his entire body clothed, contrapuntal to Halpin's brightly colored polo shirt, which hangs loosely and reveals a deep tan. Even Sandy's freer, looser hair clashes visually with Mike's combed and pomaded hair, glistening in imitation of an adult businessman. This contrast makes the "city boy" read as fey, even degenerate; he repeatedly affects ennui. A pelican stands on the dock, neatly dividing the two boys into separate halves of the frame. Mike teases Flipper and calls him "blubberhead." Sandy, dismayed and perplexed by this response to his beloved pet, engages Mike in a bout of wrestling, a moment of violent aggressiveness that becomes sensual as the two tumble—arms and legs entwined, making them into one plank—into the water, a splash of white spray enveloping them as they thrash. Sensationalizing music overanxious to highlight the drama feels at odds with the sunny cinematography and with the eroticism of the sudden meeting of these two incompatible modes of being in the world.

In *Flipper*, outsiders like Mike exemplify the figure Lee Edelman calls the "sinthomosexual." By this, Edelman means a figure who embraces the chaotic and ungovernable pleasure of *jouissance* in all its destabilizing, violent glory. When Mike takes off—against Sandy's protestations—in a racing boat owned by a friend of the Ricks family, he careens around the lagoon in fast circles, whipping around sea plants again and again, almost drowning after he finally sinks the boat. Just before capsizing, he looks full of joy, reveling in the sheer, repetitive pleasure of his high-speed looping. When Porter asks why he has behaved so destructively, Mike replies: "I thought I'd try it, for kicks," expressing an embrace of unreasoned jouissance.[1] Porter suggests a more wholesome activity: scuba diving. Scubaing, Mike and Sandy find a sunken ship containing what look like bars of silver. Before leaving Coral Key, Mike persuades Sandy to secretly take one last dive, back to this sunken treasure, which Mike wants to salvage. Mike—not intentionally, but there are still echoes of the possessive antihero in Patricia Highsmith's *The Talented Mr. Ripley* (1955), similarly wan and with the object of his lust another golden boy—sets a death trap: the two inevitably get stuck in the tangled, messy wreck and must send Flipper for a rescue that comes only in the nick of time.

The sinthomosexual, for Edelman, refuses compassion and futurity, instead embracing an antiteleological pursuit of "continuous satisfaction that the drive attains by its pulsions" (72–73). Flipper himself might qualify, since he (unnaturally) does not travel in a pod; as a solitary, bachelor dolphin, he rejects the sociality characteristic of his species. That Mike, with his aimless and gleeful theft of the speedboat, embodies such a position is brought home when it turns out that what he had thought to be silver bars were actually, Porter says sternly, "Lead! Ballast! This is what you risked your life for!" But what was for Porter an unjustifiable expense was for Mike justified by the sadomasochistic pursuit of pleasure. As valueless waste matter, the lead has an association with anality (Freud 125–133) and, for Mike, this gift remains a gift whatever its exchange value, the lead as good as gold. It had, after all, generated proximity to Halpin's vulnerably mortal body through a refusal of morality. Edelman presents the sinthomosexual as deadly serious in his embrace of the death drive, but a figure like Mike allows us to see him also as one of camp. Mike's dandyish veneer and appreciation for surface over substance—for glimmering treasure whose monetary worthlessness diminishes his appreciation not at all—chimes with camp's embrace of kitsch. In "The Misanthrope" (S1 E15, 1964), a similar dynamic is at work: when the two villains rob a houseboat at the episode's start, one laments that their plunder is only costume jewelry. But her partner argues that they have still made off with a good haul, emphasizing a pleasure in the surface of the valueless but superficially striking.

Stockton writes that in dark camp, darkness might "bend back tenderly toward the objects of . . . cruelty" (210). In "City Boy," Mike continues to hold the pain of parental loss and outsider status, as reflected in his stark refusal of closure. Although his stepfather finally rescues him from the wreck, he still refuses to call him "Dad," which would have been the most efficient way to recuperate his criminality, since in the episode's opening moments he notes how he dislikes it when his stepfather calls him "son." Mike wants to exist outside of kinship, and while the painful pressures of normativity cannot be rehabilitated, they are joined with a criminal campiness. As Booth notes, "All his life, the camp person remains a naughty child checking his elders. The targets of this mockery—conventional morality, good taste, marriage and the family, suburbia, sport and business—should help to throw the camp personality into relief" (57).

Crucially, while the exogamous moral impurity of *Flipper*'s queerly campy villains provides narrative thrust, it is primarily indicated visually. It is communicated through the various criminals' modes of dress, appearance, and coiffure: a matter of looking and of seeing the world in terms "of artifice, of stylization" which is, Sontag and others argue, very camp (Glick 16). In "The Misanthrope," the houseboat robbers present themselves as a bodybuilder and his female companion, whom he lifts in the air in a brief acrobatic display. This performance, evoking circus strongman acts, is designed to distract the boys as they prepare to rob another Key denizen. Bud exclaims, "Wow, look at those muscles! Do you think I'll ever have muscles like that?" and, later, "Anybody with muscles like that has gotta be a right guy!" Linked to kitschy sideshow acts and giving an overblown display of masculinity, the bodybuilder is a specimen of "macho camp" (Booth 148). The lure of muscles as a sign of adulthood and bodybuilding as a pedagogic process in which Bud would participate are shown to be a smokescreen, an alluring but sinister façade for robbery.

Camp Naturalism

I have been arguing that *Flipper*'s queerly coded villains introduce an element of dark camp into the show, partly through their rejection of norms and partly through the way they draw attention to surface. It is not only bodies, however, that receive a great deal of surface attention abstracted from narrative in *Flipper*: extended tracking shots documenting nature are its bread and butter. The "beautiful underwater photography" was repeatedly cited in reviews as the "outstanding feature of this show" (Kaufman, "Flipper"). Given the central place of underwater photography, what might be most perverse for a camp-inclined viewer in *Flipper* is its passion for the natural since, Sontag writes, "nothing in nature can be campy" (291). Sam See argues against this long-unquestioned tenet, proposing a contrary understanding of "queer feelings like camp as natural on the Darwinian logic that nature itself is queer, or endlessly transformative and defiant of material or conceptual normativity" (644). *Flipper* makes a similar insight, linking camp and nature through its fusion of aestheticized human body and spectacular undersea life.

This admixture of nature and campy culture is evident in "Love and Sandy" (S1 E19, 1965), an episode in which Bud clutches a small hedgehog curled into a ball, saying "Isn't he beautiful? Look at those markings." Bud's love for pattern and admiration for beauty in the organic is compared, through a long parallel action sequence, to Sandy's crush on a girl (one of the only times a female love interest for him is posited); the episode includes one of the few shots in the series' run to divide Sandy's body into part objects, as the camera lingers in a tight close-up on his leg for several seconds. The parallel moments equate erotic looking and appreciation of organic beauty. "Second Time Around" (S1 E11, 1964) revolves around Linda, a former champion water-skier recently paralyzed in an accident. The boys idolize her: Sandy says, "Flipper was born in the water, for him it's just natural. But to learn to ski like Linda Granville—boy, that would be really something." Sandy's fantasy is to live, like Linda, in another element as if it were his own but which for a human will always be unnatural. Linda's paralysis—she now uses a wheelchair—figures disability as an alternative state of unnaturalness: while Sandy longs for her dolphin-like facility with navigating aquatic environments, Linda envies his easeful negotiating of terrestrial space. In the end, both make peace with their respective impulses to absorb themselves in potentially unwelcoming environments.

Both of these episodes blur the borders between human and animal in ways that make nature available as camp in the sense of its aesthetic appeal and its openness to the mediation of those not "naturally" designed to inhabit it. The viewer's experience of the extended undersea spectacles is often self-reflexively compared to the Ricks': in many episodes, they utilize an "underwater television" attached to the hull of their boat which sends a live stream of the undersea world to a small monitor near their steering wheel, and the footage is often identical with that seen by the viewer full-screen in later shots. This self-reflexivity again destabilizes the nature/culture binarism and is in keeping with the self-referentiality characteristic of much 1960s camp television (Phillips and Pinedo 30).

In mobilizing the cinematic pleasures of the underwater, *Flipper* built on the avant-garde 1920s films of Jean Painlevé, which generated intense public interest because of their ability to record the alien underwater world. But while Painlevé's early films were advertised as being shot underwater, technical limitations in fact necessitated they be filmed through aquarium glass; other early underwater film was shot through portholes in submersibles (Cahill 164–173). By the 1940s, with figures like Jacques Cousteau shepherding innovations in waterproof cameras and new lighting technologies allowing the murky depths to become visible, a genuinely underwater cinematography emerged. Crucially, some of those involved in *Flipper* were active contributors to the importation and development of these technologies in the United States, notably underwater cameramen Lamar Boren and Jordan Klein (Rubin). Producer Ivan Tors built an entire career of bringing the undersea world into cinematic and televised spectacles such as *Flipper* and the James Bond entry *Thunderball* (1965). Co-creator Ricou Browning, who first worked with Tors on the syndicated series *Sea Hunt* (1958–61), had extensive underwater experience. Season-one finale "Flipper's Monster" (S1 E30, 1965), directed by Browning, makes a self-reflexively campy callback to his starring role as the "Gill-Man" in the three *Black Lagoon* films (1954–56, Universal). Browning, donning a monster costume that here is treated as comically fake, reprises his role in a shamelessly cheesy film being shot at Coral Key.[2]

At its most interesting, the camp arrogation of supreme significance to surface so often associated with campy villains bleeds into the naturalistic underwater sequences to which Tors and team devoted such attention. In "The Most Expensive Sardine in the World" (S3 E16, 1967), the rich Mrs. Sharp of Palm Beach has come to Coral Key to get away from the travails of more sophisticated life. This *Green Acres*–type narrative, like "Aunt Martha," provides an opportunity for the camera to linger on ostentatious jewelry and clothing in a moment of more overt camp facilitated by a wealthy female outsider. Sharp makes an exaggeratedly enthusiastic performance of feeding sardines to Flipper, but as she does so, her expensive diamond bracelet falls off and lands on a lobster deep below. The lobster scurries away as the dramatic score flares. Eventually Flipper is able to track down the speedy lobster and return the bracelet to Sharp, as seen in Plate 22. Sharp feeds Flipper a reward of caviar—which he does not like. In extended segments tracking the lobster's scuttle, the creature's spines and claws offer immense visual interest, as do the coral it traverses and the other sea creatures it encounters. Nature is aestheticized, abstracted, and polluted by human-made artifacts, and thus denatured (Heise 93–97). Though nature and culture intermix, the underwater footage avoids the overt anthropomorphism characterizing, say, Painlevé's surrealist-inflected films such as *The Octopus* (1928), in which an intertitle compares an octopus's eye to a human's. A clear but non-anthropomorphic overlay of the natural and artificial is visualized in the long shots of the bejeweled crustacean, which recall the *locus classicus* of queer engagements with aestheticized animality: the gem-clad turtle owned by Des Esseintes, protagonist of J.-K. Huysmans's novel *À rebours*

(1884), as depicted in a contemporaneous illustration in Plate 23. The novel, its title often translated as *Against Nature*, is widely considered the "yellow book" in Oscar Wilde's *The Picture of Dorian Gray* (1890), and its embrace of decadence—epitomized by the bejeweled turtle—sets an important precedent for twentieth-century camp's inversions of what is normatively considered natural.

Flipper consistently interweaves nature and culture without resorting to anthropomorphism. Even Flipper's anthropomorphized quality is only partial: human intelligence is his hallmark, but many episodes hinge on his brute stupidity, as when he veers toward unexploded mines against the boys' command in "Flipper's Hour of Peril" (S2 E4, 1965) or dashes in front of a dart in "Dolphins Don't Sleep" (S3 E18, 1967). In his autobiography, producer Tors naturalizes the series' premise by telling an anecdote about its preproduction, when a dolphin—unsolicited and of its own volition—suddenly took Tors's young son, who was "about the size of a baby dolphin," on a trip on its back. But Tors instantly denaturalizes this foundational myth by comparing Halpin and his son to the Greek myth of Arion, a boy who rode dolphins (140). Culture suddenly sets the precedent for nature, rather than vice versa.

This treatment of the natural world as itself decadent, campy, and always-already aestheticized disturbs the notional ethos of purity and naturalness governing the program. Homoeroticism linked to the male body—and often associated with criminal figures such as the bodybuilder or the counterfeiter—is rooted in, and constantly compared to, the natural. Moreover, if naturalness itself is cast in doubt, the imputed unnaturalness of same-sex attraction which organized homophobic discourses throughout the twentieth century is problematized. In a dialectical move characteristic of dark camp, the stigma of this imputed phobic unnaturalness is brought to the fore but also destabilized by *Flipper*'s nature photography, which shows nature itself as open to deviation and aestheticization.

Camp Receptions

Flipper generated a "secret public," one founded on a collective, purposefully queer viewing of the show (Nealon 99–140). For those viewing *Flipper* as camp, its chief pleasures were formal: the pleasure of looking at the aestheticized male body, and the pleasure of looking at the undersea world, each afforded a degree of plotless fixity. *Flipper*'s mainstream success hinged on its appeal to youth audiences through engaging, *Lassie*-like plots, and Halpin's star power; he received breathless treatment in *16 Magazine*, *Teen Life*, and *Tiger Beat*. A wide array of merchandise stimulated *Flipper* fandom, including novels, toys, and collectible cards. But for many nascent gay viewers in the 1960s and, via reruns since at least 1990, the show proved a formative experience in a more specific way.[3] Gripping encounters with either Kelly's or Halpin's body are attested by a wide array of comments posted on internet message boards over the past decade. Media geared toward young audiences had in previous decades featured aestheticized male actors, but these memories suggest that *Flipper* took this trope to new heights (Dennis). That is, the dual address that facilitated *Flipper*'s secret public is rooted in an overdetermined attunement to the show's camp aestheticism. Phillips and Pinedo argue that camp should be understood as a precedent for the cult TV viewing practices that are commonly said to cohere in the 1990s; many of the responses to *Flipper* from that decade exemplify a cult attitude toward the show, and as such *Flipper* lends further credence to this argument. In this last section, I examine fan responses and the afterlife of *Flipper* in experimental literature and art to see how these readings, evidence of *Flipper*'s secret public, chime with my own darkly campy reading of *Flipper* in what has preceded.

DataLounge, a popular gay message board launched in 1995, has hosted many discussions of *Flipper* over the ensuing years. In threads with titles like "Who were the men that caused you [sic] sexual awakening?" and "Shows that told you you were gay when you were a kid," Halpin and Kelly are regularly named by anonymous posters. Sometimes dissent erupts over which was more attractive, suggesting that for its young proto-gay audience, Bud provided a useful identificatory figure and, depending on taste, Sandy's swimmer's body or Porter's Rock Hudson–style physique satisfied a nascent same-sex desire. "Flipper was such a conundrum for me as a gayling. Did I want the dad or the kids—so torn," writes one commentator. "The kid was an Uber twink and the dad was an Uber daddy. Best of both worlds," resolves another ("OMG"). "The dolphin was apparently supposed to be the focus, but all I could see was Sandy (Luke Halpin) parading around in wet cutoffs," remembers one writer ("Homoerotic"). In the thread "OMG . . . Remember Flipper?," comments include: "I had such a crush on Luke Halprin [sic]" and "I used to wait for the episodes where the father took his shirt off. Masterbation [sic] material!" The latter provoked a reply: "So you coined that phrase 'Flog the dolphin'?" A wonderful example of "camping" in the sense of flamboyant repartee, this exchange reveals a tension between self-exposure and anonymity, sincerity and tease. Personal narratives of self-realization can be shared through the safe channels of fandom's communities, though the drama of "sexual awakening" seems offset by the banality of "flogging the dolphin."

Watching *Flipper* helped cope with the closet, allowing for the articulation and satisfaction of desires through licit channels:

> Growing up in Kentucky in the mid 1960s . . . I was obsessed with the tv show "Flipper." Not because it was some great show, but because Luke Halpin was the object of my teenage masturbatory fantasies for a good 5 years! Funny enough, my mother pointed him out to me on the cover of a "Tiger Beat" magazine that belonged to my sister when we were cleaning out the basement. "Here's that boy that you like so much!" she told me. ("Were you")

As such posts attest, *Flipper*'s secret public hinged on eroticized viewing, producing a specifically camp way of reading the show, focusing on its bodies "not simply because they are appropriate to the plot, but as fascinating in themselves" (Babuscio 22). They also hint at the pain of queer adolescence in a heteronormative society: like Mike's storyline in "City Boy," the posts are tender records of gaining a sense of one's self that nevertheless remains tinged with the ache of secrecy and outsider status, as in the moment of near-outing described in this post, its comedy inflected by the sting of a secret knowledge hidden in plain sight.

Nowhere is this camp-cult reception more evident than in the most devoted expression of interest in Halpin's body: a website founded in 1999 entitled "The Luke Halpin Gallery." The site's mission is "to promote appreciation of Luke's handsome physical image with one of the largest collections of Luke Halpin pictures on the internet: thousands of pictures, scans, and screencaps carefully arranged in over 600 galleries" (cpps90). As an expression of fandom, the continually updated site collects hundreds of screenshots of every *Flipper* episode. One section, "The Remarkable Body of Luke Halpin," is "offered to aid the study of the finer details of Luke Halpin's physical form." The prose sprinkled throughout this section is worshipful; subsections use cropped screenshots to analyze "Luke Halpin's Chest," arms, biceps, shoulders, legs, back, abs, lats, and serratus muscles. Each of these pages isolates hundreds of close-ups of the body part under analysis, making the website a rendition of the poetic trope of blazon, in which individual stanzas or poems describe separate parts of one body. The site embraces the threat of excess traditional blazon forcibly contains (Parker 131) in a nonproductive manner: many of the pictures are near-identical, a repetition as much disorienting and deranging as organizing. Halpin becomes tessellated and kaleidoscopic. Like other websites created in the 1990s to celebrate cult TV shows, the site devotes obsessive attention to an under-sung show. Its excessive concern for superficial detail—Halpin's body—rather than *Flipper*'s world-building or characters qualifies it as camp as well as cult. This camp, though, shades into creepiness, a term I use here in both its ordinary language sense and that proposed by Jonathan Alexander, who advocates "forms of creepiness that are really more about curiosity and the desire to make connections" (120). Scopophilia pervades, and the website clearly objectifies Halpin—a reminder that all this fandom originates in the appealing but forbidden body.

The question of creepiness is engaged by several experimental literary and artistic responses to *Flipper* that have surfaced since the 1990s. A particularly disturbing undercurrent is brought to the surface in "Jerk," a 1993 short story by Dennis Cooper in which a character, Dean, repeatedly kills teenage boys as he has sex with them, producing snuff films in the process. Dean grooms only victims who physically resemble the young male stars of 1950s and 1960s television shows. This repeated scenario originates with a victim who resembles Halpin. Like a puppeteer, Dean mimics the voice of the star whose looks his now-dead victim approximates: "I'm . . . the actor who played the older of the two sons on the TV show 'Flipper'" (19). Given my reading of *Flipper*'s criminality, Cooper does not so much invent this darkness as posit it as latent in the show and exacerbate it. A narrator, who has witnessed these murders, comments: "since those characters are only what you see on screen they have no interior life at all, unlike real human beings who are really complex and impossible to understand . . . when Dean imagined his victim was, like, Luke Halpin, he felt he knew exactly who he'd killed down to the tiniest detail, and that knowledge made the death more meaningful and complete" (22–24). "Jerk" thus gets at the dark side of fandom: the murderous impulse is said to emerge from the fan's knowing the star better than they know themselves. Cult spectatorship is taken to a homicidal extreme. For Matias Viegener, "Jerk" shows that "It is only death which provides the ultimately empty object on which to cathex one's desires, but this death takes the physiognomy of the television character imprinted as the object of desire in the first place. This object is oddly blank" (109). Dean's incorporation of mass culture into obsessive fantasy hinges on the idea of "no interior life," on surface rather than depth, much like "The Body of Luke Halpin" campily arrogates significance exclusively to superficial anatomy. In a dialectical move, this camp is joined to the recognition of emptiness, absence, and death.

Halpin also appears in collages visual artist Larry Clark made between 1989 and 1993 that, like Cooper's prose, link his ephebic body with violent crime. Clark's work, like Cooper's, can be roughly classified within what was theorized in the early 1990s as "abject art," art that reflects on themes including violence, sexual abuse, trauma, and obscenity, often with a great deal of ambiguity and discomfort (Foster). Gathered in the 1993 book *The Perfect Childhood*, several of Clark's collages incorporate Polaroids shot while watching *Flipper* on the small screen. One work features a magazine centerfold of Matt Dillon, age seventeen, leaning shirtless against a tree, at left; to his right is a row of four Polaroids of Halpin, as Sandy, on a boat. Photographing the television screen has turned the ocean into a twinkling, decorative background; a tonal distortion from interlacing underscores that this is a record of television spectatorship. To the right of the Polaroids is a gelatin silver print—one of Clark's own earlier works—depicting an ithyphallic nude man, perhaps in his twenties, with long hair and mustache. The Halpin snapshots connect the other two images, resting above both like stitches. The pattern is repeated at the collage's center, with four additional *Flipper* Polaroids overlapping a second Clark shot of the same mustached model. Is Clark comparing different notions of what an ideal youth might look like, or ironizing the very notion of a "perfect childhood"? Contrasting the family-friendly moderated eroticism of Halpin and Dillon with the desublimated, frank sexuality of the grinning adult, that is, juxtaposing the soft-core and hard-core? Or, conversely, implying that the pornographic subtends the idyllic, with both Dillon and Halpin associated with the pastoral by virtue of their outdoor settings? Tracing a before-and-after sequence of adult sexuality's unfolding? At the rightmost edge of the collage, Clark has added a folded copy of the Princeton undergraduate newspaper's front page, detailing an escalation in sexual harassment at the university circa 1987. This insertion adds further ambiguity to the collection of images: Clark may be comparing the mass media's spectacularizing treatment of young actors to sexual harassment or endorsing a normative "boys will be boys" ethos that arguably connects all four disparate image sources. The collage's pared-down structure gives equally incomplete evidence for both interpretations. This indeterminacy also works on a formal level. The collage evokes scrapbooks or the poster-clad teen bedroom, forms of visual culture with connotations of both fandom and camp (e.g., the collages of Jack Smith or Joe Brainard). Its repetition of images, incorporation of mass-cultural detritus (as in Bruce Conner's *A Movie* [1958]), and emphasis on celebrity also place it within the realm of camp. But the stalker's obsessive inventorying and the serial killer's collaged ransom note are equally palpable visual analogs.

Clark's collages put their viewers in an uncomfortable position: potentially sutured into a pederastic gaze or a conservative homoeroticism disguised as, and propping up, an aggressive heteronormativity (Muñoz). Eugenie Brinkema has tracked the varied responses to Clark's oeuvre: for some he is a perceptive commentator on the authentic experience of American adolescence, while for others he exploits and sexualizes his subjects. If Clark is eroticizing the adolescent body in these collages, this illicit fetishizing again, as in Cooper, takes *Flipper*'s criminal dynamics to an extreme. Like Brinkema, though, I want to bracket the questions of intentionality and Clark's potential investments in his subjects—an important topic beyond the scope of this chapter—and underline what she posits as his key formal operation: a "brutalizing of visual language by paring down to a radical program of exclusion" (248) that "deploys the body to reveal precisely the shortcoming of the prevailing assumption that the stuff of the corpus can be converted, put to use" in a properly signifying activity (263). It is precisely the irresolvability of the questions the collages raise that, in connection with *Flipper*'s dark camp, evokes the senselessness of the body, as focus of attention but also a "blank," as in Cooper's story. Clark's collage montages its elements without synthesizing the disparate materials into a coherent whole; rather, it reflects a failure to assemble meaning. Consider another work from the series, which places a 1983 page from the *New York Times*—headline: "L.I. Teen-ager Is Arraigned in Slaying of Newspaper Boy"—above a sequence of five Polaroids of Halpin, in another *Flipper* scene, gazing in different directions. With the oceanic backdrop again abstracted and jewel-like, Halpin is framed as aesthetic object in a pastoral setting, and yet the large clipping just above de-idealizes him—or perhaps, for Clark, suggests a subtext of criminality always already underpinning Sandy's innocence. If things went wrong in Coral Key, would Sandy be heartless killer or defenseless victim? In the collage, he is brutally blank and indeterminate. From this perspective, Clark's film *Bully* (2001) constitutes a rewriting of *Flipper*: its Florida teens jibe in age and class with the Ricks boys, but succumb to murderous and sadistic impulses. Both collages are creepy; one of the connections their creepiness makes is between criminality and "the perfect childhood." They are productively difficult objects because they reflect a failure to synthesize the two poles central to Flipper's dark camp, the nostalgic/innocent/kitschy and the unnatural/perverse/criminal.

Not all camp appropriations of *Flipper* take such dramatically abject approaches. Hernan Bas, whose art often reflects on homoerotic themes in a Floridian setting, painted a series of watercolors of Halpin as Sandy in 2005, including *Lazy Day (Luke Halpin)* and *Someone's in Danger (Luke Halpin)*. Critic Elizabeth Schambelan describes Bas's work as "Sometimes sadomasochistically charged, but more often suggesting the listless longeurs of love gone bad or unrequited lust." His sources include Hardy Boys novels, Boy Scout manuals, and the nineteenth-century decadence epitomized by Huysmans's *À rebours* (Hobbs). His work is, in the words of one critic, more "anodyne" than that of Cooper and other artists of the previous generation such as Clark (Berardini). This comparatively anodyne quality opens onto what Schambelan describes as a "postcamp" ethos in the work's Huysmansian decadence. The "postcamp" style responds to what the artist terms "fag limbo": a space in which a "new class of [heterosexual] boys ... that flirts with the sort of 'model' behavior typical of what is considered to be a bit sissy" can freely move (Hobbs 55). This untying of "sissy," or traditionally camp-coded aesthetics, from non-normative sexual object choice—in the sense that "fag limbo" is characterized by the appropriation of queer aesthetics by straight men—parallels the commercialization of camp from the 1960s to the present.

Produced in the early stages of Bas's meteoric rise to market success, *Someone's in Danger* depicts a moment similar to that rephotographed by Clark: Halpin at sea, in his small skiff. But Bas pulls back, giving us a wider "shot" so we can see him surrounded by a menacing, stormy ocean, recalling earlier images of maritime disaster such as Géricault's *Raft of the Medusa* (1818–19). In Clark's blurred Polaroids, by contrast, the ocean's narrative dimension is replaced by gaudy, picturesque blurs. Large, brushy strokes filling in both fore- and background render sky and ocean in gloomy steel gray and muddied turquoise, in contrast to Halpin's linear, penciled-in (traces of graphite remain visible), and largely blank body. As in Clark's collages and Cooper's story, there is a sense of Halpin as a surface for cult fan projections, and of his body as a vacant form which may constitute an aesthetic event but which produces little to no meaning aside from its surface. Bas's "postcamp" approach to this subject matter, with its more palatable treatment of *Flipper* and return to traditional notions of painterliness, acknowledges camp's own marketability. But the watercolor nevertheless tries to eke out possibilities for genuinely unexpected pleasures—including pleasures bound up in danger, such as the storm Halpin-as-Sandy confronts here—within the increasingly mainstream territory of camp. Cooper, Clark, and Bas each figure Sandy at moments of crisis, reading the show in relation to risk, criminality, death—and camp.

Flipper's dark camp encompasses the echo of stigma coupled with nostalgic glee captured in online discussions and the yoking of violence and innocence, or gore and aestheticism, in the artworks I have surveyed. Dark camp responses to *Flipper* constitute a particular way of engaging its dual address within the framework of other television of the era. Naïve camp, *Flipper* shows, continued to populate the airwaves in the 1960s, providing a platform for queer coming of age that left room for grappling with the pains of not fitting in and of the closet, even of reckoning with a feeling of being unnatural. The camp that undermined *Flipper*'s overt celebration of the sincere and the natural was a ground for confronting the mixture of a sense of perversion and darkness with a sense of joy and pleasure, affects more often associated with camp. Noting that, from the 1960s through the present, camp has often reproduced racist, phobic, or violent content in order to paradoxically generate bonds within minoritarian counterpublics, Julia Bryan-Wilson suggests that camp works as a "conversion operation or a translation machine, permitting the most repellent aspects of society to be switched into something more lighthearted—though of course this reinterpretation is wholly contingent on reception" (56–57). *Flipper* and its receptions productively stall or suspend this simple switching, retaining ambivalence and acknowledging the repellent. As scholarship on camp begins to examine its previously overlooked unglamorous, gritty side (Hortz-Davies), *Flipper* and its receptions provide an important and unexpected 1960s TV precedent.

Notes

1. Similarly, in "Second Time Around" (S1 E11, 1964), the character Linda refuses to evacuate Coral Key in the face of an oncoming hurricane because she feels it will be an "experience," an embrace of destructive pleasure Porter derides.
2. *The Munsters* (1964–66, CBS) also evoked the Universal film series' Gill-Man character in the figure of Uncle Gilbert ("Love Comes to Mockingbird Heights," S1 E31, 1965) (Hook 101). However, the camp humor of the performativity associated here

with the outmoded and overtly fake costume has more in common with the furry creature in the *Lost in Space* (1965–68, CBS) episode discussed by Wissner (228). There, *Lost in Space* similarly mocks its own application of camp via intentionally poor costuming. Here, the B-movie being shot on Coral Key is an object of derision as a result of its association with deliberate camp, which *Flipper*'s otherwise naïve camp allows. Both point more broadly to the aesthetic performance of camp connected to the history of drag that is reformulated as television comedy by marking its deliberateness in shows such as *The Monkees* (1966–68, NBC) and *Gilligan's Island* (1964–67, CBS) (Phillips and Pinedo 32–34; Amernick 184), where the intentionally poor cross-dressing fools the male antagonists in the story—but never the audience, who are "in" on the "joke."

3. Though said to have intermittently aired in syndication in the 1970s and 1980s, between 1990 and 1996 *Flipper* was "seen daily on Nickelodeon" (Sanz), possibly contributing to the flood of *Flipper* responses I track beginning around 1990.

Bibliography

Alexander, Jonathan. *Creep: A Life, a Theory, An Apology*. Punctum, 2017.
Babuscio, Jack. "Camp and the Gay Sensibility." *Camp Grounds: Style and Homosexuality*, edited by David Bergman, University of Massachusetts Press, 1993, pp. 19–37.
Berardini, Andrew. "Cruising Richard Hawkins." *Mousse Magazine*, no. 12, January 2008, pp. 4–5, 108–110.
Bersani, Leo. "The Gay Outlaw." *Homos*. Harvard University Press, 1995, pp. 113–181.
Booth, Mark. *Camp*. Quartet, 1983.
Brinkema, Eugenie. "Spit * Light * Spunk: Larry Clark, an Aesthetic of Frankness." *Abjection Incorporated*, edited by Maggie Hennefeld and Nicholas Sammond, Duke University Press, 2020, pp. 243–267.
Britton, Andrew. "FOR Interpretation: Notes Against Camp," *Gay Left: A Gay Socialist Journal*, no. 7, Winter 1978–79, pp. 11–14.
Bryan-Wilson, Julia. *Fray: Art and Textile Politics*. University of Chicago Press, 2017.
Cahill, James Leo. *Zoological Surrealism: The Nonhuman Cinema of Jean Painlevé*. University of Minnesota Press, 2019.
Clark, Larry. *The Perfect Childhood*. LCB in association with Thea Westreich, 1993.
Cooper, Dennis. *Jerk*. Artspace Books, 1993.
cpps90. "The Luke Halpin Gallery." October 1999, http://www.cpps90.com/luke/index.html.
Dennis, Jeffrey P. "The Light in the Forest Is Love: Cold War Masculinity and the Disney Adventure Boys." *Americana: The Journal of American Popular Culture*, vol. 3, no. 1, 2004, https://americanpopularculture.com/journal/articles/spring_2004/dennis.htm.
Edelman, Lee. *No Future: Queer Theory and the Death Drive*. Duke University Press, 2004.
Foster, Hal. "Obscene, Abject, Traumatic," *October*, no. 78, pp. 107–124.
Freud, Sigmund. "On Transformations of Instinct as Exemplified in Anal Erotism." *Standard Edition of the Complete Psychological Works of Sigmund Freud*, vol. 17, edited by James Strachey, Vintage, 1975, pp. 125–133.
Glick, Elisa. *Materializing Queer Desire: Oscar Wilde to Andy Warhol*. SUNY Press, 2009.

Heise, Ursula K. *Sense of Place and Sense of Planet: The Environmental Imagination of the Global.* Oxford University Press, 2008.

Hobbs, Robert. "Hernan Bas' 'Fag Limbo' and the Tactics of Reframing Societal Texts." *Hernan Bas: Works from the Rubell Family Collection*, edited by Mark Coetzee, Miami, Rubell Family Collection, 2007, pp. 55–85.

"Homoerotic TV Opening Themes—The Rifleman." *The DataLounge*, April 23, 2011, https://www.datalounge.com/thread/10371948-homoerotic-tv-opening-themes-the-rifleman.

Hotz-Davies, Ingrid, et al., editors. *The Dark Side of Camp Aesthetics: Queer Economies of Dirt, Dust and Patina.* Routledge, 2018.

Huysmans, Joris-Karl. *À Rebours.* Charpentier, 1884.

Kaufman, Dave. "Flipper." *Variety*, September 20, 1965, p. 18.

Kaufman, Dave. "'Flipper' Butters Kelly's Bread; Format Switched." *Variety*, January 18, 1967, p. 17.

Muñoz, José Esteban. "Rough Boy Trade: Queer Desire/Straight Identity in the Photography of Larry Clark." *The Passionate Camera*, edited by Deborah Bright, Routledge, 1998, 167–177.

Nealon, Christopher. *Foundlings: Gay Historical Emotion Before Stonewall.* Duke University Press, 2001.

"OMG . . . Remember Flipper?" *The DataLounge*, January 21, 2016, https://www.datalounge.com/thread/16355400-omg...remember-flipper-.

Parker, Patricia. *Literary Fat Ladies: Rhetoric, Gender, Property.* Routledge, 1987.

Phillips, W. D., and Isabel Pinedo. "Gilligan and Captain Kirk Have More in Common Than You Think: 1960s Camp TV as an Alternative Genealogy for Cult TV." *Journal of Popular Television*, vol. 6, no. 1, 2018, pp. 19–40.

Rubin, Steven Jay. "Boren, Lamar." *The Complete James Bond Movie Encyclopedia.* Contemporary Books, 1995, pp. 46–48.

Sanz, Cynthia. "In the Wake of the Dolphin." *People*, July 19, 1993. Reprinted in "The Luke Halpin Gallery," http://www.cpps90.com/luke/html/articles/people_1993.html.

Schambelan, Elizabeth. "Hernan Bas," *Artforum*, vol. 43, no. 4, December 2004, p. 197.

See, Sam. "The Comedy of Nature: Darwinian Feminism in Virginia Woolf's *Between the Acts.*" *Modernism/modernity*, vol. 17, no. 3, 2010, pp. 639–667.

"Shows That Told You You Were Gay When You Were a Kid." *The DataLounge*, April 13, 2011, https://www.datalounge.com/thread/10346943-shows-that-told-you-you-were-gay-when-you-were-a-kid.

Sontag, Susan. "Notes on 'Camp.'" 1964. *Against Interpretation and Other Essays.* 1966. E-book, Farrar, Straus and Giroux, 2013, pp. 238–305.

Stockton, Kathryn Bond. *Beautiful Bottom, Beautiful Shame: Where "Black" Meets "Queer."* Duke University Press, 2006.

Tors, Ivan. *My Life in the Wild.* Houghton Mifflin, 1979.

Viegener, Matias. "Men Who Kill and the Boys Who Love Them." *Critical Quarterly*, vol. 36, no. 1, 1994, pp. 105–114.

"Were You a Boy-Crazy Boy?" *The DataLounge*, January 3, 2016, https://www.datalounge.com/thread/16262260-were-you-a-boy-crazy-boy.

"Who Was the Hottest Vintage TV Twink?" *The DataLounge*, July 4, 2011, https://www.datalounge.com/thread/10611343-who-was-the-hottest-vintage-tv-twink-.

"Who Were the Men That Caused You Sexual Awakening? And How Old Were You?" *The DataLounge*, May 5, 2019, www.datalounge.com/thread/23797554-who-were-the-men-that-caused-you-sexual-awakening-and-how-old-were-you-.

Media

Batman. 1966–68. Television Series. Seasons 1–3. USA: ABC.
Bully. Directed by Larry Clark, Lionsgate Films, 2001.
Creature from the Black Lagoon. Directed by Jack Arnold, Universal Pictures, 1954.
Flaming Creatures. Directed by Jack Smith, 1963.
Flipper. 1965–67. Television Series. Seasons 1–3. USA: NBC.
Gilligan's Island. 1964–67. Television Series. Seasons 1–3. USA: CBS.
Lost in Space. 1965–68, Television Series. Seasons 1–3. USA: CBS.
The Monkees. 1966–68. Television Series. Seasons 1–2. USA: NBC.
A Movie. Directed by Bruce Conner, 1958.
The Munsters. 1964–66. Television Series. Seasons 1–2. USA: CBS.
The Octopus. Directed by Jean Painlevé, 1928.
Sea Hunt. 1958–61. Television Series. Seasons 1–4. USA: Syndication.
Thunderball. Directed by Terence Young, United Artists, 1965.

12
Camp TV, *The Beverly Hillbillies* (1962–71), and Flip Wilson's (1970–74) Geraldine Jones
Negativity, Trans Gender Queer, and the Comedy of Manners

Ken Feil

The 1964 publication of Susan Sontag's "Notes on 'Camp'" inspired numerous critics to formulate lists and lineages of exemplary works, and like Sontag, they often disregarded the fledgling medium of television.[1] TV merited no references in Sontag's essay, and it earned just one mention in Gloria Steinem's 1965 *Life* magazine piece "A Vest-Pocket Guide to Camp," for professional wrestling shows (84).[2] Television's low cultural status coupled with its associations with domesticity and femininity nevertheless contributed to its camp potential, as evocative of "so-bad-it's-good" and the "artifice" of gender (Sontag 279–280, 292). Calvin Trillin shored up all these connections in a 1965 *New Yorker* short story about a wannabe hipster hero who "idly switched on the television set and saw two middle-aged ladies from Ohio . . . playing 'Buckle Down, Winsocki' by pulling window shades up and down on portable window frames," an action that prompts the poser to ponder if "Ted Mack's 'Original Amateur Hour' was Pop, and maybe even Camp" (40).[3] Steinem intimated similar sentiments reviewing Jacqueline Susann's 1966 bestseller *Valley of the Dolls*, whose "Unconscious Low Camp" blossomed in "television-bad dialogue" penned by "a former TV actress" (Steinem, "Massive Overdose" 11). Novelist Susann likewise confirmed television's camp proteanism, which now carried with it a queer patina, just three years later in her second bestseller *The Love Machine*, in which one network television executive remarks on "two shows that *had* to flop and instead they came off as 'high camp' successes"; speculating about

Ken Feil, *Camp TV*, The Beverly Hillbillies *(1962–71), and Flip Wilson's (1970–74) Geraldine Jones* In: *Camp TV of the 1960s*. Edited by Isabel C. Pinedo and W. D. Phillips, Oxford University Press. © Oxford University Press 2023.
DOI: 10.1093/oso/9780197650745.003.0013

the show's producer, he continues: "There are even rumors that he's queer" (Susann 484).

Mark Booth formalized a position about TV's campiness in the monograph *Camp* (1983), which furnished Cultural Studies with a pithy and lasting definition: "*To be camp is to present oneself as being committed to the marginal with a commitment greater than the marginal merits*" (18).[4] Booth follows this axiom by isolating the foremost form of socially constructed piffle, "the traditionally feminine" (18), and in the ensuing chapters solidifies a trajectory of camp "democratisation" that travels from aristocratic culture to mass culture, "no longer the prerogative of an economic elite, but the birthright of all . . . who watch camp comedians on peak-time television" (175–176). Coalescing "stylized effeminacy" with the low cultural status of TV, Booth's example of the British sitcom *Are You Being Served?* (1972–85, BBC) also references an element that permeates camp narratives, the theatrical comedy of manners (also called manners comedy). An illustration of this sitcom, which takes places in a London department store, shows the flamboyant, ambiguously gay men's clothing clerk Mr. Humphries (John Inman) embracing a male mannequin in front of his associate Mrs. Slocombe (Molly Sugden), whom Booth compares to a character from William Congreve's eighteenth-century manners comedy *The Way of the World* (176). Booth's gesture locates in a sitcom qualities of the camp theatrical genre discussed earlier in his book, which originated in Restoration theater and "shifted the emphasis from moral dilemmas to stylistic ones," a dynamic eventually appropriated by "bourgeois," queer playwrights the likes of Oscar Wilde, Noël Coward, and Joe Orton (Booth 52–53, 62, 122–123).[5] If the high culture, camp comedy of manners promoted the patently aristocratic credo of style over substance, Booth suggests continuity with Camp TV, recipient and broadcaster of camp's "irresponsible and slightly dangerous pleasure" (52, 175).

The violation of conventional "good taste" and its reflection in gender performance and sexual orientation comprised a camp comedy of manners that set the stage for the programs of Camp TV, as well as its fans. Manners comedy surfaced in the Camp TV of the 1960s and 1970s alongside features identified by W. D. Phillips and Isabel Pinedo: parody, satire, self-reflexivity, and gender performativity (27). Camp TV enacted, moreover, a "larger challenge to normative values and institutions" (Phillips and Pinedo 28), also a key impulse of the "subversive" manners comedies that David L. Hirst dissects, plays such as Noël Coward's *Hay Fever* (1925) and *Design for Living*

(1932) in which "bohemian" sophisticates living according to the credo of style conquered the forces of bourgeois tastefulness (Hirst 3–4, 60–61, 64–66). In Camp TV, dedication to the marginal linked high culture with low through a common delight in the devalued, effeminized taste for stylization, theatricality, flamboyance, and as Matthew Tinkcom encapsulates, "the passionate failure to strive for a compulsory identity" (15). On the reception end, furthermore, fans flaunting their camp connoisseurship enacted a cultural comedy of manners by parading cultural knowledge that lacked legitimacy, a flurry of taste making that was funny because it was "incongruous" to bourgeois tastefulness (Booth 16; Tinkcom 20; Cohan 1, 8).

The contestation of "compulsory identity" in Camp TV manners comedy not only disrupted tasteful performances of class, gender, and sexuality but also race and ethnicity. Camp theory tends to remain colorblind and as a result, José Esteban Muñoz and Pamela Robertson Wojcik inform, replicates the white, gay, male, and middle-class historical norms of camp (Muñoz 129; Wojcik 20). Recent work by Racquel J. Gates unearths, however, the proximity between camp and what Gates calls "negative" Black texts that challenge racialized norms of tastefulness (*Double Negative* 19, 27–28, 34). Quinlan Miller consequently illuminates the cisgendered and white assumptions of camp theory, as well as the racialized, "trans gender queer" dimensions of gender performance that underpin camp TV of the 1950s and 1960s (40).

This chapter applies both Gates's and Miller's paradigms toward analyses of camp manners comedy in the sitcom *The Beverly Hillbillies* (1962–71, CBS) in addition to Flip Wilson's drag performances as Geraldine Jones on *Rowan & Martin's Laugh-In* (1968–73, NBC) and *The Flip Wilson Show* (1970–74, NBC). Wilson's Geraldine and *The Beverly Hillbillies* both resonate as Camp TV comedy that derives humor from the interruption of conventional good taste, and both resonate in the history of trans gender queer camp TV. *The Beverly Hillbillies* provides a vivid example of how trans gender queer camp works in concert with manners comedy to undermine heteronormative constructions of gender and sexual desire. Wilson's Geraldine exemplifies a negative camp text whose reception by some notable Black culture critics of the period deemed it stereotypical and regressive, yet has been reappraised more recently for Wilson's complexly racialized, gender-nonconforming performance. As a negative camp text in Black gay and trans culture, Wilson's Geraldine signified as both an alternative to normative gender performance and the means to ridicule gender nonconformity. Locating the significance of Wilson's camp TV comedy as Geraldine involves exploring various kinds of negativity surrounding the comedian's reception, in addition to signs of Wilson's "secondary circulation" in Black queer and trans culture (Gates, *Double Negative* 31, 33). Bruce Morrow's "A Play" (1993) and the documentary *Disclosure* (2020) provide ambivalent meditations on Geraldine as a figure of camp TV comedy, an ambivalence addressed by Laverne Cox in the documentary and redefined in Cox's own camp comedy performances.[6]

Camp, the Comedy of Manners, and *The Beverly Hillbillies*

US network television in the 1960s stocked mass culture with comedies of manners hewn from a camp sensibility. David Pierson argues that sitcoms such as *The Beverly Hillbillies* personified this manners comedy, but Pierson virtually negates its subversive camp; focusing on the triumph of agrarian values over style, decadence, fantasy, and the comedy of gender failure, Pierson only hints at the confusion of gender roles and sexualities that Miller unveils as the same series' camp features (36–40). Miller's conception of trans gender queer camp also evokes the workings of manners comedy—the triumph of style and theatricality over bourgeois conceptions of morality and taste—by arguing that the standardized norms of the sitcom consolidate formulaic elements that subvert binary gender performance. Miller particularly focuses here on character "eccentricity," "drag performance," "tropes of crossed wires and missed connections," dialogue strewn with double-entendre, and incongruous heterosexual coupling (9, 14–16, 29, 111). Pierson and Miller seize on what they both call the "contradictions" underpinning Nancy Kulp's character Jane Hathaway; taken together, they both illuminate the trans gender queer contradictions riddling the show's situational comedy of manners as well as provide the tools to trace further manifestations of queer camp manners comedy in the character Jethro Bodine (Pierson 37, 40; Miller 6, 9, 72).

Pierson's fruitful identification of *The Beverly Hillbillies* as a comedy of manners nevertheless overlooks what Booth views as manners comedy's governing sensibility, camp, discernible since the origins of the genre in seventeenth-century theater: Restoration comedy and the plays of Molière (Booth 52–53, 121). Pierson defines manners comedy as "the critical exploration of . . . social manners and mores," and notes the foundational irony generating "the corrective nature of the comedies' social satire," that "restoring the traditional order" at the conclusion "appears strained and absurd, which represents the order as socially false and hollow" (36). Booth also discerns the implausible resumption of social order at the conclusion of manners comedy narratives but identifies this ironic "restoration" as the stimulus for camp pleasure:

> The repentance of the fops at the end of Restoration comedies does not convince . . . Their disguises, affectations and so on are represented as in no way regrettable, but rather as aspects of a world that is more amusing, more luxurious and more fun than that outside the theatre. A good production of a Restoration play can make us feel that life might be better if it were more camp. (121)

Pierson upholds, by contrast, that the pleasure and potency of manners comedy in *The Beverly Hillbillies* stem from a critique of modernity that unambiguously rejects all the elements that camp manners comedy ironically recuperates: "social-climbing, money, and the latest fashion fads and trends" (37). This perspective negates Booth's camp contention that the decadent stylishness seemingly being critiqued in manners comedy actually acts as a camp wish-dream of style, insincerity, theatrics, and sensuous pleasure that evades both moralistic plot mechanics and life "outside the theatre."

Overlooking camp in the comedy of manners minimizes the genre's queer history, most evidently embodied in the effeminate "fops" and "dandies" that Booth anoints as camp icons. Raymond-Jean Frontain notes the historical compatibility (if not the equation) among gay culture, camp, and the "satiric mode" of manners comedy, which reverberates with "artificiality" and wordplay (161). Frontain contemplates that marginalization from heteronormative conventions of marriage and family motivated the gay writers of manners comedy, in addition to fulfilling the socially constructed roles of camp tastemaker and wit (161–162). With echoes of Pierson, Frontain notes the "arch, yet humorous, self-awareness of social foibles" in gay manners comedies and invokes Booth when extolling "the comic indulgence of behavioral excess" in Ronald Firbank's novels, Tom of Finland's homoerotic artwork, and Charles Ludlam's Ridiculous Theatrical Company (163). Frontain's concentration on gay male culture nevertheless ignores the historical genderqueerness of camp manners comedy. Miller avers, "This term *trans gender queer* is a placeholder for the genderqueer within pop culture products assumed to be exclusively cis" (3), and enlisting Booth's reasoning, brilliantly teases out the trans gender queer activity of camp parody as well as the centrality of camp in the standardized sitcom formula of the 1950s and 1960s (4–5, 12–14). Trans gender queer camp indeed pertains to additional cultural forms besides sitcoms, such as musical theater, cabaret, and stand-up comedy, and circling back to dramatic theater, surely surfaces in the style-conscious, masquerading, and duplicitous characters of theatrical comedies of manners (Miller 6, 183n11; Booth 18–19, 52–54). Miller and Pierson both explore the comedic contradictions of *Beverly Hillbillies*, and by connecting their arguments as well as extending them, this chapter fosters a clearer picture of how manners comedy figures into the gender performativity of Camp TV and, in turn, the centrality of manners comedy to the trans gender queer pleasures of this particular camp TV sitcom.

Pierson concentrates on *The Beverly Hillbillies* as a satire of modernity orbiting around a traditional moral center, the agrarian family patriarch Jed Clampett (Buddy Ebsen), and the critic concedes that "the sitcom is generally perceived as having a conservative perspective toward gender roles and politics" (39–40). Before unpacking this position, though, Pierson proffers, "the sitcom is not without its share of contradictions" (40). These contradictions include the educated, single secretary Jane Hathaway (played by Nancy Kulp), whose "unrequited" desire for Jed's muscular nephew Jethro Bodine (Max Baer Jr.) surprises conventions; even though Hathaway embodies the "unlikable, unsympathetic stereotype" of the "older woman lusting over a much younger man," Hathaway is redeemed as "the most decent, honorable, non-familial character in the show" (40). Pierson's secondary reflections on gender and sexuality regarding this "non-familial character" prove primary for Miller, while Miller's reasoning consistently dovetails with the goals and delights of the comedy of manners. *The Beverly Hillbillies* endures as "relevant—indispensable—to the study of camp TV" largely due to the work of Nancy Kulp; the situations in which Hathaway's character mocks "marriage, marriages of convenience, and single (lack of) status" are endemic also to manners comedy (111–112). Among many typecast character actors of the period, Kulp's performative "eccentricity," visible in Video 12.1, combined with other standardized features of the sitcom to generate trans gender queer camp in terms proximate to the comedy of manners: ironizing the stereotype of the "man-hungry old maid," and undermining the ridicule underlying connotations of "lesbian," "desexualized," and "sexually aggressive" (Miller 6, 9, 72) ▶. TV critics and scholars tend to confer both heterosexual desire and cis gender on Hathaway, but when the character is perceived from a perspective aware that "gender crossing of the kind common in camp is possible, pleasurable, and productive," Kulp's Hathaway instead emerges as "queerly effeminate," a "desiring subject [who] is male-identified and masculine-presenting" (72). Analyzing an appearance by Kulp on another sitcom, Miller observes a similar "campily masculine, effeminate gender expression" that scrambles presumptions about gender constructs and sexual desire (9, 73). In Hathaway's mission of winning over Jethro, returning to Pierson's example, Kulp's gender slippage enacts a queering of both heteronormative gender and desire, a dynamic that further implicates Jethro, as seen in Figure 12.1, as either an objectified male hunk or a variation on the camp fop (Miller 70–71, 86).

When Hathaway chases Jethro, exemplified in Video 12.2, Kulp's fluid embodiment of "male-identified," "masculine-presenting," and "queerly effeminate" transforms Jethro into a variety of camp figures ⊙. Jethro's visible evocation of Al Capp's popular comic strip hero Li'l Abner underscores the

Figure 12.1 The camp coupling of Jane Hathaway and Jethro Bodine on *The Beverly Hillbillies*. "Meanwhile, Back at the Cabin" (S1 E3, 1962, *Beverly Hillbillies*, CBS Broadcasting Inc.).

character as a gay object of desire, just predating Kenneth Anger's underground classic *Scorpio Rising* (1963), which famously outed Capp's comic strip hillbilly's "strongly homoerotic" overtones, and following Paramount's 1959 movie musical adaptation *Li'l Abner*, which rivals *Gentlemen Prefer Blondes* (1953) in its spectacularly, hilariously choreographed objectification of men's bodies (Harkins 188; Brennan 22, 25; Doty 138–140). Other of Jethro's qualities push the character toward camp theatricality in terms of the fops and dandies of manners comedy: as "a social climber," in Pierson's words, "easily influenced by the latest media fads and fashions"; and as someone devoid of "common sense," in pursuit of "an improbable range of fantasy-like occupations" (40). Paraphrasing Sontag, Jethro embodies the key traits of camp texts, "unpretentiousness and vulgarity," being "extreme and irresponsible in their fantasy—and therefore touching and quite enjoyable" (284–285). Combined with the character's failure to conform to bourgeois taste and heteronormative expectations of marriage, career, and family, Jethro deviates from the show's status quo moral code of agrarian values (Pierson 40). Jethro's pursuit of status remains nonreproductive, theatrical, and artificial and, like the fops, dandies, and bohemians of manners comedy, presents both a negative moral example and camp source of pleasure, a camp force of disruption perpetually stalling fulfillment of the patriarchal, heteronormative "success" narrative (Pierson 40; Halberstam 120).

Like the fops who signal "a world that is more amusing, more luxurious and more fun than that outside the theatre" (Booth 121), the camp manners comedy of Jane Hathaway and Jethro Bodine gestures beyond restrictive, naturalized constructs of binary gender and sexual desire. By contrast to the theater's fops, though, who at least experience a cosmetic (if "unconvincing") "repentance" at a play's conclusion, Hathaway and Jethro are irreparable, perpetually returning to their basic situational "eccentricities" every week. Camp TV's comedy of manners exhausts socially and institutionally mandated constrictions through its standardized gender parody "by signifying within constraints," such as when Miller opines, "Coupling and sexism are camp points of focus and focal points for camp" (72, 111). Parodying social reality is "more fun" because it hints at life beyond the limits of dominant norms and, quite tellingly, such playfulness in the comedy of manners has been criticized as "immoral and unpleasant." According to Hirst, the comedy of manners "is undoubtedly the most anti-romantic form of comedy . . . [in which] conventional moral standards are superseded by the criterion of taste, of what constitutes 'good form'" (2). Camp TV manners comedy defines "good form" differently from the typical theatrical comedy of manners, surely, enthroning eccentricity and scrambled gender as styles of distinction and sources of pleasure.

Negative Camp TV: The Manners Comedy of Flip Wilson's Geraldine Jones

Camp TV manners comedy further flourished in comedy-variety shows of the late 1960s and early 1970s, within the context of the sexual revolution, counterculture, anti-war movement, and the movements for Black Power, women's liberation, and gay liberation. *Rowan & Martin's Laugh-In* openly entertained the label "camp," as I have explored in prior work, signified in the show's style, content, and reception: a "McLuhenesque," "New Wave," rapid-fire editing style; topical humor involving heterosexuality, homosexuality, transsexuality, and interracial sexuality; a variegated audience address to children, youth culture, and intellectuals; and the reputation for "borderline taste" and "reverse sophistication" (Levine 21–22, 172–173; Bodroghkozy 149–151; Feil 8, 26, 41, 63–64, 104).[7] *The Flip Wilson Show* most obviously contributed to Camp TV through the host's iconic, fabulously popular drag character Geraldine Jones, a version of which Wilson had performed early in the second season of *Laugh-In* (see Plate 24). A fearless and flamboyant force bedecked in *haute couture* and engaging in transgressive behavior—often involving male celebrity guests (see Video 12.3)—Geraldine Jones's comedy of manners also received criticism at the time for invoking racist stereotypes ⏵. The phenomenon of Wilson's drag performance as Geraldine illuminates connections between camp and manners comedy in US network TV comedy of the late 1960s and early 1970s. Just as importantly, Wilson's contributions to Camp TV flag the insufficiency of camp theory to fully grasp the sensibilities and social constructions that Geraldine's manners comedy parodies, and the impact of Geraldine's manners comedy on a variety of audiences.[8]

If, as Tinkcom elucidates, "camp emerges as a concealed [queer] knowledge that travels with some commodities" (10), this idea joins with the gender performativity of Camp TV that Phillips and Pinedo credit with spurring "active viewership" (31–32). Phillips and Pinedo submit that Camp TV of the 1960s functioned on a secondary level of interpretation akin to resistant taste. Referring to "narrative strategies such as parody and satire, intertextuality, self-reflexivity and an overt emphasis on performativity that included (but was not limited to) the treatment of gender," they assert that "Camp TV both allowed for the mobilization of an active viewer and enabled that viewer to recognize the contestability of the texts' surface-level representations" (27). Camp TV essentially furnishes the conditions for such "contestability" through self-reflexive parody and satire, beginning on the level of taste and style and stretching to gender and sexuality.

Racquel J. Gates suggests additional forms of "concealed knowledge" embedded in camp as well as the oppositional reading strategies it spurs. Addressing scholarship on trash and sleaze, siblings to camp, Gates confirms what Pamela Robertson Wojcik notes as "the degree to which camp is assumed to be white" (Wojcik 20). Gates reasons, "we should productively trouble these existing discussions of taste and culture by first acknowledging that . . . all of these descriptors are still referring to *white* culture," that "an analysis of black mass culture necessitates both a different framework and a different category than those mainstream cultural texts associated with 'trash'" (*Double Negative* 27). Considering "the racially specific nature of the production, consumption, and circulation of black texts," Gates formulates a process for retrieving and reappraising Black cultural works disqualified as "negative": devalued by "normative, white hegemonic standards of quality" as well as "the politics of respectability" dictating "positive" Black representations (*Double Negative* 16, 21–22). Gates also conceives of "negativity" as an "alternative reading strategy," comparable to camp both in its commitment to culturally marginal texts and as a means of contesting dominant meanings (*Double Negative* 18, 20). Gates queries, "how might we see the work that negative texts are doing in the service of race, gender, sexuality, and class, when, as Matthew Tinkcom argues about camp, the work is disguised as something else, such as stereotypes?" (*Double Negative* 19–20). The normative dismissal of queer camp further compares to the disregarding of negative texts as an erasure of both Black creative work and Black audience pleasure (*Double Negative* 206n16).

Negativity neighbors Camp TV spectatorship and routinely intersects with it. Gates maps a process that "reclaims black texts that have been excluded from more traditional black film and television canons," one that depends upon the spectator's "understanding of the relation between dominant and contested meanings" and that "emphasizes the significance of black audiences and intertextuality to confer meaning" (*Double Negative* 18, 30). Negative texts and Camp TV, additionally, recurrently emerge in "the frivolous spaces of comedy" (Gates, *Double Negative* 30). By demonstrating the racialized dimensions of marginalized taste and a taste for the cultural margins, Gates not only prompts a rethinking of Camp TV but also the manners comedy in camp works and the comedy of manners that camp fandom initiates: the fan's assertion of negative camp taste as the triumph of style.

Gates evaluates reality shows such as *The Real Housewives of Atlanta* (2008–present, Bravo), for instance, by first revealing how discourses of taste, race, and social manners drive critical disapproval toward this program, which "overwhelmingly converged on the women's femininity, speech patterns, and mannerisms: sites where preconceived notions of 'upper class,' 'successful,' and 'housewife' (historically underscored by an implicit vision of whiteness) did not match the image that the Black Atlanta housewives projected" ("New Jack Black" 142; *Double Negative* 33). Gates avers that "we as viewers . . . can choose to embrace unruly women who lapse into the territory of 'ghetto,'" but acknowledges the high stakes of this *manners comedy of reception*, "given the history of racial representation in the media. It is, in fact, a *privilege* to be able to ignore the ways that racialized images have operated throughout history, one that African Americans have not traditionally been able to afford" ("New Jack Black" 153, 154).[9] Gates asserts this privilege in the language of style and taste endemic to manners comedy, both among the cast of *Real Housewives of Atlanta* and their audience. Addressing the objections of one cultural activist to the show's focus on "successful women" who manifest "ratchetness"—"behavior that is crude, socially unacceptable, and, more often than not, associated with lower-class black vernacular culture"—Gates challenges binary taste codes that overlap with constructions of race and gender: "more radically," she asks, "might it be possible for the 'successful women in Atlanta' to *also* be ratchet?" (*Double Negative* 25, 144). Gates's reclamation of *Real Housewives* involves the intersecting discourses of taste, race, and gender and coincides here with Miller's trans gender queer camp by "rejecting racist norms of perception, identity, and attraction enacted through binary gender" (Miller 15). This perspective guides perceptions of disenfranchised culture and the risks of both representation and audience pleasure. In viewing Flip Wilson's drag character Geraldine Jones as Camp TV we must consider, consequently, how Wilson performed a comedy of manners about the intersecting etiquettes of race, gender, and sexuality, a taste-making maneuver recounted by Mel Watkins as "imposing an African-American perspective" as well as "a black comic voice," for which Wilson was criticized "as a throwback to Sapphire of *Amos 'n' Andy* infamy" (Watkins

523). Wilson's Geraldine represented "a power differential on a sliding scale," in Marjorie Garber's words, "a cultural rhetoric of difference doubly inflected by race and gender," and one with "a remarkable—and dangerous—history of representation. *The issue of who manipulates the image and whose pleasure and power it serves is, in the specter of black transvestitism, brought to a state of crisis*" (274). In the overlapping contexts of Black mass culture and Camp TV, the negative reception of Geraldine represents this "crisis" as concern about the degree of "contestability" for the comedian's stereotypical character. Black audiences could comprehend Wilson's self-reflexive parody and performativity within a larger representational and cultural history, while concerns arose that white audiences ignorant of this history perceived Geraldine as a confirmation of racist norms (Watkins 41; Garber 273, 274; Acham 72–73; Haggins 37–38, 48–49). Bambi Haggins illuminates this representational crisis through "the use of drag . . . as either a liberating device utilized to interrogate stereotypes or as a means of rearticulating (and, arguably, recodifying) them within the context of black comedy. When Wilson did drag, it was both" (45). Haggins questions the degree of gender liberation by pointing out that "during Geraldine's heyday the black man playing a black woman was given greater comic license than actual black comediennes—as well as greater mainstream acceptance" (48). Geraldine also maintained an ambiguous relationship to gay culture; Wilson resisted the association of his drag with gay culture, an effort supported by some Black critics and indirectly validated by homosexual assimilationists who disputed the stereotypical equation of effeminacy with gay identity (Martin 195; Haggins 249n65; McBride 371–372; Alwood 139). Then again, Haggins counters, "Wilson attained a degree of drag credibility," an assertion that might also attest to the compatibility of Black and gay discourses of cultural resistance (Haggins 45, 249n65).

Secondary recirculation of *The Flip Wilson Show* and Geraldine Jones provides the foundations for negativity and camp to reclaim the character: drawing into relief what Gates refers to as Wilson's "variety of characters from black experience" (48) and extending that logic to Black gay, queer, feminist, and trans perspectives. Geraldine corresponds to a variety of categories of negativity envisioned by Gates: "formal negativity," here pertaining to a Black male comedian engaging in drag and employing Black cultural forms for a mixed mass audience; "comparative negativity," something Haggins identifies "when one juxtaposes the Chitlin' Circuit-informed, broad ethnic humor of Wilson's show . . . and the social relevance dramatic programming emerging on network television"; "circumstantial negativity," the criticism Wilson accrued for recycling racist stereotypes; and "strategic negativity," which Gates defines as "media texts . . . taking advantage of their distance from the politics of respectability to explore topics that their positive counterparts do not typically address" (*Double Negative* 32–34; Haggins 45–46, 48). Garber helps pinpoint Geraldine's strategic negativity through a comment by Wilson during an *Ebony* magazine interview: "Geraldine is an attitude . . . Flip Wilson might hold back on saying something but Geraldine will jump down your throat" (qtd. in Garber 298); Garber comments, "the black male comedian was here empowered by his female double. 'Geraldine' could speak when 'Flip Wilson' deemed it prudent to remain silent; she could get away with things that were still transgressive for him" (298). This particular "transgressive" gambit relied on, Haggins contends, "a problematic construction of black womanhood as overtly sexual, as possessing questionable intellectual acuity (at least, in academic terms), and as more than slightly assertive and outspoken" (46). As Garber considers, "the kind of 'success' involved in a black male comedian's impersonation of an assertive and flamboyant black woman as a vehicle for his own professional and economic liberation repeated as many patterns as it reversed" (298–299).

Wilson concocted the voice associated with Geraldine in stand-up sets, and he purportedly first performed as Geraldine for a 1969 NBC TV special in a sketch opposite Jonathan Winters playing Maude Frickert (Garber 298; Tafoya 93; Haggins 41). Even before the NBC special, though, Geraldine appeared (sans moniker) early into the second blockbuster season of *Rowan & Martin's Laugh-In*, on October 21, 1968 (Feil 4–6). Immediately following NBC's "in living color" promotional segue, the episode opens on a figure in a pink satin gown with matching parasol, standing center foreground, back to the audience and facing upstage. As we see in Video 12.4, an effeminate man in a beret and equestrian jacket rushes downstage and quickly proclaims, "You're perfect, absolutely perfect for Scarlet O'Hara in our new remake of *Gone with the Wind*! . . . Except, there's just one thing wrong." The begowned figure twirls frontward, now recognizable as Flip Wilson in drag, the last detail of the outfit punctuating the reveal: a blond wig. Without delay, Wilson's proto-Geraldine replies, "You mean my New York accent?" ⓘ A little while later, after Goldie Hawn makes typical mincemeat of a line reading, a close-up of Wilson cuts in, now sporting auburn ponytails. "That's easy for you to say, honey," kids Wilson's character, whereupon Hawn replies, "Not really, Sapphire." Hawn's punchline builds on the ostensible comic surprise of

Wilson's drag character by collapsing her with Sapphire Stevens on the radio and TV sitcom *Amos 'n' Andy* (NBC and CBS radio, 1928–60; CBS television, 1951–53), the same character that just a few years later *Ebony* magazine editor Lerone Bennett Jr. would recall to critique Wilson's Geraldine and present troubling reasons behind this particular character's popularity (Feil 4–6; Moody 46; Sutherland 64).

The humor in the opening bit surpasses the jokey revelation of cross-dressing and reverberates with reflexive camp negativity. The device of redirection provides one layer of humor; Wilson's charged, racialized drag as an antebellum blond belle with a voice redolent of Butterfly McQueen in *Gone with the Wind*, to whom Garber likens Geraldine (298), is displaced by the incongruous mismatch of regional—but no less racialized—accents, sounding like someone from the "Big Apple" rather than a Georgia peach. Drag here becomes (recalling Haggins's argument) "a liberating device utilized to interrogate stereotypes" (Haggins 45), racialized, gendered, and regional, in addition to spotlighting the country's racist history and Hollywood's racist criteria for casting, choosing stories, and determining audience appeal. Wilson's exchange with Hawn, by contrast, relates an ironic ambivalence that recirculates the comedic stereotypes of *Amos 'n' Andy* uncritically (Feil 81, 94, 97; Haggins 45). Wilson's bodily grace, comic timing, and sense of irony in the first bit empower the character as a flamboyant, confident commentator. Framing and staging in the second bit challenge Wilson's performative agency, limited to a headshot and spatially separated from Hawn. The bit initially entitles Wilson's character on the racialized terrains of language and gender comportment—mildly mocking the blond, white Hawn's garbled delivery—but then Hawn, with perfect diction, interpellates Wilson's character with a name that strikes as a ridiculous stereotype, a put-down rather than an inside joke.

Manners comedy furthermore intertwines with Geraldine's strategic and formal negativity, with the character's contradictory language of flamboyant style serving as Wilson's vehicle for both gendered cross-dressing and racial crossovers. Haggins references, for instance, the "hip" style Wilson fashioned for Geraldine, one that combined diverse cultural constructions of Blackness and femininity: "part Sapphire, part Foxy Brown (and, in terms of fashion sensibility, part *That Girl*'s Ann Marie)"; featuring "perfectly coiffed hair and miniskirted designer wear"; and "carefully crafted to at least approximate the (hip) everywoman" (44–45). Garber similarly observes how "'Geraldine,' the transvestite in her wig and Puccis, opened the door for blacks to mainstream

TV comedy" (299). By contrast to prior examples of TV drag comedy, moreover, "Wilson attained a degree of drag credibility," a pronouncement that Haggins substantiates through Wilson's recollection in 1993 of a drag performer who thanked him during a show "'for making what we do possible and . . . for your contribution to the well being of the gay community.' Despite his wariness about the use of drag being equated with homosexuality, Wilson was touched by the impromptu tribute, stating, 'That stopped me right in my tracks'" (Haggins 45, 249n65). In the terms of manners comedy, style not only wins through the liberties of high fashion, drag, and camp but also authorizes subaltern subjects. With respect to spectators, Geraldine's victory enables a range of identifications as well as unifies hitherto alienated communities, cultural practices, and practitioners.

Wilson affirmed Geraldine's gay drag significance in the wake of Dr. Frances Cress Welsing's 1991 book *The Isis Papers: The Keys to the Colors*, another example of the comedian's "circumstantial negativity." Welsing attacked Wilson, as Dwight A. McBride relates, for perpetuating the "epidemic" of "Black male passivity, effeminization, bisexuality and homosexuality" (369). Welsing exemplified these "disorders" in Wilson's Geraldine and Jimmie Walker's character J. J. on the sitcom *Good Times* (1974–80, CBS), "weekly insults . . . to Black manhood that we have been programmed to believe are entertainment and not direct racist warfare . . . a loss of respect for Black manhood while carrying that loss to even deeper levels" (Welsing qtd. in McBride, 369, 371–372). Wilson's recollection of his gay drag queen encounter also occurred the same year as the publication of Bruce Morrow's short story "A Play" in the Black literary journal *Callaloo*. What Welsing views as Geraldine's corruptive influence becomes, in Morrow's negative camp reclamation, access to a preexisting, vibrant Black gay male culture and a validation of sorts, despite the reverberations of reductive stereotypes. Morrow's protagonist, a young man perched on a metaphorical theatrical stage, reviewing his familial and romantic relationships while awaiting the results of an HIV test, tries to come out to his parents by way of explaining what a "drag queen" is. Alongside the narrator's show of taste, formulating an intertextual chain of camp figures, Morrow validates the formal and strategic negativity of Wilson's character in light of Welsing's critique by appropriating Geraldine as an ambiguous implement for coming out:

> Momma? Are you out there? Dad? . . . What's a drag queen? Oh, that's a guy who thinks he's royalty. You know, like Ivana Trump. See, it doesn't

have to be real royalty, it could be a disco queen, like Thelma Houston or Sylvester, Barbara Streisand, of course, or Vicky Sue Robinson. You know what I mean? Diana Ross-like. I know how much you hate fake Diana, but she's like royalty. It's sorta like Flip Wilson doing Geraldine. Remember that show? They call it transvestitism. Some of them are good. You should see the outfits. These boys can sew. I've never even worn a dress, Momma. . . . I like to watch, go to shows and see the outfits, see the boys. I told you I was gay. (312–313)

Morrow's narrator positions Geraldine in a multiracial, multimedia spectrum of icons and practices that vividly embody negative camp in addition to the "interracial collaborative affair" of Black popular culture, the idea "that hybridity need not undermine the specific blackness of a cultural product" (Gates, *Double Negative* 13–14, 29). The intersection of negativity and camp here in Morrow's reclamation of Geraldine furthermore evidences Marlon B. Ross's exploration of camp in Amiri Baraka's writing:

> The dozens and camp cannot be kept disentangled as "subcultural" modes of identity invective, given the constant underground cultural interchange between blacks and white homosexuals in the urban centers at least since the 1920s. Camp should not be identified solely with white urban homosexuality, for black homosexuals' inventive use of identity invective reveals a specific interaction between the dozens and camp so indeterminate that defining where one "site" or "role" begins and the other ends in their verbal contests would be absolutely impossible. (305)

As a negative means of "reconstitution," Geraldine also signifies as an ambiguous "placeholder" (applying Miller's term) in the trans media history explored in the 2020 documentary *Disclosure*. The first image to appear following the film's opening sequence, Geraldine belts "All of Me" from the pilot episode of *The Flip Wilson Show* as actress, activist, and producer Laverne Cox reminisces about "my first interactions with what it meant to be transgender happening on television . . . even when characters weren't necessarily trans identified." Further scenes of Geraldine appear, first as a sexy nurse opposite Bill Cosby, then singing seductively to Ray Charles, always greeted by applause and laughter, as Cox's voice-over continues: "And one of those early images for me was the character of Geraldine from *The Flip Wilson Show*. I remember I would watch it with my mom and my brother. And my mother loved Geraldine and would laugh at that character, so it was something that existed in the realm of humor." A little later Cox reflects on the racialized context and, as if debating Welsing, deduces that the comedy of "a Black man in a dress" defuses the "legacy of trauma around the historic emasculation of Black men in America" and that the comedic scene "takes away the threat. 'Oh, we can laugh now.'" Although the documentary film here pictures different spectacles of Black men in drag than Wilson's Geraldine, Cox's critique and that of several more witnesses suggest how Geraldine provided both a figure of identification and alienation, someone admired yet also limited to "the realm of humor." Cox discerns a dynamic neighboring what Alfred L. Martin Jr. examines as comedic "gayface," which transforms the "thin and one-dimensional construction of blackface" into "a practice whereby heterosexual actors, writers, and producers are the purveyors of mass-mediated representations of black gay men," a representation "rooted in a possessive investment in heterosexuality" (Martin 193). Although the critique of Geraldine as the butt of laughter enables a concomitant critique of hegemonic constructions of race and gender, we should not forget the terms of negative reception outlined above, particularly responses that cast Wilson and Geraldine as retrogressive forces due to the socially constructed proximity of Blackness with trans gender queerness.

Revisiting Haggins's and Miller's insights in the context of Gates's negative framework, Wilson's drag provided a comedic means to challenge stereotypes of gender, race, and taste in addition to providing an ambiguous, mobile representation of/for Black cis women, trans women, and gay men, a shifting placeholder for a range of (dis)identifications. Wilson's drag nevertheless also caricatured the style and strength of Black femininity across the gender spectrum, as ridiculous costume play and the source of demeaning identification. Cox's testimony about Geraldine Jones and Black male drag challenges the limits of self-reflexivity and contestability in Camp TV and, added to its roots in trans gender queer camp and comedy, returns us once again to Gates's emphasis on the "*privilege* to be able to ignore the ways that racialized images have operated throughout history" ("New Jack Black" 154). Rather than perceiving a trans gender queer camp stylist in the manner that Miller views Kulp's Jane Hathaway, Cox engages Geraldine as a negative text in this instance to disrupt the camp comedy of manners associated with Black male drag because the historical impact renders trans identity laughable without self-reflexively scrutinizing the construction of heterosexual masculinity.

Laverne Cox's performance as the trans character Dr. Frank N. Furter in the TV remake of the camp musical classic *The Rocky Horror Picture Show: Let's Do the Time Warp Again* (2016) suggests that representational agency makes more of a difference to the actress when assessing what "negative" means. The pleasure of trans gender queer camp is at least partly concentrated in turning the normative comedy of gender trouble into material ironically productive of gender nonconformity, and what better way to represent the power of this performative intervention than in actual performance? As the "sweet transvestite from Transsexual Transylvania," Cox intervenes into a camp comedy of manners that parodies the sexual revolution and bursts with trans gender queer delight, yet also bears a transphobic history in addition to associations with a largely white cult following. Cox turns the negative "labor" of being a Black trans spectator within a limited commercial media landscape into the joyful "work" of artistic performance (Gates, *Double Negative* 152; Tinkcom 2). Broadening the field of identification by playing "negative" roles riddled with camp "contestability" such as Frank N. Furter, Cox becomes the author and victor of her own cultural comedy of manners, a Black and trans role model-as-camp tastemaker.

Notes

1. As Sontag observes, such "best of the bad" lists qualify as "the greatest popularizer of Camp taste today" (278).
2. Sontag's aversion to television was legendary, which Andrew Ross discusses as evidence of Sontag's cultural elitism.
3. Disingenuous or not, Trillin's example of *Original Amateur Hour* as a camp text encourages further investigation into the variety format as a particularly fruitful modus operandi for producing camp and, related to that, the institution of vaudeville. Not only did vaudeville and similar variety shows on the TOBA (Theatre Owners Booking Association) circuit produce a litany of camp practitioners, from Mae West to Jackie "Moms" Mabley, vaudeville's variety structure and persistent theatricality also provide, in Richard Henke's estimation, "a fruitful metaphor for camp." Henke reasons, "Not only does vaudeville indicate camp's favorite axiom that life is theater, but it indicates what type of theater it is—a music hall review which eschews linear narration and instead asks its audience to negotiate a series of unrelated acts of jugglers, comedians and singers.... I propose that what the camp spectator identifies

with is not representation but rather the process of representation, the vaudeville of representation" (n.pag).
4. Ross uses this definition in "The Uses of Camp," the 1988 publication (reprinted in his 1989 *No Respect: Intellectuals and Popular Culture*) which coincided with the emergence of queer theory and camp scholarship.
5. Although Booth discusses Coward and Orton repeatedly, he does not directly label them as writers of manners comedy as Hirst does, linking Coward's and Orton's comedies of manners to gay camp sensibility (Hirst 3–4).
6. Since I initially wrote this in August 2020, Sid Cunningham's "'Something to Disclose'—Notes on *Disclosure* and the Possibility of Trans Camp" appeared in the spring 2021 issue of *Jump Cut*. A fascinating essay, we touch on some overlapping material, such as Gates's theory of negativity, in addition to Cunningham's close discussion of Cox's comments on Wilson's Geraldine character. My work spends more time considering Wilson/Geraldine in an African American historical context, primarily through the research of Bambi Haggins, Marjorie Garber, and Mel Watkins, in addition to exploring Black gay responses to Geraldine such as Bruce Morrow's.
7. The variety format of *Laugh-In* attests to Richard Henke's personification of camp as vaudeville (quoted earlier), as a "review which eschews linear narration and instead asks its audience to negotiate a series of unrelated acts of jugglers, comedians and singers," and a show that self-reflexively impresses "the process of representation, the vaudeville of representation" (n.pag).
8. As I have discussed in previous work on *Laugh-In*, "camp" coexisted with neighboring sensibilities that rethought the logic of good/bad taste in relation to social identity, such as "hip." Like camp, hip was appropriated from a marginalized subculture and popularized such that the racialized roots of hipness could remain relatively invisible (Torres 334–340; Klinger 140).
9. I work through similar arguments in my recently published book *Fearless Vulgarity: Jacqueline Susann's Queer Comedy and Camp Authorship* (Wayne State University Press).

Bibliography

Acham, Christine. *Revolution Televised: Prime Time and the Struggle for Black Power.* University of Minnesota, 2004.
Alwood, Edward. *Straight News: Gays, Lesbians, and the News Media.* Columbia University Press, 1996.
Bodroghkozy, Aniko. *Groove Tube: Sixties Television and the Youth Rebellion.* Duke University Press, 2001.
Booth, Mark. *Camp*. Quartet, 1983.
Brennan, Patrick S. "Cutting through Narcissism: Queer Visibility in *Scorpio Rising*." *Genders*, July 2, 2002, colorado.edu/gendersarchive1998-2013/2002/07/02/cutting-through-narcissism-queer-visibility-scorpio-rising. Accessed June 28, 2020.
Cohan, Steven. *Incongruous Entertainment: Camp, Cultural Value, and the MGM Musical.* Duke University Press, 2005.

Cunningham, Sid. "'Something to Disclose'—Notes on *Disclosure* and the Possibility of Trans Camp." *Jump Cut*, no. 60, Spring 2021, https://www.ejumpcut.org/archive/jc60.2021/Cunningham-Disclosure/text.html.

Doty, Alexander. *Flaming Classics: Queering the Film Canon*. E-book, Routledge, 2000.

Feil, Ken. *Fearless Vulgarity: Jacqueline Susann's Queer Comedy and Camp Authorship*. Wayne State University Press, 2023.

Feil, Ken. *Rowan & Martin's Laugh-In*. Wayne State University Press, 2014.

Frontain, Raymond-Jean. "Comedy of Manners." *Gay and Lesbian Literary Heritage*, edited by Claude J. Summers. E-book, Taylor and Francis, 2002, pp. 161–163.

Garber, Marjorie. *Vested Interests: Cross-Dressing & Cultural Anxiety*. Routledge, 1992.

Gates, Racquel J. *Double Negative: The Black Image & Popular Culture*. Rutgers University Press, 2018.

Gates, Racquel J. "New Jack Black. Keepin' It Reality Television." *Watching While Black: Centering the Television of Black Audiences*, edited by Beretta E. Smith-Shomade, Rutgers University Press, 2013, pp. 141–156.

Haggins, Bambi. *Laughing Mad: The Black Comic Persona in Post-Soul America*. Rutgers University Press, 2007.

Halberstam, Jack. *The Queer Art of Failure*. Duke University Press, 2011.

Harkins, Anthony. *Hillbilly: A Cultural History of an American Icon*. Oxford University Press, 2005.

Henke, Richard. "*Imitation of Life*: Imitation world of vaudeville." *Jump Cut*, no. 39, 1994, pp. 31–39, http://www.ejumpcut.org/archive/onlinessays/JC39folder/imitationLife.html. Accessed December 5, 2022.

Hirst, David L. *Comedy of Manners*. Methuen & Co., 1979.

Klinger, Barbara. *Melodrama and Meaning: History, Culture, and the Films of Douglas Sirk*. Indiana University Press, 1994.

Levine, Elana. *Wallowing in Sex: The New Sexual Culture of 1970s American Television*. Duke University Press, 2007.

Martin, Alfred L., Jr. "Norman . . . It's Not about You: Decentering Black Gayness in *Norman . . . Is That You?*" *Beyond Blaxploitation*, edited by Novotny Lawrence. Wayne State University Press, 2016, pp. 180–200.

McBride, Dwight A. "Can the Queen Speak? Racial Essentialism, Sexuality and the Problem of Authority." *Callaloo*, vol. 21, no. 2, Spr. 1998, pp. 371–372.

Miller, Quinlan. *Camp TV: Trans Gender Queer Sitcom History*. Duke University Press, 2019.

Moody, David L. *The Complexity and Progression of Black Representation in Film and Television*. Lexington Books, 2016.

Morrow, Bruce. "A Play." *Callaloo*, vol. 16, no. 2, 1993, pp. 312–313.

Muñoz, José Esteban. "Flaming Latinas: Ela Troyano's *Carmelita Tropicana: Your Kunst Is Your Waffen*." 1993. *Ethnic Eye: Latino Media Arts*, edited by Chon A. Noriega and Ana M. López, University of Minnesota Press, 1996, pp. 129–142.

Phillips, W. D., and Isabel Pinedo. "Gilligan and Captain Kirk Have More in Common Than You Think: 1960s Camp TV as an Alternative Genealogy for Cult TV." *Journal of Popular Television*, vol. 6, no. 1, 2018, pp. 19–40.

Pierson, David. "American Situation Comedies and the Modern Comedy of Manners." *The Sitcom Reader*, edited by Mary M. Dalton and Laura R. Linder, SUNY Press, 2005, pp. 35–46.

Ross, Andrew. *No Respect: Intellectuals & Popular Culture*. Routledge, 1989.

Ross, Marlon B. "Camping the Dirty Dozens: The Queer Resources of Black Nationalist Invective." *Callaloo* vol. 23, no. 1, Winter 2000, pp. 290–312.
Sontag, Susan. "Notes on 'Camp.'" 1964. *Against Interpretation and Other Essays*. Farrar, Straus and Giroux, 1966, pp. 275–292.
Steinem, Gloria. "The Ins and Outs of Pop Culture." *Life*, August 20, 1965, pp. 73, 76, 79–89.
Steinem, Gloria. "A Massive Overdose." *New York Herald Tribune (Book Week)*, April 24, 1966, p. 11.
Susann, Jacqueline. *The Love Machine*. Grove Press, 1997.
Sutherland, Meghan. *The Flip Wilson Show*. Wayne State University Press, 2008.
Tafoya, Eddie. *Icons of African American Comedy*. E-book, ABC-CLIO, 2011.
Tinkcom, Matthew. *Working Like a Homosexual: Camp, Capital, Cinema*. Duke University Press, 2002.
Torres, Sasha. "'The Caped Crusader of Camp': Camp, Pop, and the *Batman* Television Series." *Camp: Queer Aesthetics and the Performing Subject: A Reader*, edited by Fabio Cleto, University of Michigan Press, 1999, pp. 330–343.
Trillin, Calvin. "Barnett Frummer and Rosalie Mondle Meet Superman: A Love Story." *New Yorker*, April 17, 1965, pp. 40–43.
Watkins, Mel. *On the Real Side: A History of African American Comedy*. Lawrence Hill Books, 1999.
Wojcik, Pamela Robertson. *Guilty Pleasures: Feminist Camp from Mae West to Madonna*. Duke University Press, 1996.

Media

Amos 'n' Andy. 1951–1953. Television Series. Seasons 1–2. USA: CBS.
Are You Being Served? 1972–1985. Television Series. Series 1–10. UK: BBC.
The Beverly Hillbillies. 1962–1971. Television Series. Seasons 1–9. USA: CBS.
Disclosure: Trans Lives on Screen. Directed by Sam Feder, Netflix, 2020.
The Flip Wilson Show. 1970–1974. Television Series. Seasons 1–4. USA: NBC.
Gentlemen Prefer Blondes. Directed by Howard Hawks, Twentieth Century Fox, 1953.
Gone with the Wind. Directed by Victor Fleming, Metro-Goldwyn-Meyer, 1939.
Good Times. 1974–1979. Television Series. Seasons 1–6. USA: CBS.
Li'l Abner. Directed by Melvin Frank, Paramount, 1959.
The Real Housewives of Atlanta. 2008–present. Television Series. 1–13. USA: Bravo.
The Rocky Horror Picture Show: Let's Do the Time Warp Again. Directed by Kenny Ortega, Fox Television, 2016.
Rowan & Martin's Laugh-In. 1968–1973. Television Series. Seasons 1–6. USA: NBC.

13

"Far Right, Far Left, and Far Out"

Mainstreaming Camp on American Television

Moya Luckett

Despite its embrace of artifice, its reclamation of the near irredeemable, and its affiliation with sexual/political/subcultural/aesthetic outsiders, camp's marginal status is perhaps its most precarious quality. As Metropolitan Museum of Art's "Camp: Notes on Fashion" (2019) demonstrated, the mainstream often finds camp irresistible, whether it takes the guise of a museum exhibit or Broadway adaptations of John Waters's *Hairspray*. Despite its historical links with non-heteronormative social critique and rebellion, camp has more conservative uses that reroute its characteristic impulses to question or render ludicrous aspects of mainstream culture. While its political and subcultural allegiances mock, interrogate, and even threaten accepted norms, camp's aesthetics often draw on mainstream American taste (in particular, its *bad* taste) displaying its capacity to reinvent and reorient the mundane. This quality was particularly attractive to TV networks during the 1960s as they courted both hip, urbane, youthful viewers and older, more "square," heartland audiences. While better known for its countercultural borrowings, 1960s Camp TV's play with boundaries invited the more conservative reappropriations examined below. Here, its playful, colorful, performative qualities signaled the fusion of aesthetics and cultural politics endemic in both camp and its mainstream appropriations.

Potentially troubling, less visible, and out of keeping with critics' own political sensibilities (including my own), conservative uses of camp are often elided or presumed not to exist. While camp is undeniably a reception practice rooted in oppositional and queer interpretative communities, writings from period critics like the *Saturday Evening Post*'s John Skow point to its appeal for conservatives seeking to reclaim the margins for the mainstream during a time of change (Meyer). Despite their youth-friendly mien, shows like *Green Acres* (1965–71, CBS), *Get Smart* (1965–69, NBC; 1969–70, CBS), *Batman* (1966–68, ABC), and *Rowan & Martin's Laugh-In* (1968–73, NBC) invited socially and politically conservative viewers to claim a version of camp's playful, novel, and energetic sensibility as their own. Drawing on camp's own inversions, these programs potentially rendered the square hip and the mainstream bizarre all while reasserting the values of traditional masculinity for a modern, even futurist world. In a similar vein, the *New York Times* referred to *The Avengers* (1961–69, UK, Associated British Corporation; 1966–69, ABC) "as a domestication of pop that takes it away from teenagers" (T. Miller 27). Inverting much of the original's subcultural politics, this conservative, cynical camp was both reception-driven and had its own textual manifestations, perhaps most famously epitomized in Richard Nixon's 1968 cameo on *Laugh-In* (Feil 15, 62, 118).

This form of camp shared its more radical counterpart's fascination with boundaries, particularly in terms of their capacity to other, but here the joke was on the counterculture as the mainstream used television to reassert its own centrality. Abetting these reterritorializations, popular right-leaning American magazines like *The Saturday Evening Post* endorsed Camp TV shows while mocking their more radical, progressive, and intellectual antecedents (Skow 95). During the second half of the 1960s, the bimonthly *Post* discussed television just a few times a year but tellingly focused almost exclusively on Camp TV, reclaiming these texts for a resolutely unhip audience who were presented as in on the joke. *Get Smart*, *Batman*, *The Monkees* (1966–68, NBC), *Laugh-In*, and *Dark Shadows* (1966–71, ABC) all received high-profile essays, sometimes with accompanying covers, signifying their position as cultural touchstones *and* as programs of particular interest to their readers. Dressed up in academic jargon, including discussions of Susan Sontag's "Notes on 'Camp,'" these articles pointed to Camp TV's integration into a more conservative, middle-American zeitgeist. This process recalls Andrew Ross's observation that "camp can be seen as a *cultural economy* at work from the time of the early 1960s. It challenged, and, in some cases, helped to overturn legitimate definitions of taste and sexuality. But we must also remember to what extent this cultural economy was tied to the capitalist logic of development that governed the mass culture industries" (326).

Camp TV: Politics and Taste

Camp TV emerged in the mid-1960s as a youth- and advertiser-friendly production trend whose bright aesthetics appealed to networks converting to new all-color schedules (Phillips and Pinedo 21–24). With their "camp elements such as irony, farce, performativity and theatricality," these programs shared "Pop Art's bold colour schemes and similarly foregrounded its ironic and satiric treatment of mainstream culture," emphasizing artifice to critique "the constructedness of all images—in both art specifically and life generally" (21, 24, 25). Like most of the era's programming, it was designed for diverse audiences, including loyal mainstream Heartland viewers whose politics were far from radical or progressive. Around the same time, America's general interest magazines like *Look* and the *Saturday Evening Post* adopted a similar colorful, graphic modern look, testifying to widespread fascination with the period's self-conscious modernity among even the politically and socially conservative. Related formal characteristics also helped "update" TV's most "square" shows like *The Lawrence Welk Show* (1951–55, KLTA; 1955–71, ABC; 1971–82, syndicated) and *Hee Haw* (1969–71, CBS; 1971–93, syndicated), revealing that graphic sets, modish dress, quick cuts, and zooms were not necessarily the preserve of the young and hip (Johnson 73–75, 81). More than mere style, Camp TV mobilized active viewing practices, addressing audience foreknowledge and playing with televisual conventions (Phillips and Pinedo 25, 27). A markedly self-aware and ambiguous form, it should not be surprising that it stimulated both progressive and conservative readings: after all, as Quinlan Miller has pointed out, "Camp is the experience of being both, of embodying supposed contradictions" (16). These qualities both extended to and shaped its politics. While discussions of camp's ambiguity typically explore its links to more radical, queer sensibilities, these shows seeded visions of modernity that right-wing commentators could use to reinvigorate conservatism as edgy, contemporary, and as the bastion of mainstream tradition.

When it came to taste, both television and camp were typically allied to the marginal and dubious. There were, of course, obvious differences: camp was innately playful, always at a winking distance from objects that alternately embodied failed aspirations, the mundane, or outright vulgarity (Sontag). With its more middlebrow Heartland sensibility and its markedly different audience, television was often sincere, sometimes crass but rarely defiantly vulgar. Rather than integrating these different forms and taste cultures, Camp TV juxtaposed them, foregrounding their differences to produce new, more modern pleasures that did not radically disturb the medium's innate conservativism. Some of camp's more progressive aspects would have clearly been antithetical to a medium that then imagined its audiences as "'low' in terms of taste and cultural sensibilities, [but whose] 'averageness' is also periodically invoked in ideal terms—as reliably majoritarian, unswayed by fads, and, therefore, allied with stability, traditional values, and the smooth functioning of representative democracy" (Johnson 12).

Oscillating between coastal hip and Midwestern solidity, Camp TV self-consciously adopted fads while juxtaposing them to the average, the stable, and the traditional, establishing a dynamic allied to a broader series of political/cultural territorializations. This took several forms, including the representation of the heartland as itself bizarre, epitomized throughout *Green Acres*, and the presentation of solid, American masculinity as camp, but not necessarily in ways that might undermine more normative, traditional values (*Get Smart*, *Laugh-In*, and, arguably, *Batman*). With its signature take on camp's dual (or multiple) address, *Acres* offered up a range of political readings, most obviously via New York transplant Oliver's repeated patriotic heartland speeches (Phillips and Pinedo 28). These simultaneously invited sincere (conservative) interpretations, progressive camp contestation, and comic dismissal, the latter coming from Hooterville's residents who might share his patriotism but not his urbane pretensions. Like much Camp TV, *Green Acres* supports Anne Pellegrini's observations about camp's politics: "In some contexts camp is conservative; in others radical; in still others it may have little or no politics at all—or it might be a little bit country and a little bit rock and roll all at once" (170). This was particularly the case in terms of the ways *Acres* challenged and confounded critical assessments of bad taste, cultural knowledge, and habitus.

By exposing the public to camp content, Camp TV also instructed viewers in its signature modes of reception. As Pellegrini has shown, "One has to learn to 'read' and 'get' camp. Eventually you can try it at home in 'private'—but this does not make it any less public or shared" (179). Extensive media coverage of the genre spread awareness of camp's characteristics and reading strategies even as it potentially diluted and contested its politics. While camp could be opaque, difficult to read, and sometimes esoteric, Camp TV was innately more populist, performing some of the audience's work for them. As Phillips and Pinedo point out, the form depended on "spectatorial foreknowledge to a greater degree than most modes of expression, yet at the same time [it] tends to make the recognition of difference as easy as possible for the audience," effectively tutoring them in these processes (25). In making camp public, such programming arguably helped shift it toward the conservative, highlighting how "the political meaning of camp depends not on some ontology of camp . . . but on '*who* is using it, *how* it is done, and *where* its effects are concentrated'" (Pellegrini 170). Much Camp TV links camp's self-referentiality, recycling, and its play with often dated or obsolete mass culture forms to a certain knowledge of the medium and its form, making it more available to mainstream audiences. It thereby granted its public the status of insiders, allowing them to claim this aesthetic, its pleasures, and its politics as their own. A show like *Green Acres* is exemplary here in terms of the way it situated itself within the world of television, foregrounding its conventions and making them central to its comedy. As a spin-off, it referenced an already established fictional world, set in the fictional Hooterville, near Pixley, home to *Petticoat Junction* (1963–70, CBS) and within the region formerly inhabited by *The Beverly Hillbillies* (1962–71, CBS).

Green Acres: Ambivalence, Boundaries, and Conservative Camp

While undoubtedly bizarre, *Green Acres* was firmly situated in the world of television, rendering it simultaneously strange and familiar. Closely aligned to the medium, Hooterville's residents loved watching TV, while figures famous from other, often canceled, programs appeared as guests, such as Mr. Ed cast as a former star who had wasted all his money on horse races ("The Birthday Gift," S4 E12, 1969). Drawing on viewers' knowledge of these shows and, crucially, their (camp) obsolescence, *Acres* played with rural, urban, and *televisual* sensibilities to alternately support, counter, or distance the mainstream, here drawing on the ambivalence integral to its overtly fictional, rural setting. An important program that points to Camp TV's formal elasticity, *Green Acres* was stylistically muted. Aside from Lisa's technicolor outfits, it favored a more naturalistic color palette of browns, tans, oranges, and grays, and, overall, its aesthetics were less contemporary than the likes of *Batman*, *The Girl from U.N.C.L.E* (1966–67, NBC), *The Avengers*, and *Get Smart*. Its more mainstream look arguably rendered its play with television conventions all the more visible while simultaneously locating camp in realms beyond the counterculture and (urban) youth.

The tellingly named "A Square Is Not Round" (S2 E12, 1966) foregrounds not only the show's bizarre logic, but that of television more generally, rendering it both strange and ambivalent. One of Lisa's hens starts laying square eggs, attracting the attention of a chicken breeder, Mr. Moody. Meanwhile the Douglases' toaster will only work if the user says "five," which bothers Oliver whose lawyerly logic typically compromises his ability to master rural life. While it all turns out to have been Oliver's dream, *Green Acres* undermines TV's conventional use of this device to restore the status quo, here via a final scene where the fridge door opens when Lisa utters "Mabel." This ending points to the limits of televisual logic, while supporting the hyper-rural and the illogical, offering points of entry for camp critique amid its play with boundaries, tellingly a reading easily accessible to viewers. "Das Lumpen" (S3 E10, 1967) provides another example of the show's characteristic play with TV form. Lisa confuses Oliver when she utters "Two weeks later" as the words appear on screen and then clarifies that she was just reading the text from over his head. Later on, the image puckers and flickers like an old-fashioned film stuck in the gate, finally stopping as she confesses to overdramatizing her story of their marriage which structured the accompanying flashback.

While rendering its world offbeat, *Acres*'s camp sensibility was allied to rural and heartland America, not youth, counterculture, or overt modernity. Throughout its run, it accordingly presented television and Lisa's brightly colored but conservative socialite fashions as the apex of period pop culture. Potentially reassuring in terms of its assertion of stability during a time of change, this move was also self-evidently bizarre both in terms of its camp inversions and the more general strangeness that marked *Acres*'s diegetic world. Marginalized throughout a show whose protagonists, Oliver and Lisa Douglas, were resolutely middle-aged and childless, the period's youth culture indirectly influenced the show through its surreal take on its world and through its use of Arnold the pig, a gesture replete with its own camp ambivalences. One of the few episodes to address period youth culture directly, "The Youth Center" (S5 E8, 1969) frames it as both somewhat dull and mundane and as a threat to rural life (see Video 13.1) ⓟ. Inverting period media priorities that spotlight the young, vital, modern, new, and urban, Hooterville's teenagers are presented as an essentially indistinguishable and highly generic group, quite unlike the show's spirited and offbeat older residents. After the village population drops from sixty-eight to forty-eight in just one year, Oliver's barn is requisitioned as a youth club to persuade local teens to stay home and work on the village farms, but they are soon too tired to get up for work. Brightly lit and barely decorated, the club has no trace of the countercultural. Presented much like other (inauthentic) sitcom images of youth, the young dance to markedly generic music, some in bright fashions while others, mainly boys, wear plaid shirts and jeans just like Hooterville's older residents.

Acres's most surreal character, Arnold Ziffel, acts as its dated, conservative, yet deeply strange representative of youth. The youngest member of the regular cast, he has resolutely old-fashioned tastes: rather than following fads, he hangs out with the older residents at Drucker's store, visits the Douglases' home, and attends town meetings. More a child of the 1950s than mid-late 1960s, he loves watching TV, particularly Westerns, has a paper route, and walks to school carrying his books in his mouth using a leather strap. He is also bizarrely talented and fortunate: he paints (and is nicknamed "Porky Picasso"), writes novels, wins competitions, and, unlike his peers, has no desire to leave Hooterville for the city. Played by a series of young pigs, Arnold functions as a surreal take on mainstream ideals of young masculinity, one open to both conservative and progressive/countercultural interpretations. "I Didn't Raise My Pig to Be a Soldier" (S2 E3, 1966) points to this ambiguity as it both addresses anti–Vietnam War sentiments and more conservative frustrations with government bureaucracy. Throughout this episode, the Douglases try to convince administrators that third-grader Arnold is a pig and therefore not eligible for the draft. Treated as both human and animal by everybody but Oliver, Arnold both embodies and explodes camp's signature investments in boundaries, territorialization, and the construction of community.

In 1966, the *New York Times* highlighted *Acres*'s ambiguity and knowingness while it parsed its mixed reviews, stating "Maybe it's surrealism and maybe it's corn" (Stone, "Two Who Discovered"). Writer Judy Stone, author of a better-known piece on *Batman* from earlier that year, "Caped Crusader of Camp," distinguished two sets of critics, those acclaiming the show as "surreal," and linking it to the progressive avant-garde and those considering it "the bottom of the barrel" (Gould, "Too Good"). Such verdicts were clearly rooted in viewers/critics' own sensibility, with their respective middlebrow/mainstream or elite habitus accordingly shaping their interpretations of *Acres* as literal or surreal. These discussions of taste were nevertheless distinctly localized: *Variety* consistently dismissed *Acres* as "aimless rube humor," with its middlebrow reviewers slamming *Acres* as mere "corn" (Mor; Stone, "Two Who Discovered").[1] Notably, this form of bad taste did not involve vulgarity, taboos, or overstepping boundaries but instead pointed to contempt for a certain kind of mainstream American culture, one *Variety* dubbed "the chillingly morbid face of American life" (Bill). Here, again, television's own seemingly innate bad taste was on trial, with the paper's Mor concluding, "There was also something about a pig that watches westerns on television which may be a reflection of the attitude of the writers . . . to its audience" (Mor).

Camping the Square: Reasserting Heteronormative Masculinity

Like *Green Acres*, *Batman*, *Laugh-In*, and *Get Smart* were all mainstream hits that used camp's capacity to rejuvenate older values. During the mid-1960s, the hyper-stylized *Batman* and *Laugh-In* rapidly became America's most watched shows and media sensations in their own right, with the former popularizing camp and the latter casting light on its potentially conservative appropriations. The *Saturday Evening Post* gave *Get Smart*, *Batman*, *The Monkees*, and *Laugh-In* cover features, all framing these programs in a decidedly mainstream light far from the realms of radical youth culture. A June 1966 feature presented *Get Smart*'s Don Adams/Maxwell Smart as an earnest, decent everyman with whom their readers might identify: "Maxwell is fumbling and bumbling. The average guy looks at Bond or the U.N.C.L.E. hero and they're suave, beautiful, perfect and the guy knows he could never do it their way. Most people are not like that . . . Maxwell tries to be these things, but he misses. He's not superhuman. But he believes in what he is, and wants to do his best" (Smith 32). Arguing that Smart and Adams shared a "peculiar seriousness" that anchored *Get Smart*, the *Post*'s Gene Smith downplayed the show's (camp) performativity in favor of a more traditional sincerity: "'Maxwell,' [Adams] says, 'is serious, dedicated, awkward, forgetful, pompous to a certain degree, sentimental,'" qualities the actor admitted to sharing (33). His wife concurred: "'Definitely he's Maxwell'" (33). Likely inadvertently, the *Post* opened up heteronormative, white, middle-class American masculinity to another set of camp reversals here, undermining its authority and presenting it as somewhat absurd. *Batman* received similar treatment, with the *Post* dubbing its eponymous hero "so square that he is cubical," while pointing to a fan base that extended well beyond "teens and college students . . . taken [in] by 'the climate of foolishness [that] produces wins of idiocy'" (Skow 92). Indeed, no less a person than "Federal Communications Commission Chairman E. William Henry, who knows better, appeared at a Washington benefit recently wearing a Batman suit" (92). Questions of knowledge, so central to camp, were thereby annexed to more conservative interpretations of these shows, seen, for example, in references to older fans who were not taken in by "foolishness" and "know better" but still appreciated *Batman*'s camp playfulness. In the process, such awareness is pivoted away from "a closely guarded form of subcultural knowledge exclusive to (white) gay men," to one linked instead to the *Post*'s own milieu and that of its readers (Q. Miller 61). Moreover, this sensibility affirmed the domestic values of both hard-working, white, middle-aged, heterosexual men and the government and corporations they represent.

While annexing camp to more traditional values, these magazine articles performed another reversal, using it to facilitate the adoption of an "outsider status" among those who feared their values were increasingly perceived as dated. As Victoria E. Johnson points out, the period's widespread adoption of the term "square" testified to the mainstream's distance from traditional archetypes as it became more in thrall to youth culture (17). Conservative camp used this very distance to its own ends, allowing it to simultaneously lay claim to both the center and margins. In the process, it contested the marginalization of the square in hip (media) circles while also standing behind an unfashionable traditionalism, which it linked to another kind of outsider perspective. Repurposing camp's associations with the margins, it attacked the dominance of an erstwhile counterculture that, for some, was becoming all too central. This use of camp represented a very different kind of survival tactic as cultural and political conservatives fought back against perceived efforts to marginalize the traditional. Camp's foundational ambivalence here pointed to broader cultural struggles around perceptions of power in a changing world, targeting a culture seemingly in thrall to cutting-edge tastes. By participating in camp, erstwhile "square" viewers might not only gain cultural power but also demonstrate a playful sophistication that could be used toward more avowedly political ends, most famously seen in Richard Nixon's brief appearance on *Laugh-In* discussed below.

Laugh-In: Formal Innovation, Conservative Politics

Camp TV's playfulness was often associated with modern visual styling that drew on other self-consciously contemporary movements like Mod, Op Art, and Pop Art.[2] Influencing camp but not always conterminous with it, these forms had roots in both high art and popular culture, signifying camp's own play with cultural hierarchies. Formally, much 1960s Camp TV favored a retro-futuristic aesthetic, embracing a kitschy, materialistic space-age future that foregrounded its own artifice, thereby facilitating a range of reception practices and cultural reclamations. In an era where novelty was particularly important for even the most staid audiences, elements of camp spread across conventional programming. The flashy, display-oriented formal strategies that distinguished the likes of *Batman*, *The Monkees*, and *Get Smart* helped "update" other more traditional formats, leading to the juxtaposition of traditional genres and youth culture that characterized much mid-to-late 1960s American TV. Camp's performative, direct address was particularly easily co-opted by variety and talk shows as it was in keeping with their vaudeville roots, while its propensity for bright, colorful mod-style sets influenced even the likes of *The Lawrence Welk Show*. Surprisingly popular with urban viewers, *Welk* tried to increase its youth audience by introducing new dances and adopting more camp, mod aesthetics. Its later ABC episodes featured "vividly bright lighting . . . Not only are the colors splashy, with clashing contrasts, but the television technology is revved up with floor camera transitions that simulate rapidly animated movement . . . characteristic of shows marked by counterculture appeal such as . . . *Laugh-In*" (Johnson 73).[3]

Unlike *The Smothers Brothers Comedy Hour* which laced radical politics and period youth culture into a conventional variety format, *Laugh In* surrounded its besuited and often bemused hosts with mod aesthetics and young stars, who adopted a more countercultural mien (Bodroghkozy 123–163; Feil 56–57). Rather than simply pivoting young, countercultural, and hip against "square" and stolid middle America, *Laugh In* revealed camp's investment in reterritorialization, with its hosts steering the show's campiness and overt modernity toward more conservative ends (see Figure 13.1). As Ken Feil points out:

> [its] greatest innovation (and ultimate put-on) might have been perfecting the pose of playful ambivalence and the strategy of deliberate ambiguity. *Laugh-In* presented prime-time audiences with the unprecedented means to enjoy countercultural, anti-Establishment transgression through the indulgence of "bad taste" and, reassuringly, conveyed the sense that the show represented the Establishment's investment in containing such defiant delights. (1–2)

Figure 13.1 Even on black-and-white sets, *Laugh-In* juxtaposed youth culture—as seen in the set design, cross-dressing, and the presence of guest star Tiny Tim (center)—with traditional TV aesthetics and conservative values represented most obviously here by host Dick Martin and guest star John Wayne (kneeling) (S5 E8, 1971, *Rowan & Martin's Laugh-In*, Wikimedia Commons).

More an example of Camp TV than camp itself, *Laugh-In*'s flashy visuals and rapid pacing connoted a seemingly oppositional viewpoint that was often belied by its content. As the *AV Club*'s Noel Murray recently acknowledged:

> to call *Laugh-In* progressive would be a stretch. In 1968, the show added Alan Sues, a gay comedian in the Charles Nelson Reilly/Paul Lynde mode: coy about his actual sexuality but willing to play the stereotyped, over-the-top, fashion-obsessed pansy. (In the "What did you do this summer?" montage, Sues' answer is "camp.") *Laugh-In*'s portrayals of the hippie generation also tended toward the cartoonish, showing the younger set as spaced-out, unwashed druggies in shabby clothes. Even the title of the series was a spoof of the whole protest-movement era . . . And *Laugh-In*'s treatment of women? Not exactly sterling.

288   CAMP TV OF THE 1960S

With a writing staff that included progressives and hard-core conservatives, like season 1–2's head writer, Paul Keyes, *Laugh-In* was not as radical as its campy humor and mod veneer might suggest. Instead, "its fluctuating political positions, indecisive cultural allegiances, and efforts to broaden the audience address . . . communicated ambivalence about the radical subculture of the 1960s" (Feil 37). The most notable example was also one of the show's most famous moments: Richard Nixon's five-second appearance from the show's second-season premiere, September 16, 1968, when the presidential candidate quizzically and stiltedly uttered "Sock It to Me?" against a sober brown background (see Video 13.2) ▶. A notoriously untelegenic politician (see Plate 25), Nixon had shunned the medium after his disastrous appearances in 1960s debates: at that time, he had not been on a mainstream political talk show for over two years, making his cameo all the more remarkable and newsworthy (Daugherry). It was also likely conservative in its roots and political intent. Nixon's friend, *Laugh-In*'s Paul Keyes, a right-wing comedy writer who helped write Nixon's speeches, had persuaded him to appear on the program in order to improve his image, to make the dour politician look more humorous and relatable (Daugherry; Feil 15, 62).

Nixon's spot constitutes a prime—if notably brief—example of right-wing camp. His characteristic discomfort is here used for comedic ends as he mis-utters the show's catchphrase as a question. His cameo captures camp's ambiguity as it is unclear whether he is lost in this contemporary maelstrom or in on the joke, performing a caricature of himself as an unknowing "square," or simply questioning all that surrounds him. Like other establishment guest stars such as Van Johnson and Greer Garson, *Laugh-In* nevertheless granted him a modicum of sincerity and respect, "providing the normative square voice that . . . appeased more conservative voices, and redeemed the Establishment as hip" (Feil 4). Rather than peeking out of the show's psychedelic wall, he is framed in close-up against a sober brown background that visually distinguishes him from the colorful modernity around him. His straightness remains resolute, but it is coupled with a potential self-awareness. As such, the values he upheld can be reinforced and rendered *more* vital through camp, precisely because they—and Nixon—are strong enough to risk looking ridiculous as he participates in something that resembles the period's dynamic youth culture. As Feil points out:

> Couched between silly slapstick and double entendres, the program also positioned Nixon in the middle of square and hip. Was he an ambassador

of the Establishment temping among the weirdos to court votes for himself and higher ratings for the show? Was the program mocking the presidential race as mere entertainment and mocking Nixon as a failed entertainer? Was Nixon naive camp unaware of his failed seriousness, or was he a hip trickster in on the joke? Apropos for the put-on, *Laugh-In* refused to answer. (62)

While it is unclear whether the show helped Nixon to win that year's close presidential race as some have suggested, his cameo indicates that *Laugh-In*'s audience, whether young or old, might be potentially receptive to his values (Daugherry). Indeed, one of his campaign ads aired during the show's commercial breaks. Presented by singer Connie Francis who claimed "Nixon would put matters right if elected," this spot coupled celebrity appeal with themes of waning international respect for the United States (Gould, "TV Review"). The idea that a faded pop star like Francis could speak on such matters based on her experience of touring the world was itself potentially camp, just like her campaign song, "Nixon's the One," with the *Times* claiming the ad "embraced all the ills of the over-simplified campaign spot" (Gould, "TV Review").

While there was far more to *Laugh-In*'s often contested politics, the prominence of this single five-second cameo offers insight into the conservative potential of Camp TV's dual or multiple address, as this "put-on could be interpreted as either mocking Nixon or, to his credit, as attributing a sense of hip, self-deprecating humor to the stony presidential candidate" (Feil 62). The show's hosts performed a similar function, helping mainstream viewers reorient the show and its navigation of the counterculture along more conservative lines (51–52). Dan Rowan and Dick Martin were Republicans who were both photographed with Nixon, most tellingly at an October 1968 rally in *Laugh-In*'s suburban hometown, Burbank, California. In November 1968, Rowan told the *Saturday Evening Post* "he had campaigned for Rockefeller and McCarthy," extolling his conservative beliefs while bizarrely likening the "antimaterialism" of the youth and counterculture to that of the military, an exemplary part of the establishment: "I think you can be optimistic . . . It's the sort of getting down to basic standards that you find in combat veterans" (Dietz 74). While seemingly a stretch, such convoluted interpretations allying youth culture to the traditional reveal how aspects of supposedly hyper-modern Camp TV shows could potentially be reframed along conservative lines. No show's politics can be reduced to those of its hosts, of course, but Rowan and Martin's off- and on-screen personae constituted forms of conservative camp that helped reclaim the show's avowed modernity for more reactionary ends. The Vegas-style persona they adopted on the show may have been campy, but it reaffirmed their own politics, while print media imbued both men with a self-awareness that was simultaneously in keeping with the spirit of the age *and* far from progressive (Kentfield 19). As high-profile examples of conservatism and camp, Rowan and Martin demonstrated that both could coexist off-screen as well as on the show where they "redeemed the establishment as hip" via personae that "shifted from urbane sophisticates to voyeuristic squares patronizing the counterculture for thrills" (Feil 117, 99).

Such conservative and mainstream reclamations nevertheless transform camp, undermining key aspects of its politics: as Richard Dyer notes, "something happens to camp when taken over by straights—it loses its cutting edge, its identification with the gay experience, its distance from the straight sexual world-view" (116). *Laugh-In*'s politics were similarly ambivalent. Its hyper-visible subcultural influences were subsumed within a more conservative, mainstream point of view that both rendered the square marginal and in on the joke—positions central to camp. In the process, *Laugh-In* pointed to the logic of double-reversal that underpins camp's more conservative uses while acknowledging its broader appeal, its links to pleasure, community-building, and irresistible fun. Such conservative and mainstream reappropriations reorient the logic of camp's far more progressive antecedents, ultimately claiming its playful spirit for themselves while affording "some audiences the acquisition of hipness without identifying with the margins" (Feil 16).

Reclaiming/Dismissing Camp

While the term "camp" received some mainstream exposure in magazines like *Time* and *Life* around the time Sontag published "Notes on 'Camp'" (1964), it gained more widespread exposure after ABC used it as part of their marketing for *Batman* in 1966 (Phillips and Pinedo 25). Besides its use in reviews like "Campy *Batman* Flying High on TV" and "Too Good to Be 'Camp'" the term was also interrogated in general interest periodicals like the *Saturday Evening Post*, partly to explain and demystify it, but also to steer it toward more conservative, traditional values. At one level, this meant addressing its challenges to taste cultures, gender ideals, and the work-based nationalistic ethos central to American capitalism. At another, it meant finding a place for these values, using camp to reify more traditional ideals. As the primary vehicle through which camp entered American homes, television was central here, opening up a conversation that would be further developed in mainstream magazines and newspapers. Such commentary foregrounded camp's ambivalence as it tried to reterritorialize it for a more mainstream, conservative public. Unlike the *New York Times* "Campy *Batman*" article which used the word but made no effort to define or clarify what it meant, likely because it assumed a knowledgeable reader, the *Post*'s Skow parsed its qualities, wrangling with and ultimately dispensing Sontag's "Notes on 'Camp'" as he sought to validate the (more conservative) pleasures he found in *Batman* and Camp TV.

In his January 1966 review of *Batman*, the *New York Times*'s Jack Gould both alludes to camp ("instant books, folk-rock sheet music, Andy Warhol and the design of the new CBS building on West 52nd Street") and the fears of those who are "insecure in [their] judgment of what is camp," words that highlight the cultural stakes of apprehending camp. While he focuses on Pop Art and camp's affection for bad taste (here finding *Batman* just "a little *too* good"), the *Post*'s Skow interrogates the dichotomies of taste at camp's very heart. To this end, he foregrounds the hard work involved in creating a wildly popular show like *Batman*, noting that its appearance and performances are not "bad" (as in inept) but rather deliberate and careful choices. As *Batman*'s chief writer and editorial adviser Lawrence Semple Jr. pointed out: "We started out to do a pop-art thing and we're doing it." Displaying his own knowledge of camp, Skow adds "the dialogue is supposed to be solid mahogany, and so Batman always speaks in a camp-counsellor baritone" (95, 94). Linking the show's absurdity to its morality, he points to the challenges facing its writing staff: Semple "drew up a list of commandments for other writers. Killing, for instance, is forbidden . . . This makes our plotting more difficult: there isn't much for the villains to do except steal things . . . But the taboo is necessary" (95).

For Skow, *Batman*'s morality, hard work, professionalism, and widespread popularity rendered it the very antithesis of camp's pretensions and elitism, yet he still claimed aspects of this sensibility for more conservative ends. Much of his critique rests on undermining the poles of art/trash, high/low that he perceived (perhaps incorrectly) as central to both camp and the work of left-wing intellectuals: "*Batman*, faithfully translated from one junk medium [comic books] into another junk medium [television], is junk squared. But it is thoroughly successful and—this troubles critics for whom good and bad are art's only poles—it can be surprisingly likable" (95). Rather than dismissing camp shows like *Batman* for their perceived artistic failings, he celebrates their economic success and optimism, qualities he sees as innately conservative.

> There is a captivating theory, advanced by citizens who become irritable and depressed when they count other people's money, that *Batman* is a success because it is television doing what television does best: doing things badly. *Batman*, in other words, is so bad, it's good. Howie Horwitz, the show's producer, is not sympathetic to this view. "If all we had to do was be bad, we wouldn't be working so hard." (Skow 95)

While the logic of the marketplace and conservative ideals of meritocracy underpin these statements about *Batman*'s success resulting from hard work and an awareness of the zeitgeist, Skow's reference to one of camp's foundational tenets reveals his broader interest in interrogating and dismissing its associations with progressive elites:

> Members of the mind-bending profession—admen, art hustlers, TV reviewers—call *Batman* "camp," however, not junk. "Camp," "campy" and "camping" are this season's vogue words. The notion behind camp is mean-spirited: a sneering fake-enthusiasm for whatever is pretentious and not quite successful, a jeering private laugh at anyone square enough to take the pretension seriously. Oddly enough, camp owes its popularity to an article in the indomitably dense quarterly, *Partisan Review*. It was written by a young critic named Susan Sontag, who owes *her* popularity to her ability to make totally obscure references in such a way that the reader feels intellectually unclean for not understanding them ... Camp, in short, is contempt set in code. That is why *Batman* is not camp. (95)

Central to this onslaught is the question of territorialization as Skow highlights camp's capacity to undermine those outside these intellectual/subcultural worlds through its density and oblique, insider references. In reclaiming *Batman* (and Camp TV) for the mainstream, he uses its popular success, its accessibility, and sense of fun to distance them from camp's "contempt set in code." Foregrounding his own knowledge of this practice/

sensibility as well as his mastery of the opaque, he rails against camp for rendering the mainstream marginal. In the process, he uses his insider knowledge—shared with his readers to demystify it—to assert the value of an outsider perspective, one camp typically attributes to the very mainstream it shuns. He therefore contests camp countercultural origins. Lauding *Batman*, he both calls for camp's demystification and delivers it to a public that was far more likely to be allied to the mainstream than the counterculture.

Conclusion

Given the prominence of 1960s Camp TV, its wide-ranging popularity, and its appearance amid the decade's culture wars and political polarizations, its openness to conservative and traditional interpretations should not be surprising. While it is difficult to trace the range of political and cultural strategies mid-to-late 1960s viewers used to make sense of these shows and to integrate them into their worldviews, their capacity to make camp visible and render it available to the American public would have clearly resonated, particularly as politics itself became more centered on cultural boundaries. In flaunting these limits, Camp TV invited viewers to take up positions as insiders or outsiders that, as Skow scornfully admits, tie into questions of knowledge, cultural competence, and political/social capital. Shows like *Green Acres* and *Laugh-In* ("from beautiful, downtown Burbank") further point to the importance of regionalism, the intersections of taste, and widely varied American values, placing them in purposefully playful, ambiguous forms that opened up readings both against or in support of the grain.

Even as camp evokes boundaries between insider and outsider, high and low, urban and rural, elite and mass, both ratings and the critical/public reception of 1960s Camp TV programming point to their elasticity. Skow's argument, while not entirely coherent or dispassionate, reveals this slippage as he alternately claims and contests an outsider perspective for a broader, mass audience, all while attacking camp's perceived elitism. Bringing together different audiences, Camp TV granted camp a more public face, one that inculcated an awareness of the ways these differences mapped onto cultural and, implicitly, political power. Both manifestations grant the outsider value, whether in terms of camp's putative queer, progressive intellectuals or in terms of the perceived othering of the mainstream that Skow rails against.

In the process, they ironically reclaim their objects for a public that then becomes the insider. As Pellegrini points out, the politics of camp depend on *who* it belongs to, particularly for those who take advantage of the series of reversals it offers to annex its sensibilities to their own ends: "To put a finer point on the matter: where politics is so openly and cynically performative, what remains of camp as an oppositional strategy? The answer to this question depends in large part on *whose* camp we are talking about" (169).

Other later reclamations of camp similarly position their aficionados as marginal outsiders in order to express a range of political views that veer into the reactionary. Characteristically camp objects, like bad films, have been annexed to such ends, linking the conservative to the subcultural to reclaim its political energy. Despite their often queer and progressive roots, the love for what Jeffrey Sconce has dubbed "paracinema" became a matter of more public fascination after the hyper-conservative commentator, Michael Medved, co-authored *The Fifty Worst Films of All Time* in 1978 and then co-launched the Golden Turkey Awards two years later. Today, online reactionaries like 4Chan, 8Chan, and the Alt-Right adopt aspects of this conservative camp, embracing an ersatz playfulness and mockery while adopting an outsider perspective to undermine the avowed elitism of a more progressive sensibility. These twenty-first-century movements can trace their roots to practices opened up by conservative reclamations of 1960s Camp TV, a form whose play with insider and outsider sensibilities opened camp up to other forms of politicization.

Notes

1. *Variety*'s reviewers typically went by one-word pen names, like "Mor" and "Bill." Full names are not available.
2. Derived from British youth culture, Mod borrowed from Op Art and Pop Art to connote its investment in the present and future: as Christine Feldman points out, Mod's evocations of perceptual change and self-reinvention pointed to its fusion of rebellion and commerce. As its largely working-class, postwar British roots attest, Mod had few connections with camp's political and social ethos and was both associated with rebellion and a consumerist individuality centered on the desire for social mobility. Its stylization nevertheless pointed to a performativity, modernity, and celebration of difference that influenced Camp TV (Feldman 3–7).
3. In *Heartland TV* Victoria E. Johnson notes that "Welk attracted his largest nationwide audience... from 1965–68" (73).

Bibliography

Bill. "*Green Acres.*" *Variety*, October 1, 1969, p. 51.
Bodroghkozy, Aniko. *Groove Tube: Sixties Television and the Youth Revolution*. Duke University Press, 2001.
Cleto, Fabio, editor. *Camp: Queer Aesthetics and the Performing Subject: A Reader*. University of Michigan Press, 1999.
Daugherty, Greg. "Did Nixon's Laugh-In Cameo Help Him Win the 1968 Election?" History.com, October 19, 2018, https://www.history.com/news/richard-nixon-laugh-in-cameo-1968. Accessed August 1, 2020.
Dietz, Lawrence. "*Laugh In:* Where TV Comedy Is At." *Saturday Evening Post*, November 30, 1968, pp. 32–37, 74.
Dyer, Richard. "It's Being So Camp as Keeps Us Going." Cleto, pp. 110–116.
Feil, Ken. *Rowan and Martin's Laugh-In*. Wayne State University Press, 2014.
Feldman, Christine. *We Are the Mods: A Transnational History of a Youth Subculture*. London: Peter Lang, 2009.
Gould, Jack. "Too Good to Be Camp." *New York Times*, January 23, 1966, sec. A, p. 109.
Gould, Jack. "TV Review: *Laugh-In* Team Back with a Nixon Line." *New York Times*, September 17, 1968, p. 95.
Johnson, Victoria E. *Heartland TV: Prime Time Television and the Struggle for U.S. Identity*. New York University Press, 2008.
Kentfield, Calvin. "Far Right, Far Left and Far Out." *New York Times*, April 14, 1968, pp. D19–D20.
Lintelman, Ryan. "In 1968, When Nixon Said 'Sock It to Me' on 'Laugh-In,' TV Was Never Quite the Same Again." Smithsonian Magazine, N.D., https://www.smithsonianmag.com/smithsonian-institution/1968-when-nixon-said-sock-it-me-laugh-tv-was-never-quite-same-again-180967869/. Accessed August 1, 2020.
Meyer, Moe. "Introduction: Reclaiming the Discourse of Camp." *The Politics and Poetics of Camp*, edited by Moe Meyer, Routledge, 2011, pp. 1–22.
Miller, Quinlan. *Camp TV: Trans Gender Queer Sitcom History*. Duke University Press, 2019.
Miller, Toby. *The Avengers*. British Film Institute, 1997.
Mor. "*Green Acres.*" *Variety*, September 28, 1966, p. 35.
Murray, Noel. "A Very Special Episode Nixon Gets Socked in *Laugh-In*'s Most Famous, and Influential, Five Seconds." *The AV Club*, September 13, 2012, https://tv.avclub.com/nixon-gets-socked-in-laugh-in-s-most-famous-and-influe-1798233570. Accessed August 1, 2020.
Pellegrini, Anne. "After Sontag: Future Notes on Camp." *Blackwell Companions in Cultural Studies: A Companion to Lesbian, Gay, Bisexual, Transgender, and Queer Studies*, edited by George E. Haggerty and Molly McGarry, Oxford Wiley-Blackwell, 2007, pp. 168–193.
Phillips, W. D., and Isabel Pinedo. "Gilligan and Captain Kirk Have More in Common Than You Think: 1960s Camp TV as an Alternative Genealogy for Cult TV." *Journal of Popular Television*, vol. 6, no. 1, 2018, pp. 19–40.
Ross, Andrew. "Uses of Camp." Cleto, pp. 308–329.
Sconce, Jeffrey. "'Trashing' the Academy: Taste, Excess, and an Emerging Politics of Cinematic Style." *Screen*, vol. 36, no. 4, 1995, pp. 371–393.
Skow, John. "Has TV (Gasp!) Gone Batty?" *Saturday Evening Post*, May 7, 1966, pp. 92–97.

Smith, Gene. "Would You Believe Don Adams?" *Saturday Evening Post*, June 4, 1966, pp. 32–33.
Sontag, Susan. "Notes on 'Camp.'" 1964. *Against Interpretation and Other Essays*. New York: Picador, 2001, pp. 275–292.
Stone, Judy. "Caped Crusader of Camp." *New York Times*, January 9, 1966, p. 75.
Stone, Judy. "Two Who Discovered Gold Amid the Alien Corn." *New York Times*, April 10, 1966, Arts and Leisure, p. 101.

Media

The Avengers. 1961–1969. Television Series. Season 1–6. UK: Associated British Corporation; USA: ABC.
Batman. 1966–1968. Television Series. Seasons 1–3. USA: ABC.
The Beverly Hillbillies. 1962–1971. Television Series. Seasons 1–9. USA: CBS.
Dark Shadows. 1966–1971. Television Series. USA: ABC.
Get Smart. 1965–1970. Television Series. Seasons 1–5. USA: NBC, CBS.
The Girl from U.N.C.L.E. 1966–1967. Television Series. Season 1. USA: NBC.
Green Acres. 1965–1971. Television Series. Seasons 1–6. USA: CBS.
Hee Haw. 1969–1997. Television Series. Seasons 1–26. USA: CBS; syndicated.
Lawrence Welk. 1951–1982. Television Series. Seasons 1–31. USA: KLTA; ABC; syndicated.
The Monkees. 1966–1968. Television Series. Seasons 1–2. USA: NBC.
Petticoat Junction. 1963–1970. Television Series. Seasons 1–7. USA: CBS.
Rowan & Martin's Laugh-In. 1968–1973. Television Series. Seasons 1–6. USA: NBC.
The Smothers Brothers Comedy Hour. 1967–1969. Television Series. Seasons 1–3. USA: CBS.

Afterword

Questions of Taste and Pre-cult/Post-cult

Matt Hills

This collection does a sterling job of building and developing on the journal article reprinted as its opening chapter. Offering a wider range of case studies and arguments than can be provided by W. D. Phillips and Isabel Pinedo's concentrated analysis of "Camp TV" as "pre-cult," here we encounter the complexities of trans gender queer "negative camp" (in Ken Feil's Chapter 12) as well as "conservative camp" (Moya Luckett, Chapter 13), not to mention combinations of naïve and deliberate camp (in Andrew J. Owens's Chapter 5) theorized alongside much-needed work on camp sonic style, diversifying TV studies away from its treatment of the televisual (as Reba A. Wissner demonstrates in Chapter 10).

Something recurs across many of these chapters—not only the matter of Camp TV's distinctiveness, that is, how it is to be defined and delimited, but also the issue of its cultural *distinctions*. Perhaps one name is repeated more than any other—unsurprisingly, that of Susan Sontag ([1964] 1999). But a second name surely ghosts this, almost inaugurating a "fantastic family sitcom" (Spigel) of theoretical founding mothers, fathers, and family resemblances: Pierre Bourdieu. If camp and pre-cult are always questions of taste, then surely they are also questions of cultural capital—as Moya Luckett observes, Camp TV invites "viewers to take up positions as insiders or outsiders that . . . tie into questions of knowledge, cultural competence, and political/social capital" (293). The relationship between Sontag's version of camp—picked over in fragmentary notes rather than defined in essayistic form—and Bourdieu's camp is a telling one. In their monograph *Kitsch! Cultural Politics and Taste*, Ruth Holliday and Tracy Potts suggest that

> In describing camp, Sontag at once supports and departs from Bourdieu's analysis of taste. Whereas Bourdieu highlights the seriousness of taste, and

298 AFTERWORD

the symbolic violence that middle-class taste meted out to those who escape or deny its orthodoxies, Sontag cites camp as profoundly playful, an 'unserious' taste, as "above all, a mode of enjoyment, of appreciation—not judgment . . ." However, at the same time camp certainly operates as an effect of (sub)cultural capital—as "something of a private code, a badge of identity even." (118)

Nicholas C. Morgan's outstanding work on *Flipper* in Chapter 11 perhaps gets closest to this Bourdieusian "(sub)cultural capital" in his analysis of the show's camp receptions, noting that "*Flipper* generated a 'secret public,' one founded on a collective, purposefully queer viewing of the show . . . For those viewing *Flipper* as camp, its chief pleasures were formal . . . [including] the pleasure of looking at the aestheticized male body" (245).

But a range of chapters also reflect on Camp TV as "a badge of identity" whereby pre-existing forms of cultural capital can be enacted by making a "knowing" interpretation—in Chapter 2, Andrea Comiskey and Jonah Horwitz consider how *Fractured Flickers*, via its remixing of silent cinema, offered up a "dual" address, partly to youth audiences appreciating its broad comedy but partly also to established, older fans of silent film who could revel "in sophisticated, 'adult' viewing strategies: the celebratory, satirical, even subversive possibilities of audiovisual remixing, and in the masquerades, double meanings, and sense of play associated with camp" (71). Here, cultural capital is implicitly aligned with "adult" or cinephile responses, while a less tutored reading remains more youthful or cartoonish. As Comiskey and Horwitz themselves observe, this approach to Camp TV's "split" address echoes the work of Phillips and Pinedo, who separate out the "participatory" and "interpretive" dimensions of cult TV, arguing that its pre-cult precursors have been neglected due to their academic (and fan and aca-fan) positioning as lacking in cultural capital, supposedly being juvenile, or excessively low-cultural, rather than occupying the "higher-order" of later cult aesthetics:

> The lack of attention to these programmes . . . by cult television scholars can be partly justified by the historical conceptualization of the television audiences for these shows as either specifically juvenile or infantilized by the networks' audience discourse of that era. The absence of Camp TV programmes (individually and collectively) in the accepted pre-history of cult television and the identification of 1960s science fiction/fantasy programmes as the dominant predecessor of Cult TV allowed scholars to

differentiate between the higher-order *interpretive* viewing strategies and the merely *participatory* audience practices associated most often with juvenile cult fandom. (Phillips and Pinedo 21)

Indeed, Phillips and Pinedo self-reflexively remind readers that if they use a participatory/interpretive binary in their own analysis, then this very much runs the risk of repeating "critical hierarchies inherent within much scholarship" (26n11). The danger, then, is that Camp TV becomes speciously aligned with 1960s discourses of TV's "vast wasteland" in order, precisely, to counterpose later forms of cult TV as elevated, historically important, valorized television. The complexities of Camp TV—brilliantly highlighted across this collection—would be problematically reduced to a singular mode of address and viewed only as puerile by such a maneuver. But as Emily Hoffman in Chapter 3 rightly counters, even animated figures such as Hanna-Barbera's Snagglepuss, "best known as the star of *Snagglepuss*, a series of cartoon shorts included in *The Yogi Bear Show* (1961–62, syndicated), that depicts him as a pastel pink mountain lion who dreams primarily of becoming a stage and screen star" can be re-read as a "ground-breaking choice" to textually oppose hegemonic masculinity at the start of the 1960s, reducing its purveyors instead to ephemeral guest stars (75, 91). Snagglepuss, by contrast "an obviously non-normative character," is granted "the privileged status of camp protagonist" (91). The ambivalences and intricacies of programs such as *The Addams Family*, *The Munsters*, and *Bewitched* are similarly revisited in these pages (see Jamie Hook's Chapter 4 and Andrew J. Owens's Chapter 5) in order to firmly disconnect them from the sickly domain of Newton Minow's "vast wasteland" and reposition them via newfound bids for cultish "quality" status. And in fact, these critical moves are not always so very different from the "bat-bids for quality" that are analyzed by Benjamin Kruger-Robbins in Chapter 7: in terms of *esprit*, there are many academic crusaders for camp contributing to this volume.

But if camp acts as an "effect of (sub)cultural capital," then does revisionist TV history not likewise and inevitably iterate "critical hierarchies" via the performance of (sub)cultural capital? Subcultural, because the move is readily recognized in the eyes of TV studies' beholders, and a matter of cultural capital because credentialed education and expertise are mobilized to mark out this territory of rereading. If we accept such a charge, then pre-existent (sub)cultural capital would seem to be merely replayed here, as if we're left with reruns of the same cultural distinctions, forever in syndication.

However, in "Watching 'Bad' television: Ironic Consumption, Camp, and Guilty Pleasures," Charles Allan McCoy and Roscoe C. Scarborough argue that Sontag and Bourdieu are more closely aligned than Holliday and Potts (118) allow for:

> In Sontag's view, a cultural object can be enjoyed in a camp style when there is a "failed seriousness." This occurs when an object, that is so full of exaggeration and extravagance that it cannot be taken seriously, is esthetically redeemed as camp.... "[C]amp sensibility" is not about ridicule or even condemnation. Instead, it is a form of admiration; "Camp is a tender feeling" (Sontag, 1999 [1964], p. 62) that replaces the ordinary esthetic values of good and bad with its own standards of valuation. Exercising this "camp sensibility" is a contemporary form of elitism that allows one to transcend the "nausea" of popular culture ... Bourdieu takes a similar line in *Distinction* (1984) when he discusses the concept of "kitsch." He argues that culturally savvy less wealthy consumers (i.e. intellectuals and artists) can "outflank" the dominant cultural tastes and gain cultural capital by redefining cultural objects "less obviously marked out for admiration [e.g., Westerns, comic strips, and graffiti]" (1984: 282) as worthy of esthetic evaluation. (45)

This again seems to reinforce camp directly as a "form of elitism," produced via the possession of cultural capital. But the redefinition of cultural objects "less obviously marked out for admiration," whether this is *F Troop* (in Cynthia J. Miller's Chapter 6) or *The Monkees* (as discussed in Chapter 8 by Dan Amernick), doesn't simply rerun cultural capital after all. Instead, new cult(ural) objects are effectively and affectively produced by and through interpretive communities—cultural capital is rerouted through new circuits and projected or accumulated in new ways. Rather than being repeated, there is a *transformative cultural capital* at work through Camp TV, as much as through Warhol's Pop Art where fresh symbolic capital was generated by articulating economic and cultural capital in unexpected ways (see Cook 73). To paraphrase Andrew Ross's work on the "Uses of Camp," we can view Camp TV—as seen in this volume—as "irradiated, this time around, with the glamor of resurrection. In liberating the objects and discourses of the past from disdain and neglect, camp [TV] generates its own kind of economy. Camp [television], in this respect, is the *re-creation of surplus value from forgotten forms of labor*" (Ross 151).

This might be argued to restate some of the terms of cult film debate that have occurred between Mark Jancovich (2002) and Jeffrey Sconce (1995); where Jancovich alleged that cult movie status re-enacted distinctions of academic and fan cultural capital, Sconce saw what he called "paracinema" (trash or badfilm) as the creation of a new cultural space for innovatively activated (sub)cultural capital, albeit performed by alienated yet highly educated graduate students. Whether or not we can agree that Camp TV is genealogically pre-cult, it appears to be caught up in the same underlying, structuring processes of taste-cultural valorization/elevation that cult film and television (Jancovich and Hunt) have been enmeshed in for their fans and scholars. Akin to "para-paracinema" (Hills 2007; Mathijs and Sexton 94), the cinematic detritus that was first adjudged to be too mainstream-generic or not outré enough to be reclaimed as "trash," but which has eventually been elevated by a further generation of aca-fan cinephiles, Camp TV finds itself code-switching here from the vast wasteland of critical neglect into the subject of skillful close reading and textual redemption.

It may not seem unusual, at this point in the normalization of aca-fan identities, to align progressive Camp TV scholars with cult or paracinema fans. However, prior work on cult television has witnessed occasional spats between cultists and TV studies' professors—most notably, perhaps, in Toby Miller's "Trainspotting *The Avengers*." Despite Miller's self-professed attempt to interpret the show as transgressive—somewhat akin to the reading of its historical place in the "pop camp" destabilization of hegemonic masculinity that is convincingly set out by Craig Haslop and Douglas McNaughton in Chapter 9—Miller instead encountered *Avengers* fans for whom the program enabled a reactionary performance of settled, superior self-identity:

> Such cults are entirely self-directed forms of life—self-formation is their alpha and omega. Collective consciousness about the show does not lead to collective investigations of gender politics on TV, or postcolonialism, or the fashion industry and tie-ins, or product placements, or the politics of fun. (T. Miller 193–194)

These cultists compiled lists of errors in Toby Miller's work (191) by way of demonstrating their moral ownership of *The Avengers*, eventually leading him to suggest that as a specific group of participatory-interpretive fans, they were "close to the sovereign consumer beloved of the right[-wing]" (192).

Gallingly for Miller, as a left-wing TV/cultural studies' scholar, these fans also seemed to be

> Straightforwardly dedicated to replicating a college of aficionados, who by their knowledge of the great elevating texts are somehow superior. This sounds familiar and, if anything, somewhat regressive to me. It replicates the very forms of quality discourse that were supposedly toppled by anti-canonical cultural studies. Instead, the best readers of the best texts are back, armed with their best interpretations. No, thank you. . . . [C]ount me out of cultism as a supposedly progressive tendency. Leave spotting trainspotters to trainspotters. (195)

This seemingly rather affronted (and dramatically under-cited) assault on the concept of cult TV and its fans as progressive finds a parallel in Moya Luckett's impressive analysis of "conservative camp" preceding this Afterword. Cult and camp media become "a perfect site for this sort of power game," as Greg Taylor notes (5), with their political valence being open to recontextualization by active (fan) audiences as a range of texts are valorized, typically against the readings of "mainstream" viewers. Luckett explores a particular spin on the double-coding of insiders and outsiders. Where Toby Miller was treated as an outsider intruding on *Avengers* cultists' expertise, Luckett's work on *Rowan & Martin's Laugh-In* shows how conservative camp posits progressive interpretation as part of a "hip" insiderdom, contrasting with conservative readers' own sense of "square" outsider status. Of course, this insider/outsider binary is very much a construction of meaning, and one that enables conservatives to draw "on camp's own inversions," to render "the square hip and the mainstream bizarre all while reasserting the values of traditional masculinity" (278). This enables right-wing readers to celebrate their own performed marginality, playing out a politicized script of the underdog fighting back against progressive/liberal mainstream media positioned as dominant.

Moya Luckett goes on to narrate a connection between this 1960s maneuver and present-day cultural politics:

> Characteristically camp objects . . . have been annexed to such ends, linking the conservative to the subcultural to reclaim its political energy. . . . Today, online reactionaries like 4Chan, 8Chan and the Alt-Right adopt aspects of this conservative camp, embracing an ersatz playfulness

and mockery while adopting an outsider perspective to undermine the avowed elitism of a more progressive sensibility. These twenty-first-century movements can trace their roots to practices opened up by conservative reclamations of 1960s Camp TV, a form whose play with insider and outsider sensibilities opened camp up to other forms of politicization. (294)

Combined with Miller's early/mid-noughties' attack on right-wing cult TV fans, this suggests not only a far longer history to contemporary "reactionary fandom" (Stanfill) but also points to an enduring development of both camp and cult television toward a mixed cultural-political ecology where transgressive-progressive readings and "hip to be square" counter-interpretations can coexist among different audience fractions.

In part, these politicized reappropriations can be viewed as a logical outcome of the fact that camp, cult, and kitsch (see Holliday and Potts 149) have all been understood as admixtures of textual content and contextual/audience activations. Phillips and Pinedo observe that both "Cult TV and camp (TV and otherwise) . . . hinge significantly . . . on a symbiosis of textual properties and audience awareness and agency in the construction of a purposeful differentiation from mainstream texts and behaviours" (26). Consequently, rather than only focusing on issues of taste in terms of cultural capital—or fixing this as a debate between transgressive/political camp and de-politicized camp (Bould 106)—we need to restore questions of taste as they are linked to the wider sense of left-wing and right-wing politics played out through camp and cult valorization. This complicates the analysis of cult, taste, and cultural distinction set out by Mark Jancovich and Nathan Hunt, given that the "mainstream" isn't only relationally othered to cult or camp but can also be variously constructed as a conservative *or* progressive mainstream-Other. As a result, subcultural capital becomes not simply a matter of recognition in the eyes of the relevant beholder but also a form of capital that can be dramatically contextualized, or fragmented, via subculturalized versions of oppositional alt-right politics or "social justice fandom" (De Kosnik 182).

Alongside theorizing Camp TV textualities of the 1960s, Phillips and Pinedo and their contributors also innovatively explore—whether explicitly or implicitly—camp television of the era as a form of "pre-cult" TV. The original series of *Star Trek* plays a key role in this timeline, analyzed in Reba A. Wissner's Chapter 10 via a bravura reading of an infamous scene from

"The Trouble with Tribbles," but also discussed in Phillips and Pinedo as a—perhaps *the*—textbook cult text:

> The existing literature on Cult TV ... focuses, in its genealogical account, almost exclusively on the science fiction programmes of the 1960s, such as *Star Trek* (1966–69) in America and *Doctor Who* (1963–89, 2005–present) and *The Prisoner* (1967–68) in Britain. Roberta Pearson recently referred to television's *Star Trek* as the "fount and origin of all things cult" ("Observations" 9). Through its avid viewership in first broadcast and then syndication, its letter-writing campaign to stave off cancellation, its establishment of a constellated community of fans via fanzine publication and circulation, the actual congregation of that community at fan conventions and the continued activation of that community through a multi-media, multi-text, shared universe, *Star Trek* did, in many ways, "establish the pattern for the cult television programme" (Gwenllian-Jones and Pearson xvi) and serve as a "prototype" (Reeves et al. 25) for later Cult TV. (Phillips and Pinedo 21)

Camp TV, as revalorized here, is set against this conventional scholarly narrative. But has *Star Trek* always been viewed in this way? For example, although Roberta Pearson certainly has discussed the program as a "fount" of cult, she also refers to it as displaying attributes of TVII and TVIII (demographically oriented niche TV, and brand-oriented digital TV) during the era of supposedly mass-audience television: "[Newton] Minow and [Rod] Serling routinely criticized the dominant medium's timidity and sameness. Opposition to the putatively gutless mainstream, a hallmark of cult and quality television in TVII and TVIII, was a significant aspect of [Gene] Roddenberry's producer brand at the height of TVI" ("Cult Television" 112). As such, Pearson makes the same argument about *Star Trek*-as-cult that is pursued by Phillips and Pinedo in relation to camp TV, given that they also suggest that "television audience interpretive and participatory practices more commonly associated with programmes and viewers in the TVII (post-network cable) and TVIII (digital content delivery) eras, within which Cult TV first developed and now thrives, can also be found productively in TVI (network era) environments" (35). Although Pearson describes *Star Trek* as a kind of originary cult TV, then, she actually understands it—and *The Twilight Zone* even earlier—in much the same way as Camp TV has been positioned as cult's genealogical predecessor in this volume. In a sense, whether we call 1960s *Star Trek* cult or camp, it is still being analyzed in each case via challenges to TV history's periodizations and as a kind of "classic cult" (Lavery 3) or "pre-cult." Catherine Johnson even uses the latter category for *Trek*, while recognizing that it could be contentious:

> It may seem strange to propose *Star Trek* as an example of pre-cult television. The series has generated an active and vociferous fan following since its initial broadcast in the US in the second half of the 1960s, and it has subsequently been the subject of numerous studies of the active fan, making it a seemingly clear example of a cult text. Yet within its context of production *Star Trek* is quite different from the cult television of more recent years, such as *Buffy the Vampire Slayer*. In fact, when *Star Trek* originally aired in the US (and in the UK) "cult television" was not a particularly widespread concept. Rather, television was understood, within both the industry in particular and society in general, as a mass medium, a medium of nation-building . . . The idea of "cult" television, with its connotations of exclusivity and specialness, would seem to run counter to the aims of television broadcasters at this time to produce programmes that appealed to consensus national audiences. (136)

Oddly, it may well be the case that as well as all the Camp TV exemplars analyzed so eloquently here, supposedly textbook cult TV such as 1960s *Star Trek* can also be readily grouped together with "pre-cult" texts such as *Gilligan's Island*, *F Troop*, *Get Smart*, *The Man from U.N.C.L.E.*, *Green Acres*, *Batman*, and *The Monkees*. Cult is often a retrospective, retroactive categorization reaching back into TV history, and previous industrial eras, to confer the recontextualizations of later active audiences. For instance, Pearson sees *The Twilight Zone* as another "post-hoc designated cult" show ("Cult Television" 119). But cult status can surely also decay or fade over time, with pre-cult and camp shows like *Bewitched* (see Chapter 5's excellent application of Sontag's naïve and deliberate camp) arguably entering a post-cult phase, as has been discussed in Catriona Miller's recent *Cult TV Heroines*:

> *Bewitched* remains in the public consciousness due to its regular syndication, though fan activity is more muted than lively. Fanlore.org reports a variety of online communities and mailing lists, some defunct, with Endora memes the most active. The design of the show has also remained popular, with the house and its interior designs still widespread on sites like

Pinterest, and Samantha's outfits also featuring on Pinterest ... especially following the success of *Mad Men* ... which raised the profile of midcentury design. There is a wiki ..., though it is rather sparsely populated ... The imaginative play with *Bewitched*'s suburban paradise seems to have died down. (80–81)

The present book's contributors, by impressively picking up the baton of Phillips and Pinedo's historicizing "pre-cult" argument, also enable us to think about how camp and cult television have developed beyond their TVI precursors and TVII and III entrenchments. Justin Smith has argued that "perhaps we should more accurately consider the present time as being ... 'post-cult,'" whereby related "kinds of cultural consumption have become commodified and fragmented to the point of individuation. Subcultural distinction has been elided through hegemonic processes to the extent that the cult is almost totally recuperated ideologically, and reproduced commercially to feed ... personalised media culture" (215; Hills, "Cult Cinema"). In Smith's account, which could be argued to link up with TVIV streaming culture, cult becomes individualized, cut adrift from collective readings and interpretive communities as well as stable performances of (sub)cultural capital. Projecting a "mainstream-Other" starts to become more difficult and tenuous than before. Thorsten Botz-Bornstein has argued that the individualization of targeted tastes has likewise impacted on understandings of kitsch: "In a neoliberal world ..., the respect of individual tastes is a priority. Kitsch is only what I see as kitsch ... The assumption that kitsch exists (saying that something *is* kitsch) is incompatible with liberal relativism holding that all (aesthetic) values are alike and need to be respected" (46). If camp, cult, and kitsch—each of which has previously been theorized as textually identifiable and audience-activated—have tipped further toward neoliberalized consumer sovereignty, attenuating their connections to specific (sub)cultural groups and communities (T. Miller 192), then the analyses of Camp TV established here do not only illuminate cult television's industrial and cultural prefigurations. By highlighting how camp fed into cult's similarly doubled quality of being both created and found (Hills, *Fan Cultures* 98), these essays also point to the longer consumer-cultural history through which "post-cult" and its unbalancing of objective textual attributes and (inter)subjective appropriations (in favor of the neoliberal, relativist latter) are already structured into 1960s Camp TV's subjective/objective tensions.

Where scholarly expertise has sometimes sought to "objectify" cult status by removing or minimizing audience inputs, waves of neoliberal (re)commodification have underpinned an increasing—though not absolutely total—subjectification of cult. Camp, we might suggest, has similarly migrated from scholarly expertise aimed at disconnecting it from queer audience activations in order to render it as a secure textual object for cultural capital (Bould 106), becoming more of a neoliberal targeting of markets and a personalized embrace of streamed, branded content. But nuanced scholarship of the kind provided in *Camp TV of the 1960s* helps to critically reconnect text-based and audience-based analyses of both camp and cult television, at the same time as laying waste to shibboleths of American TV's "vast wasteland" of the 1960s.

Bibliography

Abbott, Stacey, editor. *The Cult TV Book: From* Star Trek *to* Dexter, *New Approaches to TV Outside the Box*. Soft Skull Press, 2010.
Botz-Bornstein, Thorsten. *The New Aesthetics of Deculturation: Neoliberalism, Fundamentalism and Kitsch*. Bloomsbury Academic, 2019.
Bould, Mark. *Routledge Film Guidebooks: Science Fiction*. Routledge, 2012.
Bourdieu, Pierre. *Distinction*. Translated by Richard Nice. Harvard University Press, 1984.
Cook, Roger. "Andy Warhol, Capitalism, Culture, and Camp." *Space & Culture*, vol. 6, no. 1, 2003, pp. 66–76.
De Kosnik, Abigail. *Rogue Archives: Digital Cultural Memory and Media Fandom*. MIT Press, 2016.
Gwenllian-Jones, Sara, and Roberta E. Pearson, editors. *Cult Television*. University of Minnesota Press, 2004.
Hills, Matt. "Cult Cinema and the 'Mainstreaming' Discourse of Technological Change: Revisiting Subcultural Capital in Liquid Modernity." *New Review of Film and Television Studies*, vol. 13, no. 1, 2015, pp. 100–121.
Hills, Matt. *Fan Cultures*. Routledge, 2002.
Hills, Matt. "Para-Paracinema: The *Friday the 13th* Film Series as Other to Trash and Legitimate Film Cultures." *Sleaze Artists: Cinema at the Margins of Taste, Style, and Politics*, edited by Jeffrey Sconce, Duke University Press, 2007, pp. 219–239.
Holliday, Ruth, and Tracy Potts. *Kitsch! Cultural Politics and Taste*. Manchester University Press, 2012.
Jancovich, Mark. "Cult Fictions: Cult Movies, Subcultural Capital and the Production of Cultural Distinctions." *Cultural Studies*, vol. 16, no. 2, 2002, pp. 306–322.
Jancovich, Mark, and Nathan Hunt. "The Mainstream, Distinction, and Cult TV." Gwenllian-Jones and Pearson, pp. 27–44.
Johnson, Catherine. "Cult TV and the Television Industry." Abbott, pp. 135–147.
Lavery, David. "Introduction: How Cult TV Became Mainstream." *The Essential Cult TV Reader*, edited by David Lavery, University Press of Kentucky, 2010, pp. 1–6.

Mathijs, Ernest, and Jamie Sexton. *Cult Cinema*. Wiley-Blackwell, 2011.

McCoy, Charles Allan, and Roscoe C. Scarborough. "Watching 'Bad' Television: Ironic Consumption, Camp, and Guilty Pleasures." *Poetics*, vol. 47, 2014, pp. 41–59.

Miller, Catriona. *Cult TV Heroines: Angels, Aliens and Amazons*. Bloomsbury Academic, 2020.

Miller, Toby. "Trainspotting *The Avengers*." Gwenllian-Jones and Pearson, pp. 187–197.

Pearson, Roberta E. "Cult Television as Digital Television's Cutting Edge." *Television as Digital Media*, edited by James Bennett and Niki Strange, Duke University Press, 2011, pp. 105–131.

Pearson, Roberta E. "Observations on Cult Television." Abbott, pp. 7–17.

Phillips, W. D., and Isabel Pinedo. "Gilligan and Captain Kirk Have More in Common Than You Think: 1960s Camp TV as an Alternative Genealogy for Cult TV." *Journal of Popular Television*, vol. 6, no. 1, 2018, pp. 19–40.

Reeves, Jimmie L., et al. "Rewriting Popularity: The Cult Files." *"Deny All Knowledge": Reading* The X-Files, edited by David Lavery et al., Syracuse University Press, 1996, pp. 22–35.

Ross, Andrew. *No Respect: Intellectuals & Popular Culture*. Routledge, 1989.

Sconce, Jeffrey. "'Trashing' the Academy: Taste, Excess, and an Emerging Politics of Cinematic Style." *Screen*, vol. 36, no. 4, 1995, pp. 371–393.

Smith, Justin. *Withnail and Us: Cult Films and Film Cults in British Cinema*. I. B. Tauris, 2010.

Sontag, Susan. "Notes on 'Camp.'" Cleto, pp. 53–65.

Spigel, Lynn. *Welcome to the Dreamhouse: Popular Media and Postwar Suburbs*. Duke University Press, 2001.

Stanfill, Mel. "Introduction: The Reactionary in the Fan and the Fan in the Reactionary." *Television & New Media*, vol. 21, no. 2, 2020, pp. 123–134.

Taylor, Greg. *Artists in the Audience: Cults, Camp, and American Film Criticism*. Princeton University Press, 1999.

Index

For the benefit of digital users, indexed terms that span two pages (e.g., 52–53) may, on occasion, appear on only one of those pages.

Figures are indicated by *f* following the page number

1950s
   culture, 28–29, 196–98
   television, 12–13, 24, 25–26, 54–57,
      58–59, 77, 124–25, 143–44,
      168–69, 196–98, 219, 221,
      248–49, 258, 260–61
1970s
   culture, 13–14, 120, 125–26,
      134, 196–97
   television, 9, 13–14, 29–30, 34, 69–70,
      114, 134, 143–44, 146–47, 158,
      171–72, 209, 225, 257–58, 264
1980s 69–70, 225
1990s. *See also Flipper*: queer reception in the 1990s
   culture, 154–55
   television, 14, 26–27, 69–70, 236–37,
      245–46

À rebours (1884) (novel), 244–45, 251
ABC (American Broadcasting Company)
   audience, 9, 23–24, 29–30, 124–25,
      154–60, 162–68, 171–72
   broadcasts, 55–57, 60–61, 140–41
   reputation, 17, 124–25, 154–75
ABC (Associated British Corporation), 195–96, 202–3
abject art, 249–50
Ackroyd, Peter, 38–39
Adams, Don, 140–41, 226, 284–85
Addams, Charles, 99, 100–1
Addams Family, The (1964–1966), 14, 15–16, 34–35, 97–119, 121, 299
Addams, Gomez, 99, 104, 105, 106–7, 108–9, 110, 112–13
Addams, Morticia, 99, 100–1, 104, 105, 108–9, 110–11, 112–13

Addams, Pugsley, 99, 104–5, 110
Addams, Wednesday, 99, 104, 110
Adler, Margot, 128, 129–30
Adventures of Rocky and Bullwinkle and Friends, The (1959–1964), 15, 20, 51. See also *The Bullwinkle Show*; *Rocky and His Friends*
aesthetic. *See also* camp aesthetic
   aestheticization of nature, 242–43, 244–45
   aestheticized body, 242–43, 245–46, 250–51
   black-and-white aesthetic, 41, 98
   cartoon aesthetic, 76–77
   mod aesthetics, 285–86
   Pop Art aesthetic, 28–29, 30–31, 83–84, 219, 279 (*see also* Pop Art)
Agarn, Randolph, 140, 145, 146–49
Agent 86. *See* Smart, Maxwell
Agent 99 33, 40–41, 226–27
Alarcó, Paloma, 28–29
Alexander, Jonathan, 247–48
All in the Family (1971–1979), 9
alternative interpretation, 25–26, 218–19, 265. *See also* oppositional interpretation
Altman, Rick, 3–5
Alvey, Mark, 124–25
American International Pictures (AIP), 120–21, 168
Amernick, Dan, 9–10, 17, 176–94, 300
Amos 'n' Andy (radio, 1928–1960; television, 1951–1953), 266–67, 268–69
Anchors Aweigh (1945), 82
Anger, Kenneth, 5–6, 262–63
anthropomorphism, 82–83, 244–45

Are You Being Served? (1972–1985), 209–10n.2, 257
"Astaire Time" (1960), 8
Auslander, Philip, 181–83
Austen, Jake, 178–79, 180–82, 185–86, 189
authenticity, 176–94
Avengers, The (1961–1969, UK; 1966–1969, US), 17–18, 195–96, 199, 202–4, 208–9, 277–78, 301–2

Baba Looey, 77, 79–80, 86–87
Babuscio, Jack, 5, 30, 62–63, 171, 236–37, 247
Baccolini, Raffaella, 150
Badenov, Boris, 184–85
Ball, Lucille, 38–39, 108
Bankhead, Tallulah, 39–40, 156–57
Bara, Theda, 62–63
Baraka, Amiri, 271
Barbarella (1968), 6–7
Barbera, Joseph, 81–84. *See also* Hanna-Barbera
Barker, Simon J., 198–99, 201, 203–4
Barlow, Aaron, 142
Barnes, Alan, 209
Barrymore, John, 59, 65–66
Bas, Hernan, 251–52
Basinger, Jeanine, 145
Batman (character), 33, 36, 158, 164–65
Batman (film) (1966), 162–63
Batman (TV show) (1966–1969), 14, 19–20, 25, 103, 154–65, 179–80, 305
  audience, 17, 23–24, 25–26, 41, 103, 155–60, 162–65, 277–78, 284–85
  commercialism, 36, 158–59
  gender fluidity, 38, 39–41, 184
  influence, 1–2, 29–31, 179–80, 223, 224, 285–86, 290–91
  campy music in, 221–23
  reception, 17, 23–24, 160–65, 171, 236, 278, 284–85, 290–93
  references in other media, 5–6, 20, 31–32, 34–35, 191
  satire, 33
  self-awareness, 36, 154, 236, 237–38
  use of color, 28, 30–31, 281
Batmania (fanzine), 31–32
Beatles, The, 57, 113, 177–78, 180–81, 189

Becker, Christine, 176–77, 181
Bennett, Harve, 17, 125–26, 157–58
Benshoff, Harry, 14, 98, 101, 103, 218, 220–21
Bergman, David, 23, 30–31
Bergson, Henri, 146
Berle, Milton, 11–12, 38–39, 149–50
Beverly Hillbillies, The (1962–1971), 9, 19, 258–64, 280–81
Bewitched (1964–1972), 12, 14, 16, 120–36, 140–41, 157–58, 305–6
Beyond the Valley of the Dolls (1970), 6–7
Big Sleep, The (1946), 202–3
Birds, The Bees and The Monkees, The (1968) (album), 189
Blackman, Honor, 202–4
Black Widow (*Batman*), 39–40, 156–57
Bodine, Jethro, 259, 261–64
Bodroghkozy, Aniko, 9, 37, 125–26, 158, 168, 171–72, 179, 264, 286
Bogart, Humphrey, 202–3
Bond, James, 31–32, 36, 226, 243–44
  camping of 6–7, 199, 226
  comparisons, 199–200, 205, 224, 284–85
  influence, 23–24, 36, 184–85, 199, 223–24
Boo Boo (*The Yogi Bear Show*), 79–80, 86–87
Booth, Mark, 13–14, 220, 239, 241, 242, 257–58, 259–61, 263–64
Bordwell, David, 54
Bore, Inger-Lise, 176–77, 181
Borscht Belt, 138, 149–50
Botz-Bornstein, Thorsten, 306
Bourdieu, Pierre, 20, 297–98, 300
Brinkema, Eugenie, 250–51
Britton, Piers D., 198–99, 201, 203–4
Bride of Frankenstein (1935), 101
British television. *See* television
Broadway, 80, 112–13, 277
Brooker, Will, 222
Brown, Foxy, 269–70
Brown, James, 166–67, 168–70
Browning, Ricou, 243–44
Bryan-Wilson, Julia, 252
Buffy the Vampire Slayer (1997–2003), 13, 14, 24–25, 26–27, 305

INDEX   311

Bullwinkle Show, The (1961–1964), 58, 61, 184–85. See also *Rocky and His Friends*; *Adventures of Rocky and Bullwinkle*
Bully (2001), 250–51
Burns, Allan, 59–60
Butler, Daws, 80, 85
Butler, Judith, 38
Butsch, Richard, 109

Caine, Mark, 207, 208–9
camp
　camp aesthetic, 1–2, 5–6, 41, 58, 114, 121–23, 138, 200–1, 218, 245–46, 277 (*see also* aesthetic)
　　in music, 215–16, 217, 220, 222, 224, 227–28, 230, 231–32
　　mainstreaming camp aesthetic, 280–81
　camp coding, 10–11, 155–56, 161–62
　camp humor, 3, 15, 20, 77, 102–3, 201, 258–59, 288
　　as self-conscious humor, 16–17, 51, 55–56
　camp performativity, 17, 19–20, 111–12, 180–81, 182–83, 187–88, 205, 252–53n.2, 277, 285–86 (*see also* performance/performativity)
　camp sensibility, 14, 15–16, 30–31, 36, 52, 64, 81, 106, 115, 122, 124, 129, 137, 195–96, 209, 221–22, 259–60, 282–83, 300
　　camp as "sensibility" 1–2, 4–5, 7, 98, 121–22, 129, 200–1
　　mainstreaming camp sensibility, 19–20, 277–78, 291–94
　camp style, 7, 18, 23–24, 29–32, 81–82, 110–11, 130, 204, 216, 219, 232, 279
　　camp as "style" 1–2, 12–13, 23, 30–31, 300
　　style over content, 106, 200–1, 207–8, 215–2, 217, 257, 259–60
　camp taste, 1–2, 121–22, 128–29, 215, 265–66, 279–80, 291, 297–98 (*see also* taste)
　conservative camp, 13–14, 15–16, 19–20, 277–96, 297, 302–3

　countercultural camp, 15–16, 114 (*see also* counterculture)
　dark camp, 18–19, 236–37, 241, 242, 245, 250–51, 252
　deliberate camp, 3–4, 6–7, 17, 122–23, 124–30, 133–34, 218, 297
　democratized camp, 7, 13–14, 43n.8
　de-politicized camp, 7, 33, 303
　feminist camp, 13, 100 (*see also* feminist)
　het[erosexual] camp, 7, 115n.2
　mainstreamed camp, 4–5, 7–8, 15–16, 19–20, 29–30, 51–52, 183–84, 277–96, 302–3
　mass camp, 1, 7, 12–13, 14, 15, 29–30, 33, 41–42
　musical camp, 217, 220–22
　naïve camp, 18–19, 122–23, 124, 126, 130–34, 179–80, 236–37, 252, 288–89, 297
　negative camp, 258–59, 265–66, 269, 271 (*see also* negativity)
　pop camp, 7, 17–18, 23–24, 29–30, 196–97, 201, 202–4, 208–9, 301
　trans gender queer camp, 12, 258–59, 260–62, 266–67, 272–73 (*see also* trans gender queer; Miller, Quinlan)
Camp (1965, Andy Warhol), 5–6
campification, 32–34, 81, 84, 183, 184–85
Canote, Terence Towles, 141
Capp, Al, 262–63
Car 54, Where Are You? (1961–1963), 139–40
Catwoman, 34–35, 40–41, 156–57, 162–63
CBS (Columbia Broadcasting System), 9, 101, 154–55, 165, 168–70, 171–72, 191
Chaney, Lon, 51, 60, 65–66
Chaney, Lon, Jr., 52, 61
Chaplin, Charlie, 54
Chapman, James, 195–96, 198–99, 202–5, 208
Chavo, 229–30
Cheyefsky, Paddy, 160–61
Chiaro, Delia, 150
Chief (*Get Smart*), 184–85, 226

312 INDEX

cinema
  avant-garde cinema, 5–6, 15, 52, 68, 69, 243–44
  cult cinema/film, 14, 26, 100–1, 301
  film cycle, 4 (*see also* genre cycle)
  found footage, 15, 52, 68, 70
  midnight movies, 13–14
  silent cinema/film, 143–44
    Fractured Flickers' treatment of silent cinema, 65–67, 68, 70–71, 298
    reuse in other media, 15, 53–57, 58, 59, 100–1
    use in *Fractured Flickers*, 15, 51, 52, 58, 59–60, 62–63, 64–68
Circus Boy (1956–1958), 177–78
Civil War, 143–44
Clampett, Jed, 261–62
Clark, Larry, 249–52
classical music, 215, 216–17, 227–29. *See also* music
Cohan, Steven, 81–82, 88–89, 137, 217, 257–58
Cohen, Jeffrey, 150–51
Cold War, 32–33, 145, 184–85, 197–98, 218, 224–25
collage, 5–6, 28–29, 67–69, 70, 249–52
Collins, Joan, 13
color. *See also* aesthetic
  American television's transition to, 2, 12–13, 25, 27–29, 83–84, 140–41, 279
  as aesthetic, 28, 41, 82, 83–84, 98, 157–58, 189, 285–86
  as bearer of meaning, 3–4, 21, 29, 30–31, 41, 77–78, 200–1, 204, 221–22, 281, 282–83, 288
  related to race, 19, 145, 258–59, 264–73
  versus black and white, 18, 21, 27–28, 30–31, 218–19, 221–22, 232
colorblind, 19, 258. *See also* racial representation
Columbia Pictures, 177–78, 186–87
comedy 15–16, 97, 133–34, 221, 264, 269–70. *See also* sitcom
  comedy of manners, 19, 256–76
  comedy-variety shows, 264 (see also *Rowan & Martin's Laugh-In*; *Smothers Brothers Comedy Hour*)

  silent comedy, 54, 55, 57
  slapstick comedy (*see* slapstick)
Comiskey, Andrea, 15, 20, 51–74, 298
Confidential (tabloid), 88–89
Conner, Bruce, 15, 52, 68–69, 249–50
Connery, Sean, 31–32, 199–200
Conried, Hans, 59–60, 61–64, 65–67
conservative. *See* camp: conservative
CONTROL, 34, 226, 227
Cooper, Dennis, 248–52
Coral Key, 238–39, 240–41, 243–45, 250–51
Core, Philip, 111
Corman, Roger, 120–21
counterculture. *See also* camp: countercultural
  audience, 2, 103, 124–26, 157–58, 159–60, 171
  in the 1960s 102, 105, 120, 123–24
  on Camp TV, 32–33, 37, 38, 98, 105, 113–14, 133–34, 158, 177, 186, 188, 189–90, 191–92, 231–32, 264, 278, 283, 285–86, 289–90
Cousin Itt, 112–13, 117n.18
Cousin Lester. *See* Wolf Man
Coward, Noël, 88–89, 257–58
Cowardly Lion, 80–81, 83–84, 88
Cox, Laverne, 258–59, 271–73
Creature from the Black Lagoon (1954), 101, 243–44
cross-dressing, 11–12, 37, 38–41, 78, 184, 202–3, 269–70, 287f, *See also* drag
cross talk, 25–26, 34–35, 184–85
Crusader Rabbit (1950–1951, 1959), 58
cult TV, 14, 26–27, 56–57, 247–48
  Camp TV as precursor to, 3–4, 24–27, 31, 34, 38, 40–42, 196, 209, 298–99, 301–7
cultural capital, 20, 297–301, 303, 306–7
cultural resistance, 2, 5, 266–67
Curse of Frankenstein, The (1957), 100
Curtin, Michael, 161–62

Danger Man (1960–61, 1964–67), 195–96, 197–200, 202
Dangerous When Wet (1953), 82–83
Dante, Joe, 70
Dark Shadows (1966–1971), 115n.6, 157–58, 278

DataLounge, 246–47
Davis, William A., 124
DC Comics, 75–76
demographics, 9, 17, 103, 124–26, 304–5
Dennis, Jeffrey P., 79–80, 245–46
Department S (1969-1970), 17–18, 195–96, 204–9
Desilu Productions, 60–61
Disclosure: Trans Lives on Screen (2020), 258–59, 271–72
distinction
   class distinction, 109
   cultural distinction, 297, 299, 303
   subcultural distinction, 306
   taste distinction, 77
Dobbs, Hannibal, Private, 140, 147–48
Doctor Who (1963–1989, 2005–present), 24–25, 209, 304
Dolenz, Micky, 37, 38, 176–94
domestic sitcom. *See* sitcom
Doty, Alexander, 80–81, 129, 262–63
Douglas, Lisa, 35–36, 281, 282–83
Douglas, Oliver, 35–36, 280, 282–83
Douglas, Susan, 127–28, 132
Dozier, William, 1, 23–24, 33, 154–57, 159–65, 167–68, 170–72
drag, 6–7, 11–12, 29–30, 38–39, 183–84, 207–8, 266–70, 271–73.
   See also cross-dressing
   drag performance, 19, 258–59, 264, 266–70, 271–73
   drag queen, 126, 270–71
   macho drag, 17–18, 206
   same-sex drag, 21, 76–77, 79, 81, 89
Drake, John, 197–201
Drew, William, 53–54
Drop Kick, The (1927), 64–65
Drushel, Bruce, 9–10, 218
dual address, 2, 3–4, 12–13, 15, 18–19, 21, 23–24, 25–26, 33, 63–64, 159–60, 165–66, 237–38, 245–46, 252, 298
Dudley Do-Right, 58–60
Duffy, Trooper, 140
Dunstan, Dinky, 51, 64
Dyer, Richard, 109, 200–1, 205–6, 290
Dynasty (1981–1989), 13

Edelman, Lee, 159–60, 240–41
elitism, 291–92, 293–94, 300, 302–3
El Kabong, 78–80. *See also* Quick Draw McGraw
El Kazing, 78–80. *See also* Snagglepuss
Endora, 126–28, 129–30, 132–33, 305–6
Engelhardt, Tom, 143
espionage, 34, 195–96, 198–99, 200–1, 202–4, 208–9, 223–24
Exit Stage Left: The Snagglepuss Chronicles (2018) (comic), 75–77, 90–91, 91n.3

F Troop (1965–1967), 9–10, 16–17, 20, 32–33, 34, 38, 40–41, 137–53, 300
Factory (Warhol), 5–6
failed seriousness, 64–65, 68, 130, 288–89, 300
family. *See also* sitcom: fantastic family sitcom
   camping the American family, 15–16, 97, 102–3, 105, 110–11, 114, 121, 241, 262–63
   family-centered narratives, 15–16, 97, 121, 157–58, 236
   questioning family life in the 1960s 38, 97, 98–99, 125–26, 158–59, 260–61
fandom, 25–26, 31–32, 162–63, 236–37, 245–50, 265–66, 298–99, 303
fantasy genre, 25–26, 199, 203–4, 298–99
Fatale, Natasha, 184–85
Federal Communications Commission (FCC), 8–9, 12–13, 35, 154, 158–59, 161–62, 218
Feehan, Mike, 75–76, 90–91
Feil, Ken, 10–11, 19, 256–76, 277–78, 286–90, 297
Feldon, Barbara, 226
femininity, 36, 83–84, 238–39, 256–58, 269–70, 272–73
   challenging norms of, 40–41, 202–3, 266–68
   exaggerated femininity, 126, 128, 238–39
   versus masculinity, 150–51, 157–58, 196–97, 201–4, 208–9 (*see also* masculinity)
feminism, 128–29, 201–2, 223

feminist, 126, 127. *See also* camp: feminist; second-wave feminist movement
Feuer, Jane, 13, 124–25
Fielding, Jerry, 230–31
Fields, W. C., 69–70
film. *See* cinema
Finch, Mark, 13
Fisher, Terence, 100
Flaming Creatures (1964), 5–6, 236–37
Fleming, Ian, 23–24
"Flicker Flashbacks" (1943-1948), 54, 69–70
Flip Wilson Show, The (1970–1974), 19, 258–59, 264, 267–68, 271–72
Flipper (character), 236, 238, 240–41, 242–43, 244–45
Flipper (1964–1967), 18–19, 236–55, 298
 queer reception in the 1990s 18–19, 245–52
Foltz, Tanice, 126
"For Pete's Sake" (1967) (song), 189–90
Foray, June, 59–60
Fort Courage, 137, 139–40, 141, 142, 147–49
found footage. *See* cinema
"Fractured Fairy Tales" 20, 58, 59
Fractured Flickers (1963–1964), 12–13, 15, 51–54, 58, 59–71, 298
Francis, Connie, 289
Frankenstein (1931), 101
Frawley, James, 36–37
Freed, Arthur, 80–81
Freed Unit, 81–82
Frees, Paul, 59–60, 62–63
Fried, Gerald, 229
Frontain, Raymond-Jean, 260–61
Furter, Frank N., 273

Gale, Cathy, 202–4
Galef, David, 218, 220, 232
Galef, Harold, 218, 220, 232
Garber, Marjorie, 38–40, 266–70
Gaslight Follies (1945), 54, 55–56, 67
Gates, Racquel J., 19, 258–59, 265–68, 271, 272–73
gay labor, 15, 76–77, 81, 85–86
gender
 gender fluidity, 38–41, 58–59, 85–86, 185, 203, 204

gender performance, 17–18, 19, 25–26, 35, 38–41, 62, 64–65, 76–77, 85–86, 146, 206, 256–76 (*see also* drag)
gender politics, 127–28, 157–58, 200–2, 301
gender queer (*see* queer)
gender representation, 10–11, 32, 38–41, 107–11, 126–27, 137, 224–25, 238–39
gender roles/norms, 16–17, 19, 38–41, 107–11, 121–22, 132–33, 137, 146, 150, 157–58, 196–97, 223, 256–76
gender swap, 184
genre. *See also* comedy; fantasy; horror; melodrama; police procedural; science fiction; sitcom; space opera; spy-fi; spy genre; variety shows; Westerns
 boundaries of genre, 102–3, 150–51, 170–71, 179, 189, 230, 278
 film and TV genres, 4–5, 221
 genre cluster, 7, 32, 41–42, 141–42
 genre conventions, 4–5, 196, 205–6
 genre cycle, 4, 7–8, 9–10, 13–14, 24, 32, 164–65
George of the Jungle (1967–1970), 58–59, 62–63
Get Smart (1965–1970), 18, 19–20, 32–33, 34–35, 40–41, 184–85, 223–24, 226–27, 284–85
Gilligan, 35, 71n.2
Gilligan's Island (1964–1967), 11–12, 34, 35, 38, 40
Gill-Man, 101, 243–44
Girl from U.N.C.L.E., The (1966–1967), 281
Gitlin, Todd, 9, 134
Gledhill, Christine, 4–5
Goddard, Michael, 209
Goffman, Erving, 102–3, 104
Goldenson, Leonard, 158–60, 166–67
Goldsmith, Jerry, 224
Goldstein, Marilyn, 124
Gone with the Wind (1939), 268–69
Good Times (1974–1980), 270
"Goofy Movies No. 4" (1934), 53–54, 69–70
Goon Show, The (1951–1960), 57
Goostree, Laura, 36–37, 183, 185–86
Gorbman, Claudia, 221

Gould, Jack, 160–61, 283–84, 289, 291
Grade, Lew, 198–99, 205
Grant, Ginger, 35
Granville, Linda, 242–43, 252n.1
Great Escape, The (1963), 227
Green Acres (1965–1971), 19–20, 32–33, 34, 35–36, 40, 244–45, 280–84, 293
Green Hornet, The (1966–1967), 163–64
Greenway Productions, Inc., 154–55, 159–60, 163–65
Griffith, D. W., 55–57, 59
Grossberg, Lawrence, 181–82
Gwenllian-Jones, Sara, 14, 24–25, 26–27, 304
Gwynne, Fred, 101

Haggins, Bambi, 266–70, 272–73
Haines, Mike, 166–67, 169–70
Halberstam, Jack, 131–32, 165, 262–63
Halpin, Luke, 237–38, 240, 241, 245–52
Hammer Film Productions (Hammer Studios), 100, 120–21
Hands of Orlac, The (1924), 66–67, 100–1
Hanna, William, 81–84. See also Hanna-Barbera
Hanna-Barbera, 15, 75–76, 77, 79–80, 83–84, 86, 90–91, 299
Haralovich, Mary Beth, 98–99, 106
Hard Day's Night, A (1964), 57, 177–78
Haslop, Craig, 17–18, 195–212, 301
Hathaway, Jane, 259, 261–64, 272–73
Hawn, Goldie, 268–69
Haydn, Joseph, 216–17, 228–29
Hayward, Chris, 59–60
Headquarters (1967) (album), 178–79, 188–90
Hee Haw (1969–1971), 9, 279
Hefti, Neal, 221–22
Hekawi tribe (*F Troop*), 138, 140, 148–50
Helm, Matt, 6–7
Help! (1965), 57
Henning, Paul, 35–36
Henry, Buck, 33
Hills, Matt, 20, 297–308
Hine, Thomas, 9–10
Hirst, David L., 257–58, 263–64
Hitchcock, Alfred, 97
Hoffman, Emily, 10–11, 15, 75–93, 299

Hogan's Heroes (1965–1971), 20, 146–47
Hogg, Christopher, 209
Holliday, Ruth, 297–98, 300, 303
Hollywood
  Hollywood productions, 11–12, 14, 53–54, 56–57, 69–70, 79–80, 100–2, 114
  Hollywood references in Camp TV, 34, 101–2, 112–13
  Hollywood's gay labor and racism, 15, 76–77, 81, 85–86, 88–89, 269 (*see also* gay labor; racial representation)
Hollywood Squares (1966–1981), 3, 12, 20, 129
"Homosexuals, The" (1967) (documentary), 169–70
Hood, Robin, 87–88, 89–90
Hook, Jamie, 7, 15–16, 97–119
Hooterville, 34, 40, 280–81, 282–83
horror, 15–16, 97, 99, 100–2, 111, 114–15, 120–21
Horton, Edward Everett, 20, 58, 62, 138
Horwitz, Howie, 292
Horwitz, Jonah, 15, 20, 51–74
Hour of Silents (c. 1957–1958), 56–57
House Un-American Activities Committee (HUAC), 12–13, 75–76
Hoyt, Eric, 53–54, 55
Humphrey, Hal, 160–65
humor, purpose of, 146, 150–51. *See also* camp humor
Hunchback of Notre Dame, The (1923), 51, 56–57, 65, 66–67
Hunt, Nathan, 26–27, 301, 303
Hurst, Annabel, 204–5, 208
Huysmans, Joris-Karl, 244–45, 251

I Dream of Jeannie (1965–1970), 115n.1, 184–85
I Love Lucy (1951–1957), 38–39
Indigenous people, 137–38, 144, 148–50
Instrumentation, 18, 215, 229. See *also* music
Interpol Calling (1959), 197–98, 204–5
intertextuality, 3–4, 25–26, 34–35, 63–64, 77, 79, 84–85, 101–2, 179–80, 184–85, 265–66

irony
    as element of camp, 2, 25–26, 29, 30, 55, 200–1, 259–60
    examples of irony in camp, 23–24, 58–59, 80, 143–44, 156–57, 195–96, 200–1, 208–9, 261–62, 269
Isherwood, Christopher, 5, 9–10

Jagose, Annamarie, 129
Jancovich, Mark, 26–27, 301, 303
Jason King (1971–1972), 17–18, 204–5
Jay Ward Productions, 20, 51, 58.
    See also Ward, Jay
jazz, 215, 221–22, 225–26
Jenkins, Henry, 40–41
"Jerk" (1993) (Dennis Cooper), 248–49
Jerry Mouse, 79–80, 82–83, 86–87
Jetsons, The (1962–1963), 115n.1, 124–25
Johnsen, Grace, 167–69, 171–72
Johnson, Catherine, 304–5
Johnson, Victoria E., 161–62, 168–69, 279–80, 285–86
Joker, the, 156–57, 222
Jones, Carolyn, 100–1, 112–13
Jones, Cyrano, 230
Jones, Davy, 34–35, 38, 176–94
Jones, Geraldine, 19, 258–59, 264, 266–73
Judd, Clinton, 169–70
Judd, for the Defense (1967–1969), 169–70

Kane, Bob, 154–56
KAOS, 33, 34, 35, 226–27
Karloff, Boris, 100–1
Keaton, Buster, 57, 59–60, 67–68
Keel, David, 202–3
Kelly, Brian, 236, 237–38, 245–47
Kelly, Gene, 82
Kerr, Paul, 124–25
Keyes, Paul, 288
Kich, Martin, 142
Killiam, Paul, 55–57, 64
King, Jason, 17–18, 195–96, 204–9
King, Rob, 55
Kirk, James T., Captain, 230–31
Kirshner, Don, 17, 178–79, 186–87, 189, 190, 191–92
kitsch, 20, 106–7, 200–1, 241, 242, 250–51, 285–86, 300, 303, 306

Kitt, Eartha, 156–57
Knapp, Raymond, 216–17, 218–19
Kovacs, Ernie, 56–57
Kruger-Robbins, Benjamin, 17, 154–75, 299
Kuchar, George, 5–6
Kulp, Nancy, 259, 261–63, 272–73
Kuryakin, Ilya, 225–26

Lahr, Bert, 80–81
Lamas, Fernando, 82–83
Larson, Randall, 221–22, 224, 227–28
Laurel and Hardy, 35, 59, 69–70
Laurent, Lawrence, 160–61, 162–63
LaVey, Anton, 123
Lawrence, Eddie, 68–69
Lawrence Welk Show, The (1951–1982), 58–59, 279, 285–86
LeShan, Eda, 161–62, 166–67
Lester, Richard, 57
Levine, Elana, 125–26, 157–58, 168–69, 264
Lichtenstein, Roy, 28–29, 83–84
Liddle, Audrey, 203
Life (magazine), 29–30, 256–57, 290–91
Li'l Abner (1959), 262–63
Lincoln, Elmo, 59, 62–63
Lloyd, Harold, 54, 59–60
Look (magazine), 100, 279
Looney Tunes (1930–1969), 84–85
Loretta Young Show, The (1953–1961), 66–67
Los Angeles Times, 61, 79, 120–21, 160–61, 163–65
Lost in Space (1965–1968), 18, 115n.1, 164–65, 227–30, 252–53n.2
Love Machine, The (1969) (novel), 256–57
Luckett, Moya, 13–14, 15–16, 19–20, 277–96, 297, 302–3
Lurch, 100–1, 113
Lynde, Paul, 6–7, 10–11, 12, 62, 126, 128–29, 130–32, 287

Mack, Ted, 256–57
Macnee, Patrick, 202–4
MAD Magazine, 6–7, 70–71
Mad Men (2007–2015), 305–6
Mad Movies with the L.A. Connection (1985–1986), 69–70

INDEX   317

Major Minor, 83, 84–85, 86–87, 89–90
Malinowska, Ania, 2, 10–11, 13–14, 137–38, 218–19
Maltese, Michael, 80, 84–85
Man from U.N.C.L.E., The (1964–1968), 18, 23–24, 27–28, 31–33, 34, 199, 223–26, 227–28
Mankoff, Robert, 146, 150–51
manners comedy. *See* comedy of manners
Man's Genesis (1912), 55–56
Marc, David, 181
Mark of Zorro, The (1940), 79
Marlin, Robert, 144, 146–47
Marlow, Phillip, 202–3
Marshall, P. David, 176, 181–82
Martha Raye Show, The (1954–1956), 10–11
Martin, Alfred L., Jr., 266–67, 271–72
Martin, Dean, 6–7
Martin, Dick, 289–90
Marubbio, M. Elise, 143–44
Marx, Groucho, 84–85
Marx, Harpo, 38–39, 187–88
Marwick, Arthur, 196–97
Mary Tyler Moore Show, The (1970–1977)
masculinity
  American masculinity, 80, 138, 280, 284–85 (*see also* masculinity: traditional masculinity)
  changing representations of, 16–18, 137–38, 142–46, 150–51, 195–212
  heteronormative masculinity, 201–2, 272–73, 284–85
  hypermasculinity, 62–63, 82, 86–87, 144, 149–50, 206–7, 242
  masculine performance, 15, 80, 205–9, 239
  masculine power, 146–47, 148
  non-normative masculinity, 15, 80–81, 82–83, 140, 195–212
  queer masculinity, 80–81
  subverting hegemonic masculinity, 17–18, 38–39, 90–91, 195–212, 299, 301
  traditional masculinity, 15, 82–83, 86–89, 149–50, 277–78, 283, 302
  versus femininity, 150–51, 157–58, 196–97, 201–4, 208–9 (*see also* femininity)

Mashon, Mike, 162–63
Maverick (1957–1962), 143–44
Mayberry R.F.D. (1968–1971), 9
McBride, Dwight A., 266–67, 270
McCallum, David, 225
McCoy, Charles Allan, 300
McGoohan, Patrick, 197–202, 205
McHale's Navy (1962–1966), 137–38, 146–47
McLuhan, Marshall, 133–34
McNaughton, Douglas, 17–18, 195–212, 301
Medhurst, Andy, 36, 155–57, 195–96, 200–1, 205, 207–8, 209
Medved, Michael, 294
Mellencamp, Patricia, 38–39, 89–90
melodrama, 4–5, 55–56, 59, 143–44
Meredith, Burgess, 154, 162–63
Metropolitan Museum of Art, 19–20, 277
Metz, Walter, 35, 121–22, 126, 128–29, 132–33
Meyer, Moe, 5, 29, 81, 117n.24, 200–1, 228, 277–78
MGM (Metro-Goldwyn-Mayer), 53–54, 79–82, 217
middlebrow, 1, 279–80, 283–84
middle-class, 15–16, 19, 28–29, 98–99, 109, 125–26, 128–29, 167–68, 238–39, 258, 284–85, 297–98
midnight movies. *See* cinema
military
  draft, 34
  satirical representations in the 1960s 32–33, 37, 137–53, 227
Miller, Catriona, 305–6
Miller, Cynthia J., 9–10, 16–17, 20, 137–53, 300
Miller, Quinlan, 9–13, 19
  camp, 11–13, 126, 215, 218, 279, 284–85
  guest stars, 10–12, 77, 90–91, 133–34
  music and sound, 218–20
  sitcoms, 10–11, 124, 129–30
  trans gender queer, 10–12, 58–59, 129–30, 258–59, 260–62, 263–64, 266–67, 271–73 (*see also* trans gender queer)
Miller, Toby, 195–96, 201, 277–78, 301–2, 303, 306

Minow, Newton, 8–9, 35, 125–26, 154, 158–59, 160–62, 165–66, 167, 218, 299, 304–5
Mittell, Jason, 58, 89–90
Mod Squad, The (1968–1973), 158, 168
Molière, 259–60
Molly, the Riddler's assistant, 39–40, 184
Mondo Cane (1962), 68
Monkees, The (TV show) (1966–1968), 9–10, 11–12, 15, 17, 32–33, 34–35, 36–40, 54–55, 57, 176–94, 284–85, 300
Monkees, The (album) (1966), 178
Monkees, The (band), 17, 36–37, 176–94
Monroe, Alph, 40
Monroe, Marilyn, 35, 75–76
Monroe, Ralph, 40
"Monster Mash" 100, 116n.10
monstrosity, 97, 102, 105, 113, 115
Montez, Maria, 236–37
Montgomery, Elizabeth, 126
Moore, Christopher, 216–17, 220
Moorehead, Agnes, 126, 127
More of the Monkees (1967) (album), 178
Morgan, Nicholas C., 18–19, 236–55, 298
Morreall, John, 146, 150–51
Morrow, Bruce, 258–59, 270–71
Movie, A (1958), 15, 52, 68–69, 249–50
Movie Museum (1954–c. 1957), 52, 56–57
Movie Orgy, The (1968), 70
Mr. Ed, 281
MTM Enterprises, 171–72
multivalence, 21, 76–77, 79, 82–83, 90–91, 115
Mulvey, Laura, 206–7, 225
Muñoz, José Esteban, 250–51, 258
Munster, Eddie, 99, 104, 109, 113, 114
Munster, Grandpa, 99, 101, 104, 105, 112, 113
Munster, Herman, 99, 101–2, 105, 108, 109, 112, 113, 114–15
Munster, Lily, 99, 101–3, 105, 108, 109, 112, 113
Munster, Marilyn, 99, 102–3, 109, 112
Munsters, The (1964–1966), 4–5, 15–16, 97–119, 121, 299
Murray, Noel, 287
music. *See also* classical music; instrumentation; jazz; musicals; pop; rock

influence on/from camp, 13, 26–27, 100, 291
music as camp, 18, 68–69, 215–35
musical authenticity, 17, 36–37, 176–83, 185–90, 191–92
musical camp, 217, 220–22
musical coding, 21
musicals, 80–83, 177–78, 217, 260–61, 262–63, 273
My Fair Lady (1964), 112–13
My Favorite Martian (1963–1966), 124–25, 227–28
My Mother the Car (1965–1966), 71n.4, 160–61
Myra Breckenridge (1970), 6–7
Mystery Science Theater 3000 (1988–1999; 2017–present), 14, 52, 69–70

Nagel, Thomas, 146
Naremore, James, 4–5
National Association of Broadcasters, 8, 60
National Legion of Decency (NLD), 219–20
NATO, 197–99
NBC (National Broadcasting Company), 9, 154–55, 161–63, 165, 168–69, 171–72, 180–81, 268–69
negativity, 258–59, 262–63, 265–68, 269–73. *See also* camp: negative camp
neoliberal, 306–7
Nesmith, Michael (Mike), 36–37, 38, 176–94
Newhart, Bob, 62, 64–65
Newkirk, Peter, Corporal, 146–47
Newmar, Julie, 34–35
New York Times, 1, 23–24, 28, 29–30, 99, 161–62, 168–69, 277–78, 283–84, 290–91
New Yorker, 99, 256–57
Nixon, Richard, 13–14, 168–69, 277–78, 285, 288–90
"Notes on 'Camp'" 1–2, 9–10, 29–30, 51–52, 98, 179–80, 256–57, 278, 290–91. *See also* Sontag, Susan
Number Six (*The Prisoner*), 197–202, 204, 208–9
Nurmi, Maila, 100–1
N.Y.P.D. (1967–1969), 17, 154–55, 165–72

occult, 16, 120–26, 133–34, 157–58
O.K. Crackerby! (1965–1966), 158
Olé, Mark, 225–26
Oliver! (stage production), 177–78
oppositional interpretation, 13–14, 26–27, 265, 277–78, 287, 293–94, 303. See also alternative interpretation
O'Rourke, Morgan, Sergeant, 140, 145, 146–49
Orton, Joe, 257
Our Man Flint (1966), 6–7
Owens, Andrew J., 16, 120–36, 157–58, 297, 299

Painlevé, Jean, 243–45
paracinema, 14, 20, 43n.11, 294, 301
Paramount Pictures, 262–63
Parmenter, Wilton, Captain, 40, 137–38, 139–40, 145, 147–49
parody
　as trait of camp, 25–26, 32–34, 58, 143–44, 182–83, 207–8, 220–21, 228–29
　of the American frontier, 137, 138, 143–44
　of crime and spy genres, 195–96, 199, 203–4, 223–24, 226
　of gender, 38–40, 58–59, 129–30, 263–64
　of silent films, 57
　queer and trans gender queer parody, 6–7, 260–61, 273
　self-parody, 39–40, 62, 266–67
Partisan Review, 98, 292
passing, 15, 38, 79, 85–91
patriarchy, 8–9, 16–17, 102–3, 128, 201–2, 262–63
Patty Duke Show, The (1963–1966), 10–11
Peabody Awards, 171–72
Pearson, Roberta, 14, 24–25, 26–27, 303–5
Peel, Emma, 17–18, 202–4
Peeping Tom (1960), 97
Pellegrini, Anne, 280–81, 293–94
Penguin, the, 33, 154, 222
Perfect Childhood, The (1993) (book), 249–50
performance/performativity. See also camp performativity
　as trait of camp, 35, 38–41, 85, 185, 200–1, 264–65

drag performance, 19, 258–59, 264, 266–70, 271–73
gender performance, 17–18, 19, 25–26, 35, 38–41, 62, 64–65, 76–77, 85–86, 146, 206, 256–76 (*see also* drag)
masculine performance 15, 80, 205–9, 239
queer performance, 1, 11–12, 79, 98, 257–59
Pertwee, Jon, 209
Peters, Brian, 9–10
Petticoat Junction (1963–1970), 141–42, 280–81
Phillips, W. D., and Isabel C. Pinedo, 1–22, 23–48
　camp as precursor to cult TV, 23–48, 150, 209, 245–46, 297, 303–5, 306
　color, 83–84 (*see also* color)
　defining Camp TV, 51–52, 89, 103, 179–80, 196 (*see also* camp)
　four traits of Camp TV, 84–85, 98, 183, 257–58
　viewing strategies, 58, 70–71, 264–65, 280–81, 298–99, 303
Phil Silvers Show, The (1955–1959), 146–47
Pickett, Bobby "Boris" 100, 116n.10
Picture of Dorian Gray, The (1890), 244–45
Pierson, David, 142, 259–63
Pinedo, Isabel C., and W. D. Phillips. See Phillips, W. D., and Isabel C Pinedo
Pink Flamingos (1972), 13–14
Pinter, Junior, 186–87
Pisces, Aquarius, Capricorn & Jones, Ltd. (1967) (album), 189
Pistols 'n' Petticoats (1966–1967), 143–44
Plan 9 from Outer Space (1957), 100–1
police procedural, 165–66, 168–69, 171, 197–98
Pop Art, 12–13, 23–24, 28–29, 103, 164–65, 179–80, 195–96, 285–86, 291, 300. See also aesthetic: Pop Art
pop music, 6–7, 181–82, 196–97
Portmeirion, Wales, 195–96, 198–99, 200–1, 208–9
postmodern, 14, 43n.13, 207
Potts, Tracy, 297–98, 300, 303
Powell, Michael, 97
Poulenc, Francis, 216, 217, 229

prime time
  as vast wasteland, 8–9, 21, 158–59, 160–61
  camp prime-time programs, 7–8, 23–25, 58, 164–65, 176–77
  controversial topics on prime time, 37, 108, 154–56, 158, 165–68, 286
  color, 2, 4, 25, 27–29, 30–31, 41
  family dynamics on prime time, 108, 109, 114
  queer visibility on prime time, 154–56, 165–67
  silents on prime time, 55–57, 69
Prisoner, The (1968–1969), 17–18, 195–96, 197–202, 204, 205, 208–9
Private Property (1960), 219–20
Pryor, Thomas M., 164–65
Psycho (1960), 97
Purvis, Philip, 217

Quasimodo, 51, 60
queer, 129–30, 242. *See also* trans gender queer
  ABC's queer programming, 154–60, 165–72
  camp and queer, 2, 5, 9–14, 29–30, 77, 112–13, 126, 154–58, 201, 216, 236, 256–57
  queer audiences and interpretation, 18–19, 103, 156–57, 159–60, 236–38, 245–47, 251–52, 267–68, 277–78, 293–94, 298, 307
  queer performance, 1, 11–12, 79, 98, 257–59
  queer portrayals of characters, 75–93, 128–30, 131–32, 165–67, 169–70, 205, 207–9, 239–40, 260–63
  queer visibility on prime time, 154–56, 165–67
Quick Draw McGraw 77–80, 85, 86–87, 90–91
Quick Draw McGraw Show, The (1959–1961), 77–80, 83, 84, 85–86

racial representation, 19, 258–59, 265–70, 271–73. *See also* Indigenous people
racism, 105, 252, 264, 266–68, 269, 270. *See also* colorblind

Rafelson, Bob, 177–78, 185–87, 191–92
Real Housewives of Atlanta, The (2008–present), 266–67
reappropriation, 277, 290, 303
reception
  camp as mode of reception, 1–2, 30, 280–81
  negative reception, 257–58, 266–67, 271–72
  reception practices, 25, 26–27, 41–42, 144, 150, 236–38, 245–52, 277–78, 285–86, 293–94, 298
reflexivity, 4–5, 15, 51, 55–56, 64, 98, 206, 207, 269
  as trait of camp, 25–26, 35–37
  self-reflexivity, 85, 100, 185, 243–44, 264–65, 266–67, 272–73
Reilly, Charles Nelson, 287
restoration comedy, 259–60
Ricardo, Lucy, 38–39, 89–90. *See also* Ball, Lucille
Rickles, Don, 149–50
Ricks, Bud, 236, 237–38, 242–43, 246–47
Ricks, Porter, 236, 237–38, 239–41, 246–47
Ricks, Sandy, 236–38, 239–41, 242–43, 246–47, 249–52
Riddle, Nelson, 222
Riddler, the, 39–40, 222
riffing, 52, 53, 58–59, 65–66, 69–70
Rigg, Diana, 17–18, 202–3
Riot on the Sunset Strip (1967), 168
RKO Pictures, 54
Robertson, Pamela. *See* Wojcik, Pamela Robertson
Robin (*Batman*), 36, 39–40, 154, 158, 160–61, 184
rock music, 37, 113, 176–77, 181–83, 197, 280, 291
Rocky and His Friends (1959–1961), 58. See also *Adventures of Rocky and Bullwinkle*; *The Bullwinkle Show*
Rocky Horror Picture Show, The (1975), 13–14
Rocky Horror Picture Show: Let's Do the Time Warp Again, The (2016), 273
Roddenberry, Gene, 304–5
Rohauer, Raymond, 59–60, 67–68, 69–70
Romero, Cesar, 62, 156–57, 162–63

Rose, Ralph J., 112–13
Rose, Reginald, 63–64
Ross, Andrew, 5–6, 102, 122, 123, 127, 196–97, 278, 300
Ross, Kristin, 102–3
Ross, Marlon B., 271
Rowan & Martin's Laugh-In (1968–1973), 9–10, 19–20, 258–59, 264, 268–69, 277–78, 280, 284–90, 293, 302
Rowan, Dan, 289–90
Ruff and Reddy, 79–80, 86–87
Ruff and Reddy (1957–1960), 79–80
Running Jumping & Standing Still Film, The (1959), 57
RuPaul's Drag Race (2009–present), 13
Russell, Mark, 75–76, 77, 90–91

Saks, Sol, 126
Sargent, Dick, 126
satire, 3–4, 25–26, 29, 32–34, 41, 142–44, 161–62, 184–85, 259–60, 261–62, 264–65
Saturday Evening Post, 176, 277–79, 284–85, 289–91
Saturday Night Live (1975–present), 76
Scarborough, Roscoe C., 300
Schambelan, Elizabeth, 251
Schickel, Richard, 52, 56–57
Schneider, Abe, 177–78, 186–87
Schneider, Alfred, 158–59
Schneider, Bert, 177–78, 186–87, 191–92
Schwartz, Sherwood, 34, 160
science fiction, 6–7, 24–26, 121, 199, 203–4, 227, 298–99, 303–4
Sconce, Jeffrey, 14, 43n.11, 294, 301
Scorpio Rising (1963), 262–63
Scott, Bill, 51, 58, 59–60, 65, 68–69
Scott, Montgomery (Scotty), 230–31
secondary meaning systems, 25–26, 98, 143–44, 150
second-wave feminist movement, 110
See, Sam, 242
Self, Robert O., 145
self-reflexivity. *See* reflexivity
Sellers, Peter, 57
Semple, Lorenzo, Jr., 33, 155–57, 291
Sennett, Mack, 54, 59–60

Serling, Rod, 63–64, 121, 160–61, 162–63, 304–5
Sgt. Pepper's Lonely Hearts Club Band (1967) (album)
Shakespeare, William, 78, 84, 86–87, 130
Shoes (1916), 53–54
Silencers, The (1966)
Silents Please (1960–1962), 56–57, 70
Silvers, Phil, 149–50
Simpsons, The (1989–present), 89–90
sitcom
 as a genre, 4–5, 15–16, 97, 139–40, 142
 authenticity in, 176–77, 179, 181–83, 185–86, 187–88, 190–91
 British sitcoms, 13, 257
 characters, 89–90, 128
 conventions and tropes, 110–11, 114, 130–31, 179, 187, 190, 259, 260–62, 282–83
 domestic sitcom, 97, 98–99, 109, 111, 114, 158–59
 fantastic family sitcom, 16, 121, 157–58
 guest stars, 77, 90–91
 production, 140–41, 181
 Quinlan Miller's study of, 10–12, 58–59, 77, 90–91, 124–25, 129–30, 133–34, 218
 working-class sitcoms, 106
Skal, David, 100
Skow, John, 277–78, 284–85, 290–94
slapstick, 15, 33, 52, 55, 57, 64–65, 186–87, 288–89
Smart, Maxwell (Agent 86), 33, 34, 40–41, 184–85, 226–27, 284–85
Smith, Gene, 284–85
Smith, Jack, 5–6, 236–37, 249–50
Smith, Justin, 306
Smith, Pete, 53–54
Smith, Venus, 203
Smothers Brothers Comedy Hour, The (1967–1969), 158, 168–69, 286
Snagglepuss (character), 15, 75–81, 82–91, 299
Snagglepuss (1961), 3–4, 15, 75–77, 81, 83–86, 88–91, 299
Snark, Marvin D., 67–68
Society of Cinema Arts, 69
Solo, Napoleon, 31–32, 224, 225–26

Sontag, Susan. *See also* "Notes on 'Camp'"
  artifice and exaggeration, 16, 121–22, 180–81, 183, 242
  as popularizer of camp, 1–2, 9–10, 29–30, 51–52, 98, 179–80, 256–57, 278, 290–91
  being-as-playing-a-role, 35, 111–12
  camp as sensibility, 4–5, 122, 200–1
  defining camp, 1–2, 5, 30, 98, 121–22, 137, 242, 262–63, 297–98
  deliberate and naïve camp, 122–23, 130, 179–80, 236, 305
  failed seriousness, 64–65, 300
  music, 215, 217, 228–29
  serious about the frivolous, 2, 102–3, 124, 128–29
  style over content, 106, 200–1, 217
space opera, 18, 215–16, 223, 227–32
Spigel, Lynn, 28, 40–41, 57, 121, 157–58, 297. *See also* sitcom: fantastic family sitcom
Spock, Mr., 231–32
Spooner, Dennis, 208
spy-fi, 17–18, 195–96, 199, 202, 203–4, 208–9
spy genre, 18, 23–24, 184–85, 195–96, 197–98, 202–3, 215, 218, 223–27
Standells, The, 113
Star Trek (1966–1969), 3, 18, 24–25, 31–32, 227, 230–32, 303–5
Steed, John, 17–18, 202–4, 205, 207–9
Steinem, Gloria, 256–57
Stephens, Darrin, 126, 127, 128–29, 132–33
Stephens, Samantha, 126, 127, 128–29, 130–31, 132–33, 305–6
Steve Allen Show, The (1956–1964), 55–56, 57
Stevens, Sapphire, 266–70
stigma
  dark camp, 18–19, 236–37, 245, 252
  social difference, 38–39, 102, 105
Stockton, Kathryn Bond, 236–37, 241
Stone, Judy, 1, 23–24, 29–30, 283–84
Stonewall riots, 13–14, 169–70
Storch, Larry, 137–38, 140–41, 149–50
subaltern, 6–7, 13–14, 269–70
suburban, 38, 99, 121, 125–26, 131–32, 241, 305–6

Sues, Alan, 287
Sullivan, Ed, 84–85
Sullivan, Stewart, 204–5, 206, 208
Susann, Jacqueline, 256–57
Swanson, Gloria, 57
Szathmary, Irving, 226

Tandem Productions, 171–72
Tarzan, 58–59, 62–63
Tarzan of the Apes (1918), 59, 62–63
taste. *See also* camp taste
  bad taste, 19–20, 121–22, 218, 232, 277, 280, 283–84, 286, 290–91
  cult taste, 13–14, 301
  cultural taste, 102, 106–7, 112–13, 300, 303, 306
  marginalized taste, 265–67
  mass taste, 161–62, 167
  tastemaker, 260–61, 273
  violation of conventional "good taste" 19, 257–59, 262–67, 270, 272–73, 278
Taylor, Greg, 5–7, 13–14, 302
Taylor, Rip, 191
television. *See also* 1950s television; 1970s television; 1980s; 1990s television
  British television, 3, 13, 17–18, 20, 196, 197–98, 209, 257
That Certain Summer (1972), 171–72
theatricality, 25, 29, 41, 86–87, 126, 209, 217, 257–58, 259, 262–63
"(Theme from) *The Monkees*" (1966) (song), 189–90
Thing (*The Addams Family*), 34–35, 100–1
Thin Man, The (1934), 202–3
Third Doctor, 209
This is Your Life (1952–1961), 84–85
Thomas, Howard, 202–3
Three Musketeers, 87–88, 89–90
Three Stooges, 11–12, 38–39
"Thrills of Yesterday" (1931), 53–54
Thunderball (1965), 243–44
Time (magazine), 29–30, 123, 133–34, 290–91
Tinkcom, Matthew, 5–6, 257–58, 264–65, 273
Tom and Jerry (1940–1958), 79–80, 86
Tom Cat, 79–80, 82–83, 86–87

Tork, Peter, 34–35, 176–94
Torres, Sasha, 23–24, 155–57, 179–80, 236
Tors, Ivan, 243–45
transgender, 271–73
trans gender queer, 10–13, 58–59, 129–30, 256–76. *See also* camp: trans gender queer
Trillin, Calvin, 256–57
Tropiano, Stephen, 168–70
"turn toward relevance," 8, 9, 134
TVI, 41–42, 304–5, 306
TVII, 41–42, 209, 304–5, 306
TVIII, 41–42, 209, 304–5, 306
TVIV, 306
TV Guide, 1
Twilight Zone, The (1959–1964), 8, 121, 162–63, 304–5
Twin Peaks (1990–1991), 24–25, 209

Uncle Arthur, 12, 126, 128–33
Uncle Fester, 99, 108
Uncle Gilbert. *See* Gill-Man
United States Cavalry, 144, 146–47
Universal Pictures, 53–54, 100, 101–2
"Unshod Maiden, The" (1932), 53–54

Vadim, Roger, 6–7
Vahimagi, Tise, 124–25
Valiant Years, The (1960–1961), 8
Valley of the Dolls (1966), 256–57
Vampira Show, The (1954–1955), 100–1
Van Hise, James, 100–1, 221–22
Vanderbilt, Trooper, 140, 147–48
Variety, 164–65, 283–84
variety shows, 11–12, 38–39, 55, 57, 273–74n.3, 274n.7, 285–86. *See also* comedy-variety shows
vast wasteland, 8, 21, 24, 35, 63–64, 125–26, 161–62, 218, 299, 301, 307
vaudeville, 5–6, 11–12, 16–17, 38–39, 80, 107, 137, 140, 149–50, 273–74n.3, 274n.7, 285–86
Vaughn, Robert, 31–32, 225–26
Veidt, Conrad, 66–67
Vidal, Gore, 160–61
Viegener, Matias, 248–49
Vietnam War, 124–25, 145, 168–69, 283

violence
  against homosexuals
    in American society, 15, 76–77, 85–86, 89–91
    on television, 15, 76–77, 83, 85–86, 89–91, 169–70
  in dark camp, 236–37, 240–41, 249–50, 252
  on television (general), 8, 55, 58, 165–66, 168

Wagner, Richard, 215, 228–29
Wagon Train (1957–1965), 143–44, 227
Walker, Jimmie, 270
Ward, Burt, 38–40, 154, 156–57, 184
Ward, Jay, 15, 20, 51, 52, 58–61, 63–64, 67, 69–71. *See also* Jay Ward Productions
Ward, Jeff, Detective, 166–67, 168–70
Warden, Jack, 166–67, 168
Warhol, Andy, 5–6, 28–29, 83–84, 103, 291, 300
Warner Bros. Pictures, 53–54, 84–85, 140–41
Warner, Jack, 141
Washington Post, 160–61, 162–63
Waters, John, 13–14, 277
Watkins, Mel, 266–67
Watts Gnu Show, The (1959), 59–60
Weber, Lois, 53–54
Weissmuller, Johnny, 58–59, 62–63
Weldon, Michael, 108
Welsing, Frances Cress, 270, 271–72
Wertham, Fredric, 36, 155–57
West, Adam, 156–57
Westengard, Laura, 142
Westerns, 53–54, 87–88, 143–44, 150–51, 168–69, 227, 283–84, 300
Whale, James, 101
Wild Angels, The (1966), 168
Wild Wild West, The (1965–1969), 3, 20, 143–44
Wilde, Oscar, 5, 29, 81, 129, 205, 244–45, 257
Williams, Esther, 82–83
Williams, John, 227–28
Willis, Paul, 76–77
Wilson, Flip, 19, 258–59, 264, 266–73

Winters, Jonathan, 268–69
Wissner, Reba A., 18, 215–35, 297, 303–4
Wizard of Oz, The (1939), 80–81
Wojcik, Pamela Robertson, 13, 100, 258, 265
Wolf Man, 101
Wood, Bob, 9
Wood, Robin, 97, 99, 102
World War II, 52–53, 144, 145, 197
Wrangler Jane (Angelica Thrift), 40, 137–38, 140, 147–48
Wyngarde, Peter, 204–6, 207–9

X-Files, The (1993–2002), 24–25, 209

Yockey, Matt, 33, 36, 158, 223
Yogi Bear, 75–76, 79–80, 85, 86–87
Yogi Bear Show, The (1961–1962), 15, 75–77, 79, 80, 83, 84–86, 299
York, Dick, 126
You Bet Your Life (1950–1961), 84–85
Youngson, Robert, 57
youth culture, 19–20, 37, 40, 55, 57, 100, 264
    conservative views and youth culture, 282–83, 284–86, 288, 289–90

Zappa, Frank, 36–37, 191–92
Ziffel, Arnold, 34, 35–36, 40, 282–83
Zorro, 78, 79

Printed and bound by CPI Group (UK) Ltd, Croydon, CR0 4YY